PRAISE FOR
THE GERTRUDE STEIN READER

"There have been many Anthologies, Chrestomathies, and Readers of Gertrude Stein's work, a multiplicity corresponding to the diversity and development of the writings she produced with such astonishing continuity all her life. In his lively selection, Mr. Kostelanetz has successfully represented one aspect of Stein's repertoire and provided a characteristic introduction which surely identifies his particular insight into her work. As Gertrude Stein says in *Tender Buttons*: 'a line in life, a single line and a stairway.' Congratulations all round!"

—Pulitzer Prize–winning poet **Richard Howard**

"Kostelanetz does it again, gathering Stein's lively, liberating, and cleansing words (the words, as she says, we hold in our hands) in a fine new anthology that includes 'Many Many Women,' 'Wherein the South Differs from the North,' 'Three Sisters Who Are Not Sisters,' and 'How Writing Is Written'—testimony all to Stein's prescient originality and Kostelanetz's lifelong commitment to it."

—**Brenda Wineapple**, author of *Sister Brother: Gertrude and Leo Stein*

"Here's proof—in readings bound to tease, perplex, and delight—that Stein was the Great American Pioneer in the avant-garde of twentieth-century literature."

—**William C. Carter**, author of *Marcel Proust: A Life*

"Richard Kostelanetz is right—again. Gertrude Stein is the great American pioneer of the avant-garde. Kostelanetz shows us Stein in all her bounty, ingenuity, and originality."

—**Catharine R. Stimpson**, dean and university professor, New York University, and editor of the Library of America's two-volume *Gertrude Stein: Writings*

"Gertrude Stein always did things her own way, with no apologies given. Editor Richard Kostelanetz captures the contradictory aspects of her domineering personality and towering presence. He makes quite clear that Stein was a woman for all seasons and for all times."

—**June Skinner Sawyers**, editor of *The Lost Generation Reader*

THE
GERTRUDE STEIN
READER

The Great American Pioneer
of Avant-Garde Letters

THE
GERTRUDE STEIN
READER

Edited with an Introduction by
RICHARD KOSTELANETZ

Cooper Square Press

First Cooper Square Press edition 2002

This Cooper Square Press paperback of *The Gertrude Stein Reader* is an original publication. It is published by arrangement with the editor.

Published by Cooper Square Press
A Member of the Rowman & Littlefield Publishing Group, Inc.
200 Park Avenue South, Suite 1109
New York, NY 10003-1503
www.coopersquarepress.com

Distributed by National Book Network

Library of Congress Cataloging-in-Publication Data

Stein, Gertrude, 1874–1946.
    The Gertrude Stein reader : the great American pioneer of avant-garde
letters / edited by Richard Kostelanetz.— 1st Cooper Square Press ed.
        p. cm.
Includes bibliographical references.
    ISBN 0-8154-1238-X (cloth: alk. paper) — ISBN 0-8154-1246-0 (pbk. : alk.
paper)
    I. Kostelanetz, Richard. II. Title.
    PS3537.T323 A6 2002
    818'.5209—dc21
                                        2002008713

Manufactured in the United States of America

∞™ The paper used in this publication meets the minimum requirements of
American National Standard for Information Sciences—Permanence of
Paper for Printed Library Materials, ANSI/NISO Z39.48-1992.

*"Any human beings putting words together
had to make some sense out of them."*
—**Gertrude Stein**, *in an interview
with Robert Haas (1946)*

*"Composition is not a process but a process that displays the growth of the
form that the work renders—a process in which statement and observation
occur simultaneously. Rendering the process which evolves the work
collapses the time of reading, the writing of writing, and diegetic time
into the single moment of presence."*
—**Bruce Elder**, "The Films of Stan Brakhage
in the American Tradition" *(1998)*

Pour Marc Dachy,
après vingt-huit ans

CONTENTS

PREFACE

Remarkable family Stein
There's Ep and there's Gert
And there's Ein
Ep's sculpture is junk,
Gert's poetry is bunk
And nobody understands Ein.

Once I discovered that there was more to Gertrude Stein than *Three Lives* and *Toklas*, I came to regard her among the greatest modern writers—in her idiosyncratic ways the equal of William Faulkner and James Joyce. What I had to discover was AnOther Stein, or at least a Stein other than the minor realist who authored those two familiar books. My reading mechanisms were opened by the titles that Stein had self-published in the 1930s (or, more precisely, that her devoted companion Alice B. Toklas had published for her as the Plain Edition). Long scarce in America, these titles were reprinted in the 1960s by the great Dick Higgins under the imprint of Something Else Press (SEP), which I've characterized in my *A Dictionary of the Avant-Gardes* as an educational institution as important to the 1960s avant-garde as Black Mountain College was to the 1950s. My SEP copies of *Geography and Plays*, *G. M. P.*, *The Making of Americans*, and *How to Write* were well thumbed and annotated over the past three decades.

I realized then that Stein had two reputations. Where conservative critics thought her a minor realist who also wrote a lot of inscrutable texts, I ranked her the Great American Person of Avant-Garde Letters whose "bunk" roughly in the genres of fiction, poetry, drama, and exposition was monumentally innovative. Whereas earlier Stein anthologies and criticism focused upon the realist Stein, I've favored the radical Gertrude Stein, first in a series of critical appreciations, then in an anthology drawn exclusively from the volumes posthumously published by the Yale University Press (my *The Yale Gertrude Stein*, 1980, and still in print), third in an anthology of criticism concentrating upon the more radical work (*Gertrude Stein Advanced*, 1990), and finally in this new collection. My gratitude goes to Michael Dorr and his associates at Cooper Square Press for commissioning this book and Steven Dekovich for careful and conscientious proofreading.

In selecting items for this volume, I have drawn mostly upon less familiar texts initially published abroad. Within that bias, I've favored versions that have previously appeared in print, because that is how I know them, while acknowledging the heroic efforts of Ulla Dydo and Edward Burns, among others, to produce more definitive versions from Stein's handwritten manuscripts. When proofreading this text against original publications, we discovered oddities of spelling, grammar, and punctuation, which were sometimes corrected using brackets ([ ]) to indicate such an editorial change. In ordering the selections, I've tried to follow the outlines of the second half of my extended introduction. Headnotes appear only when necessary.

INTRODUCTION

"I found myself plunged into a vortex of words, burning words, cleansing words, liberating words, feeling words, and the words were all ours and it was enough that we held them in our hands to play with them; whatever you can play with is yours, and this was the beginning of knowing; of all Americans knowing, that it would play and play with words and the words were all ours— all ours."
                                                        —**Gertrude Stein,**
            "American Language and Literature" (undated)

"The *Homme de Lettres, homme* not *femme.*"   —**Virgil Thomson**

Though Gertrude Stein died more than fifty years ago, her writings have survived her. Nearly every year something she wrote is reprinted and a book at least in part about her appears. No longer the epitome of inscrutable preciosity in modern literature, she is now ranked among its greatest inventors, whose best writings still seem very, very contemporary. It is hard for a reader today to believe that Stein, born February 3, 1874, belongs chronologically to the generation of Theodore Dreiser (b. 1871), Stephen Crane (b. 1871), H. L. Mencken (b. 1880), and Eugene O'Neill (b. 1888). While her genius as an art collector was often acknowledged during her lifetime, only after her death have her literary achievements been so widely honored. In the 1950s, Yale University Press published several volumes of previously unpublished texts, including the monumental poem "Lifting Belly," while Something Else Press in the 1960s reprinted Stein texts that were first published only in Europe decades before, such as *The Making of Americans* (1926) and *G. M. P.* (1932). Back in 1926, she wrote in her inimitable style, "For a very long time everybody refuses and then almost without pause almost everybody accepts. In the history of the refused in arts and literature the rapidity of the change is always startling. Now the only difficulty with the *volte-face* concerning the arts is this: When the acceptance comes, by that acceptance the thing created becomes a classic." She continued, "And what is the characteristic quality of a classic. The characteristic quality of a classic is that it is beautiful. . . . Of course it is beautiful but first of all beauty in it is denied and then all the beauty of it is accepted." In her familiarity with the career of avant-garde art, Stein implicitly predicted that by the twenty-first century her own much-scorned scribblings would be regarded as, yes, beautiful and classic.

It is perhaps a tribute to the originality and integrity of her more difficult writings that they, in contrast to other dimensions of her achievement, have taken so long to be recognized. Back in the 1930s, Stein became a celebrated eccentric, thanks mostly to *The Autobiography of Alice B. Toklas* (1933), which became a best-seller, and then her highly publicized U.S. lecture tour in the wake of the book's success. For the next decade, her most conspicuous activities were reported in the newspapers, often with whimsy, rarely with undiluted cultural respect. When American soldiers took back France from the Nazis during World War II, she gained notoriety for entertaining the Americans in her home.

This exploitation of her personality was, like her art collection, merely incidental to what she considered her primary interest, which was her writing. From 1902, when she began her first novel, to her death forty-four years later, Stein wrote steadily, producing some of the most extraordinary books in modern literature—texts so original that they still strike many literate people initially as "unreadable."

A short stocky woman, Stein favored heavy shirts, long brown corduroy skirts, and jackets with loose pockets, as well as sandals and idiosyncratic hats—in sum giving her a public appearance that was neither masculine nor feminine but somewhere in between. In his pioneering 1948 biography, journalist W. G. Rogers found "a distinguished and beautiful face, strong, open, molded massively on big, generous lines and planes; it reminded me of eighteen-inch sculpture which mysteriously produces an eighteen-foot effect. The mouth was wide, the complexion weathered, the dark brown eyes mellow and magnetic." In the 1970s, I remember meeting people who had seen her forty years before, more than one remembering her head as unusually "well-formed."

In 1905, Pablo Picasso, then twenty-four, briefly saw Stein in an art gallery; and though he had previously spurned the use of live models (and was unaware of her reputation as an art collector), he found her appearance so infatuating that he asked to paint her portrait. Her hair was then long and dark, with gentle curls that, as in the Picasso painting, were pulled back across the crown of her head. Not until twenty years later did she adopt the close-cropped haircut that became her instantly recognizable trademark. In both her art and her life, Stein mixed semblances of affectation with genuine style. It seems that Stein's major passion, after writing, was eating; and though only five feet two inches tall, she reportedly weighed over two hundred pounds. When she sat down, she resembled, it was commonly said, "a living Buddha." What was more commanding than her physical presence, however, was her personality—alert, articulate, cordial, imperious, and quarrelsome. Rarely bothered by illness, avoiding alcohol and other deleterious drugs, she retained her strengths to her death.

Especially after her split from her slightly older brother Leo, with whom she lived for most of her thirties, she tended to dominate all public situations; and if, perchance, someone else upstaged her, Stein did not stay long. This urge to dominate perhaps explains why Stein's favorite kind of social gathering was the Saturday soirée in her own house where guests, offered nothing stronger than tea or an occasional liqueur, could be awed by both her collection of recent paintings and her brilliant conversation. One of her biographers, John Malcolm Brinnin, characterizes her monologue as typically "a mixture of small talk and *pronunciamento*." The British writer known as Bryher remembers that Stein "would pick up a phrase and develop it, ranging through a process of continuous association until we seem to have ascended through the seven Persian heavens and in the process to have turned our personalities inside out." She coined the term "lost generation" to define younger writers diametrically unlike herself. Like her sometime friend Ernest Hemingway, she seems to have implanted something of herself in nearly everyone she met.

This remarkable cosmopolitan was born not along the eastern seaboard, as one might expect, but in Allegheny, Pennsylvania, just outside of Pittsburgh. Her father was a prosperous clothing merchant whose ancestors had emigrated from Germany only a few decades before. Gertrude was the last of five children; when she was still an infant, her father, Daniel Stein, moved his large family from Pittsburgh to Austria, in part because he wanted a cultural atmosphere more conducive to the education of his children. When he returned to the United States in 1878, mostly to amass more money, the rest of the family moved to Paris. Two years later, all the Steins came back to the United States, settling in Oakland, California, where Gertrude and her closest brother, Leo, were educated by governesses at home and then in the local public schools. She later remembered her particular enjoyment of grammar, which she described as "very exciting. I really do not know that anything has ever been more exciting than diagramming sentences. . . . I like the feeling the everlasting feeling of sentences as they diagram themselves." Precociously intelligent, she devoured the English classics as a child, "living continuously," as she later put it, "with the rhythms of the English language."

Either no one told Gertrude that women were supposed to be intellectually inferior, or she never got the standard Victorian message. From a young age she developed the romantic notion of herself as a "genius" who could transcend mortal conventions in favor of her own rules; and since both of her parents died before she turned eighteen, Gertrude was free of another source of possible restraint. After a year living with relatives in Baltimore, she applied for admittance into Harvard, where Leo Stein was already studying. Although she had not officially graduated from high school (and did not know Latin, which was then required for entrance), Radcliffe accepted her as a special student. Her favorite teacher was the philosopher William James, from whom she learned much about psychology and even more about philosophical empiricism. While an undergraduate, she joined a male graduate student in doing original research in automatic writing. It is commonly assumed that this instilled a pre-Freudian interest in her own unconscious, but that is not true. As Stein herself once testified, "Gertrude Stein never had subconscious reactions," and her writing was never anything less than fully conscious.

Graduated magna cum laude, she rejoined Leo in Baltimore and studied medicine for five years at the Johns Hopkins Medical School. In addition to doing research in brain tracts and taking private lessons in boxing (with men), she assisted in the delivery of African American infants (and thus gained firsthand material for her story "Melanctha"). Just short of finishing a medical degree, she once again followed Leo, this time to Europe. After brief trips to Italy, London, and then back to New York, she joined him at 27 rue Fleurus, their first Parisian residence. Meanwhile, her eldest brother, Michael Stein, had assumed management of the family finances, shrewdly supervising modest investments that freed them from the need for jobs and yet kept them parsimonious. Gertrude frequently characterized their financial condition as "reasonably poor."

Astute investors in spite of themselves, Leo and Gertrude Stein scrimped and saved to buy numerous then-recent paintings by young artists with names like Matisse and Picasso, adventurously establishing one of the first percipient collections of modernist art. Whenever Gertrude's regular income was insufficient, pieces from this collection would provide a sure source of instant money.

Michael Stein also told several other San Franciscans, including Alice Babette Toklas, to call upon his siblings during a projected European trip in 1907. Though Alice and Gertrude were totally opposite in certain respects—Alice being thin, practical, and deferential—they became best friends for life, married in all but name. In 1910, Alice came to live at 27 rue Fleurus, and by 1913 Leo moved out, leaving his sister, at thirty-nine, finally free of her last constraint.

Alice B. Toklas became a dutiful housekeeper and an accomplished cook, whose choice recipes were eventually gathered into a popular cookbook. Once she became fully integrated into Gertrude's habitual routines, Alice would typically begin her mornings by typing the handwritten pages that Gertrude had left the night before, and it was Alice, rather than their author, who submitted manuscripts to prospective publishers. With both a private income and a loyal helper, Stein was as free of mundane cares as any artist can be. Though Gertrude Stein spent nearly all of her adult life abroad, mostly because a comfortable, job-free existence was more feasible in Europe, she was scarcely an expatriate. She never considered herself French, and she disliked reading, even newspapers, in any language but English. In her will, she described herself as "legally domiciled in Baltimore, Maryland, but residing" in Paris. Throughout her life, her frame of reference, her cultural tradition, her imagination, her sense of audience, her home life, her friends, her language, and her income all remained primarily American.

Even by 1913, she was a persevering, if unrecognized, author. A decade before, she had finished her first novel, entitled *Q.E.D.*, a stylistically realistic portrait of her female protagonist's apparently frustrated affection for another woman. In part because of its unusual subject, it did not appear in print until 1950 (and then in a limited edition). Having worked on a translation of Gustave Flaubert's *Trois Contes*, she wrote around 1905 a similarly structured fiction, initially entitled "Three Histories," that also portrayed female sexual frustrations. This new book, like *Q.E.D.*, contained finely constructed psychological portraits that echoed not only the writings of Flaubert but also those of her favorite teacher's younger brother, Henry James.

She sent the manuscript to college friends back in the United States, and they submitted it to several East Coast publishers, all of whom refused it. Rather than let her text accumulate surplus dust, Stein followed the good example of earlier American authors (Poe, Whitman, Crane) and paid a small publisher $660 to print one thousand copies of *Three Lives* (1909). Reviews were few at the time, while sales were negligible (and the publisher gratuitously insulted Stein's competence in the English language). However, not only has the best of these novellas, "Melanctha," been frequently reprinted, but *Three Lives* has since become one of Stein's two most popular works. It is also a litmus test of one's taste in Stein: readers and critics who are especially fond of it tend not to like her more difficult works, and vice versa.

Meanwhile, Stein had been working on her most ambitious single book, *The Making of Americans*, whose principal quality is linguistic repetition. Customarily retiring to her work table just before midnight, she wrote until dawn in a studio filled with contemporary paintings and then slept into the afternoon. The final draft ran over 550,000 words (in comparison, say, to the 379,000 of James Joyce's *Ulysses*), and one of Alice B. Toklas's first gifts of love was typing the monumental manuscript for 2,428 pages, nineteen lines to a page. As this book too did not initially find a publisher, Stein turned to writing a shorter novel, *A Long Gay Book*, which combined a personal curiosity about unconventional human relationships with her literary interest in stylistic permutations and potentialities. Stymied again by possible publishers, Stein wrote a series of much shorter pieces, some of which she submitted to magazines in both England and America. Not until 1912, when Alfred Stieglitz took two prose pieces for his prestigious *Camera Work*—she was thirty-eight years old at the time—did any editor, entirely on his own volition, accept her work for publication.

Though Stein was then writing, writing, writing all the time, her efforts to place book-length manuscripts did not immediately succeed. Beginning in 1931, Carl Van Vechten, a prominent reviewer and publicist at that time, generously sponsored her manuscripts with the larger American book publishers. Some of them snickered when the manuscripts arrived, while others returning them shamelessly vented arrogance based upon irate ignorance. The London publishers she tried were rarely more sympathetic. Short pieces would occasionally appear in better magazines or in folios issued by a Parisian art dealer, while two freshly founded New York small presses issued Stein books—*Tender Buttons* (1914) and *Useful Knowledge* (1928), respectively—in small editions that, like their publishers, quickly disappeared. In the 1920s, H. L. Mencken, who was then both a critic and an editor, smugly numbered Stein among the "Ten Dullest Authors."

Nonetheless, younger writers like Sherwood Anderson and Ernest Hemingway were seeking her out and citing her influence, for it was commonly known within the literary world that Gertrude Stein was doing something special. Still book publishers refused, oblivious to both the presence of a public for her work and its professional distinction. (The industry's next historian might note that the editorial sinners included some of the more honored names in U.S. publishing.)

With typical generosity, Carl Van Vechten followed Stein's pre-Xerox request to put her manuscripts away for safekeeping; and after her death, he became Stein's literary executor. Perhaps because she seldom regarded herself as either female or Jewish, she never publicly blamed her publishing problems on sexual and/or religious discriminations (which did exist, nonetheless, in literary milieus). Her "genius" and originality were, in her judgment, far more troublesome.

In 1922 appeared a collection of her very best short pieces, *Geography and Plays*, published by a small Boston firm, Four Seas, which asked its authors to defray the costs of printing. Four years later, she had to promise Robert McAlmon's Contact Editions that her family would purchase fifty copies (or 10 percent) of the original printing of *Americans*. In the mid-1920s, Stein and Toklas began to spend their summers at Bilignin in the Rhône valley; but every time they returned to Paris in the fall, the cabinet filled with unpublished manuscripts depressed them. In 1930, Toklas simply sold a spare Picasso to Mrs. Averell Harriman in order to found Plain Edition, as she called it. Under that imprint appeared five new Stein books. Stein even contributed her American money to the Paris publication of a book that included French translations of her work. Not until 1933, when Gertrude Stein was fifty-nine years old (and had been a full-time writer for thirty years) did any prominent U.S. publisher invest its name and its own money in her work; and that fact is scarcely a testimonial to the industry's pretensions of literary intelligence.

The book that changed Stein's career was *The Autobiography of Alice B. Toklas* (1933), a gossipy memoir published under her own name. The device of using "Toklas" as a first-person narrator induced Stein to simplify her style, as well as conveniently enabling her to become her own Boswell—to boast about herself in the third person, as "she" and "her." What was initially conceived as a brazen literary stunt became a graceful springboard into American fame. As an effective bit of press-agentry, this extended essay in self-appreciation also generated the first public myths about "Gertrude Stein." Partially serialized in *The Atlantic Monthly*, more influential then than now, *The Autobiography* became a best-seller that no doubt capitalized upon a larger public's salacious interest in Parisian bohemia. Since Stein and Toklas were very hospitable, nearly everyone of cultural importance passed through their house and thus the pages of this book. A year later, Virgil Thomson's musical setting of her opera libretto, *Four Saints in Three Acts*, became a hit in both New York and Chicago, the fame of one work implicitly abetting the other.

No longer a private enthusiasm, Stein suddenly became a public celebrity who was invited to celebrate her sixtieth year with a lecture tour across her native land. Returning to America for the first time in thirty years (and the last time in her life), she gave interviews that made the front pages of newspapers, while her lectures captured an emerging generation of serious readers. Her postlecture repartee was so brilliantly imposing that spectators could recall her exact remarks decades later. Bennett Cerf's Random House agreed to publish only Stein's new manuscripts; but those appearing after *Everybody's Autobiography* (1937) were considerably weaker than their predecessors. At worst, her tone becomes arrogant, the exposition coy, the language cute, and her perceptions glib. Simply, success had made her into a flaccid suburban entertainer. It seems in retrospect that once Stein found a large audience, she became more predisposed to the undistinguished practice of giving her readers what she and her publishers thought they wanted.

Random House's Modern Library reprinted *Three Lives*, and it commissioned Van Vechten to edit and introduce *The Selected Writings of Gertrude Stein* (1946), which incidentally reprinted some of the earlier, more difficult pieces, including *Tender Buttons*. Another New York publisher issued a severely abridged edition of *The Making of Americans* (1936), which thus became available in two drastically different versions. (Back in the 1970s, the Harbrace paperback of this shorter edition mentioned nothing about abridgment.) All this fame notwithstanding, no one wanted to publish Stein's rich cache of earlier, still-unpublished manuscripts;

so one provision of her will was a subsidy to support eight large volumes that the Yale University Press issued between 1951 and 1958. "It has always been my hope," she wrote in 1937, "that some day some one would print everything," and until the 1960s that "some one" was finally herself.

Stein's books fall into two categories—the simple ones and the more difficult texts. Although these terms are themselves too simplistic to provide much critical insight, they have their truth. The "simple" books are those enjoyed by moderately sophisticated readers of realistic fiction: not only *Q.E.D.* and *Three Lives*, but the two autobiographies, *Alice B. Toklas* and *Everybody's Autobiography*, and then the later novels like *Ida* (1941) and *Brewsie and Willie* (1946), in addition to the later memoirs, such as *Paris, France* (1941) and *Wars I Have Seen* (1945). And these remain her more popular works. Nearly everything else can justly be considered "difficult." However, the fact that these works are frequently dismissed as "inscrutable" does not mean they cannot be understood.

One reason that even experienced readers find Stein's prose so difficult is that they expect elements that simply are not there. In her fictions, they look for full-bodied characters but instead find only caricatures; instead of comprehensive descriptions, they find repetitious declarations. Instead of plots that come to a climax, there is uninflected narrative. In her essays, they expect developed definitions and instead find circuitous, indefinite encirclings around an ostensible subject; in lieu of representation, they find abstraction. Even those readers accustomed to the classic modernists—to Joyce, Proust, Eliot, et al.—often find Stein's work opaque, largely because her innovations are not like theirs. What readers often miss is that an understanding and appreciation of Gertrude Stein starts with her style.

Whereas Pound and others experimented primarily with literary structures, Stein concentrated on language. "I like writing," she once wrote. "It is so pleasant, to have the ink write it down on the paper as it goes on doing." Gertrude Stein was almost incapable of writing a common sentence. Even in personal letters, she is continually shifting the order of words, so that the syntactical parts of a sentence fall in unusual places. Adverbs that conventionally come after their verbs now appear before; ditto with prepositional phrases. The object of a clause becomes the subject (i.e., "the ink write it down"), and both adjectives and prepositions have ambiguous referents. Some parts of speech are omitted, while others are duplicated. All these essentially mechanical devices enabled her to express rather simple sentiments in remarkably striking forms: "William Aspinwall Bradley our agent came to stay. After a little while I asked him to go away, not because he was not a pleasant guest because he was but because after a time they are part of the way we live every day or they am not and I prefer them to be not." In some of Stein's works, the sentences are usually short; in others, they are alarmingly long. From sentences of every length, she usually removed all internal punctuation, thus increasing the possibility of ambiguous comprehension; and she favored participles as well, in part to create a sense of interminable continuity. Reading Stein is the best preparation for reading more Stein, for nobody teaches readers how to read Stein better than Stein herself.

Another trick of hers is the use of a severe limitation, such as writing a piece with words of only one syllable, or severely restricting the vocabulary of a passage (and thus necessitating the repetition of those few words):

> Very fine is my valentine.
> Very fine and very mine.
> Very mine is my valentine very mine and very fine.
> Very fine is my valentine and mine, very fine very mine and mine is my valentine.

Always responsive to linguistic possibilities in mundane experience, she once wrote prose that intentionally imitated the rhythms that her dog made while lapping food; other passages imitated sounds in the street or waves hitting the shore. According to Virgil Thomson, she wrote *Lucy Church Amiably* (1930) against a background of streams and waterfalls.

It could be charged that she was "playing games with language," but her decisions were always based upon literary style. Nothing she wrote was gratuitous. What at first seems "mad" is ultimately quite sane. Among her underlying purposes was rescuing printed prose from spoken English: "Because everybody talks as newspapers and movies and radios tell them to talk the spoken language is no longer interesting and so gradually the written language says something and says it differently than the spoken language." A reporter once asked, "Why don't you write the way you talk?" She replied, quite rightly, "Why don't you read the way I write."

Early in her career, she assimilated a primary strategy of experimental art—doing the opposite of convention. If most writers strive for variety of expression, she would repeat certain words and phrases in numerous slightly differing clauses. ("It's not all repetition," she once told a reporter. "I always change the words a little.") If literate writers customarily strive to display a rich vocabulary, along with allusions and other literary connotations, she confined herself to common words and their immediate meanings. She avoided myth and most kinds of metaphor. In lieu of balanced sentences, she decided to explore imbalance. Instead of instilling emotion through rhetoric and flowery language, she keeps her prose generally free of adjectives and adverbs. Typically, she eschewed not only the naturalism then fashionable in fiction writing but the symbolism favored by French poets. As an American individualist, she was neither a surrealist nor a dadaist, neither a futurist nor a constructivist, to cite several European terms that have erroneously been applied to her work. Always, always, Gertrude Stein was something else.

It is a tribute to her genius that she could turn all these counterconventional attitudes to literary advantage, such as transforming a limited vocabulary into something astonishingly evocative. Soon after her break with Leo, she wrote a paean to liberation that reads in part:

> In working when she did what she did she worked all she worked and she did all she did when she did what she did. She did what she did and she worked. She felt what she felt and she did what she did and she worked. She did what she did and she felt what she felt when she was doing what she did when she worked. She felt what she felt when she did what she did when she worked. She worked when she did what she did. She felt what she felt when she did what she did. She worked when she did what she did and she felt what she felt when she worked, when she did what she did.

On her personal stationery was the much-cited motto: "Rose is a rose is a rose is a rose." In Stein's judgment, repeating the noun over and over again raises a supplementary connotation: "I'm no fool," she once told a university audience. "I know that in daily life we don't go around saying [that], but I think that in that line the rose is red for the first time in English poetry for a hundred years." Her most elaborate experiment with linguistic repetition as a device for realizing emphasis, structure, nuance, and rhythm was *The Making of Americans*, which ostensibly relates the history of her own family (disguised as the "Herslands"). The plot is incidental, however, to the linguistic experiments that really interest Stein; for whereas conventional novelists were more concerned with inventing plot and characters, Stein's forte, here and elsewhere, is inventions in language. The true "subject" of *Americans* is not the Hersland family or the complex system for classifying character mentioned in the book's opening pages, but the potentialities of American English.

Repetition was only one Stein stylistic strategy, as the attempt to emancipate language from conventional syntax led swiftly (and logically) to a more radical effort to separate language from context. In short pieces written around 1911 and collected as *Tender Buttons*, the texts often have no apparent relation to their subtitles; yet the rhythms of the words, or their taste (especially if read aloud) relate to one's experience of that declared subject. An example is "Custard," which reads in its entirety:

> Custard this is. It has aches, aches when.
> Not to be. Not to be narrowly. This makes a whole little hill.
> It is better than a little thing that has mellow real mellow.
> It is better than lakes whole lakes, it is better than seeding.

In "Salad Dressing and an Artichoke," Stein writes:

> Please pale hot, please cover rose, please acre in the red stranger, please butter all the beef-steak with regular red faces.

According to Toklas, it was one of Stein's aims "to describe something without mentioning it." Their close friend, the composer Virgil Thomson, finds that "Each description is full of clues, some of them easy to follow up, others put there for throwing you off the scent." One of her best critics, Donald Sutherland, suggests, "One has to give her work word by word the deliberate attention one gives to something written in italics."

In later Stein, such as "Preciosilla" (1926) and certain chapters of *Geography and Plays* (1922), adjacent words have even less syntactical relation to each other:

> Lily wet lily wet while. This is so pink so pink so pink in stammer, a long bean which shows bows is collected by a single curly shady, shady get, get set wet bet.

But, especially if this passage is read aloud, one can hear unities in diction, rhythm, and alliteration, as well as in more subtle qualities like timbre, density, and other nonsyntactical kinds of relatedness:

> In the win all the band beagles which have cousin lime sign and arrange a weeding match to presume a certain point of exstate to exstate to exstate a certain pass lint to exstate a lean sap prime Io and shut shut is life.

In passages like these Stein achieved a scrupulously nonrepresentational prose—language that is intended to be appreciated simply as language, apart from anything else; and those I quoted above strike me as beautiful and really quite classic.

As Sherwood Anderson put it, "She is laying word against word, relating sound to sound, feeling for the taste, the smell, the rhythm of the individual word." Thanks to her experimental attitudes toward the mechanics of prose, Stein created not one original style but a succession of them, all of which are highly personal and thus eventually inimitable. As Sutherland testifies, "Though many other things attach me to Gertrude Stein, what really holds me is her overwhelming rhetorical agility."

What Stein had done was recapitulate in language the history of modernist painting. Her initial scrambling of syntax could be considered an appropriate literary analogy for painterly cubism, which likewise scrambled the viewer's perspective upon an identifiable subject. As in painting, such techniques not only distort the representation of the worldly reality but they also flatten the work's form (by diffusing the traditional ways of focusing its space and time). As cubism brought the reorganization of visual space, so Stein revised the frame of literature. Another analogy is the history of atonal music, as composers who avoided the tonics and dominants of classical harmony found other ways of organizing musical sound. All these developments give mediumistic qualities more prominence than they had before; and just as cubist painting forces the viewer to pay closer attention to two-dimensional composition, so Stein's sentences always call attention to themselves as language. What you read is most of what there is.

The next step, in both postcubist painting and Stein's own writing, was the elimination of an outside subject, once again in order to emphasize the essential properties of the artist's medium. If the materials indigenous to painting are paint and two-dimensional canvases, the mediumistic writer dealt with words and words alone, as in this marvelous passage from "A Sweet Tail (Gypsies)":

> Able there to bill bawl able to call and seat a tin a tin whip with a collar. The least license is in the eyes which make strange the less sighed hole which is nodded and leaves the bent tender.

Like the modernist painters, Stein was interested not in new ideas and new subjects but new perspectives, new perceptions, new forms, and new mediumistic possibilities; yet the kinds of perceptual shifts that an experienced viewer makes before an abstract painting are rarely made in perusing print. As nonrepresentational prose makes no pretense about referring to any reality beyond itself, it need not be "interpreted." What you read is all there is.

By this leap Stein realized another great modernist idea of emphasizing certain dimensions of an art, while completely neglecting others. Both Matisse and Picasso had neglected the photographic purpose of painting, the former emphasizing coherences of color, while the latter concentrated on alternative ways of organizing lines and shapes on a canvas. "Since Picasso," she once wrote, "no painter uses a model at least no painter whose painting interests anybody. The only thing that is outside them is the painting they have just been painting and all the others which of course are always around them." By neglecting not just conventional syntax but the representational purposes of language, Stein was thus free to emphasize its indigenous elements. Though such writing is frequently called "musical," it actually emphasizes qualities peculiar to words and to them alone, such as puns and incantation. What all of Stein's styles had ultimately accomplished was, quite simply, a reinvention of literary English. Perhaps because she lived so long in places where English was scarcely heard, she wrote original English that is so different from what is commonly heard.

Whereas Pound and Eliot, say, initially thought of themselves as poets who also dabbled in essays and plays, Stein's initial medium was prose; only later did she turn to poetry and drama. This might explain why those poets' plays tend to be fairly conventional as drama; Stein's plays and opera librettos, by contrast, represent a radical departure in the history of dramatic writing. As with her prose, Stein made her theatrical advances by emphasizing certain dimensions while totally neglecting others. Her scripts say nothing about costumes, timing, scenery, phrasing, décor, or direction. Many lack any sense of plot, action, protagonist, antagonists, character development, conflict, climaxes, or denouement. Her texts are customarily printed as just a series of unattributed lines (which are occasionally extended into short paragraphs), so that even when the head of the text announces the play's characters, it is frequently hard to tell which passage belongs to which character. Stein further confuses dramatic exposition by violating the conventions of organization. Thus, her plays have any and all number of scenes and acts, while a "Scene II" sometimes follows "Scene III" that had followed an earlier "Scene II." Early in *Four Saints*, she writes: "Repeat First Act." No theatrical texts written before were ever like these.

An extreme example that nonetheless exemplifies Stein's playwriting style is "A Curtain Raiser," which was written in the 1910s:

Six,
Twenty,
    Outrageous
Late,
Weak.

    Forty.
More in any wetness.
Sixty three certainly.
Five
Sixteen
Seven.
Three.
More in orderly. Seventy-five.

That is the play's *entire* text, which typically emphasizes verbal style to the neglect of everything else. To the critic Donald Sutherland, these evocations of sound and image are plays, rather than fictions, because they are designed to be performed and because they present "movement in space, or in a landscape." They are organized not as narratives but as a series of joyous moments, each of which is as important as every other. Rather than telling "what happened," they are happening. Sutherland continues, "These plays of hers do not tell you anything. They merely present themselves, like a drama or a circus or any play that is really a stage play." Though a text like Stein's allows its director enormous liberties, the verbal style still bestows particular qualities upon the final production. Stein became the historical precursor of a popular contemporary practice of writing scripts so unorthodox in form that the performances they generate would necessarily be comparably eccentric.

    The first major production of a Stein text was Virgil Thomson's of *Four Saints in Three Acts*, and in his spectacular use of musicians, dancers, setting, and even a choir, Thomson created a marvelous, distinctly American opera that elegantly enhanced Steinian lines like these:

Pigeons on the grass alas. Pigeons on the grass alas.
Short longer grass longer longer shorter yellow grass. Pigeons large pigeons on the shorter longer yellow grass alas pigeons on the grass.

As this much-praised, widely remembered production became a persuasive alternative to the theatrical realism that then dominated the American stage, it became a precursor of subsequent antirealistic, "absurd" theater. This theatrically abundant operatic style has informed subsequent productions of Stein texts, such as those by Al Carmines and Lawrence Kornfield at New York's Judson Memorial Church during the 1960s. One reason why directors have so far favored such festive formats is that Stein's own sense of theater is primarily visual and kinetic. In fact, she preferred Russian ballet, Isadora Duncan, operas, bullfights, and football games (which may have influenced her enthusiasm for numbers in "A Curtain Raiser"). However, as the poet-playwright Dick Higgins once told me, "It does not have to be that way. I'd like to see a moody, Scandinavian production." Stein also wrote poems, few of which were published during her own lifetime. They are as nonrepresentational as her most abstract prose, completely eschewing subject, and yet observing selected conventions of poetry—meter, alliteration, and consistent diction. They exemplify what Stein once called "really writing." As Stein's poems are scarcely appreciated by either critics or anthologists, they remain the most neglected dimension of her achievement.

Almost from the beginning of her professional career, Stein wrote essays about the world around her. Just as her perceptions are invariably original, so the best of these essays are stylistically remarkable. The earliest notable efforts were the "portraits" of Matisse and Picasso, which emphasize certain points not by elaboration but by repetition. (Thus, Matisse is "expressing something struggling," while Picasso is "certainly working" and "completely charming.") From portraits she moved eventually into "geographies," as she called them, or portraits of places, which mixes detail with impressions, going around their subjects rather than at them. Some of these were reportedly done by Stein's concentrating upon a particular subject and then writing down whatever flashed into her head, for she hoped to record in print the characteristic image and sound of her subjects. As she put it, her aim was "exactitude in the description of inner and outer reality." Beginning in 1922, with an essay called "An Elucidation," Stein also began to write prolifically about her own work; but rather than providing simple, Aristotelian guidance (and compromising certain integrities), she pursued her earlier stylistic predilection and wrote essays that explain by example—elucidating within the essay, rather than through it or by it. Nonetheless, in this respect too, the best preparation for reading Stein is Stein herself.

It is in her essays that Stein most clearly reveals the paradoxical qualities of her mind. They show, for instance, how she was using intelligence to deny those literary qualities customarily associated with intelligence, such as analysis and human insight, all in the interests of a supposedly higher intelligence about literary art. This predilection might also explain the remarkably limited range of subjects in nearly all her writing—herself, her immediate friends, and U.S. history. Though enamored with speculations, she was also an empiricist, who meant what she said; yet in spite of this empirical bias, her writing is riddled with quirky prejudices and hokey ideas. Typically, for all of her perceptions into her cultural enthusiasms, she was absolutely smug about what she did not like, and her terms of dismissal were invariably as curt as "uninteresting" or "no longer interesting."

Though she rarely wrote about either herself or her companion Alice Toklas as Jewish, I find that Stein reflects Judaism in her interests in abstraction and in incantatory, mantric writing. The French among whom she lived and died thought her Jewish. Special arrangements had to be made to protect her from the occupying Nazis during World War II; and when she died, she was buried where her body still remains—in a section of the famous Père Lachaise (Paris) Cemetery reserved exclusively for Jews.

Mostly because nothing in her experience, until the Second World War, led her to question the conservative social-political attitudes of her youth, her remarks about politics and economics are often embarrassing. "To be avaricious I think the greatest value in the world and I say so and I do want to be so." In *Everybody's Autobiography* are some particularly hair-raising passages about all the difficulties in keeping reliable servants. Early in the Second World War, which she spent in occupied France, Stein began to translate into English the speeches of Marshal Pétain, a Nazi collaborationist whom she somehow regarded as the French George Washington. She hoped they would be published in America. Though she had a romantic conception of her artist's self, her aesthetic is counterexpressionistic, and that tension explains why her art is frequently sabotaged by her ego. What explains these paradoxes to me is my impression that her intellect did not equal her great aesthetic intelligence.

It would not be improper to call Stein the Totemic Mother of modern art, mostly because of her influence on young artists—not only those she knew personally, like the composer Virgil Thomson, the painter Picasso, and the writers Ernest Hemingway, Thornton Wilder, and Sherwood Anderson, but the many creative people who read and assimilated her work. Hemingway reveals Stein's influence particularly in his use of a mundane vocabulary, his outright repetitions, and his syntactical shifts, such as placing the adverb after the verb instead of prior to the verb or after the object (e.g., "He poured smoothly the buckwheat batter."). In my judgment, Stein probably influenced William Faulkner's use of excessively long sentences and John Dos Passos's penchant for dropping parts of speech, as well as E. E. Cummings's syntactical shiftings, Samuel Beckett's uninflected prose, and Norman Mailer's habit of impersonating Alice B. Toklas—speaking of himself not as "I" but "Mailer" or "Aquarius."

Adventurous young authors customarily ignore the recently dominant figures to discover possibilities in previously neglected precursors. The declining influence of Faulkner and Pound accompanies the rise of Stein, who is presently having yet another round of influence. Unlike before, however, now the more radical works seem most alive. I hear the impact of this Stein in the non-representational poetry of John Ashbery, Clark Coolidge, Bruce Andrews, and those customarily classified with epithets emphasizing the word Language, among others. Andrews once told me, "Repetition seems like a very personal mark that does not open doors for us, but the idea of non-syntactical organization stands ready for any of us to use. Once syntax is abandoned or attenuated, and need no longer function as the organizing principle for the signifiers, there is a tremendous and unprecedented freedom in the ways words can be organized." I also hear Steinian aesthetics in the modular music of Philip Glass, Steve Reich, Terry Riley, and Meredith Monk, in which fixed motifs—modules, phrases—are repeated through a succession of otherwise changing relationships.

Perhaps because her works were neglected for so long (and then commonly regarded as largely inaccessible), remarkably little has been written about Gertrude Stein. There are several biographies, none of which would rank as definitive, all of which tend to echo excessively Stein's own autobiographies. The keystone in Stein criticism has been Donald Sutherland's brilliant *Gertrude Stein: A Biography of Her Work* (1951), which is filled with spectacular perceptions and speculations. Some of the earlier attempts to understand her work, such as Edmund Wilson's chapter in *Axel's Castle* (1931), now seem superficial and mistaken, while passing references to her work, even in literary journals, are often inaccurate and inept. Stein's works suggest many other interpretations that have scarcely been broached—not only of such technical matters as her idiosyncratic representation of space and time, but also her subject matter.

The crucial questions raised by Stein's writing have scarcely been answered. It is indicative that though her works are commonly acknowledged as "uneven," even professionals disagree drastically over which books are the masterpieces. Whereas some favor *Three Lives* and *The Autobiography*, I personally prefer the more difficult ones— not only *The Making of Americans* and *Geography and Plays*, but *Painted Lace* (1955), which strikes me as collecting the most extraordinary examples of previously uncollected works. These are great American books; no European could have possibly written them.

At a time when readers of literature have successfully assimilated the innovations of, say, Faulkner and Pound, Stein's more difficult works still seem very, very strange. If one were not otherwise informed, he or she would initially suspect they were written yesterday. Their sole peer in this respect is Joyce's *Finnegans Wake*. Fifty years ago, Robert Penn Warren suggested that "the study of Faulkner is the most challenging single task in contemporary American literature for criticism to undertake." I thought thirty years ago when I first read Warren's statement that the current challenge was the study of Stein; it still is.

The other major American artist closest to her is the composer Charles Ives, who was curiously born in the same year of 1874. Likewise declining to earn a living through art, he composed pieces that were for decades unperformed, much as Stein's manuscripts were unpublished. Each received great recognition just before their deaths—1946 for Stein, 1954 for Ives. There is no evidence that they ever met each other. Perhaps the surest way I have of gauging their originality is that I can identify what each of them did with terms that come from my understanding of subsequent avant-garde art, using such terms as minimalism, simultaneity, uninflected form, and so on; but since such ideas were not known in the early twentieth century, I can barely imagine what they thought they were doing.

One reason Stein's writings seem so contemporary is that they suggest further possibilities in literary art; another is that they force even experienced readers to re-adjust—to stretch if not expand—their perceptual capabilities. Reading a lot of Stein induces you to pay closer attention to the language of English sentences. A half-century ago, when writers praised the avant-garde Gertrude Stein, they were talking about works that were not commonly available. Fortunately, that is no longer true. American readers are finally free to discover what Stein knew all along—that she was indeed "a genius" and that her best writing is spectacularly original.

INTRODUCTION

Those who like to construct superlative-filled hierarchies in American writing might say that Stein was the foremost literary alumna of a "seven sister" college, probably the greatest writer of Jewish descent, perhaps the principal woman writer, and one of the two great homosexual writers (as well as, incidentally, the best art collector and the greatest fat author). However, these are partial and thus minor accolades. It is more important that as a literary inventor she ranks with Ezra Pound and Walt Whitman; but unlike them, she made decidedly innovative contributions not to just one genre or two but several. In American literary history she has had no equal as a pioneer of avant-garde letters.

RICHARD KOSTELANETZ
New York City
May 2002

INTRODUCING

Sensing more Steinian resonance in the title than perhaps was intended, I find this an appropriate opening to this book.—R. K.

One was a completely young one and this one was very clearly understanding this thing, clearly understanding that this one was a young one then and this one was one very clearly explaining this thing to every one and some indeed quite a number listened to him then and some of those listening were young ones then and some of those listening then were not young ones then.

The one who was completely a young one was one certainly very clearly then understanding this thing and quite clearly explaining this thing and explaining this thing clearly and quite often.

This one was one who was doing something and another thing and another thing and in a way he was doing each thing in the same way as he was doing each other thing and in a way there were differences and in a way certainly there were not any differences at all. He was a young one and he was clearly understanding this thing and he was certainly often very clearly explaining this thing. He was

From *Useful Knowledge* (1928).

I

doing something and he certainly did it for sometime and it was certainly something he should then be doing. Some one might be thinking that he might be more successfully than doing some other thing but really not any one thought he should not be doing the thing he was doing when he was doing the thing and certainly he was very steadily doing the thing, the thing he was doing when he was doing that thing. In a way he had been doing a number of things, in a way he was always doing the same thing. He was a young one and he was completely clearly understanding this thing and he was completely when he was explaining this thing completely clearly explaining this thing.

He certainly was understanding something. He certainly was understanding and clearly explaining being a young one in his being a young one. Certainly he was listening and listening very often. Certainly he was understanding something, he was clearly understanding his being then a young one. He certainly was listening very much and very often. He certainly was sometimes explaining something. He certainly was clearly explaining his being a young one, he certainly was clearly understanding and clearly explaining this thing.

He could certainly pretty clearly ask what was the meaning of anything he was hearing. He certainly could ask quite clearly what was the way that something could come to have the meaning that thing had in being existing. He could almost completely clearly ask about something that some one had been explaining. He could completely clearly ask a question, he could almost completely clearly then ask another question, he could not quite completely clearly ask another question about that thing, he certainly could not completely clearly ask a question then again, ask another question then. He could certainly completely clearly explain being a young one in being then a young one, he certainly could completely clearly explain this thing, he certainly could completely clearly understand this thing.

He certainly did do a thing and go on sometime and go on and steadily go on doing that thing and certainly he did begin getting to explain quite clearly why he was doing that thing, what he was doing then, what he was not doing then. Certainly he did then explain quite clearly about his doing that thing and he was then certainly completely steadily doing that thing. He was quite steadily doing that thing, he certainly was quite completely then understanding his doing that thing, he certainly was very steadily doing that thing. He certainly was very steadily doing another thing then, he certainly quite completely understood his doing that thing then, he certainly quite completely and clearly understood his doing that thing then. He certainly did that thing very steadily then. He certainly quite completely clearly understood his doing that thing then. He certainly did another thing then, he certainly quite steadily quite entirely steadily did that thing then. He certainly quite clearly understood his doing that thing then. He certainly very steadily did that thing then. He certainly quite completely understood his doing that thing then. He certainly did another thing then. He certainly very steadily did that thing then. He certainly quite completely, he certainly quite clearly understood his doing that thing then.

He certainly did listen and listen again and again, he certainly quite steadily did this thing. He certainly quite clearly asked a question then. He certainly did sometimes quite clearly ask another question then. He did certainly sometimes did and quite clearly ask another question then, and certainly then he commenced listening again and he went on then listening and he continued then being listening.

He certainly was not ever about the same thing asking the same question again. He certainly was listening again to the same thing, he certainly was not asking the same question about the same thing again. In a way then he was not one asking the same questions again and again. He certainly was not asking the same question about the same thing and he certainly was one understanding clearly his being a young one and he certainly was quite often quite clearly explaining this thing and he was doing something and he was completely steadily doing that thing and he was completely clearly understanding his doing that thing. He certainly did amuse some and he certainly did interest some and he certainly did not disappoint some and he certainly did go on being living and certainly he did quite clearly understand being a young one in being a young one and he certainly did very nearly completely clearly and quite often explain this thing to some who were and to some who were then not themselves then young.

ADVERTISEMENTS

This can be read as a compressed cycle of compressed short stories.—R. K.

I was winsome. Dishonored. And a kingdom. I was not a republic. I was an island and land. I was early to bed. I was a character sodden agreeable perfectly constrained and not artificial. I was relieved by contact. I said good-morning, good evening, hour by hour. I said one had power. I said I was frequently troubled. I can be fanciful. They have liberal ideas. They have dislikes. I dread smoke. Where are there many children. Where are there many children. We have an account. We count daisy. Daisy is a daughter. Her name is Antonia. She is pleased to say what will you have. Horns and horns. Nicholas is not a stranger. Neither is Monica. No one is a stranger. We refuse to greet any one. We like Genevieve to satisfy us. I do not like what I am saying.

How can you describe a trip. It is so boastful.

He said definitely that they would. They have. It's a little late. I hope the other things will be as he states them. I have confidence.

From *Geography and Plays* (1922).

I have not eaten peaches. Yes I have. I apologize. I did not want to say the other word that was red. You know what I mean.

Why can I read it if I know page to page what is coming if I have not read it before. Why can I read it. I do.

I didn't.

Let me see. I wish to tell about the door. The door opens before the kitchen. The kitchen is closed. The other door is open and that makes a draft. This is very pleasant in summer. We did not expect the weather to change so suddenly. There seem to be more mosquitoes than ever. I don't understand why I like narrative so much to read. I do like it. I see no necessity for disclosing particularity I am mightily disturbed by a name such as an English home. An English home is beautiful. So are the times.

A dog does not bark when he hears other dogs bark. He sleeps carefully he does not know about it. I am not pained.

This is the narrative. In watching a balloon, a kite, a boat, steps and watches, any kind of a call is remarkable remarkably attuned. A resemblance to Lloyd George, bequeathing prayers, saying there is no hope, having a french meeting. Jenny said that she said that she did not believe in her country. Any one who does not believe in her country speaks the truth. How dare you hurt the other with canes. I hope he killed him. Read it. I believe Bulgaria. I have pledges. I have relief.

I Am Not Patient

I am interested. In that table. I like washing gates with a mixture. We get it by bringing up melons. White melons have a delicious flavor.

I am not patient. I get angry at a dog. I do not wish to hear a noise. I did not mind the noise which the client made. I wished to see the pearls. How easily we ask for what we are going to have. By this we are pleased and excited.

The hope there is is that we will hear the news. We are all elated. Did you see her reading the paper. I cannot help wanting to write a story.

A woman who had children and called to them making them hear singing is a match for the man who has one child and does not tell him to play there with children. Heaps of them are gambling. They tell about stitches. Stitches are easily made in hot weather and vegetation. Tube roses are famous.

I could be so pleased. It would please me if Van would mention it. Why is an index dear to him. He has thousands of gesticulations. He can breathe.

White and be a Briton. This means a woman from the north of France. They are very religious. They say blue is not a water color. It should be a bay. We are pleased with her. She washes her hair very often.

Do not tremble. If she had an institution it is the one excluding her mother. Her native land is not beautiful. She likes the poet to mutter. He does. The olive.

We had that impression. Do speak. Have they been able to arrange matters with the proprietor.

I will not please play. I will adorn the station. It has extraordinarily comfortable seats.

To Open

Not too long for leading, not opening his mouth and sitting. Not bequeathing butter. Butter comes from Brittany. In the summer it smells rancid. We do not like it. We have ceased use of it. We find that oil does as well. We can mix oil with butter but we have lard. We use lard altogether. We prefer it to butter. We use the butter in winter. We have not been using it before the winter. We mix lard and oil. We will use butter.

Do Let Us Be Faithful and True

I do not wish to see I do not wish to see Harry I do not wish to see Harry Brackett I do not wish to see Harry Brackett.

A Grape Cure

What did we have for dinner we had a melon lobster chicken then beet salad and fruit. How can you tell a melon. You tell it by weight and pressing it. You do not make mistakes. We are pleased with it. Do we like a large dog. Not at all.

Battle

Battle creek. I was wet. All the doors showed light. It is strange how Brittany is not attractive as Mallorca and yet butter does make a difference. We are perfect creatures. What is a festival. Saturday to some. Not to be dishonored. Not to be tall and dishonored they usually aren't but some are, some are tall and dishonored. By this I mean that coming down the mountain faces which are shining are reflecting the waving of the boat which is there now. I distrust everybody. Do sleep well. Everywhere there is a cat. We will leave by boat. I am not pleased with this. I will get so that I can write a story.

Fastening Tube Roses

I understand perfectly well how to fix an electric fan. Of course it makes sparks but when the two black pieces that do not come

together are used up you get this. I do it without any bother. I am
not certain I could learn it. It is not difficult. We do not find that
it does away with mosquitoes. We use it in the night. Sundays there
is no electricity.

They Do It Better Than I Do

I can. I can be irritated. I hate lizards when you call them
crocodile. She screamed. She screamed. I do not know why I am
irritated.

It Is a Natural Thing

Do not do that again. I do not like it. Please give it away. We
will not take it to Paris. I do not want the gas stove. It has a round
oven. It does not bake. We use coal by preference. It is very difficult not to bathe in rain water. Rain water is so delicious. It is
boiled. We boil it.

Loud Letters

Look up and not down.
Look right and not left.
And lend a hand.
We were so pleased with the Mallorcans and the wind and the
party. They were so good to offer us ice-cream. They do not know
the french names.
Isn't it peculiar that those that fear a thunder storm are willing
to drink water again and again, boiled water because it is healthy.

All the water is in cisterns rain water. There are no vegetables that is to say no peas. There are plenty of beets. I like them so much. So do I melons. I was so glad that this evening William came and ate some. It would not go back as if it hadn't been good.

Pleasures in Sincere Wishes

I wish you to enjoy these cigarettes. They are a change from those others. I understand that you had some very good ones. You are not able to get these any more. I have tried to get them. They tell me that they cannot say when they will come. They do not know that about them. We sleep easily. We are awakened by the same noise. It is so disagreeable.

An Exhibition

I do not quite succeed in making an exhibition. Please place me where there is air. I like to be free. I like to be sure that the dogs will not be worried. I don't see how they can avoid crickets. They come in. They are so bothersome. We must ask Polybe to wish.

The Boat

I was so disappointed in the boat. It was larger than the other. It did not have more accom[m]odation. It made the noise which was disagreeable. I feel that I would have been willing to say that I liked it very well if I had not seen it when it was painted. It is well never to deceive me.

Threadneedle Street

I am going to conquer. I am going to be flourishing. I am going to be industrious. Please forgive me everything.

Present

This is a ceremonial. When you are bashful you do not think. When a present is offered you accept it you accept the bracelet worn by the nun so that it rusted. You do not know what to do with it. You describe its qualities. It is a pleasure to have it. You will give it. You are steadily tender. You say the beginning is best. Why do you say Englishman. You say Englishman because he wished it. Do not hurry.

Evian Water

Evian water is very good. Sometimes I am not sure it is put up by them at least now when there is a war. I say it is fresh. When I do not like a bottle I throw it away. I throw the water away.

BUSINESS IN BALTIMORE

"Business in Baltimore" depends upon repetition of an euphonistically attractive phrase announced in its title. My hunch is that it began with a title and is thus initially about the poetic qualities available in these words, climaxing with a spectacular conclusion.—R. K.

Nor narrow, long.
    Julian is two.
    How many and well.
    And days and sank.
    Thanks to having.
    Business in Baltimore thanks to having and days and sank how many and well Julian is two not narrow, long.
    Julian is two how many and well thanks to having.
    Once upon a time Baltimore was necessary.
    How and would it be dressed if they had divided a bank and tan. It connected at once it connected twice it connected doors and floors.
    This is in May.

From *Useful Knowledge* (1928).

So they say.

How many places for scales are there in it.

Weigh once a day.

In Baltimore there are the ferns the miles the pears the cellars and the coins.

After that the large and small stones or stepping stones.

This is why they have every reason to be arranged and every morning to be morning and every evening to be evening.

This is the reason why they have every Sunday and Tuesday and Monday.

Who finds minds and who lines shines and two kinds finds and two kinds minds. Minds it. She never wanted to leave Baltimore anywhere and was it.

Business in Baltimore.

He did and peppers see he did and three.

He did and three he did and see he did and three and see and he did and peppers see and peppers see and three he did.

It is so easy to have felt needed and shielded and succeeded and decided and widened and waited. No waiting for him Saturday Monday and Thursday.

All of them are devoted to it to doing what was done when it was begun and afterwards all sashes are old. Forget wills.

The best and finally the first, the first and formerly the rest all of it as they have it to do to do to do already in their house. Suppose in walking up and down they sat around.

Imagine vines, vines are not had here imagine vines that are not to be had here and imagine rubbers had here and imagine working working in blue that means over it. Each one of these had to give away had to have to had to give way. How many others brothers and fathers.

He had held him he had held her he had held it for him he had held it for her, he had hold of it, and he had had days.

How many days pay, how much of a day pays and how difficultly from thinking. I think I thought I said I sought I fell I fought I had I ought to have meant to be mine.

Not as funny as yet.

Imagining up and down. How many generations make five.

If another marries her brother, if another marries their brother, if their brother marries another, if their brother and a brother marry another and the sister how many pairs are there of it.

It is easy not to be older than that.

Do you hear me.

It is easier.

How many papers can make more papers and how many have to have her. Have to have her. How many papers can make more papers and how many have to have to have it.

How many have to have to have it and how many papers make more papers. It makes a little door to-day.

Put it there for him to see. He knew how and how to have he knew how to have and accepted so much as much or much much of it for it, for it is and in either direction might be saved, saved or so and while it is while it is while it is near near while it is while it is near having monthly in use. To hear them and as it has to be at and for and as it has to be for and mine and as it has to be powder and ice and as it has to be and as it has to be louder and there and as it has to be louder and there and I hear it.

And in there.

When he could not remember that when he could not remember it at all when he could remember it all and when he could remember it all. It started and parted, partly to them and for most. Foremost is a way they have to have used here.

The first time they ever had it, heard it and had it, the first time they ever had it.

In their favor as a favor as a favor or favorable.

Having forgotten how it sounds, have they forgotten all the sound remind them.

The first reason for having seven is six and a half, six and a half and as seldom. After that the real reason for six more than a half and as seldom the real reason for six more and a half and as seldom is six more six more and a half more and six more and a half more and six more and a half more and seldom.

Please put it in paper there.

A little place and for fortunately. Did he and they have a lake to-day. Nearly.

Having at it and at once a noise and it, it could be just as much more also. Have a sound of or a sound of or, or Alice. Miss Alice is might it.

The very easy how do red horses have a pair. This makes Arthur and no name. He made him go.

Come near come nearly come nearly come near come near come nearly. Come near. Come near come nearly. He had a haul and I said do you do that and he did and he said not to-day. Anybody can say not to-day.

There was once upon a time a selfish boy and a selfish man, there was once upon a time a selfish man. There was once upon a time a selfish man. There was once upon a time there was once upon a time a selfish man there was once upon a time a selfish boy there was once upon a time a selfish boy there was once upon a time a selfish boy there was once upon a time a selfish man. How selfish. There was once upon a time a selfish man. There was once upon a time a selfish boy, how once upon a time a selfish boy how once upon a time a selfish man.

Nobody knows whose wedding shows it to them. Business in Baltimore makes a wedding first at first business in Baltimore makes a wedding at first first. Business in Baltimore makes a wedding at first at first. Business in Baltimore makes a wedding at first at first first. Business in Baltimore makes a wedding first at first. Business in Baltimore at first makes a wedding first makes a wedding at first. Business in Baltimore makes a wedding at first.

Business in Baltimore makes a wedding at first.

Business in Baltimore at first.

In heights and whites, in whites and lights, in lights in sizes, in sizes in sides and in wise, or as wise or wiser. This not to be the first to know.

To know.

Altogether older, older altogether.

Not following hearing or a son or another. No one spells mother or brother.

To them or then or then by then it was mostly done by them.

Who has had had it had. Had it, he had it and following he had it, he had it. Following he had it.

Business in Baltimore following he had it. Business in Baltimore following he had it following he had had it. Business in Baltimore following he had had it. Following he had had it following he had had it business in Baltimore following he had had it.

Business in Baltimore.

How easy it is to see voices. How easy it is to see.

How easy it is to see voices and very much of it put as a rug. Supposing a whole floor was covered and on the cover where he stands has a place for it which is attached to them and of this kind. Could it have been made before a boat and no one follows. How many have had hands.

When they were sung to sung to see when they were sung to sung among when they were snugly sung to see, see seeds for that to eat and for and have the size and no more satchels made at all. Satchels may be held loosely. When they are sung and sung and sung and little have to have a hand and hand and two and two hands too, and too and two and handled too to them, handed to them, hand and hands. Hands high. This can be Baltimore and or and Baltimore and for and Baltimore and more and Baltimore and for and Baltimore and or. It does not sound like it.

When he older than that when he older than this when he older than this when he as old as he is, he is as old as he is, he is as old he is as old and would they know that fifty are fairly plenty of later hats. Hats cannot be used as mats not for selling or for much as much. He certainly was amused by it.

Devoted to having a whole a half a half a whole, a whole or told it. Devoted to having a half, a whole a whole or told or it. Devoted to having a whole a half a half a whole a whole or told it. Devoted to having a half a whole a whole a whole a half a whole or told it.

She did see fortunes fade.

Who did see fortunes fade.

Nobody saw fortunes fade. Nobody saw fortunes nobody saw fortunes fade.

A whole a half a half a whole, fortunes fade who never saw fortunes fade he never saw fortunes fade. A half a whole he never saw he never saw fortunes he never saw fortunes fade or faded. He never saw fortunes he never saw fortunes fade.

How much business is there in Baltimore.

And how many are there in business in Baltimore.

And how have they had to have business in Baltimore.

And how has it been how has it been how has he been in business in Baltimore.

He has been in business in Baltimore and before and before he was in business in Baltimore he was not in business he was not in business before he was in business in Baltimore.

He had been in business before he had been in business in Baltimore he had been in business before in Baltimore. How had he been in business in Baltimore. He had been in business before in Baltimore he had not been in business before he was in business in Baltimore.

Business in Baltimore before, before business, before business in Baltimore.

Business in Baltimore is business in Baltimore.

Business in Baltimore in business in Baltimore and business in Baltimore is this business in Baltimore.

How many more are there in business in Baltimore than there were before.

How many more are in business in Baltimore than were in business in Baltimore before.

This business in Baltimore.

That business in Baltimore.

A business in Baltimore.

Business in Baltimore.

Who says business in Baltimore. Who says business in Baltimore and before, and who says business in Baltimore more business in Baltimore more business in Baltimore than before.

Pleases me, and while they have to have eaten eaten it, and eaten eaten it and eaten eaten it eaten eaten eaten eaten eaten it. Then a list is useful. Useful soon, useful as soon. As useful as soon. As useful as soon. Some time and shown. Who has to say so say so. They easily have after and soon.

It was said at once to them that they had it. Afterwards it was said at once to them that they had it. Afterwards it was at once said to them that they had it. It was said to them it was afterwards said to them at once that they had it. It was afterwards said at once said to them afterwards said to them that they had it. It was afterwards said to them that they had it. It was afterwards at once said to them that they had it.

How much easier how much easier, how much easier and how much easier. Forty makes forty and forty-four makes forty-four and forty-four makes four and forty four makes forty-four. Business in Baltimore makes counting easy.

If he had had and had had given and had had given to him what he had had how many more are there to have held it in this way away. One and he was famous not for that nor for provision nor for in addition nothing, nothing too much, not anything more and it was not said to be said. It takes many times more to make many times more and not to make many times more and not to make many times more many times more. Not many times more. Read riches. Anything that begins with r makes read riches and this is as twice and once and once. Once is it once, twice is it twice is it twice once and is it once twice.

This is the way they make the day they make the day they make the day this is the way they make the day, once a day and it is a reason for having heard of it. Now at last it is well known that not because he did he did not hurry he did not hurry because he did and did not hurry and who asked him. That is what they say who asked him.

Forgetting a name.

Not to be transferred to Baltimore and so to say so so much. If you do not hear him speak at all louder then not to speak at all louder, not to speak at all louder not to hear him speak at all louder not to hear him speak at all louder and so not to speak at all louder. He does not speak louder and so not to speak louder and so not to speak louder at all.

She was as well as he was as well as he was as well as she was as well as all that.

All that as well as all that and having forgotten all the same having forgotten having forgotten and all the same all the same as having forgotten and to hear it hear it heard it heard it hear heard it heard it, heard it and all the same as forgotten having heard it all the same and all the same and having forgotten and having heard and all the same. Having heard it all the same having heard hear it hear it all the same having forgotten and hear it and having forgotten and hear it and all the same and all the same and hear it and heard it.

So much and so much farther as much and as much farther, and as much farther and so much and hear it and having heard it and all the same and having heard it and all the same and hear it and all the same and hear it and heard and having heard and all the same and hear it. Here and hear it. They are all the same as heard it as hear it all the same as heard it all the same and as heard it. All the same and heard and as heard it and as heard it and as all the same and heard it. All the same. Hear it. All the same hear it all the same.

The same examples are the same and just the same and always the same and the same examples are just the same and are the same and always the same. The same examples are just the same and they are very sorry for it. So is not business in Baltimore. And so it is not and so is it not and as it is not and as it is and as it is not the same more than the same. This sounds as if they said it and it sounds as if they meant it and it sounds as if they meant it and it sounds as if they meant and as if they meant it. Everybody is disappointed in Julian's cousin Julian's cousin too, everybody is also disappointed is disappointed in Julian's cousin too. Julian and everybody is disappoointed in Julian's cousin and everybody too is disappointed in Julian's cousin too. How many days are there for it. There are as many days for it as there are ways to see how they do it. Do it too. Julian and a cousin too. Two and two, and two and two and lists and remembered and lists. To commence back further and just as far and as far back and just as far back. Just as far back as that. Just as far back as that and Julian remembers just as far back as that and Julian remembers just as far back and remembers Julian remembers just as far back as that.

Everybody knows that anybody shows shows it as soon as soon and at noon as carefully noon as carefully soon, everybody knows, everybody shows, everybody shows anybody knows carefully as soon carefully and noon carefully at noon everybody knows everybody shows carefully at noon carefully soon carefully soon carefully at noon, everybody knows carefully at noon carefully as soon anybody knows everybody shows everybody shows everybody knows carefully as soon, anybody knows carefully as soon, anybody knows carefully at noon everybody knows carefully as soon everybody knows carefully as soon, anybody knows carefully as soon everybody knows carefully as soon.

Everybody knows carefully as soon, everybody knows carefully at noon everybody knows carefully as soon.

Entirely exposed too.

And how many in passing turn around. Just how many in passing just how many turn around. One can always tell the difference between snowy and cloudy everybody can always tell some difference between cloudy and snowy.

Every one can always tell some difference.

Every one can always tell some difference between cloudy and cloudy between snowy and snowy between cloudy and snowy between snowy and cloudy.

Not as to dinner and dinner.

How many are a hundred and how many are two hundred and how many are a million and three. This is for them to answer and in this way more in Baltimore. Business in Baltimore consists of how many and how often and more at once and a half of them there.

Business in Baltimore is always a share a share and care to care and where where in Baltimore. Where in Baltimore. How many kinds are there in it.

There are many and as many there are as many as there are streets, corners, places, rivers and trees in Baltimore. Squares can be mentioned too and stones and little and at once to approach. Who changes all changes.

All changes who changes.

Do not hurry to winter and to summer. Do not hurry to winter. Do not hurry to summer. Do not hurry to summer. Not to hurry to winter. Not to hurry to winter and to summer and to winter and not to hurry to summer and not to hurry to winter.

He can hear they can hear they can hear that they do hear her. They can hear that they do hear him. They can hear that they do hear him. They can hear that they do hear her. They can hear that they can hear him.

They can hear winter, they can hear summer they can hear that they do hear summer, they can hear that they do hear that they can hear winter, they can hear summer they can hear winter. They can hear that they hear him they can hear that they can hear her they do hear that they can hear that they do hear her that they do hear winter that they do hear her that they can hear her that they can hear that they do hear him that they do hear him that they can hear that they do hear that they hear that they can hear summer and hear hear her here hear him here that they can hear her that they can hear. They do hear that they can hear winter. They do hear that they can hear summer.

Business in Baltimore for them and with them with them and as a tree is bought. How is a tree bought. Business in Baltimore and for them and by them and is bought how is it to be bought and where is it to be bought. Business in Baltimore and for them and adding it to them and as it has the half of the whole and the whole is more if it is best shown to be more used than it was here and nearly. This and a result. Take it in place, take it to a place take it for a place and places and to place and placed. Placed and placing should a daughter be a mother. Placed and placing should a father be a brother. Placed and placing should a mother be a sister altogether. All this makes it easy that very many say so and very many do so and very many do so and very many say so.

He can so easily amuse himself and so can he so very easily amuse himself and so can he so very easily and so can he so very easily amuse himself and so can he so very easily and so can he so very easily amuse himself and as it were to be they had to have it largely and more and when they needed it all. To begin.

How many houses were there in it. And to go on. And how many houses were there in it.

How to depend upon it. And how many houses were there in it. And how to depend upon it and how many houses were there in it. How many houses are there in it.

There were as many houses as there were in it.

There were as many houses in it as there were as many houses in it. There are as many houses in it. How many houses are there in it. There are as many houses as there are in it. After that streets, corners, connections and ways of walking. There were more houses than there were in it. There were more corners than there were in it. There were more streets than there were in it. How many streets are there in it. How many corners are there in it. How many streets are there in it. How many houses were there in it. Everybody counting. Call somebody Hortense. Please do. And David. Please do.

A little makes it all stop and stopped. A little makes it all stopped and stop. A little makes it all stop. A little makes it all stopped.

It is a great pleasure for Hilda and for William for William and for Hilda. It is a great pleasure for either. If a home and a house and as often as hurry and hurried, they need to and do, they need to do they did need to they did and they did need to and they do and they do and they did need to do it too. Does she look as much like it as the newspaper would suggest.

Plainly make it mine. Plainly make it plainly make it mine.

This is as least not as well said as ever.

Having forgotten to hear, what and having forgotten to hear what had not been forgotten and not forgotten to hear.

They have please they have please they have please. Business in Baltimore they have please.

Did they like five.

Did they like five of five.

Business in Baltimore and more. More seated.

Business in Baltimore need never be finished here when it is there when it is commenced there when it is completed here when it is added to here when it is established there. In this they mean he means to too and two.

Never to be used at last to last and never as it was as if it was a horse. They have no use for horses.

Never as it was as if it was because they had to have a way of counting one to make one.

Could be sitting around faced that way and lean and if he did would he not having been as payed follow to a home. Follow to a home for him.

Two cannot make room for two and two both seated cannot make room for two both seated. Two both seated cannot make room for two both seated.

This is one date.

Two cannot make room for two both seated.

Yes and yes and more and yes and why and yes and yes and why and yes. A new better and best and yes and yes and better and most and yes and yes and better and best and yes and yes and more and best and better and most and yes and yes. And yes and yes and better and yes and more and yes and better and yes, and yes and yes and more and yes and better and yes and more and yes and yes and yes and more and best and yes and yes and better and most and yes and yes and more and better and best and most and yes and yes and most and better and yes and yes and most and more and yes and yes, and more and yes and yes and better and yes and yes and most and yes and yes and best and yes and yes and better and yes and more and yes and best and yes and better and yes and more and yes and most and yes and more and yes and yes and better and yes and yes and most and yes and yes and best and yes and yes and yes and yes and better and most and yes and yes and better and most and yes and yes and more and most and yes and yes and better and most and yes and yes and more and better and yes and yes and yes and yes and more and best and yes and yes and more and best and yes and yes and more and yes and yes and best and yes and yes and more and yes and yes and better and yes and yes and best and yes and yes and more and yes and yes and better and yes and yes. And yes and yes and and more and better and yes and yes and better and yes and yes and more and yes and yes and better and and yes and yes and better and yes and yes and more and yes and yes and best and better and yes and yes and most and more and yes and yes and yes and yes and better and yes and best and most and better and more and best and better and yes and yes and yes and yes and yes and yes and more and yes and yes and better and yes and yes and more and yes and yes. And more and yes and yes. And more and better and yes and yes and best and more and yes and yes and better and yes and yes and most and yes and yes and best and more and yes and yes and yes and yes and better and more and better and yes and yes and most and better and more and yes and yes and yes and yes. And better and yes and yes and more and yes and yes and yes and yes and more and best and better and most and best and better and most and more and more and most and better and yes and yes.

A FAMILY OF PERHAPS THREE

If you want to investigate stylistic alternatives as Stein did, choose a familiar subject—in Stein's case, familial relations, presaging her mammoth The Making of Americans *(1926).*—R. K.

When they were younger there may have been three of them sisters, and a mother. When they were younger there may have been three of them one of them a brother, and a mother. When they were younger there were certainly two of them, sisters, and a mother. There was not then any father. There may have been a father living but certainly he was not then living with them. Anyway there were when they were younger two of them, two sisters, and a mother.

Perhaps the sister who was older then supported her sister and her mother. Perhaps she earned a living then for all of them. She was much older than her sister, enough older so that she could be quite certain that all her living her sister was much younger, that all her living her sister was a young one, that all her living she was earning her living, that all her living her sister was not earning her living.

From *Geography and Plays* (1922).

25

The sister the younger one was earning her living and certainly then the older one, the one who was much older than her sister who was much younger was certain that the younger one would have been earning her living all her living if she had been one commencing to earn her living. The younger was earning her living, she was not listening then to the story which was distressing of the older sister then almost not earning any living. She would listen sometime to this thing but certainly she would not listen then to this thing.

The older sister had not then any longer any mother. The younger sister then had not then any longer any mother. The older sister then had not then any longer any mother. The younger sister was not then hearing about this thing about the older sister having then not any longer any mother. Not any one then was listening to this thing to the older sister not then having any longer any mother. The older sister was then quite an old person. The younger sister was then not a young person. The younger sister was not then hearing anything about this thing about the older sister having then not any longer any mother.

They were then being living and very many knew them then, two of them, they were sisters, one was older, much older, the other was younger, some younger. They were living together then. The older was then earning some living, the younger was then sometimes hearing this thing, the younger was then not such a young one, she was quite completely hearing this thing, hearing that the older was almost earning a living, they were both living then, the younger was hearing then that the older one was almost earning a living. The younger was not listening, any more then, the older one was not earning any more of a living then. The younger one was almost not listening then.

The younger then earned her living. She was not at all a young one. The older one was not a very old person then, she was an old person then, she was almost not earning a living then. The younger one was not listening then to anything about any such thing then. She was not listening then and certainly the older one was not listening then and certainly neither of them was listening then. The older was almost not earning a living then and she was quite old then and she was not listening then. The younger one was earning a living then and was not listening then and she was not at all a young one then.

The older one was protecting the younger one from knowing where they had been when they were young ones. They both knew where they had been when they were young ones. The younger one was protected for this thing for not knowing where they had been when they were young ones.

The younger one was protected. She was protected from knowing that they were ones having been living when they were young ones, she was protected from knowing that they were not ever completely earning a living, she was protected from knowing that they were not going to be succeeding in earning a living. She was protected from these things, really she was protected from these things. Certainly every one knew everything, both of them and every one knowing them knew everything. That was a natural thing that every one should know everything. In a way they were succeeding in living. In a way the older one was succeeding in living, in a way the younger one was succeeding in living. Everybody knew everything, anybody knowing them knew everything, everybody knowing them knew it again and again, knew everything again and again, the older one knew everything knew it again and again. The younger one knew everything knew it again and again. Certainly every one knew everything. Certainly every one knew everything again and again.

The older one succeeded very well in living. The younger one succeeded very well in living. The older one was successful in being living. The younger one was successful in being living. The older one came to be certain that she was not successful in being living, that she was not succeeding in living, she came to be certain that the younger one would have been successful in living if the older one had not been one protecting the younger one from knowing this thing. The older one came to be certain that she had been successful in living, that she would not be succeeding in living. The older one came to be certain that the younger one would not really be succeeding in living. The younger one came to be certain that the older one could have been succeeding in living. The younger one came to be certain that the older one would not be succeeding in living. The younger one came to be certain that she could be succeeding in living. The younger one came to be certain that it would not be an easy thing to keep on being succeeding in living. The younger came to be certain that the older one never had been keeping on succeeding in living. The younger one was certain that one could keep on succeeding in living but that this was not an easy thing.

The older sister was not ever married. The younger sister was not ever married. This is quite common, not being married. The older sister was one whom some were certain could have been married very often. Certainly if she had been a little different she might have been married again and again. Certainly she was never married. Certainly she was not needing that thing, needing being married, needing being married again and again. She certainly was talking about any such thing, talking very often about any such thing about any being married, about any being married again and again. She certainly was one knowing very many men. Certainly very many men liked this woman. Certainly she was talking about this thing about being married very often, certainly she was very often talking about this thing. Certainly she was not ever completely needing this thing, needing marrying, she certainly was not ever completely needing marrying again and again. She was never a married one. She was not ever completely needing this thing. Certainly she could think again and again of this thing, of marrying. She certainly did think about this thing about marrying. She certainly did talk about marrying again and again. She certainly did feel something about this thing about marrying again and again.

The younger sister was never married and she might sometime have come to be married and she did not come at any time to be married. She was never married. She might talk about this thing about marrying. She might feel something about this thing about marrying. She might completely need this thing, need being married. She might have come to be a married one. She did not come to be a married one. Her sister was not ever certain that she would come to be a married one, that she would not come to be a married one. Her sister was not certain about either of them that they would never come to be married ones. They were never married neither the one nor the other and certainly each one of them knew this thing that neither one of them had come to be a married one.

Certainly the older one had done something and certainly every one was content to tell about this thing about her having done something and being one every one knowing her was remembering as having been one doing something. She certainly had done something and certainly any one knowing her remembered that thing remembered that she was one having done something. She was one going on doing that thing and certainly every one knowing her knew that thing knew that she was going on doing that thing. She was one having done something and doing that thing and certainly any one knowing her remembered that thing. It was a natural thing to remember that thing, any one, every one remembered that thing.

She was one doing something and certainly in a way she was not getting old in doing that thing and certainly in a way she was completely old in doing that thing, she was not doing that thing she was so old in doing that thing. In a way she was not old in doing that thing, in doing anything and certainly then she was completely old and not really to any one doing that thing. She was not old in doing that thing, that is to say she was doing that thing, that is to say if not anything had been changing she would not have been old in doing that thing. In a way somethings are not changing and so in a way she was not old in doing that thing. Certainly to those being then doing that thing and not being old then anything is a changed thing and certainly then she was old in doing that thing.

She was not old in being living that is to say as not anything is changing she was completely not old in being living. She was pretty nearly old in being living that is to say she was not young in being living that is to say some were old in being living and she was talking to them and they were understanding and some were young in being living and they were telling something and she was certain they were not telling any such thing. She certainly was not old in being living. She certainly was not young in being living.

The younger one was certainly not an old one. She certainly was not such a young one. In a way she was certainly a young one and certainly she was such a one in not hearing some things and in telling some things and certainly this did not astonish any one and was a natural thing and certainly she was not then a young one.

She was an older one and she was certain of this thing and this was not an astonishing thing to any one and not to her sister who was not astonished at her being a younger one at her being an older one but was certainly hoping to have had this thing happening that the younger one would have been going on being a younger one and being an older one and not be remembering anything of any such thing. Certainly the younger one came to be one almost liking to be remembering something and then again she certainly came to be quite tired of doing this thing of remembering anything, of remembering being an older one and remembering being a younger one and then she came to going on being one remembering being an older one, she was then remembering being a younger one. Certainly she came to be remembering pretty nearly everything and to going on in this thing, keeping going on in this thing, steadily enough going on in this thing.

They could both of them, they did, both of them, they would, either of them, know that they were ones having been together and they were ones having been alone. The older one certainly was one having been alone, being alone, going to be alone and certainly this thing was something that she was certain she was completely needing, was something she was certain she was completely regretting, was something that certainly she was one certain she could be feeling and certainly she was feeling this thing and certainly she would be one having been feeling this thing and certainly she could never be not feeling that this was something that was a thing she was needing, she was regretting, in which she was suffering, in which she was glorying, in which she was believing, in which she was despairing, in which and by which she was really being living.

The younger one was alone and not feeling about this thing that it was an important thing, she was feeling about this thing that it was a thing that she was needing to be changing. The older one was quite certain that the younger would never be changing anything. The younger one was not certain whether she would or whether she would not be changing anything but this was not to be an important thing, the important thing for her was to be one living where she wanted to be living and to be working if she needed to be working. Certainly her sister was one to whom any such thing was an important thing and so the younger one did not tell her sister anything about this thing until she had changed everything, that is gone to where she wanted to and working because she had to.

So each of them were ones being not living with any one and certainly the older one had that then as an important thing in being one being living.

Certainly any one could know that having been being living was an interesting thing in knowing the older one. Any one could know this thing could know that the older one had been one being living and that that was an interesting thing. She certainly had been one being living and that certainly was an interesting thing. She had been being living and this had been going on a very long time and it was all that time and later then a very interesting thing. She was being living and this was then to her then an important thing and not then so completely interesting. The younger one had been being living and this was to some an important enough thing and was to some quite an important thing and was not to any one a very interesting thing not to the older one either or to the other one herself who was one doing that living. They certainly had been both being living and were then being living. Certainly having been being living was an important thing was a completely interesting thing, any one could know that thing, certainly the older one could know that thing, certainly the younger one was not remembering that thing.

They had been together, they were together, they were not together. When they had been together the older one was almost completely succeeding in being one naturally needing that the younger one was something any one would be protecting. The older one was then going to be one being completely interesting in having been living. The older one was then almost completely brilliantly this thing being one being completely interesting in having been living. The older one was completely then succeeding in this thing in being one going to be interesting in having been living, in being one needing that any one would have been protecting the younger one. They had been together. They were together. When they were together the older one was almost needing that any one would be certain to be doing that thing certain to be sometime protecting the younger one. The older one was then certainly completely interesting in having been living and certainly then was completely interesting. She was almost then, was almost brilliantly succeeding in this thing in being completely interesting in having been living. Certainly they were both being living then and they were together then. Certainly then the older one was going on in being interesting in having been living, she certainly was then quite completely interesting. She certainly then was being living and certainly then she was almost certain that any one would be one to protect the younger one. They were together then and certainly some were not certain of this thing that any one would sometime protect the younger one. They were together then and every one was certain that the older one was completely interesting in having been living. They were together then and some were not certain that the older one was certain that any one would be protecting the younger one. Some were certain then that the older one was interesting in having been living. They were together then and any one could be certain that not every one would ever protect the younger one when the younger one would be needing any protection. Some were certain that the older one was not certain that any one would protect the younger one when the younger one would need protection. The older was almost certain that some one would protect the younger one when the younger one would need protection. The older one was almost quite certain. The older one was almost quite completely interesting in having been one being living. They were together. They were not together. The older one was certain that some one would have been protecting the younger one when the younger one would be needing protection. The older one was certain that sometime the younger one would be needing that thing would be needing protection. The younger one was not with the older one. The younger one was remembering that she was not with the older one. The younger one was remembering that she was not with the older one and was needing that the older one would be one coming sometime to remembering that thing. The older one was pretty nearly interesting in having been one being living. She was pretty nearly certain that some one would have been protecting the younger one when the younger one would have been needing that thing. They were not together then. The older one was pretty nearly interesting in having been one being living. She was quite certain that any one could have protected the younger one when the younger one would have needed that thing. She was almost remembering that they were not together then. She was almost quite remembering that thing. She was quite interesting in having been one being living. She was almost quite interesting in having been living.

AN INSTANT ANSWER OR A
HUNDRED PROMINENT MEN

"An Instant Answer" differs from other Stein texts in that each part belongs in a certain place where it and only it can be. Or at least the sequential numerical constraint (1 to 100) gives it coherence otherwise unavailable in the most experimental Steinian writing. Note that for all Stein's interest in repetition, she never repeats exactly.—R. K.

What is the difference between wandering behind one another or behind each other. One wandered behind the other. They wandered behind each other, they wandered behind one another.

Kings counts and chinamen.

A revival.

I will select a hundred prominent men and look at their photographs hand-writing and career, and then I will earnestly consider the question of synthesis.

Here are the hundred.

The first one is used to something. He is useful and available and has an unclouded intelligence and has the needed contact between Rousseau and pleasure. It is a pleasure to read.

From *Useful Knowledge* (1928).

The second one and in this case integrity has not been worshipped, in this case there has been no alternative.

The third one alternates between mountains and mountaineering. He has an anxious time and he wholly fails to appreciate the reason of rainfall. Rainfall sometimes lacks. It sometimes is completely absent and at other times is lacking in the essential quality of distribution. This has spread disaster.

The fourth one illustrates plentifully illustrates the attachments all of us have to what we have. We have that and we are worried. How kind of you to say so.

The fifth one of the fifth it has not been said that there have been three told of the gulf stream and the consul. Frank, where you have been. I have not been to London to see the queen.

The sixth one the sixth one thoroughly a pioneer. He is anchored we do not speak of anchor nor of diving he is readily thoughtful. He has energy and daughters. How often do we dream of daughters. How often. Just how often.

The seventh is mentioned every day.

The eighth. Can you pay the eighth to-day. Can you delay. Can you say that you went away. Can you colour it to satisfy the eye. Can you. Can you feel this as an elaborate precaution. Can you.

The ninth one is vague. Is he vague there where they care to insist. Is he vague there or is he inclined to tease. Is he inclined to tease. We know what we show. A little quarter to eight. I hope you will conduct him to his seat. He does not need politeness. No and he tells you so. No.

The tenth one the tenth one feels traces of terror. This does not sound wealthy nor wise nor does he plan otherwise. He planned very well. There is always this to tell of him. He can be a king or a queen or a countess or a Katherine Susan. We know that name. It has always been the same. At the same time every one shows changes. We arrange this at once.

The eleventh. Who won you. That is very sweet. Who were you. Expected pages and word of mouth, and by word of mouth.

Expect pages and by word of mouth. Who won one. Who won won. Mrs. Mrs. kisses, Mrs. kisses most. Mrs. misses kisses, misses kisses most. Who won you.

And the twelfth. The twelfth was the man who restrained Abel and Genoa. Why do the men like names. They like names because they like calling. A calling is something to follow. We no longer represent absence. I call you. Hullo are you there. I have not been as intelligent yet as I was yesterday.

Thirteen, the thirteenth has not neglected the zenith. You know how to invent a word. And so do you. You know how to oblige him with lilacs. And so do you, you know you do. And you know how to rectify an expression. Do you build anew. Oh yes you do.

The fourteenth prominent man is prominent every day of the year. Do you feel this to be at all queer. He is prominent and eminent and he is personally severe. He is not amiable. How can an amiable baby pronounce word. How can they be predominant. We know why we have reason we reason because of this.

The fifteenth is wholly exhilarated. Place air and water where they are.

The sixteenth yes indeed. Have we decreed. Yes indeed. Have we. Do we need that.

The seventeenth. The seventeenth century is older than the sixteenth. How much older. A century older. Or older than a century older. The seventeenth is a century older is older than a century older than the sixteenth.

The eighteenth one wishes to annex the Philippines.

The nineteenth one mingles with men. We say he mixes with men. We say he mixes up nothing. He does not mix things up nor does he do the opposed thing. When he does ring and he does ring, what, that is what he says, what. What does he say. He says what did I say. He says. Did I ring. I say, he says, I say did you say anything. How cleverly brothers mingle. We haven't forgotten.

The twentieth. No one forget anything and he does not forget anything. He does not forget anything when he is here. Does he forget to come again. He does not elaborate exercises. There are witnesses there.

The twenty-first nursed what was to him beaming. I can declare that they are not aware of seeming to share policing. They have increased the number of police in New York.

The twenty-second, how many more days are there in September than there were. This question has been aroused by the question asked by the prominent man who is the subject of the declaration that words may be spoken.

The twenty-third is not indicated by invasion. We all believe that we do invade islands countries homes and fountains. We do believe that the hierarchy of repetition rests with the repeaters. Now we severally antedate the memory. Do you relish powder.

Of the twenty-fourth it has been said that out of sight out of mind is not so blind. Please do not wave me away. Waves and waves they say carry wood away. Carry, does that remind you of anything.

The twenty-fifth is moderately a queen. What did you say. Anger is expressive and so are they.

The twenty-sixth has many ordinary happinesses. He is ordinarily in the enjoyment of his challenge. Do not challenge him to-day. What did you say. Do not challenge him to-day.

The twenty-seventh does measure very well indeed the heights of hills. How high are they when they are negligible. How high are they any way and where do dogs run when they run faster and faster. And why do dog lovers love dogs. Do you know everything about deer. He had a father and they made a window and windows have never been scarce.

The twenty-eighth is perceptibly loving. He has invented perfumes and portraits and he has also reconciled stamina with countenance. I do say that yesterday he was very welcome. And to-day. To-day he is very welcome. We do not say that it is wonderful to be loaned at all.

The twenty-ninth neglects the history of a mute. Mute and unavailing. The twenty-ninth does not add considerably to his expense.

He is not needed there. Where is he needed. He is needed here and there. Drive me there.

The thirtieth manages to be lavish. He washes land and water, washes them to be green, wishes them to be clean, his daughter merits her mother and her sister her brother. He himself witnesses this himself and he carries himself by special train. A train of cars. Will there soon be no trains of cars. Did you hear me ask that. Will there pretty soon be no bridling.

The thirty-first remembers that a pump can pump other things than water and because of this he says miles are astray. They have proof of this. Can you solidly measure for pleasure.

The thirty-second is an irresistible pedestrian. He has much choice, he chooses himself and then his brother and then he rides back. He can seem in a dream and he can uncover the lover. I have been so tender to-day.

The thirty-third is incapable of amnesty. Forgive me for that you dear man. Where were you born. I was born in a city and I love the whole land.

The thirty-fourth is second to none in value. Why do you value that more. Why do you value you value that any more.

The thirty-fifth why can there be naturally this one who has found it invigorating to exchange beds for beds and butter for butter. Exchange butter for butter. Do exchange more beds for more beds.

The thirty-sixth has heard of excitement. How can you be excited without a reason. How can you be an adaptable tenth. He is in the tent. There is a tent there.

The thirty-seventh for the thirty-seventh a great many to the truth, they tell the truth generously. Somebody is generous there where the rest of them care. Do they care for me. Do they. How awfully popular I am.

The thirty-eighth has held enough and he holds the rest there where there are no more edible mushrooms. Do you know how, to tell an edible mushroom. Have you heard any of the number of ways.

The thirty-ninth is contented and alarmed. Why do you share and share alike and where do you share what you share. What do you care.

The fortieth is rapidly rained on. Rain is what is useful in Europe and not necessary where you have irrigation. Do you understand me. And why do you repeat what you say I like to repeat what I say.

The forty-first one did he duck. Did he say I wish they would go away, did he describe himself, did he feel that he was married, did he entertain on next to nothing and did he furnish houses and did he candidly satisfy enquiries. Did he learn to quiet himself. Did he resemble ready money and did he inquire where they went. How can all shawls be worn all the time. Some say it is very fine to-day.

The forty-second what did you say, the forty-second came every day and yet how can he come every day when they are away. He comes anyway and he replaces what he uses and he uses it there and he promises to share what he has and he is very prominently there. We stay home every day when he comes here. I don't quite understand, I am a little confused. Does he come every day.

The forty-third one is the one that has inevitably established himself in the location which is the one that was intended as the site of the building. Did they build there. No certainly not as he had already arranged it for himself. I understand. He came first. Yes he came first and he stayed which was quite the natural thing for him to do.

The forty-fourth one married again. No one meant to come to the wedding absolutely no one and he said I am marrying and they said who is it to be and he said I know what you believe and they said how can you believe that you are to be married again. What is the marriage ceremony that you refer to. I refer to the marriage ceremony. Is that so.

The forty-fifth, all the immediate present and those immediately present, all those present will please answer that they are present now. And what do they all say. All those who are present say so. We were very nearly pioneers in this movement. And why are you so frequently referred to, because when they refer to me they mean me.

The forty-sixth prominent man is the one who connected them to their country. My country all the same they have their place there. And why do you tell their names. I tell their names because in this way I know that one and one make a hundred. It is very difficult to count in a foreign language.

The forty-seventh does do what he expected to do. He expected to have what he has include what he was to have and it did and then when he went again he went again and again. After that all the same he said all the same I am very well satisfied.

The forty-eighth placed them there. Where did he place them. Exactly what do you mean by placing them, he was asked and he answered. I placed them and they were equally distant from the different places that were near them. Is this the way you choose a capital they said. Yes indeed he said, that is as you may say the result of the influence of Spanish. Oh yes they replied not entirely understanding but really he was right. He was undoubtedly in the right.

The forty-ninth, what habits had this one formed, you may say that he can be mentioned as being the one who was bestowed again and again on elephants and mosses. It is queer that fountains have mosses and forests elephants. And why is it astonishing that we have heard him when he was mentioning that he went there, we do not know. Show me he said and they opened their eyes. Why do you stare, and why did they. We do not care. Yes do please me. We please ourselves.

The fiftieth, why did you expect me. We expected you because you had announced yourself and you are usually punctual. How did you learn to be punctual. Because we have had the habit of waiting for the rain. Does that make one punctual. It does. This is what has been bought. Buying is a vindication of roads. Bu[y] and stay, stay and buy. By and by. Yes Sir.

The fifty-first one has to say what do you command. What is sweating, that is what I like says Mike, the fifty-first one has an understanding of resisting. He had it said of him that he could countenance alarmingly the destruction of a condition. Why are conditions connected with what I have not said. I said the account, was there an account of it on account of it.

The fifty-second has as an established fact the fact that the account given is the one that makes him furnish everything. Did he furnish it all and was it wise to apprise him that there were many who had religiously speaking an interest in interpretation. This sounds like nonsense. What do you mean by spiritual, what do you. Mike said what do you mean by spiritual what do you. They wished to say that they did not wish anything tried again and again. Be rested. You be rested.

The fifty-third have you heard that fifty and fifty are evenly divided. Have you heard about the way they say it. All of them come again and say it. We say it and they say it. May we say it. I have not forgotten that the fifty-third prominent man is the one that has the most anxious air.

The fifty-fourth one is the one that has been left to study industrialism. No one asks is there merit in that. No one says that there is something noble in that. No one says how do you study a subject. No one idolises Frank. Don't they indeed.

The fifty-fifth is very pretty in any language. How do you do is one way of looking at it. He minds it the most and the shape of it very much. He is very easily offended and he believes in a reference. I refer to you and to you and to you. I always refer to you. I refer to you and I refer you to him and I refer her to them and they refer them to me. Can you see why. Do you understand why they have no need to go and come, to sit down to get up and to walk around.

The fifty-sixth measures what he has done by what he will do. He measures it all and means to react. Action and reaction are equal and possible and we relieve the strain. In this way we arrange for hope and pleasure. This is what we say unites us all to-day.

The fifty-seventh is admirably speaking radiant when he has no annoyances. And why does he continue to know that a lieutenant colonel is in command. Why does he know it. Dear me why does he know it.

The fifty-eighth one is alright. How do the hours come to be longer. Longer than what, longer than English french, Italian, North and South American Japanese and Chinese.

The fifty-ninth marries when he marries, and he is married to me. Do not fail to see him and hear him and rehearse with him and molest him. He has an organic wit.

The sixtieth is actually rested. He has come to be reasonably industrious. He had and he has come to be reasonably industrious. In this way he is successful.

The lieutenant colonel was found dead with a bullet in the back of his head and his handkerchief in his hand.

The sixty-first one has had a very astonishing career. He said that he would never mention another and he never did, he also foresaw the re-establishment of every crisis and he went ahead he went in and out and he foresaw that youth is not young and that the older ones will not seem older and then he imagined expresses. In this way he established his success. I have not mentioned his name.

The sixty-second was just the same. He entered and he came and he came away and no one cared to share expenses. No one cared to share expenses. What did you say. No one cared to share expenses. He was privileged to increase paler nights and he always measured investigation. How can you investigate privileges. By not curtailing expenses. Thank you for all your thoughts. Give you best thoughts. Thank you for all your thoughts.

The sixty-third, we all have heard of regiments called the sixty-third. Reform regiments in time and they have magnificent beginnings. Do not reform them in time and they progress fairly. Do not reform them at all and they will not necessarily decrease. I say the sixty-third one is the one who came to be celebrated because of this. Because of this he came to be the one that one of the ones that are mentioned in this list.

The sixty-fourth we are a nation of sixty-fourth. Do you remember how a great many of them sat together. Do you and do you remember what they said. My impression was that they had not spoken. My impression was that they had not spoken then. Never again. It is hard to love your father-in-law. Hard almost impossible.

The sixty-fifth, there is a standard from the sixty-fifth. This is his standard. He comes to it and he is very well indeed. Is he. Yes he is very well indeed.

The sixty-sixth, how are you when you are steady. He steadily repeats himself. Do you mean he allows you to feel that he does so. He does indeed.

The sixty-seventh has this advantage. It is an advantage that is easily enjoyed.

The sixty-eighth all small culmination meets with this as their reward. We reward when and where we reward and we reward with rewards. And this is the use of a guardian, where it is guarded it is as well guarded as ever.

The sixty-ninth how authoritative he is and he was. He was able to arrange for everything again and again and he said with hesitation why do I like to make sweets. Sweets to the sweet said some one.

The seventieth come again and listen were the origin and the beginning of his success. Come again and do not go away. Come again and stay and in this way he succeeded. He was successful. Have you meant to go away he would say. Oh no indeed he meant to stay they would say. And he meant to stay. He was successful in his heyday and he continued to be successful and he is succeeding to-day. When you say how can you feel as you feel we say, that is the way to succeed. That is just the way to succeed. He says I have succeeded.

The seventieth do I remember whether I do or I don't. I think I usually do that is to say I always have. Does that mean you always will. I think so. I gather from what I saw at the door that you wanted me to come in before.

The seventy-first believe me at first. At first we believed that that was because they were so many that had been equal to this one. And then we accompanied them. They were not regularly identified. Nor was he, why did he and because, why did he, because he did double the pansies. You understand that this is symbolical. No one has really more than doubled the pansies.

The seventy-second for in this way there is a second the seventy-second managed to see me. And where were they all. They were all in there. And why did no one declare themselves faultless. This was very nearly a dish, a nest of dishes. Do you remember that play. A nest of dishes. This and the painting of a garden scene made an astonishing measure for measure. Answer blindly to this assurance and be assured that all the pleasure is yours.

The seventy-third has nearly spoken. He said I see rapidly I compose carefully, I follow securely and I arrange dexterously, I predict this for me.

The seventy-fourth how often have both had children. I said that he should not change he should continue with girls. I said she should not change she should continue with girls. She changed and he did not. He continued with girls.

The seventy-fifth very many actually count. They count one two three four five six seven.

The seventy-sixth one is the one that has not often met nor often been met nor very often met them yet. They are there they do declare that they are there. And why publish data.

The seventy-seventh really places it. He places there with a great deal of care. And when he was twelve he sang in public. There are a great many reasons for it. This is one of them. The reason I have given is their reason. Do be satisfied with their reason. Do not be worried do not be worried at all nor do not be at all worried. Be satisfied. Be very well satisfied.

The seventy-eighth do you remember about him do you really explain when you explain that he loved lacing and unlacing and releasing and separate silence. Do you really credit this with that. Do you do so fairly.

The seventy-ninth was originally delicious, delicious as delicious as the excellent repast which was offered. Do you remember how she wrote offer, offered. Do you and do you prefer exchange that is barter to pleasure in reason. I believe in pleasure and the reason the reason for it.

The eightieth how do you manage to mention a number separately. It is a specialty a specialty of wine. That is very fine in you and it all proves to me that I have faith and a future.

The eighty-first at first the eighty-first was the one who had made the fruit house who had the fruit house made there where it was very singular that he could understand that there was land.

You see it is like this land is made to be near by so that one can see it. Land is made to be understood to be there. So there was naturally no distribution of land and land. Do you understand, Lizzie do you understand. These were naturally there here there and everywhere. We have principally met whether we need to or not. I do complain of sitting there. Not here. No not here.

The eighty-second, was it we say was it by means of a hammer or by means of a rock, was it by hammer or by rock that we felt that the future was one with the present. Do you know by what means rockets signal pleasure pain and noise and union, do you know by what means a rock is freed when it is not held too tightly held in the hand. Many hold what they hold and he held what was best to settle in Seattle. Why do you care for climate. Why do you. I know.

The eighty-third, tell me about him. I will. He was never neglected nor was he especially willing to sing, a great many ceased to secure singing. You mean they found Saturday intolerable. That is just it that is just what I wish to say, you put it in that way and certainly very certainly a great many kind of birthdays are taken for granted. Granted.

The eighty-fourth that too might be taken to be the same as if it were one number the more and yet if you think delicately and you do think so you will see why I say no it is not the same. Now supposing he were famous would he understand it as you say he does understand fame. Would he. Oh you question me so narrowly and I might say I didn't mean and then what would you say. I would say I just want to be praised. There that is permanent.

The eighty-fifth is the one did I mention that this too might be the number of a regiment. You see they say that there are more there you mean as to one thousand and four thousand, there are more there.

He has given as the reason that he knows the difference between Christmas New Year Easter and Thanksgiving. He has given this as a reason.

The eighty-sixth is the one to measure by animals. A dog another dog and a woman two lions and man a central surface a lion a dog and a man and two men and more introduction. I introduce you to him and to him. Do you introduce him too often. I do not think so. No I do not think so.

The eighty-seventh study the eighty-seventh one carefully and tell me what it is that you notice. I notice that in different positions one sees a different distinction. You mean you always distinguish him. Oh so readily. And when you smile does he smile at all, he smiles very readily when you smile at all. And does he furnish you with agreeable merriment. Very agreeably so. Tell him so it will please him. I do. I will.

The eighty-eighth furnish the eighty-eighth with the means of furnishing. We furnish everything. He furnishes everything. In this way we cannot mean what has been made clear. We cannot mean that he plans this.

The eighty-ninth remember that when you remember the eighty-ninth it was not so happily bowed to as it might have been if all pages were printed as they came. We like printing it all the same. Now just what do you mean by that. I mean that very rapidly he refreshes himself.

The eighty-ninth, forty made the eighty-ninth clearly the half of that number. There are a number of them aren't they and each one every one more than one, one and one, they all stay over there. If for instance there had been one continuation where then would they place the succession. Where would they. You don't ask where did they. You don't really ask me anything.

The ninetieth is the ninetieth one to-day. To-day come to care to stay. How do you. Dear me how can you use it as if it was a cane. How can you. Please how can you. I can do all this and all the time have you discovered anything. She did, keys and a kitchen. Not a mistake. It was not a mistake.

The ninety-first who knows about this one, it is not easy to plan for it, eat for it or trouble for it. It is not easy to manage to say to-day and yesterday and very likely every other day. It is not easy. I say it isn't easy.

The ninety-second and does he attend to all of it. Do you attend to all of it. I am not easily convinced that they attend to all of it. Do they attend to all of it. All that I know about it is that whether they do or whether they do not we have a system of triple mirrors. In this way we see where they come. Where do they come from. I see abundance geographically.

The ninety-third, every one has heard of the ninety-third. Naturally, and now what do you mean by rushing. What do you mean by rushing in here and saying am I in it. What do you mean by doing that. Even if you were in it you would not be heard from so definitely. Be reasonable, leave it all to me. When this you see remember that you are to wait for me. I can say this very quickly.

The ninety-fourth marries he marries them, now how can you know whether in saying this I mean what you mean does this bother you at all does it annoy you, can you be obstinate in asserting that we have the same meaning that you mean and that I mean that he marries them. Think about this carefully and when you are thoroughly prepared to be generous give me your answer. I answer for him.

The ninety-fifth, remember the ninety-fifth. Ninety-nine is ninety-nine, and the ninety-fifth has a very good evening. Good evening. It is not our custom to say good evening.

The ninety-sixth and more and more. You were given to reconciling floods with fire. This is a noisy day. May I look again.

The ninety-seventh hears me has heard me when I have said do no care to hear Cornelius Vanderbilt. The ninety-seventh is excellent in his way, he is very excellent in that way and does prepare his share. Do you prepare your share. And do you estimate your share correctly. Have you ever mistaken anything and put it away there with your share. No neither of you have, neither of you have ever done so.

The ninety-eighth, the ninety-eighth and the ninety-ninth, the ninety-eighth is the one we see when we look. We look and we look. How do we look. We look very pretty. Do we look well. We look very well.

The ninety-ninth who is the ninety-ninth, as for me I prefer to call tissue paper silk paper. Do you prefer to do so by the year. Tissue paper is thin paper, and silk paper is a thin paper. One might say that tissue paper is a paper made of thin tissue. It is sometimes called silk paper. It is made of the same material but is not quite so thin.

The Hundredth. When you believe me you believe me very often don't you. I believe that Andrew D. White and many worked all day and I believe that Andrew D. White and many others worked all night I believe that many others worked all day and that many others worked all night. I believe that many others are so had I not better say are often an addition. Then can you say that you do like to see. Yes I do like to see you here. And then why do you follow me. You follow me. I follow you follow you follow me. You do follow me.

One hundred and won. When this is done will you make me another one.

OLD AND OLD

"Old and Old" is sustained wordplay. If you think such writing is easy, try it sometime and discover how the constraints can be defeating.—R. K.

I. Conditions.

House plants.
Cousin to cousin the same is a brother.
Collected tumblers.
Pretty well so called, pretty careful and going all the detention.
Hopping.
Pretty well Charlie, pretty sour poison in pears, pretty well henny soon most soon bent.
Collect.
In do pot soon, in loud coal bust, in do pot soon, in chalk what.

From *Operas and Plays* (1932).

In do pot soon in hold hot. In do pot soon, in due point, in die point.

In due point and most visible.

In vain, in vain, in a vein, in a vein. In do point that. Bay weight and balk and be wet. Be wake and white and be wet. Be count and lunge and see wall, be how, be how but can than.

Be how not inches, be have no cone grass, be who come in tear, be who coat.

Collect.

Couple calling, call cuts, call peaches and way laden and brim, brims and climate, a whole paper, little holes, and little hole, little holes.

Crowd a collection with large layers, ages, ages and ages, ten, control, kill hen, hurry in, hurry. Hold up. Saw a case cool most, come with him. Come with him. Come and trim, come in, come. Come, come, come.

Call all coupling just that please and a way to irrigate is a fountain, a folding dish and a head meadow, a folding glass and a heated moan, a brittle orange and a soon, all so soon, acres sideling. Acres sudden and a pole mischurch, miss olives, miss old age collars and cuffs and rhubarb, rub roads, roll extras, rule a case of set smashes and no pillows, no pleasure pillows. No waking cases, no closed colors, no colored suddens, no votes, no viols, no mixed peas, no regular soap stones, no regular stools, no regular ones, no such bad eggs, no cold chicken no shadow, no winter seen, no bowls, no carrots, no joints, no slender peals, no cape cuts, no batter and always more, always a season.

The grass, the grass is a tall sudden calendar with oats with means, only with cages, only with colors and mounds and little blooms and countless happy eggs to stay away and eat, eat that. The high arrangement which makes colds is that. A grand stand a real old grand stand and means and trees and coats and bars and cherries and wheels and boxes and cooking and limes and bowels and butter and points and points.

Cold wets and cold woods and cold cow harness and cold in the stretch and more pleasing reason with the cheque in the book and a dress and a dress and a medium choice and a blooming chest and a passing supper and a little cheese and a white a white and a wet white tool and a pole and a straw and a little chicking bean and a little toe white and a little cow soon. A little kew a little piece of an hopeless pre barometer and jelly cups, a way both heat, a way they heat cold. A single thing is dandy, a soiled monkey eating ahead. A spoon, a coat, a collided blotter and a case.

2. Treatment.

A whole eggs in stout muds. A vest sand, a lime eater, a cold saw, a kind of stammer, a little shade, a new opera glass, a colored mule, a best winter, a spoon, a wetness, a jelly, a window and a fruit season and a ripe pear and a point in pudding in a pudding being a pudding and sometime anytime, in being a pudding and necessary and reasonable and mostly judicious and particularly flattering and seasoned, really seasoned and almost always too bad.

Cunning next.

Cunning is to be too easy to be funny. Cunning enough and a whole extra change is not necessary and all the time and particular.

A best stand is minus and it is, it just is more and any way is there a road, is there a whole way to have a belly and a bycicle and measles and oats and oranges and little whistles and balloons and old things and necessary and a pleasant day to stay and bycicles and old stretches and cold stuck and bodies and little cheeses and meat balls and sandwiches and closets and collected oils and balls and sweet breads and toads and colored choice sticks and little steady mirrors and little puddings and almost any pies and between handies and mittens and clouds and old things and butter and a soiled omelette and pieces of oat meal and a stage. Can there be any difference in any way. Can there be necessary.

A bouncing release from a whole water country and more than that makes a bed-room. It does that. It shines by day-light. It makes all the pins steal. It does show. It has moons, it has more, it had mind and molasses and everything in a thing. It is so hold.

A little be seen by a dent.

Any dent is a past time and a coach a coach why when there is wood and old iron and little things and readily quite readily.

3. Collecting Poles.

Old mans and a cost in corsets and a grand guard and a good gold flour, a good flour, a cold flower, a bad flavor, a certain decent and a request a request for a distant smell, a request for a smell, a request, a distant smell, a smell distant, a request, a smell, a smell distant, a smell, a distant smell.

That is the end of a solid tree in a fog, that is the end in noon, that is the end of a chance to sit in change, that is the end spinach and an egg much more egg, much more green.

Collected poles.

A little bit of spoiled choice, the little bit of wood and gold, the little bit of old baked gold, a little bit of water which is cake.

Then comes the decision. Supposing the utter meaning is that a loose dog is a fellow and a piece of certain exchange is places where there is a return, suppose all that necessarily, is it not soon beside that each is were in a tall and natural cane, is it not more so. A distribution.

We and cake, wake cake, wake, walk, cake, cool, sun, pale, rich, hold with a piece of half and half, whole, hold in with a canter and a choice and a little piece of clean and not too old soda.

We in between, cold spores, cool and we, so allowed wonder struck and so glass, so glass in previous notices. We change what. In when.

We in between, a button, a log, a handle, a burnt heading, a changed charlie an altogether neglected tub street.

Weak in the glass worn in the nose, perceived in the gold, chosen in the waste, and tuneless, quite coldless.

Collecting poles.

Come, come, no no no, no no no no, come, no no no, come. Come no no no come. Come, no no no, come, no no no no. Come.

Come no no no no, come. A loaf a whole little lamp shade that has a bottle, a kind of a bottle in it and is used, is used in a way, is used in a way splendidly.

Collecting poles.

A way to suggest restraint and alarm and reserve and a mistake and a single kind of neglect and a softened order to remove pieces and a messed sadness and an exchange is in the beginning and in the end definitely, is definitely useful.

Invite.

Bounce, to bounce, a head, to lead, to squeeze, to wander about, to neglect, to assuage, to please, to refuse a cold, to engage furnaces, to collect a roll of paper and to remove a best part of a snatch, all this and the whole real place, the whole real place.

A kind of business, a ready handle and a sold penny and a leading string and a powder any old returned cover, all the courtesy and a half of napkin, all this so suddenly. What is bleeding.

Cool gate, a sand lot and a sudden key and a house bent and a pleaser.

Cold thimble and agitation, a best fit and a boast and a harsh man.

Question. A lively turkey and a feather. Real hosts, ready hose. A basted clothes manger.

Age in girls age in cakes, age in opera glasses, aged plastered stools.

A coincidence that is a deal a great deal of patience and hold enough and wind out often in above. All the cow herds are stuffed. They are wide. In the cane there is a cover, a long thin cover of excellence and how is it.

Invite in a way.

Help a hook and a clothes button. Help it in a spell. Help a hangar. Help way in the nucleus of a particular delight and a change, changed hurry, or sudden white ship a little linen cheese.

Invite in a way.

Clean, clean in a horizon of rich red milk and made high made a way and a lifted helper, all that, a cousin is a bit, it is so reckless, it is so collected in a puddle, it is so seasonable with survey chants.

Beam, loaf, electricity in left cleans, extraordinary water spoons and sullen clocks secretly, sullen clocks not so seen as they are why so. So much animal roast leaves in mutton.

Colored janes and a high lip ruddy, a gook in soft bees and little holders.

Give in birdie, go on to artichokes suddenly in mean and in collections, go on to this sense, go on mind in so.

Go on particularly, night in.

Go on particularly nickels strange. Go in pour the chain for it full of china. Full of china choice up. Full of china crossed in. Full of china. Full of chin that has china. Chin and china. China.

5. A Told High Flows, [Colossal], Smell, Bell.

A tucking only a silver hose, a white lip a single tin, a solid reasoning arch representative, a single arch representative.

A single arch representative, this is so. A told countenance, this is the personnel exactly and considerately.

Curve the second to place collecting and mere ways all right. Which in bear cases and neglected suit tracks and white sails and kind of vagrant wellies and collecting verses and beads and called plates and places with soon more and white, might there, and with, all the cow bright laugh in sounds and laughter.

Heap and combine killed captures and the blame bone and the illustrious station the steady water flame breaking the called way in a change, in a silly veil storm and clutches and a time when a time table utterly and noise and nearly all the estranged speats and later spreads and last vexed coats all coats.

A ladder viciously and a keen collected wood pen and a coaxed cat in a rack and a combination, a climbed call at.

Hard all, hem stitch centrally cooled with cables in a place and strong, strong elevated horrid stones and nearly why and more the which is able to and no.

Cousins in and coal beds on and coal beds there and why the half stead which relates that which when than more go to horrid exchange.

A told in that all which has mine and beads the same which shall be shut and more to wait and all the candy, all the habited exchanged wonder resources in the best condition vacationally reduced and rectified more in that change.

Lend a stand and little eases and the whole resolved exchange of wildnesses and a lease and peas and a chat related and the nut and but to make the water steal.

Cone in cousins is bleeding with the exchange of letting out palings and whole seeds and all the little ways. Tenderly. To be let.

Cold acres, cold couches in three cities, colored cups one readily and much must be resumed and let out with magazines and care taken with takers remedy and a whole speech readily very readily external and more extra than by the side of a shirts. By the side of half and more in the miserable seat of a whole interchange between education and visit between education and visit. More in than before the last prints and idless becomings and more aged mending and little pieces. All extra.

Put in the most and delighted and believe the hay mound and little classes, believe big classes clouding and cowardly weather spittoons and grass mere, merely the same, merely believe that change, merely show towels, merely be in that gaining collapse and article.

Be wet in a chest of sucks where there is a grasp and a close a half close cup of excellent refusings a cup so more readily and behind that. Behind that.

A gentleman that vindicates addresses and pearls and loose cards and shoes and puffs and little seas and a great deal of necessary able colored watches and behind any little thing is so likely very much that benumbing and reclosed, all this means a bed room and a single center and more beneath, and not climbing with paste and crevasses and any little thing. This is no neglect of spades and all the ways and like that and orderly and a best way to sputtter when there is a distraction which a doubt can make beam, can make beam.

A little in that white wonder place which shows the slight indication of more necessarily reduced and disturbed and loosening all the regular manipulation of lessening in the challenges which make plenty a disgrace with a booth. The real thing is beside that when the return is pleased with cloth and more nearly on the sweet hold of the change which makes these.

That then more cultivated in a slight union of viciousness which is the very best representative of an incline and a message and really utility is the indication of much that is neglected by harmony and mingling and a little chapter and no counter leaving.

The best union to fit is in the shut and not in that neglected by cold scratches and a little there. Not at all then.

Peeling changes makes ready and left brooms are called that reliably and with that fair division that makes it cold and potatoey in the meadow light and in the ground and all of it, all of it.

A case to know.

Singly is enough, any way it is splendidly and be that in a way and a hold a wide hold and old told, old told in a loaf of told batter and green pleases and all that. No dirt, no copper no doubt, no doubt no dirt, no doubt, no doubt that, no doubt that that copper, no doubt that, no copper, no copper, no doubt that no doubt no copper. No copper, no copper, no doubt. No doubt. No doubt no copper, no doubt.

6. Widows.

A cold state, a kind of stable life, a kind of boiler and a gold skate, a choice hearty delicate underneath water builder and muttons muttons of useful ardent oat cakes apron. A cold state and meat pants and little losses and beneath water apples and doors and jerked barbers and little hens and leaders. All that and a best halt and little goes and wheat staffs and miss curls and hard chests and all best and little mutters. Little mutters to salt wet words, little mutters in the dew. Little is the case. Little is the case.

Go belt, go in there copiously and within and strong sudden salt works, strong sudden salt works, have cold wet nurses and cold wet noises and cold wet nuts and cold wet nurses. Cold wet nurses and cold wet noises, cold wet noses, cold wet nurses.

Cup spaces.

Cup spaces are readily seen to be local and back and never stolen and always always coincident, coincident with long angels and much much passes, much so. A little gain is a squeal it is a squeal so addedly it is a squeal, it is a squeal. It is more than the first apron it is the second. It is.

Collusion.

Collidable and covered and with stead and sturdy and neglected occasion, with neglected occasions there comes meaning and every measure with stalk.

Kinds in tables.

A learned collection of more places once, a learned recollection comes from springs and lanterns and little sides, a learned recollection of more places once, a learned recollection of more places once comes in to the kinds of a first, exchange and then collectedness and then a table a piece of expression steadily and really what is the exchange between glueing, what is the select action of real neat and sold pieces of cork. What is the best standing and more shoulders in nearly application to a rain that is stubborn and relaxed and so torn so torn with with water places and real corns with very blue soldiers and little really tall colors with blue. All the same growing is with steady and ridiculous furs, monthly the cup kind and the grass, really the grass and the considered window and any way that is crossness for, crossness is for a reason and a little change to make a bell and ringing, ringing is all the same as knocking and any way a little difference is not necessary is not more necessary than freezing not really more necessary than a settled shawl. A real way to make fingers is rather by that and that. The real white way is with a color and powders are green and roses are vacant and beets real beets have balls. Suppose there are quick ways suppose they are and a memory is told by asking in change what was the case in dream what was the case in a tall decanter what was the last case that had puddings. The answer is already.

A little afternoon makes the sun and then if there is a circumstance and the real shout is called right in with a splendid and regular delay then surely there is in between more comforts more real comforts readily. A question is a dozen. A question is the case of the revolving butter and last train and secretly really secretly, all that, and no consideration for spells and little tiny white eggs and the same in blue and in a center color. The rest is in exchange collected by long and satisfactory installation and dusting.

All pages and white thistles and little torn berries and little mass means, and the time of the stretch and a plan to carry poles and little searches and a couple of condies with a sudden best stick, and last met with a sign of a place to show touches and a little climb and a sweet hold of a more excellent and reseen oleander, a most excellent hurling, a most sand paper and a glass which shows a change in cultivating rare trees and little things which are mutton and a pet all the same close bent share of cut a way clothes brush.

The season is best with wheels.

7. Grass Trees.

Always satisfying the labor of exacting the recognition of lost references to the long case which has structure elevation and disgrace and surely there is a bald sacrament that means an extrapiece [sic] of lamp with a glass shade certainly clean. The best excuse is this. Let the right corner see more great pauses then there are practical places to search out cups and saucers. Let there remain little things nice things and exact works and little quite the best time exactly and more in the wick and sold more there and there there is doleful examples of ever ready hydrangeas. In the ease which makes all the disturbance and a center concentrated all this makes a reason why any distance is a street and a street is mathematical and wise really wise and this makes a hole makes a hole so that coming in is in.

Great bay waters and left in there makes a swim a tank and makes bugs real bugs that is bugs that have a lesson and an organ and an approach and a light change and a miserable a quite miserable interchange most readily.

Making a change quite readily is peaceable. Any cold is a species of least resemblance and love. Love is a cool cat which has them. A grain a grain is established and hesitation is so learned that almost any is put in the house patiently with no hesitation, none, no one.

Cold up with the expression of the reason when a glance and a little paste all the newly joined is in the particular clear use of more than organs.

Cold up with a climb and an ox and a sensitive birthday of pieces of cheese and a lost a long lost specimen of rose. A rose is streak a streak mentionedly and like a current which shows the circumstance of light and a cap. A cap is surrounded by blind clause which shows rain and the same.

Rest with it and make a tall mind show it. Rest with it and make no man tall more likely. The best is in the soot, a large dress shows that, a large dress is made with him.

Ground left.

Cunning seas so sweet in being little nice and covered with one. All the tough apple makes a piece of raisin all of it and eye glasses are exchanged by nearly everything naturally and in legs, again a week, any tuck makes a different thing tremble and show electricity with a vim with a lovely dog and feet, heels are careful with bursts and kindly in with black.

A mouse cow and a strange half cram filled with a surging that is particular with sound. A relief a whole church a whole lean bag necessarily.

Waist in a little piece of hurt with a head and covered covered with an ear and a long a long oar or a long a long cat called a collision. A real meet, a real met land which is copied by a latterly arranged cut up resemblance to not more than a relief from more mixing than the chance. A time climate and religion and sweet use and a pill in and a whole sound which is called met and which seems chair and which is conwheeled.

Left in when and leave leave a corn starch with a heather that is red and a pin and a likely cooled in frozen.

Cut in. Hinges.

Close to all the wide reason that there is cold and a happy warm table and a little biting egger and a puzzle mentally, in spite of despite of, relight from, all this wade later and later in lie which is the.

The rest is popular. The rest is a pole teller. The rest is pope and wheeler and a page flated, in the pay of august and more waiter and mind in page whiter, and in whiter, in white page straight in later page in later. Page. Later.

8. Cut Indians.

Come in little cubicle stern old wet places. Come in by the long excuse of more in place of bandages which send a little leaf to cut a whole condition with a pan, all the can all that can see the pen of pigs wide.

All this man is a make of chins which is to be tall and most many women, in the directory that shows why the state which is absolutely with plaster absolutely with plastering received with boast. All this in bedding.

Cut circles in Indians.

A cubicle with a reserved center and little spades and a large shade and a colored hour glass and little pieces, grand.

Colored up with bet let, leen glass cage. Colored up with let keen girk clink gage, colored up with keen get call up be seen in when call up when in bend that more wheezily. Colored up in when call that up if cost, call it up in when call that wake west, call it up in when that when it is in call and call it up in when it is when it is in when, when it is in when it is in when when it is in, when it is in when, when, it is in, in. When it is in when.

When it is in when call it up in when.

When it is in when call it up in when it is in when. It is in by the perulean repetition of amalgamated recreation of more integral and less solidifying rudeness. It is paul.

Baby mine, baby mine, have a cow come out of have a cow come out of baby mine baby mine have a cow come out with time, baby mine baby mine have a cow come neatly have a cow come sweetly baby mine baby mine have a cow come out in mine. Baby mine baby mine have a cow come out of have a cow come out of baby mine baby mine have a cow come out of have a cow come out of, have a cow come have a cow come have a cow come come come come.

A COLLECTION

What begins with the semblance of a conventional narrative gets side tracked.—R. K.

My Dear Miss Carey: A Story

There were little places to see Fernville, the town, the hospital, the lying in hospital, the sea-shore and the city.

Once we met my brother he was ringing a bell. He needed an umbrella but he would not buy it. I sent him one not prepaid. Oh yes the people are kind they all drink together. Even now. No not now. We are late.

Did you see the pear tree. It resembles the figs. They are often ripe. They grow in great abundance.

We like milk. My father likes milk and coffee.

Whenever there are flowers my mother is angry. She is even angry with me. That is to say she is generous enough and wishes

---

From *Geography and Plays* (1922).

63

everything back. We are all that way. My brother takes coal away in a little bag for use. All dark days are necessary. No permission is asked and it is given. For all day. For all day. Whenever it is needed. Not whenever it is needed. We do as we say it is best to do. Even religious people do so.

Come together in Fernville. Not I I thank you. My brother finds handkerchiefs there. For men. For men and for women. So does his wife. Many. Not very many. She brings them with her. Is that so. Many handkerchiefs are not necessary in Fernville. No indeed. We dismiss the church. We separate it. We have it to-day. A great many people call. On one another. Not altogether that. The post-office. The post-office of my brother. Now. Not now. Yes he is there now. Since the war. Yes since the war.

I remember when I was a b of c. I did not speak to old men then not when I was busy. I waited until I was tired and then we all sat down and had a cup of coffee. Coffee is very nourishing. I am very sensitive to the influence of coffee. So are we all.

Do you think that we are married. That we are all married. Mr. Weeks is married. He is going to be able to follow my advice. I advise him to go to my country. There he will do very well. The only advice I have to give him is never to live in the city. His wife does not like the city nor does she like a sunny climate. She is not able to go about with him. We are all of us leaving the end of the month.

Do not be angry.

I was very much surprised that water was the same color.

As what.

As the sun.

I feel that I must go at once.

Did you entirely forget about the other.

Drowning in water.

This is a question that I have never asked about because in the summer one does not think about it. Now it is winter but it is as warm as in summer.

Dear friends have a way of relating themselves to a town. We find in some districts that there are better ways of investing money. Some find that at the end of the war they are not able to continue paying on their houses.

Does this affect you.

Oh no because even if the father of my child is killed his sister will continue to give the money. She is obliged to by law.

This makes the whole matter very simple.

Not to me I have always been accustomed to it and have had some difficulty.

Yes we know we know that it is suddenly cold.

You are not pleased to see the sun setting. Indeed I cannot blame you.

Polybe in Port: A Curtain Raiser

Polybe in Port.

A hunter. He was not a hunter. He had a gun. I do not know whether they have permission to shoot.

Of course he must have if he has a gun. In this country they have a great many dogs who hunt rabbits. They run quicker.

We are surprised to see him.

Polybe is an ornament.

He is not thinner.

He likes the water now.

This I do not believe.

Neither do I believe there was any intention to go that way. Which way do you mean. Polybe does not remember. Me. Yes. The house. Yes. The servant. Yes. You are not mistaken.

We are not mistaken.

A great many shrubs every one of which are labelled.

Scene II.

A credit to me.

The cares and duties of a mother had been denied to Carrie Russell.

Polybe silent.

He said earnestly that it didn't matter.

Spanish Chattings

Do you keep books.

All weddings are back.

Pigeons.

Pigeons recognise persons. Do they. We saw them. They flew around.

Shooting pigeons is necessary. For what. For the sea.

I see old peppers that are dried. We do not complain. We say winds are violent and I do not wish them. Wish for them. I do not wish to see the stars. Call it out of here. You mean that pole. No indeed I don't mean Inca.

Oh yes certainly.

They Came Together

I can tell a little story. I cannot describe the character nor the color in the street nor the kind of a stone. A great many people have silver purses.

Wild Flowers

We collected wild flowers. We enjoyed it very much. In a window we saw exhibited the things that can be found in the country.

There was a satisfaction that we had the temporary installation which made it possible for us to ask another servant not to visit our servant. We did not do so. We were not neglectful of our best interests.

Will They Crush Germany

They will crush Germany. There is no doubt about it.

A PATRIOTIC LEADING

VERSE I

Indeed indeed.
Can you see.
The stars.
And regularly the precious treasure.
What do we love without measure.
We know.

VERSE II

We suspect the second man.

VERSE III

We are worthy of everything that happens.
You mean weddings.
Naturally I mean weddings.

From *Useful Knowledge* (1928).

VERSE IV

And then we are.
Hail to the nation.

VERSE V

Do you think we believe it.

VERSE VI

It is that or bust.

VERSE VII

We cannot bust.

VERSE VIII

Thank you.

VERSE IX

Thank you so much.

Long regarding this among Stein's most innovative fictions, I anthologized it three decades ago in Breakthrough Fictioneers *(1973).*—R. K.

Incline.

Clinch, melody, hurry, spoon, special, dumb, cake, forrester. Fine, cane, carpet, incline, spread, gate, light, labor.

Banking.

Coffee, cough, glass, spoon, white, singing. Choose, selection, visible, lightning, garden, conversation, ink, spending, light space, morning, celebration, invisible, reception, hour, glass, curving, summons, sparkle, suffering the minisection, sanctioning the widening, less than the wireless, more certain. All the change. Any counselling non consuming and split splendor.

From *Geography and Plays* (1922).

IIIIIIIII.

Forward and a rapidity and no resemblance no more utterly. Safe light, more safes no more safe for the separation.

M—N H—.

A cook. A cook can see. Pointedly in uniform, exertion in a medium. A cook can see.

Clark which is awful, clark which is shameful, clark and order.

A pin is a plump point and pecking and combined and more much more is in fine.

Rats is, rats is oaken. Robber. Height, age, miles, plaster, pedal, more order.

Bake, a barn has cause and more late oat-cake specially.

Spend rubber, holder and coal, high, careful, in a pointed collar. A hideous south west is always a climb in aged seldom succeeded flavoring untimely, necessity white, hour in a glaze.

Break, sky blue light, obliquely, in a cut carpet, in the pack. A sound.

COO—GE.

Press in the ink and stare and cheese. Pick in the faint and feather and white. White in the plume.

M—N H—.

No noon back. No noon settler, no sun in the slant and carpet utterly surrounded.

No pressed plaster. None.

No pressing pan and pan cake. Not related exactly. Not related.

Matter in the center of single sand and slide in the hut.
No account of gibberish. No sky lark utterly.
Perfect lemon and cutting a central black. Not such clouding.
A sugar, a lame sugar, certainly. No sobriety no silver ash tray.

M—N H—.

A co existence with hard suckling and spoons, and spoons. A co-existence with orange supper. A last mending. A begging. Should the assault be exterminated, should it.

M—N H—.

A sound is in the best society. It hums and moves, it throws the hat in no way away and in no way particularly at paving. The meanness is a selection of parts and all of that is no more a handkerchief merely and large.

Points.

The exchange which is fanciful and righteous and mingled is in the author mostly in the piece.

CH—N.

A unity is the meantime in a union. A branch case is exactly so anxious and avoided and even then is it in place of blunders, is it in the piece that makes hesitation clear.

The youth and the check board and the all color minutely, this and the chance of the bright flours inward is not in a glance. A check is an instance and more more is indwelling.

Pecked Places.

In the unconcise word that is ministered and in the blame extraordinarily the center the whole center is coupled. This is choice.

M—N H—.

Hunger is not hurry and a silence and no more than ever, it is not so exactly and the word used is there.

T—S WH—.

A cut in trusts and in black colors which are not carpets not at all likely carpets and no sucking in substance of the sacking placed only in air outside. This makes a change precious and not odd not odd in place of more use. Not odd in the meaning rapidly.

M—N H—.

The soon estate and established alternately has bright soldiers and peaceable in the rest of the stretch.

J—S B—E.

A regular walking ground is that which shows peeping and soft places between mush and this is most moist in the settled summer. So much wet does gleam and the shutters all the shutters are sober. A piece of cut grass is dangerous dangerous to smelling and to all most.

S—NS.

A dark ground is not colored black mostly and dirtily securely and much exchange is much with a sight and so much to sponge in with speeches to whittle.

J—E B—E.

A tight laundry that is piece meal is in the best astounding. Between, in, on the beside, and no more origin, more in the weed blessed.

M—N H—.

Point, face, canvas, toy, struck off, sense or, weigh coach, soon beak on, so suck in, and an iron.

W—IE C—N.

Point a rose, see a soil, see a saddle, see a monk tree, see a sand tree, trust a cold bit of pickle usefully in an oration.

||||||||.

See the meadow in a meadow light.
The blame is necessarily an interruption perpendicularly.

L—E.

The seam in between is fenceless.

E—E.

The seam in most tight legs are looser and not secure politely.

K—Y.

The separation is a sight.

R—CK.

Chocolate is alarming in old places, chocolate is thunder.
Joining jerked sour green grass is yesterday and tomorrow and
alternately.

CH—N.

Kindness is necessary and a spilled iron loan. The best choice
is a sucked place readily and much any within the cut spilling.

ALF—.

Jacket in buds and in glasses, jackets entirely in collision.
A triangle is worried with recollected socks and examples.

[Peace is in.]

No spilling and an argument, no spilling and no spilling is beckoned. A shout is particular.

CH—N.

An heroic countenance justly named and special, special and contained and in eagle.

A mark and a window glass and a splendid chew, altogether a singer.

R—CK.

Secret in a season makes the pining wetter. So much hooding, so best to saw into right pieces the clang and the hush. The held up ocean, the eaten pan that has no cut cake, the same only different clover is the best, is the best.

K—Y.

Caution, caution all, caution the cloud and the oats and the beagle and the clearing and the happy dent and the widow soaking and the climb and the correction.

||||||||||.

M—N. H—.

Shut the chamber in the door, so well and so weak and so buttered. Shut the chest out, do not shut it in.

ALF—.

Crime, crime is that way to charge safely, crime is a tooth-pick. It is. It has a credit. Any old stick that has a choking in the way that there is leather shows a mean spirit.

An eye glass, a yellow and neck lace person, a special way to date something, any pleasing register means no readily replaced mice.

L—E.

A set cold egg, a set in together is lively.

ALF—.

A barked out sunshine, a better way to arrange Monday, a cloud of neglected Thursdays, all these are together somehow.

E—E.

A white wedding cake means a white thing and so no more left in the bottle, no more water grows.

A very likely told place is that which is not best mentioned, not the very best.

The incline is in classes in coats in whole classes puzzling peculiarly.

The best way to put it all in is a bite, it is so in every way especially.

S—NS.

Cunning, very cunning. Cute, very cute, critical, not only very critical, critical, critical.

ALF—.

Climbing into the most high piece of prepared furniture is no collection. It is part of the winding old glass.

M—N H—.

A sun in shine, and a so and a so helped angle is the same as the whole right.

The Wedding

It is not for nothing that the row placed quantity without grinding. Furnishing is something, individual is pointed. Beetles, only aged sounds are hot, a can in ease and a sponge full, a can in case and a wax well come, a can, a single hole, a wild suggesting wood, a half carpet and a pillow, a pillow increasing, a shirt in a cloud, a dirty distress, a thing grey, a thing thin, a long shout, a wonder, an over piece of cool oil, a sugar can, a shut open accident, a result in a feat, a copper, any copper. A cape coat, in bold shutters, in bold shutters shutting and not changing shutters not changing climaxes and feelings and hold over the switch, the binding of a pet and a revolver, the chosen loan, the owned cake in pieces, the way to swim.

B—B—B.

A language in a bath and in a dressing gown to a precision and a likely union and a single persian and a pressing quite not colored and a gloom not a gloom, and a pin all the same, and a pin not to share and a pin with a stone.

W—IE C—N.

A sudden plunge into a forest and sudden reserve in a cup of water coldly and a dark sunshine and a squeeze, a length in all.

T—S WH—.

A kind of cataract is a hopeless stroke.

Curls

A choked part of a loud sound in an old piece of glass is happening, it is solid and all that and not by any means noisy. The best way is just to stay any way and to think. The best way is always lively by a kind of a hoarse whisper. A shutter is only light when there is a joke. This is no use.

ALF—.

A birthday cake is in the morning when there is no use in sleeping. Supposing there is time at nine, the less often there is seven the more use there is in lending a joke. Any nice way to remain is longer than was necessary and the temptation the real temptation never happens, there is a cut away and there is a kind of a mellow cheese that has just begun.

Climbing in and climbing are the ways to change and the only hope is what is there, when it is not a difference between all of it every time.

J—S B—E.

A countenance and order and a bite, really a bit and care and receiving and a vacation and a long half mounted hat box and more silver and more in silver in some and the buttons in a hat and a mild market and goats and not coats Thursday and all health and heels in front grasses and light corn cropping, all this is a toiler and much breading and a kind of a cover is the kind unoccurringly.

Keys

A wild waist and a simple jerk and bloom and best to come in a way, hut, heart, hide, have, within, a study, hard in, all which, black busts, coal car, gold nose, white wood, curly seize, half in, all which, best plant, cold carpet, in the glass.

Keys

Why are stains silky and old pieces ruddy and colored angels way built. Why are knuckles calmer and pins chunks and bold in heats frightened. Why are the savage stern and old age coming. Why are the best old seem culpable and a decision, decisive.

CH—N.

Enthusiasm, prudence, cold heart and elegant example, a winding alley and a stair case center, a complete poison slip.

CH—N and R—CK.

A clatter of curious pin cushions softly gathered by the pan that comes.

Wide in the street makes the double engagement stutter, a lean in the roll, a lean in it.

A lean in when and all came but when it was for and the hindrance and it.

A residence.

CH—N R—CK AND M—N H—.

Be advised that really no insolence is in the bicycle shop. Be advised by it.

Be advised that no belgian is strong, be wonderful.

Bet use that come in.

M—N H— AND ALF—.

An occasion to sell all cables all towels and all that is what is met, is not met.

A cold hash that means saw dust and hot enough, hot enough heating.

[Not cutting furiously.]

A single speech is in it, a soil. A single speech. A ham. A cold. A collusion. A count. A cowslip. A tune ditch. A well king. A house to let. A cut out.

B—B—B.

A shudder makes a shake. A bit of green breeze makes a whole green breeze and a breeze is in between. A breeze is canvassed by a week wet and all sold, anything dwelling, in the mist. All the whole steer, all of it.

Shout

Best to shut in broken cows with mud and splinters and little pieces of gain and more steel doors a better aches and a spine and a cool school and shouting, early mounting and a best passion and a bliss and a bliss and a bliss. No wide coal gas.

THE SUPERSTITIONS OF FRED ANNEDAY, ANNDAY, ANDAY: A NOVEL OF REAL LIFE

A "novel" so short with chapters so short and paragraphs so short was awesomely radical in 1935 and still is now.—R. K.

A cuckoo bird is singing in a cuckoo tree, singing to me oh singing to me.

It was many years before it happened that that song was written and sung but it did happen.

A cuckoo bird did come and sit in a tree close by and sing, sing cuckoo to me.

And this is the way it came to happen.

As I say the song was written and sung many years before, before this happening.

The song was written and sung in Italy.

There Fred Annday was living in a villa in Fiesole. He had been born and raised in America had Fred Anday and there in America he had naturally never heard a cuckoo sing although he had heard a cuckoo clock sing.

From *The Nassau Lit* (December 1935).

And when he first heard a cuckoo sing cuckoo, and that was in Germany he was convinced that it was a clock and not a bird and it took a great deal of argument to convince him that it really was a bird and that birds did sing cuckoo.

Then a number of years afterwards in Italy and he was thinking then of one he loved and one who loved him and he did not see a cuckoo and perhaps he did not hear a cuckoo sing but he made the song, a cuckoo bird in sitting in a cuckoo tree singing to me oh singing to me.

And then many years after in France he was thinking of how pleasant it is to be rich and he had as a matter of fact for him a fair amount of money in his pocket and all of a sudden he heard a cuckoo at a distance and he was pleased because he had money in his pocket and if you hear the first cuckoo of the season and there is money in your pocket it means that you will have money for all that year.

And then the miracle happened. The cuckoo came and did what cuckoos never do and it came and sat in a tree right close to him and he could see it and it could see him and it gave a single loud cuckoo and flew away. And this was the beginning of something for him because from that time on he was successful and he believed in superstition yes he did.

Fred Anneday knew all that and he knew better than that. He knew something else about the cuckoo. The cuckoo is a bird who occupies other birds' nests. Perhaps that is the reason he brings money and success. Because he certainly does.

And Fred Anday knew that there was a monastery where there had been monks and the monks had been forced to leave and others who were not monks had taken their place and the neighborhood gathered around at night and made cuckoo noises around the place at night. Cuckoo they said and they meant that the cuckoo takes other birds' nests and that is what these people had done. And so Fred Anneday's life was based on superstition and he was right.

What had Fred Anday done all his life.

A novel is what you dream in your night sleep. A novel is not waking thoughts although it is written and thought with waking thoughts. But really a novel goes as dreams go in sleeping at night and some dreams are like anything and some dreams are like something and some dreams change and some dreams are quiet and some dreams are not. And some dreams are just what any one would do only a little different always just a little different and that is what a novel is.

And this is what a novel is.

Fred Anneday all his life had loved not only one woman not only one thing not only managing everything, not only being troubled so that he could not sleep, not only his mother and religion, not only being the oldest and nevertheless always young enough, not only all this but all his life he had loved superstition and he was right.

He had a great deal to do with everything. This was not only because he was one and the eldest of a very large family which he was but it was because he did have a great deal to do with anything.

One of his friends was Brim Beauvais but he met him later later even than when he loved the only woman whom he ever loved and who was larger and older. And he did not meet Brim Beauvais through her although he might have. It made him think of nightingales. Everything made him think of nightingales and express these thoughts.

If any one is the youngest of seven children and likes it he does not care to hear about birth control because supposing he had not been. If one is the eldest of eight children and likes it he too does not care to hear about birth control but then any one knowing him would know what he would say if any one asked him.

If any one is an only child and likes it well then he is an only child and likes it as men or women, or as children. And they may or may not like birth control. There you are that is the answer and even superstition is not always necessary. But really it is. Of course really it is.

Fred Anneday loved a woman and it made all the difference in his life not only that but that he continued to have a great deal to do with everything only it worried him less that is to say not at all and he slept well, that is after he had found that he loved this woman.

Oh Fred Anneday how many things have happened, more than you can say. And Brim Beauvais how many things have happened to Brim Beauvais. Not so many although he thought as many did. And this goes to show how many have told how many so. And this was because Brim Beauvais did not have to count for superstition. Which is a mistake.

Fred Annday was not tall be he changed and his forehead was high. And he changed.

Brim Beauvais was fat that is to say he grew fatter which was not fair as he had been very good looking when he was thin.

Fred Anday loved one woman and she had had a strange thing happen. Not that he loved her for that but it was that which brought them together.

Listen it is very strange. But first how long has Anday lived. About thirty-eight years. And how was he feeling then. Very badly because he was very nervous and did not sleep and his mother was older and thinner and active and wore a wig but bowed as he did.

The woman that he loved was not at all like that although some men love to love a woman who might have looked like their mother if she had looked like that.

There had been a great many women in the life of Fred Anday before he loved the only woman whom he ever loved. First there was his mother.

If there where they lived there had been a mother's day she would have celebrated it eight times and Fred Anday the eldest always would have been there. He would have taken care that he was there with her to celebrate it with and for her.

What does he say and what does she say or what does she say and what does he say.

Another man was Enoch Mariner and he had a beard and violet eyes and stood and looked at one place any time a long time.

He said to her to the mother of Fred you are sixty but if everything is alright and it is it is not too late to take a lover. Did she Mrs. Anneday think he meant her. He certainly did and said so.

But nobody knew because she never told and besides her sister had just died. This did not interest Enoch Mariner. Enoch Mariner was about forty-one years old at that time.

So now there are three men and there are also more than as many women and there had been as many children.

Fred Annday had no child nor did most of his sisters and his brothers. One had a child just one and only had one child just one.

Brim Beauvais never had a child. His sister had.

Enoch Mariner never had a child and he had no brothers and no sisters to have one.

So there you have a great many things that happened and remember what a novel is it is just that.

And now every one wishes to see any one see the family Annday although a great many were very cross about them. They thought they exaggerated being what they were and that everybody had to say or do something about Fred Annday. Which once he loved the only woman he ever loved slowly nobody did. And this in a way ceased to be exciting. But the way it came about was very exciting as exciting as Dillinger and almost as many knew about it that is if you remember the size of their town and country.

A Motto.

How could it be a little whatever he liked.

Chapter II

It is impossible perfectly impossible to mention everybody with whom Anday had something to do. And why. Because there are so many of them. This is true of every one and therefore that is not what a novel is. A novel is like a dream at night where in spite of everything happening any one comes to know relatively few persons.

And superstition. Superstition does not come in in dreaming. But in waking oh yes in waking and being waking oh yes it is nothing but superstition. And that is right. That is the way it should be. And anybody likes what they like and anybody likes superstition and so did Fred Anday and the only woman he loved but not in the same way. She was not superstitious in his way and he was not superstitious in her way. But he was right right to be superstitious. Oh yes he was.

What is superstition.

Superstition is believing that something means anything and that anything means something and that each thing means a particular thing and will mean a particular thing is coming. Oh yes it does.

Fred Annday has been superstitious as a little boy. Which of course he had not better not.

Brim Beauvais was superstitious but it moved slowly and as well as not he was not.

Enoch Mariner was superstitious and if he was nobody came to ask him to like it. He liked whatever he did or did not like. He was not very alike. And he made no reference to a wound in his stomach which he had had.

And in this town was a hotel and this at any rate is so. In this town there was a hotel and there was a hotel keeper and his wife and his four children three boys and a girl and his mother and his father and his maiden sister and a governess for the daughter and a woman who helped manage everything and she was a sister of Fred Annday. She came very near being older than Fred only she was not although she felt herself to be in spite of the fact that she had an older sister who still was not older but younger than Fred for Fred after all was the older. Any superstition will help. And it did. He was the eldest and he was older. He knew to a day how he came to be there to stay.

It is not at all confusing to live every day and to meet everyone not at all confusing but to tell any one yes it is confusing even if only telling it to any one how you lived any one day and met everybody all of that day. And now what more can one do than that.

And doing more than that is this.

A Motto.

Once. It is always excited to say twice.
He came twice and she coughed.

Chapter III

Now I need no reason to wonder if he went to say farewell. But he never did. Fred Anday never said farewell to any one in a day no one ever does because every one sees every one every day which is a natural way for a day to be. Think of any village town or city or desert island or country house or anything. Of course no dream is like that because after all there has to be all day to be like that. And all day is like that. And there cannot be a novel like that because it is too confusing written down if it is like that so a novel is like a dream when it is not like that.

But what is this yes what is this. It is this.

Now having gotten a little tired of Fred Anday but not of Mariner let us begin with the hotel and the hotel keeper. Everybody can go on talking about Fred Anday at any time. When two or three or ten people are together and you ask them what are they talking about they say oh about Fred Anday and some people are like that. They just naturally are the subject of discussion although everybody has said everything about that one and yet once again everybody begins again. What is the mystery of Fred Anday. Any conversation about him is a conversation about him. That is the way it is. Does he know it. Well I do not know that he does. And if he does it does not add to his superstitions. And about that he is right it does not add to his superstitions.

How could Enoch Mariner have loved more than one woman, of course he did and could. He could even very well remember asking the first woman he asked to marry him. Not only he remembered but also everybody who saw the letter and quite a few did see it because the girl proposed to was so surprised that she had to show it to several of her friends to help her bear it.

She was going to be a school teacher and she and Enoch had met once. He sat down the next day so he said in his letter and took off his coat and he got all ready and he wrote her this letter. He said he knew she would not say yes but she would if he had said all he had to say. And he did say all he had to say and she said no. That is the way life began for Enoch and many years later any one would have married him but he was a bachelor and he had a beard and he walked well and he always proposed to any one to be their lover but was he, this nobody knows.

See how very well Fred Anday might have come to know him but as a matter of fact did he I am not at all sure that he did. And if one were to ask Fred Anday, he would not remember.

A Motto.

Pens by hens.

Chapter III

Slowly he felt as he did.

So many things happen that nobody knows that it is necessary to say that he was right to have his superstitions. Of course he is. What is the use of knowing what has happened if one is not to know what is to happen. But of course one is to know what is to happen because it does. Not like it might but might it not happen as it does of course it does. And Anday Fred Anday is never in tears. Not in consequence but never in tears.

And yet Fred Anday could be treated as if he should be in tears but he was not because he had others things. He always did have other things even when it was not true that he slept.

And best of all he knew how he did. He did it very well. And because of this they knew how to say so.

Every one said Anday was not like a hill or like a ball. They said he was not well to do but he had everything to do and he did everything. Nobody could look better than best at that.

For how many reasons was Anday loved or if not loved. Just for how many reasons. Anybody can and could tell just for how many reasons.

And just for how many reasons is a chinaman loved if he comes from Indo China. Just for how many reasons.

Just for how many reasons is everybody loved or please just for how many reasons. Best of all let this be an introduction to how they feel when they do not remember anybody's first name.

One remembers only the names one has heard.

Motto.

Why should he go with him when he stays here for him.

Chapter IV

Do not bother. Do not bother about a story oh do not bother. Inevitably one has to know how a story ends even if it does not. Fred Annday's story does not end but that is because there is no more interest in it. And in a way yes in a way that is yes that is always so. I can tell this story as I go. I like to tell a story so.

Anybody will have to learn that novels are like that.

IF YOU HAD THREE HUSBANDS

The most audacious of this sequence of unconnected paragraphs, setting the tone for the whole, is "three and three makes two."—R. K.

If you had three husbands.

If you had three husbands.

If you had three husbands, well not exactly that.

If you had three husbands would you be willing to take everything and be satisfied to live in Belmont in a large house with a view and plenty of flowers and neighbors, neighbors who were cousins and some friends who did not say anything.

This is what happened.

She expressed everything.

She is worthy of signing a will.

And mentioning what she wished.

She was brought up by her mother. She had meaning and she was careful in reading. She read marvelously. She was pleased. She was aged thirty-nine. She was flavored by reason of much memory and recollection.

This is everything.

From *Geography and Plays* (1922).

Foreword.

I cannot believe it.
I cannot realize it.
I cannot see it.
It is what happened.
First there was a wonder.
Really wonder.
Wonder by means of what.
Wonder by means of measures.
Measuring what.
Heights.
How high.
A little.
This was not all.
There were well if you like there were wonderful spots such as
were seen by a queen. This came to be a system. Really it was just
by a treasure. What was a treasure. Apart from that.
Surely.
Rather.
In their beginning what was a delight. Not signing papers or
anything or indeed in having a mother and two sisters. Not nearly
enough were mentioned by telegraphing. It was a choice.
I ramble when I mention it.
Did she leave me any money.
I remember something.
I am not clear about what it was.
When did I settle that.
I settled it yesterday.

Early Life.

They were not miserably young they were older than another. She was gliding. It is by nearly weekly leaning that it comes to be exact. It never was in dispute.

They were gayly not gaily gorgeous. They were not gorgeous at all. They were obliging. If you think so. If you think so glow. If you believe in light boys. They were never another.

It came to be seen that any beam of three rooms was not showy. They were proud to sit at mother. Slowly walking makes walking quicker. They have toys and not that in deceiving. They do not deceive them. No one is willing. No one could be cool and mother and divided and necessary and climatical and of origin and beneath that mean and be a sun. It was strange in her cheek. Not strange to them or that.

A young one.

Not by mountains.

Not by oysters.

Not by hearing.

Not by round ways.

Not by circumference again.

Not by leaving luncheon.

Not by birth.

It doesn't make any difference when ten are born. Ten is never a number. Neither is six. Neither is four.

I will not mention it again.

Early days of shading.

Make a mouse in green.

Make a single piece of sun and make a violet bloom. Early piece of swimming makes a sun on time and makes it shine and warm today and sun and sun and not to stay and not to stay or away. Not to stay satin. Out from the whole wide world he chose her. Out from the whole wide world and that is what is said.

Family.

What is famine. It is plenty of another. What is famine. It is eating. What is famine. It is carving. Why is carving a wonderful thing. Because supper is over. This can happen again. Sums are seen.

Please be polite for mother. Lives of them. Call it shall it clothe it. Boil it. Why not color it black and never red or green. This is stubborn. I don't say so.

No opposition.

If you have a little likeness and hoped for more terror. If you had a refusal and were slender. If you had cuff-buttons and jackets and really astonishing kinds of fever would you stop talking. Would you not consider it necessary to talk over affairs.

It was a chance that made them never miss tea. They did not miss it because it was there. They did not mean to be particular. They invited their friends. They were not aching. It was noiseless and beside that they were clever. Who was clever. The way they had of seeing mother.

Mother was prepared.

They were caressing.

They had sound sense.

They were questioned.

They had likeness. Likeness to what. Likeness to loving. Who had likeness to loving. They had likeness to loving. Why did they have a likeness to loving. They had a likeness to loving because it was easily seen that they were immeasurable.

They were fixed by that, they were fixed, not licensed, they were seen, not treasured, they were announced, not restless, they were reasoning, not progressing. I do not wish to imply that there is any remedy for any defect.

I cannot state that anyone was disappointed. I cannot state that any one was ever disappointed by willingly heaping much confusion in particular places. No confusion is reasonable. Anybody can be nervous.

They were nervous again.

This is wishing.

Why is wishing related to a ridiculous pretence of changing opposition to analysis. The answer to this is that nearly any one can faint. I don't mean to say that they don't like tennis.

Please be capable of sounds and shoulders. Please be capable of careful words. Please be capable of meaning to measure further.

They measured there.

They were heroes.

Nobody believed papers.

Everybody believed colors.

I cannot exercise obligation.

I cannot believe cheating.

I cannot sober mother.

I cannot shut my heart.

I cannot cherish vice.

I cannot deceive all.

I cannot be odious.

I cannot see between.

Between what and most.

I cannot answer either.

Do be left over suddenly.

This is not advice.

No one knows so well what widening means. It means that yards are yards and so many of them are perfect. By that I mean I know.

This is not so.

I am not telling the story I am repeating what I have been reading. What effects tenderness.

Not to remember the name.

Say it.

The time comes when it is natural to realize that solid advantages connect themselves with pages of extreme expression. This is never nervously pale. It is finely and authentically swollen by the time there is any rapid shouting.

I do not like the word shouting. I do not mean that it gives me any pleasure. On the contrary I see that individual annoyances are increased by it but nevertheless I am earnestly persuasive concerning it. Why soothe why soothe each other.

This is not at all what is being said.

It happened very simply that they were married. They were naturally married and really the place to see it was in the reflection every one had of not frightening not the least bit frightening enthusiasm. They were so exact and by nearly every one it was encouraged soothed and lamented. I do not say that they were interested.

Any years are early years and all years are occasions for recalling that she promised me something.

This is the way to write an address.

When they were engaged she said we are happy. When they were married she said we are happy. They talked about everything they talked about individual feeling. This is not what was said. They did not talk about disinterested obligation. They did not talk about pleasantness and circumstances. I do not mean to say that there was conversation. I do not organize a revision. I declare that there was no need of criticism. That there was no criticism. That there was breathing. By that I mean that lights have lanterns and are not huddled together when there is a low ceiling. By that I mean that it was separate. The ceiling was separated from the floor. Everywhere.

I could say that devotion was more merited than walking together. What do you mean. I mean that we all saw it.

When not by a beginning is there meadows and music, you can't call it that exactly, when not by a beginning, there is no beginning, I used to say there was a beginning, there is no beginning, when there is no beginning in a volume and there are parts, who can think.

This pencil was bought in Austria.

Length of time or times.

He agreed. He said I would have known by this time. I don't like to think about it. It would have led to so much. Not that I am disappointed I cannot be disappointed when I have so much to make me happy. I know all that I am to happiness, it is to be happy and I am happy. I am so completely happy that I mention it.

In writing now I find it more of a strain because now I write by sentences. I don't mean that I feel it above, I feel it here and by this time I mention it too. I do not feel the significance of this list.

Can you read a book.

By the time artificial flowers were made out of feathers no pride was left. Any one is proud if the name of their house is the name of a city.

I remember very well the time I was asked to come up and I said I did not want to. I said I did not want to but I was willing not quite to understand why after all there need be poison. Do not say more than a word.

No this is wrong.

Cousins and cousins, height is a brother. Are they careful to stay.

If you had three husbands I don't mean that it is a guess or a wish. I believe finally in what I saw in what I see. I believe finally in what I see, in where I satisfy my extreme shadow.

Believing in an extreme dream. This is so that she told her mother. I do not believe it can be mentioned. I do not believe it can be mentioned.

Astonishing leaves are found in their dread in their dread of that color. Astonishing leaves can be found in their dread not in their dread of that color. Astonishing leaves can be found in their dread in their dread of that color.

When it came to say I mean a whole day nobody meant a whole day. When it came not to say a whole day nobody meant a whole day. There never was a single day or a single murmur or a single word or a single circumstance or sweating. What is sweating. Not distilling. Distilling necessitates knowing. Knowing necessitates reasons and reasons do not necessitate flowers. States are flowers.

Brother to birthdays.

Twenty four days.

Not a beginning.

By politeness. It is not really polite to be unworthy. Unworthy of what unworthy of the house and of the property adjoining.

Let me describe the red room. A red room isn't cold or warm. A red room is not meant to be icy. A red room is worthy of articles.

He pleased she pleased everybody. He pleased her.

He pleased her to go. She was attracted by the time. I do not remember that there were any clocks.

I don't wish to begin counting.

All this was after it was necessary for us to be there all the time. Who were we. We were often enlivening. By way of what. By way of steps or the door. By way of steps. By way of steps or the door.

I remember very well the day he asked me if I were patient. Of course I was or of course I was patient enough, of course I was patient enough.

When it was easy to matter we were all frames not golden or printed, just finely or formerly flattered. It was so easy easy to be bell. Belle was her name. Belle or Bella. I don't mean relations or overwhelming. I don't even mean that we were fond of healthy trees. Trees aren't healthy by yesterday or by roots or by swelling. Trees are a sign of pleasure. It means that there is a country. A country give to me sweet land of liberty.

One can easily get tired of rolls and rows. Rows have one seat. Rolls are polite. In a way there is no difference between them. Rolls and rows have finished purses. Rows and rolls have finished purses.

It isn't easy to be restless.

If sitting is not developed.

If standing is not open.

If active action is represented by lying and if piles of tears are beside more delight, it is a rope.

By that we swim.

Capture sealing wax not in or color.

Ceilings.

I like that dwelling.

All the same sound or bore.

Do it.

Try that.

Try.

Why.

Widen.

Public speaking is sinister if cousins are brothers. We were a little pile.

Buy that.

There is no such sense.

Pleasant days.

So to speak.

Sand today.

Sunday.

Sight in there.

Saturday.

Pray.

What forsooth.

Do be quiet.

Laugh.

I know it.

Shall we.

Let us go ten.

One must be willing.

If one loves one another by that means they do not perish. They frequent the same day and nearly that it was six months apart.

Three and three make two.

Two twenty.

I was not disappointed.

Do as you please, write the name, change it, declare that you are strong, be annoyed. All this is not foolish.

She was doubtless not old.

Pleasant days brother. I don't mean this thing. I don't mean calling aloud, I never did so, I was not plaintive. I was not even reached by coughing. I was splendid and sorrowful. I could catch my breath.

I don't feel that necessity.

They came home.

Why did they come home.

They come home beside.

All of it was strange, their daughter was strange, their excitement was strange and painfully sheltered. Quiet leaning is so puzzling. Certainly glasses makes cats a nuisance. We really have endured too much. Everybody says the same thing.

I do not see much necessity for believing that it would have occurred as it did occur if sun and September and the hope had not been mentioned. It was all foolish. Why not be determined. Why not oppose. Why not settle flowers. Settle on flowers, speak cryingly and be loath to detain her. I don't see how any one can speak.

I am not satisfied.

Present Homes.

There then.

Present ten.

Mother and sister apples, no not apples, they can't be apples, everything can't be apples, sounds can't be apples. Do be quiet and refrain from acceptances.

It was a great disappointment to me.

I can see that there is a balcony. There never was a sea or land, there never was a harbor or a snow storm, there never was excitement. Some said she couldn't love. I don't believe that anybody said that. I don't mean that anybody said that. We were all present. We could be devoted. It does make a different thing. And hair, hair should not be deceiving. Cause tears. Why tears, why not abscesses.

I will never mention an ugly skirt.

It pleased me to say that I was pretty.

Oh we are so pleased.

I don't say this at all.

Consequences are not frightful.

Pleasure in a home.

After lunch, why after lunch, no birds are eaten. Of course carving is special.

I don't say that for candor.

Please be prepared to stay.

I don't care for wishes.

This is not a success.

By this stream.

Streaming out.

I am relieved from draught. This is not the way to spell water.

I cannot believe in much.
I have courage.
Endurance.
And restraint.
After that.

For that end.

This is the title of a conclusion which was not anticipated[.]
When I was last there I smiled behind the car. What car
showed it.
By that time.
Believe her out.
Out where.
By that.
Buy that.
She pleased me for. Eye saw.
Do it.

For that over that.

We passed away. By that time servants were memorable. They
came to praise.
Please do not.
A blemish.
They have spans.
I cannot consider that the right word.
By the time we are selfish, by that time we are selfish.
By that time we are selfish.
It is a wonderful sight,
It is a wonderful sight to see.
Days.

What are days.
They have hams.
Delicate.
Delicate hams.
Pounds.
Pounds where.
Pounds of.
Where.
Not butter dogs.
I establish souls.
Any spelling will do.
Beside that.
Any spelling will do beside that.
If you look at it.
That way.
I am going on.
In again.
I am going on again in in then.
What I feel.
What I do feel.
They said mirrors.
Undoubtedly they have that phrase.
I can see a hat.
I remember very well knowing largely.
Any shade, by that I do mean iron glass. Iron glass is so torn.
By what. By the glare. Be that beside. Size shall be sensible. That
size shall be sensible.

Fixing.

Fixing enough.
Fixing up.
By fixing down, that is softness, by fixing down there.

Their end.

Politeness.
Not by linen.
I don't wish to be recalled.
One, day, I do not wish to use the word, one day they asked to buy that.
I don't mean anything by threads. It was wholly unnecessary to do so. It was done and then a gun. By that stand. Wishes.
I do not see what I have to do with that.
Any one can help weeping.
By wise.
I am so indifferent.
Not a bite.
Call me handsome.
It was a nice fate.
Any one could see.
Any one could see.
Any one could see.
Buy that etching.
Do be black.
I do not mean to say etching. Why should I be very sensitive. Why should I matter. Why need I be seen. Why not have politeness.
Why not have politeness.
In my hair.
I don't think it sounds at all like that.
Their end.
To end.
To be for that end.
To be that end.
I don't see what difference it makes
It does matter.
Why have they pots.

Ornaments.

And china.

It isn't at all.

I have made every mistake.

Powder it.

Not put into boxes.

Not put into boxes.

Powder it.

I know that well.

She mentioned it as she was sleeping.

She liked bought cake best. No she didn't for that purpose.

I have utter confusion.

No two can be alike.

They are and they are not stubborn.

Please me.

I was mistaken.

Any way.

By that.

Do not refuse to be wild.

Do not refuse to be all.

We have decided not to withstand it.

We would not rather have the home.

This is to teach lessons of exchange endurance and resemblance and by that time it was turned.

Shout.

By.

Out.

I am going to continue humming.

This does not mean express wishes.

I am not so fanciful. I am beside that calculated to believe in whole pages. Oh do not annoy me.

Days.

I don't like to be fitted. She didn't say that. If it hadn't been as natural as all the rest you would have been as silly as all the rest.

It's not at all when it is right.
I wish for a cake.
She said she did.
She said she didn't.

Gloom.

There was no gloom.
Every room.
There was no room.
There was no room.

Buy that chance.
She didn't leave me any money.
Head.
Ahead.
I don't want to be visible or invisible.
I don't want a dog named Dick.
It has nothing to do with it.
I am obliged to end.
Intend.
My uncle will.

ROOMS

Act so that there is no use in a centre. A wide action is not a width. A preparation is given to the ones preparing. They do not eat who mention silver and sweet. There was an occupation.

A whole centre and a border make hanging a way of dressing. This which is not why there is a voice is the remains of an offering. There was no rental.

So the tune which is there has a little piece to play, and the exercise is all there is of a fast. Then tender and true that makes no width to hew is the time that there is question to adopt.

To begin the placing there is no wagon. There is no change lighter. It was done. And then the spreading, that was not accomplishing that needed standing and yet the time was not so difficult as they were not all in place. They had no change. They were not respected. They were that, they did it so much in the matter and this showed that that settlement was not condensed. It was spread there. Any change was in the ends of the centre. A heap was heavy. There was no change.

Burnt and behind and lifting a temporary stone and lifting more than a drawer.

From *Tender Buttons* (1914).

The instance of there being more is an instance of more. The shadow is not shining in the way there is a black line. The truth has come. There is a disturbance. Trusting to a baker's boy meant that there would be very much exchanging and anyway what is the use of a covering to a door. There is a use, they are double.

If the centre has the place then there is distribution. That is natural. There is a contradiction and naturally returning there comes to be both sides and the centre. That can be seen from the description.

The author of all that is in there behind the door and that is entering in the morning. Explaining darkening and expecting relating is all of a piece. The stove is bigger. It was of a shape that made no audience bigger if the opening is assumed why should there not be kneeling. Any force which is bestowed on a floor shows rubbing. This is so nice and sweet and yet there comes the change, there comes the time to press more air. This does not mean the same as disappearance.

A little lingering lion and a Chinese chair, all the handsome cheese which is stone, all of it and a choice, a choice of a blotter. If it is difficult to do it one way there is no place of similar trouble. None. The whole arrangement is established. The end of which is that there is a suggestion, a suggestion that there can be a different whiteness to a wall. This was thought.

A page to a corner means that the shame is no greater when the table is longer. A glass is of any height, it is higher, it is simpler and if it were placed there would not be any doubt.

Something that is an erection is that which stands and feeds and silences a tin which is swelling. This makes no diversion that is to say what can please exaltation, that which is cooking.

A shine is that which when covered changes permission. An enclosure blends with the same that is to say there is blending. A blend is that which holds no mice and this is not because of a floor it is because of nothing, it is not in a vision.

A fact is that when the place was replaced all was left that was stored and all was retained that would not satisfy more than another.

The question is this, is it possible to suggest more to replace that thing. This question and this perfect denial does make the time change all the time.

The sister was not a mister. Was this a surprise. It was. The conclusion came when there was no arrangement. All the time that there was a question there was a decision. Replacing a casual acquaintance with an ordinary daughter does not make a son.

It happened in a way that the time was perfect and there was a growth of a whole dividing time so that where formerly there was no mistake there was no mistake now. For instance before when there was a separation there was waiting, now when there is separation there is the division between intending and departing. This made no more mixture than there would be if there had been no change.

A little sign of an entrance is the one that made it alike. If it were smaller it was not alike and it was so much smaller that a table was bigger. A table was much bigger, very much bigger. Changing that made nothing bigger, it did not make anything bigger littler, it did not hinder wood from not being used as leather. And this was so charming. Harmony is so essential. Is there pleasure when there is a passage, there is when every room is open. Every room is open when there are not four, there were there and surely there were four, there were two together. There is no resemblance.

A single speed, the reception of table linen, all the wonder of six little spoons, there is no exercise.

The time came when there was a birthday. Every day was no excitement and a birthday was added, it was added on Monday, this made the memory clear, this which was a speech showed the chair in the middle where there was copper.

Alike and a snail, this means Chinamen, it does there is no doubt that to be right is more than perfect there is no doubt and glass is confusing it confuses the substance which was of a color. Then came the time for discrimination, it came then and it was never mentioned it was so triumphant, it showed the whole head that had a hole and should have a hole it showed the resemblance between silver.

Startling a starving husband is not disagreeable. The reason that nothing is hidden is that there is no suggestion of silence. No song is sad. A lesson is of consequence.

Blind and weak and organised and worried and betrothed and resumed and also asked to a fast and always asked to consider and never startled and not at all bloated, this which is no rarer than frequently is not so astonishing when hair brushing is added. There is quiet, there certainly is.

No eye-glasses are rotten, no window is useless and yet if air will not come in there is a speech ready, there always is and there is no dimness, not a bit of it.

All along the tendency to deplore the absence of more has not been authorised. It comes to mean that with burning there is that pleasant state of stupefication. Then there is a way of earning a living. Who is a man.

A silence is not indicated by any motion, less is indicated by a motion, more is not indicated it is enthralled. So sullen and so low, so much resignation, so much refusal and so much place for a lower and an upper, so much and yet more silence, why is not sleeping a feat why is it not and when is there some discharge when. There never is.

If comparing a piece that is a size that is recognised as not a size but a piece, comparing a piece with what is not recognised but what is used as it is held by holding, comparing these two comes to be repeated. Suppose they are put together, suppose that there is an interruption, supposing that beginning again they are not changed as to position, suppose all this and suppose that any five two of whom are not separating suppose that the five are not consumed. Is there an exchange, is there a resemblance to the sky which is admitted to be there and the stars which can be seen. Is there. That was a question. There was no certainty. Fitting a failing meant that any two were indifferent and yet they were all connecting that, they were all connecting that consideration. This did not determine rejoining a letter. This did not make letters smaller. It did.

The stamp that is not only torn but also fitting is not any symbol. It suggests nothing. A sack that has no opening suggests more and the loss is not commensurate. The season gliding and the torn hangings receiving mending all this shows an example, it shows the force of sacrifice and likeness and disaster and a reason.

The time when there is not the question is only seen when there is a shower. Any little thing is water.

There was a whole collection made. A damp cloth, an oyster, a single mirror, a mannikin, a student, a silent star, a single spark, a little movement and the bed is made. This shows the disorder, it does, it shows more likeness than anything else, it shows the single mind that directs an apple. All the coats have a different shape, that does not mean that they differ in color, it means a union between use and exercise and a horse.

A plain hill, one is not that which is not white and red and green, a plain hill makes no sunshine, it shows that without a disturber. So the shape is there and the color and the outline and the miserable centre, it is not very likely that there is a centre, a hill is a hill and no hill is contained in a pink tender descender.

A can containing a curtain is a solid sentimental usage. The trouble in both eyes does not come from the same symmetrical carpet, it comes from there being no more disturbance than in little paper. This does show the teeth, it shows color.

A measure is that which put up so that it shows the length has a steel construction. Tidiness is not delicacy, it does not destroy the whole piece, certainly not it has been measured and nothing has been cut off and even if that has been lost there is a name, no name is signed and left over, not any space is fitted so that moving about is plentiful. Why is there so much resignation in a package, why is there rain, all the same the chance has come, there is no bell to ring.

A package and a filter and even a funnel, all this together makes a scene and supposing the question arises is hair curly, is it dark and dusty, supposing that question arises, is brushing necessary, is it, the whole special suddenness commences then, there is no delusion.

A cape is a cover, a cape is not a cover in summer, a cape is a cover and the regulation is that there is no such weather. A cape is not always a cover, a cape is not a cover when there is another, there is always something in that thing in establishing a disposition to put wetting where it will not do more harm. There is always that disposition and in a way there is some use in not mentioning changing and in establishing the temperature, there is some use in it as establishing all that lives dimmer freer and there is no dinner in the middle of anything. There is no such thing.

Why is a pale white not paler than blue, why is a connection made by a stove, why is the example which is mentioned not shown to be the same, why is there no adjustment between the place and the separate attention. Why is there a choice in gamboling. Why is there no necessary dull stable, why is there a single piece of any color, why is there that sensible silence. Why is there the resistance in a mixture, why is there no poster, why is there that in the window, why is there no suggester, why is there no window, why is there no oyster closer. Why is there a circular diminisher, why is there a bather, why is there no scraper, why is there a dinner, why is there a bell ringer, why is there a duster, why is there a section of a similar resemblance, why is there that scissor.

South, south which is a wind is not rain, does silence choke speech or does it not.

Lying in a conundrum, lying so makes the springs restless, lying so is a reduction, not lying so is arrangeable.

Releasing the oldest auction that is the pleasing some still renewing.

Giving it away, not giving it away, is there any difference. Giving it away. Not giving it away.

Almost very likely there is no seduction, almost very likely there is no stream, certainly very likely the height is penetrated, certainly certainly the target is cleaned. Come to sit, come to refuse, come to surround, come slowly and age is not lessening. The time which showed that was when there was no eclipse. All the time that resenting was removal all that time there was breadth. No breath is shadowed, no breath is painstaking and yet certainly what could be the use of paper, paper shows no disorder, it shows no desertion.

Why is there a difference between one window and another, why is there a difference, because the curtain is shorter. There is no distaste in beefsteak or in plums or in gallons of milk water, there is no defiance in original piling up over a roof, there is no daylight in the evening, there is none there empty.

A tribune, a tribune does not mean paper, it means nothing more than cake, it means more sugar, it shows the state of lengthening any nose. The last spice is that which shows the whole evening spent in that sleep, it shows so that walking is an alleviation, and yet this astonishes everybody the distance is so sprightly. In all the time there are three days, those are not passed uselessly. Any little thing is a change that is if nothing is wasted in that cellar. All the rest of the chairs are established.

A success, a success is alright when there are [three] rooms and no vacancies, a success is alright when there is a package, success is alright anyway and any curtain is wholesale. A curtain diminishes and an ample space shows varnish.

One taste one tack, one taste one bottle, one taste one fish, one taste one barometer. This shows no distinguishing sign when there is a store.

Any smile is stern and any coat is a sample. Is there any use in changing more doors than there are committees. This question is so often asked that squares show that they are blotters. It is so very agreeable to hear a voice and to see all the signs of that expression.

Cadences, real cadences, real cadences and a quiet color. Careful and curved, cake and sober, all accounts and mixture, a guess at anything is righteous, should there be a call there would be a voice.

A line in life, a single line and a stairway, a rigid cook, no cook and no equator, all the same there is higher than that another evasion. Did that mean shame, it meant memory. Looking into a place that was hanging and was visible looking into this place and seeing a chair did that mean relief, it did, it certainly did not cause constipation and yet there is a melody that has white for a tune when there is straw color. This shows no face.

Star-light, what is star-light, star-light is a little light that is not always mentioned with the sun, it is mentioned with the moon and the sun, it is mixed up with the rest of the time.

Why is the name changed. The name is changed because in the little space there is a tree, in some space there are no trees, in every space there is a hint of more, all this causes the decision.

Why is there education, there is education because the two tables which are folding are not tied together with a ribbon, string is used and string being used there is a necessity for another one and another one not being used to hearing shows no ordinary use of any evening and yet there is no disgrace in looking, none at all. This came to separate when there was simple selection of an entire pre-occupation.

A curtain, a curtain which is fastened discloses mourning, this does not mean sparrows or elocution or even a whole preparation, it means that there are ears and very often much more altogether.

Climate, climate is not southern, a little glass, a bright winter, a strange supper an elastic tumbler, all this shows that the back is furnished and red which is red is a dark color. An example of this is fifteen years and a separation of regret.

China is not down when there are plates, lights are not ponderous and incalculable.

Currents, currents are not in the air and on the floor and in the door and behind it first. Currents do not show it plainer. This which is mastered has so thin a space to build it all that there is plenty of room and yet is it quarreling, it is not and the insistence is marked. A change is in a current and there is no habitable exercise.

A religion, almost a religion, any religion, a quintal in religion, a relying and a surface and a service in indecision and a creature and a question and a syllable in answer and more counting and no quarrel and a single scientific statement and no darkness and no question and an earned administration and a single set of sisters and an outline and no blisters and the section seeing yellow and the centre having spelling and no solitude and no quaintness and yet solid quite so solid and the single surface centred and the question in the placard and the singularity, is there a singularity, and the singularity, why is there a question and the singularity why is the surface outrageous, why is it beautiful why is it not when there is no doubt, why is anything vacant, why is not disturbing a centre no virtue, why is it when it is and why is it when it is and there is no doubt, there is no doubt that the singularity shows.

A climate, a single climate, all the time there is a single climate, any time there is a doubt, any time there is music that is to question more and more and there is no politeness, there is hardly any ordeal and certainly there is no tablecloth.

This is a sound and obligingness more obligingness leads to a harmony in hesitation.

A lake a single lake which is a pond and a little water any water which is an ant and no burning, not any burning, all this is sudden.

A canister that is the remains of furniture and a looking-glass and a bed-room and a larger size, all the stand is shouted and what is ancient is practical. Should the resemblance be so that any little cover is copied, should it be so that yards are measured, should it be so and there be a sin, should it be so then certainly a room is big enough when it is so empty and the corners are gathered together.

The change is mercenary that settles whitening the coloring and serving dishes where there is metal and making yellow any yellow every color in a shade which is expressed in a tray. This is a monster and awkward quite awkward and the little design which is flowered which is not strange and yet has visible writing, this is not shown all the time but at once, after that it rests where it is and where it is in place. No change is not needed. That does show design.

Excellent, more excellence is borrowing and slanting very slanting is light and secret and a recitation and emigration. Certainly shoals are shallow and nonsense more nonsense is sullen. Very little cake is water, very little cake has that escape.

Sugar any sugar, anger every anger, lover sermon lover, centre no distractor, all order is in a measure.

Left over to be a lamp light, left over in victory, left over in saving, all this and negligence and bent wood and more even much more is not so exact as a pen and a turtle and even, certainly, and even a piece of the same experience as more.

To consider a lecture, to consider it well is so anxious and so much a charity and really supposing there is grain and if a stubble every stubble is urgent, will there not be a chance of legality. The sound is sickened and the price is purchased and golden wheat is golden, a clergyman, a single tax, a currency and an inner chamber.

Checking an emigration, checking it by smiling and certainly by the same satisfactory stretch of hands that have more use for it than nothing, and mildly not mildly a correction, not mildly even a circumstance and a sweetness and a serenity. Powder, that has no color, if it did have would it be white.

A whole soldier any whole soldier has no more detail than any case of measles.

A bridge a very small bridge in a location and thunder, any thunder, this is the capture of reversible sizing and more indeed more can be cautious. This which makes monotony careless makes it likely that there is an exchange in principle and more than that, change in organization.

This cloud does change with the movements of the moon and the narrow the quite narrow suggestion of the building. It does and then when it is settled and no sounds differ then comes the moment when cheerfulness is so assured that there is an occasion.

A plain lap, any plain lap shows that sign, it shows that there is not so much extension as there would be if there were more choice in everything. And why complain of more, why complain of very much more. Why complain at all when it is all arranged that as there is no more opportunity and no more appeal and not even any more clinching that certainly now some time has come.

A window has another spelling, it has "f" all together, it lacks no more then and this is rain, this may even be something else, at any rate there is no dedication in splendor. There is a turn of the stranger.

Catholic to be turned is to venture on youth and a section of debate, it even means that no class where each one over fifty is regular is so stationary that there are invitations.

A curving example makes righteous finger-nails. This is the only object in secretion and speech.

To being the same four are no more than were taller. The rest had a big chair and surveyance a cold accumulation of nausea, and even more than that, they had a disappointment.

Nothing aiming is a flower, if flowers are abundant then they are lilac, if they are not they are white in the centre.

Dance a clean dream and an extravagant turn up, secure the steady rights and translate more than translate the authority, show the choice and make no more mistakes than yesterday.

This means clearness it means a regular notion of exercise, it means more than that, it means liking counting, it means more than that, it does not mean exchanging a line.

Why is there more craving than there is in a mountain. This does not seem strange to one, it does not seem strange to an echo and more surely is in there not being a habit. Why is there so much useless suffering. Why is there.

Any wet weather means an open window, what is attaching eating, anything that is violent and cooking and shows weather is the same in the end and why is there more use in something than in all that.

The cases are made and books, back books are used to secure tears and church. They are even used to exchange black slippers. They can not be mended with wax. They show no need of any such occasion.

A willow and no window, a wide place stranger, a wideness makes no active cent[re].

The sight of no pussy cat is so different that a tobacco zone is white and cream.

A lilac, all a lilac and no mention of butter, not even bread and butter, no butter and no occasion, not even a silent resemblance, not more care than just enough haughty.

A safe weight is that which when it pleases is hanging. A safer weight is one more naughty in a spectacle. The best game is that which is shiny and scratching. Please a pease and a cracker and a wretched use of summer.

Surprise, the only surprise has no occasion. It is an ingredient and the section the whole section is one season.

A pecking which is petting and no worse than in the same morning is not the only way to be continuous often.

A light in the moon the only light is on Sunday. What was the sensible decision. The sensible decision was that notwithstanding many declarations and more music, not even notwithstanding the choice and a torch and a collection, notwithstanding the celebrating hat and a vacation and even more noise than cutting, notwithstanding Europe and Asia and being overbearing, not even notwithstanding an elephant and a strict occasion, not even withstanding more cultivation and some seasoning, not even with drowning and with the ocean being encircling, not even with more likeness and any cloud, not even with terrific sacrifice of pedestrianism and a special resolution, not even more likely to be pleasing. The care with which the rain is wrong and the green is wrong and the white is wrong, the care with which there is a chair and plenty of breathing. The care with which there is incredible justice and likeness, all this makes a magnificent asparagus, and also a fountain.

WE CAME. A HISTORY

The punctuation device holding these fragments together—the equal sign—is unique.—R. K.

A History

We came and were pleased with what we saw. It was very much as pleasant as it could be. It was nearly with which we were to be as much as possible contented. In no time we were made where we were.

This is an introduction to residing.

A nephew of an old woman could be shot having been mistaken for a wild boar not by those who had the right to destroy the animal by themselves but by those who were doing it illegally. So then they made it be as if he had been killed. The result of which is that we have no wild hare.

One day we had two visitors they stayed not with us but in the neighborhood two days and during that time they were with us and

From *Readies for Bob Brown's Machine* (1931).

we found it agreeable to show them things that were known. What is known homes and places and lakes and churches.

An attitude of being made agreeable to those who do not care to address him. What is history. Believe them it is not for their pleasure that they do it. History is this anything that they say and that they do and anything that is made for them by them such as not speaking to them in case that he is turned away from them. This is historical. What did they do. They were willing to like them and to tell it of them in telling everything.

What is historical. Sentences are historical. They will not encourage children. This is not historical. They will be made very dependent on men and women. This might be historical. He was very much pleased with the hope of release. This is historical. What happened. He resigned himself to remaining where he was and in this way he neither endeared himself nor made them relieve him when he was willing. This is history because it is accompanied by reluctance. Reluctance is not necessarily history nor is decision.

I like white because dahlias are beautiful in color. Tube roses come from onions, in every sense of the word and the way of saying it is attractive to her.

How do you like what you have heard.=History must be distinguished=From mistakes.=History must not be what is=Happening.=History must not be about=Dogs and balls in all=The meaning of those=Words history must be=Something unusual and=Nevertheless famous and=Successful. History must=Be the occasion of having=In every way established a=Precedent history must=Be all there is of importance=In their way successively =History must be an open=Reason for needing them=There which it is as they=Are perfectly without a=Doubt that it is interested.=History cannot be an accident.=They make history they=Are in the place of it.=II=History leaves no place=For which they ask will=They be made more of=In case of the disaster=Which has not overtaken=Any one. Historically there= Is no disaster because=Those who make history=Cannot be overtaken=As they will make=History which they do=Because it is necessary=That every one will=Begin to know that=They must know that=History is what it is=Which it is as they do=Know that history is not=Just what every one=Does who comes and=Prefers days to more=Than ever which they have=History must again be=Caught and taught and=Not be that it is tiring=To play with balls.=It is not tiring to go on=And make the needle=Which goes in and out=Be careful not at all=History is made by a very=Few who are important=And history is what that=One says. History is=This it is the necklace=Which makes pansies=Be made well of stones=Which they are likely=To be. This is not=History history is made=By them they make history.=III=One who was remarkable=Addressed them as follows.=Come when you like and=Leave when you like=And send what you like=And play what you like=But and in this there=Can be no mistake=Do not care more for=Nasturtiums than for=Tube roses. It was a=Moment the moment=When there was certainty=That it was that and by=Itself they were told=That it was not different.=There are three things=That are historical.=Tube roses heliotrope and lavender.=There may be fragrant lilies=And other delights but=History is made and=Preserved by heliotrope=Lavender and tube-roses.=History is made and remains=A delight by reason=Of certainty and certainty=Depends upon a result=Achieved directly by a=Surprise not a surprise=In fact nor in thought=Nor in result but a=Surprise in the delight=And the delight is not=A surprise the surprise=Is in confirmation and so=It is undoubtedly real=That history is made=By accomplishment=And accomplishment is=A surprise which it is=So that there is not=A possibility of coming=And going historically.=This will be understood=Readily not by them.=Nor by me for them=Nor is it without doubt=That they are as for them=In elegance. In order=Not to end and finish=They will say it has=Not happened but it has.=With them in time.=The time for tasting is=Also as you may say=They have forgotten that=It is not worth while=This has to do with grapes=And barley and wheat=And also meat and rice=And also ducks and birds=And also hens and cats=And eggs. All this has=Been a history of pleasantness=In arrangement which=They made when they=Were pleased.=IV=But in duration they might=With which they please days=More just as willing pass=In neglect receive on loan=It is call of=They will be willingly here=Not as if alright lain=Made it a forgotten thing=That she could thank layers=Not without use of it=Partly as when known mind=They mind whether they do=A well which it is=Counting from this of it=In much of it owned.=Likeness makes places be where=They must have what now=Come to smoulder with our=Nearly formed alike with moist=Allowed which is in his=To make those carry here=She sleeps but is annoyed=And so she mentions them=That is arranged like it=A part of which cut=You know how like it=Known how you like it.=V=But as will which is of it=Nearly come back to help exploit it=They might in the meantime see which=In a way it is a choice=By the time that it is finished=They must have whatever they will like=It is very dangerous to help it=As they mean to hold all there=As they very well happen with it=To hope to have it like it.=VI=Please save them=For little things=In a million=They make which=It is vastly=Nor more than=As left nearly=In a tree=Which came like=A better parasol=Made into two=The like of which=Is not felt=By those who=In the meanwhile=Are better inclined=Than they were=As much as=In silently waking.=As she named.=All of it=Is made there=In quietly=Second to none=In recollection barely=Hours at a time=They will share=What they have=With those known=By their name=They will hear=What they do=In woods alike=And rhododendrons hortensias=And peppers alike=They will have=More of it=Chain of vines=Made of morning-glories=Which are renowned=And blushing pails=Which made treasure=Be happily theirs=Oh leave it=With them here=Because as a matter of fact=They will be better off.=VII=Touch butter

but not flower=Whether either or for another=Make hopes leave
it all=Never bother them with it=As very likely they will=She
knows how to refuse=Leave it for them there=They will have a
use=For it as an almanac=In splendid weather=Which they ex-
pect=VIII=Bother me with that=But it is part of it=In that case
do not leave it=But it is of no use to me=why do they not like
it.=Do not say they when you mean them=They like it very
well=They will use it for themselves=Once in a while they will not
know what to do with it.=It is the only reason for it not being
made better.=The change from all of it is well enough.=They have
it=As they like=Which they regulate.=IX=Acrobacy fools
them.=X=Just when they went=They knew as well=As if it
was=Their wish to go=In which in case=They were as often
=Left alone with it=As it might be=Too much coming
there=Without its being said=Jackets are necessary here=In a little while=Very often a veil=Is what they know=When they hear
it=In the meanwhile too=It is actually read=By the time only=In
case of separation=Two have to order=All that they need=May be
she will=But in and about=It is not likely=Which she
means.=XI=Autobiography ought to=Have made doors=They
will scare them=XII=By their help=It is usual=To succeed
nicely=Without their help=Which they give=As it is=Ought to
go=They must and=Will have whatever=They want here=By the
time=They are willing=To allow banking=Which have helped
them.=XIII=It is easy to see that they move differently=XIV=I
called it audience and then frame or form but the question is not
that it is not composition it is not that it is beginning and middle
and ending without that anybody can end and begin and the middle is easier than anything.=XV=I am not busy=When he is ne-
glected=This is not often=Because she is there=XVI=Ours are
made for them=They will ask for it=They need two rests for
it=Because it is helped more than they like by it=Because in
searching for doves=Doves are named pigeons by butter.=Do not
be blamed for failure=Ask them are they ready=But is it wise

to=Because it may annoy them=Press them to remain here=They will like it if they stay=Little by little it will help=Not to be restless like that=He wants his dinner=After it is over he will be=Just as restless=This is why they never pay any attention to what he does.=They must call him anyway.=XVII=I do not think it would do=To bathe him on a Sunday=This is the reason=It is easy to be quiet=And to give it as a reason=For coming to-day=Florence is made to George=Now listen to that.=It does surprise you=Florence is not yet married to George but they have had the dinner of betrothal which was later than noon and a good deal of bother.=The first of September Florence is to be married to George.=XVIII=Any one believes that things equal to the same thing are equal to each other. Any little way that is like a pleasure.=Just why they came=Is the same way=In which they waited=In liking having bought it=Which made them go=They went away at once.=XIX=It is easy to keep count.=One two three all out but she.=It is easy to keep count and make a mistake.=Slenderness keeps them busy.=Ought they to be busy=With it=Anything artificial is an annoyance example artificial silk.=All history is cautious.

MANY MANY WOMEN

One of the great Stein texts, this is rarely reprinted, though frequently performed, most notably by Petr Kotik with his group SEM Ensemble. At forty thousand words it is technically a novella; to my mind, it is also a masterpiece that belongs at the center of this book.—R. K.

Any one is one having been that one. Any one is such a one.

Any one having been that one is one remembering something of such a thing, is one remembering having been that one.

Each one having been one is being one having been that one. Each one having been one is remembering something of this thing, is remembering something of having been that one.

Each one is one. Each one has been one. Each one being one, each one having been one is remembering something of that thing.

Each one is one. Each one has been one. Each one is remembering that thing.

Each one is one. Each one has been one. That is something that any one having been one, any one being one is having happen. Each

From *G. M. P.* (1932).

one being one is having it happen that that one is being that one. Each one having been one is one having had it happen that that one has been that one.

Each one is one. Any one is the one that one is. Each one is one.

One who is one is remembering that she is one forgetting anything. One who is one is remembering that she is forgetting everything again and again. She is remembering this thing. She is not interested in this thing. She is remembering this thing and she is remembering that this is a quite necessary thing, it is quite a necessary thing that she is remembering that she is forgetting anything.

She is forgetting anything. This is not a disturbing thing, this is not a distressing thing, this is not an important thing. She is forgetting anything and she is remembering that thing, she is remembering that she is forgetting anything.

She is one being one remembering that she is forgetting anything. She is one not objecting to being one remembering that thing, remembering that she is forgetting anything. She is one objecting to there being some objecting to being ones forgetting anything. She is one objecting to any one being one remembering that they are not forgetting anything. She is one objecting to any one objecting to her being one forgetting anything. She is not one remembering being one objecting to any one objecting to her being one forgetting anything. She is one remembering that she is one objecting to being one remembering that they are not forgetting anything. She is one remembering something of being one objecting to some being one objecting to forgetting anything.

She is one forgetting anything. She is one remembering something of this thing. She is one repeating this thing repeating remembering something of forgetting anything.

She is one remembering that she has been having something. She is one remembering something of this thing. She has been having something, she is having something, she is remembering something of this thing. She is not objecting to having something, she is having something, she is remembering something of this thing.

She is one being that one being one having something and re-membering something of that thing. She is one being one and she is forgetting anything and she is remembering being one forgetting anything.

Any one she is kissing is one she is kissing then, not kissing again and again, not kissing and kissing, any one she is kissing is one she kissed then, is one she did kiss then, one she kissed some then.

Any one she is kissing is one needing something then, needing kissing, needing anything just then, needing some kissing then. Any one she is kissing is one having been kissed then, having been kissed some then and she was the one who was kissing that one some just then. Any one she was kissing was one whom she was kissing just then. Any one she was kissing was one who might have been needing something then, needing anything then, needing kissing then, needing a little kissing then, needing any kissing then, needing something then, needing kissing then.

She was one living and remembering that she had enough for this thing, enough for living. She was one remembering that she had enough for being living and she was remembering that she could always be needing that thing needing having enough to be living. She could remembering to remind herself and any one of this thing, she could remember that thing, she could remember to be reminded of that thing. She could remember to be one reminding herself, she could remember to be one having any one remind her quite often of this thing that she could remember that she had enough and would be always having enough to be living. She could remembering that she was needing this thing needing having enough always enough for living. She could remember enough of reminding any one of this thing. She could remember this thing remember reminding herself of this thing. She could remember something of being reminded of this thing. She could remember this thing, she could remember a good deal of knowing that she was having enough for being living and that she could always be needing having enough for living. She could remember this thing, she could quite remember that thing.

She was one forgetting anything. She was remembering something of that thing of forgetting anything. She could always remember something of that thing, remember something of forgetting anything.

In giving she was giving what she had then remembered to give then. In giving she was going to be giving. In giving she was quite often giving something. In giving she was not scolding any one. In giving she sometimes remembered that she was going to give that which she would give. In giving she was forgetting that thing the thing she was giving.

In giving she was remembering that she would be one being living. In giving she remembered something of being one needing something in being one being living. In giving she almost remembered she had enough for going on being living. In giving she was one forgetting that thing, the thing she was giving. In giving she was being one remembering something. In giving she was beginning again and again.

She was lonesome. She was not remembering all of this thing. She was not ever remembering everything of being lonesome. She was lonesome, she was not regretting this thing, she was not expecting anything from that thing, from being lonesome. She was not expecting anything in being lonesome. She was lonesome and she was not interested in the thing in being lonesome, she was not interested in not expecting anything from being lonesome. She was lonesome and was always knowing all any one could know about that thing about her being lonesome. She was lonesome and was remembering all there was to remember of the thing of her being lonesome.

She was lonesome and that was not coming to be something. Being lonesome was not coming to be anything. She was remembering enough of that thing that being lonesome was not coming to be something. She was lonesome and she was not using that thing in remembering being lonesome, she was not using very much then. She was lonesome and she remembered enough about that thing and she would be lonesome and she would be remembering all she was remembering about that thing. She was lonesome and forgetting anything and remembering something of forgetting everything.

In remembering forgetting something not anything was something she was needing in being then that one. She was not using anything for any such thing for remembering, for forgetting anything. She was often using something. She was not one forgetting, she was not one remembering having been using that thing. She was using things and forgetting then something and remembering then something and she was not using that thing in being then that one one remembering something, one forgetting anything. She was using anything she was having then to be something she might be using then. She was not remembering, she was not forgetting then to be one having been using, being using that thing.

She was going on being one using, having been using something and being then not one using anything in being that one, one forgetting anything, one remembering that thing remembering forgetting anything.

Why should not any one be certain that any one is one any one could be liking and that every one are ones being completely foolish ones in being ones being any one. Why should not any one be repeating something of some such thing, repeating quite often that any one is one any one is liking and that every one is one being a quite foolish one. Why should not any one be one saying some such thing.

She was remembering quite remembering that any one was a one any one could be liking well enough for anything and she was remembering and saying some such thing that every one is a foolish enough one and that very many are being ones being living.

She was saying this thing and any one could come to be one being certain that she was quite saying that any one is one any one can be liking in being one being living and that every one is one being a silly one in being that one. Why should not any one come to be hearing her saying this thing, quite saying this thing. She was not saying this thing and saying anything in saying this thing. She was saying this thing and any one could be one saying this thing, saying something of this thing, almost quite saying that thing.

In paying anything she was not worrying. In paying for anything she was not worrying. She had worried some. She was always worrying. In paying for anything she was not needing to be paying then. She was not knowing that thing, she was always worrying. She was paying for anything. She could have been one not paying for anything if she had not been one paying for everything. She did pay for something and then she paid for another thing. She was always worrying. She paid for very many things. She always was paying for something. She was always worrying. She was not paying for anything and certainly she did pay for everything and there were very many things that she was needing to be one paying for and she paid for them and she was always worrying and she was quite putting off then paying and she did then pay for something and sometime she paid everything and she was being one knowing this thing that she could pay for everything. She was needing almost everything and was paying then and worrying then and paying a little again and again.

She was feeding something. She was one feeding that thing, feeding being one knowing something. She was feeding something in feeding that thing. She was really feeding something. In feeding that thing she was not beginning. She was not beginning in feeding. She was not beginning, she was feeding something. She was knowing that she was one who was not beginning feeding something, she was not remembering any such thing as feeding something, she was not forgetting any such thing as feeding something. She was feeding something. She was not beginning. She was going on in that thing in feeding something. She was one feeding that thing feeding being one knowing something.

She was one knowing something of feeding knowing something. She was feeding on feeding knowing something, on feeding in this thing. She was not one forgetting everything. She was not one remembering anything.

She was one loving. She was one being loved then. She was one loving in being loved and was loving then. She was one loving then. She was one loved then. Loving is a thing that was happening some then. She was loving then, she was loved then.

Any one doing that thing doing loving is doing something of that thing, something of doing loving. She was loving some one and some one was loving her then. Both of them were loving then. They went on both of them doing something of that thing of loving. She was loving and she was content in doing that thing, and she was remembering that thing remembering doing loving, and she did not forget everything of being content in that thing in being loving. She was loving, she was remembering being content in doing some loving. She was loving, she was doing something of that thing. She was needing being content in being loving. She remembered something of that thing of needing being content in being loving. She forgot something, she forgot some of the things she was liking in loving. She did not remember anything of forgetting things she was liking in loving. She remembered something of needing being content in being loving. She was loving some and she was remembering that thing, remembering that she was loving some.

This one is one and she is that one. Each one is one. There are many. Each one is different from any other one.

Each one is one. There are many. Some of them are loving. Some of them are completely loving. One of them is completely loving. This one is living in loving being existing in that one and loving is existing in that one, completely existing in that one. That one is loving and is completely existing in loving being completely existing in that one and in the one that one is loving and in that one who is the one loving that one. This one is one completely existing as loving is completely existing in that one and one other one.

Each one is one. There are many of them. Each one is different from any other one of them. Each one is one being living. Some are ones loving. Some are ones believing in loving. Some are ones believing in loving and marrying and having children. Some of such of them are ones believing in working and believing in every one. Some of such of them are ones working and getting sick then and going on believing in everything in which they have been believing. One being such a one was one loving. She was one believing in something, she was one believing in working and marrying and having children and believing in all that she had been believing. She believed in changing in some things. She believed in something. She was loving. She was working. She was marrying. She was having children. She was believing in all she had been believing. She was one believing in something. She was a sick one. She believed then in what she had been believing.

She could be certain that she could be content to let some go on doing what they were doing. She was certain she could be content to have some come to be doing other things than the things they were doing. She did come to be certain that she could wait for something, for any one to go on doing what they were doing, for some to come to be doing some other thing than the thing they were doing.

She was one having children. She did have three of them. She was one working. She got sick then. She was one beginning again working. She was one then coming to be completely a sick one. She was one then believing what she had been believing.

She was one loving, she was one marrying. She was one believing in something and she went on believing in that thing. She went on believing in all she had been believing.

In living she was believing in that thing believing in doing that loving. She was believing that not anything was changing in being one being loving. She went on believing that thing. She changed her mind some.

She was loving and she was certain that any one doing that thing any one loving was the one not doing that thing not doing anything for loving. She went on believing that thing. She changed her mind some about some little things. She was loving and she was marrying and she was sick then and she had three children and she believed in everything in which she had always been believing. She had always been believing in working, she believing in that thing. She had always been believing that loving and marrying and having children was something that was happening, she believed in believing that thing. She believed that in doing anything nothing was changing, she believed that in arranging living any one would do that thing would arrange the living they were believing in. She went on believing in the things in which she was believing. She changed her mind about some little things and she said then that she had changed her decision. She believed in that thing she believed in working and marrying and having children and in believing in the things in which she had been believing.

She was working and loving then and marrying and being sick then and working and having children and being sick then and she was believing then in the things in which she had been, in which she was believing.

Each one is one there are many of them. Some are liking what they are doing. Some are completely liking what they are doing. Some are loving and are completely liking that thing are completely liking loving.

One was loving some one and was completely liking that thing liking loving that one. This one was completely loving that one and was completely liking that thing completely liking loving that one. This one the one loving and being loved then was one completely liking that thing completely liking loving and being a loved one.

There are very many being living. Each one is one. Each one is one being that one. Each one is like some. Each one is one. There are very many of them. There are many kinds of them. Each one is one. Each one is that one.

One is one and that one is one quite loving. This one is one needing enough of that thing enough of loving so that that one is not needing too much, needing to be doing everything. This one is one who was quite enjoying loving. She was loving. She was marrying again then. She was quite needing that thing, needing marrying so that she would not be needing too much doing everything.

She was marrying and she was needing marrying. She was doing everything and she was needing that thing she was needing doing everything. Any one doing everything can be needing that thing needing doing everything. She was needing that thing she was needing doing everything. In loving she was marrying, she was doing everything. In marrying she was doing everything. She was doing everything. She was marrying, she was needing that thing she was needing marrying. She was moving in every direction in doing everything. She was loving in marrying. She was marrying in doing everything. She was doing everything in moving in every direction.

She was needing being such a one. She was moving in every direction. She was loving. She was marrying. She was needing doing everything. She was not beginning, she was not suffering, she was not loving, she was not winning, she was going on and that was exciting, exciting enough for any living continuing. She was not sacrificing, she was not seizing, she was not losing, she was not winning, she was winning in every direction, she was not gay then, she was not exciting then, she was moving then moving in every direction, she had courage for that thing, courage for being that one, she had courage in going on living, she had courage in moving in every direction, she had courage in not winning, she had courage in not losing, she had courage in not sacrificing, she had courage in not seizing, she had courage in not being exciting, she had courage in moving in every direction, she had courage in being one loving, she had courage in being one marrying. She had courage. She had courage in being one not being a gay one, she had courage in moving in every direction, she had courage in being one moving in every direction, she had courage in being one going on living, she had courage.

She was one being living, she could be exciting and then some one could remember that she had not been one being exciting. She had courage then. She could be kissing and any one could be remembering that she had not been completely being fascinating. She had courage then. She could be succeeding and any one could be pleased then and could be remembering that thing, remembering that she always had had courage in going on being living. She was lively and any one could remember that she could be a lively one.

Any one could remember she had courage. Any one could remember that thing.

Some are living and they might if they went on living they might then not be liking that thing. Some are living and they might if they went on living they might then be liking that thing. One went on living and was happier then happier than any one. That one went on living and went on then being happier than any one. That one was then that one, one being happier than any one ever had been in being one being living.

Some are living and they might if they went on living they might then not be liking that thing. One of such of them was one going on living and she went on quite liking that thing and she was one not completing that thing not completing liking that thing liking living but she went on living and she was liking that thing and certainly then there was no reason why she should not be liking that thing, she went on living and she was liking that thing.

She would be one going on being living even though she could understand something of any one coming to be dying. She did go on being living although she could tell any one how any one could come to be a dead one. She did go on being living although she could explain how very many she was knowing were not needing such a thing needing going on being living.

She went on being living, she did that thing with enough decision, she did that thing with decision enough to be one being one doing everything, doing everything enough, doing anything just enough.

She was one whom some one married and then they had a child born to them and that child was one she was having with her and she was then finding everything a little irregular. She said the thing she should say then, she did the things she should do then. Sometimes she was repeating other things, sometimes she was changing her opinion, always she was changing her opinion, she was decided enough then to say something, she did say that thing, she told then the whole of that thing the whole of that opinion.

She was satisfied with being living. Being living is not satisfying is not completely satisfying, any one listening was hearing some explanation of this thing. She was satisfied with being living. She was satisfied with marrying. She was satisfied with being a married one. She was satisfied with her husband who was quite a satisfying man. She was satisfied with having had one child and having that child. She was satisfied that she would not have another one. She was satisfied that he went on being living, that she would not have to have another one. She was satisfied with her mother and her brothers and her sister. They were satisfactory as mother and sister and older brother and younger brother. She had opinion enough about that thing about mentioning there being existing. She was satisfied with regular living. She had opinion enough of this thing to be quite expressing any such opinion. She was satisfied with being living. She was satisfied with not any living being satisfying. She was satisfied with her living. She was important in that thing so as to be explaining satisfactory living. She did explain satisfactory living. She was satisfied with being living. She was satisfied that any living was not satisfying. She was satisfied with her living. She expressed her opinion.

Each one is one. Each one is that one. Each one is one. Each one expressing an opinion is expressing that thing that opinion.

One is expressing an opinion, one is expressing a suspicion. She is expressing the whole of that thing. She is clearly having that thing, that suspicion, that opinion. She is one clearly having that thing having that suspicion, that opinion. She is that one the one having that expression, that opinion and clearly expressing that thing that suspicion, that opinion. She is completely loving, completely lovelily loving. She is that one.

Each one is one. Each one is that one the one that one is. Each one is one. Each one is one some are knowing. Each one is one. One is one many are knowing. One is one not any one is completely certain is completely charming. That one is one being one being almost completely feeling in being almost completely charming. This one is one not completing any such thing not completing feeling, not completing feeling in being almost completely charming, not completing being almost completely charming, not completing being charming.

She was marrying, she was not then married, she was one having lost something and not remembering anything then of anything,
of having or of loving, she was marrying then again. She was married then. She was living then, she was satisfying any one being satisfied with that thing. She was satisfying herself then with being one
satisfying herself with that thing. She was not losing anything, she
was losing that thing, she was losing not losing anything.

Being that thing being one being something that was in a way
a delicate thing was something she was not having, she was not having that thing in being one being that one being the one she might
be, being the one she was. Being a delicately sensitive one was
something she was not having in being completely that one being
completely the one she might be being, in being the one she had
been being, in being the one she would be being.

She was having delicate sensitive perception in being that one
the one having such things, in being one being the one she was being, she was being one having delicate and sensitive perceptions.
She was one always having been and always being that one the one
quite having delicate and sensitive perceptions.

She was interested in being any one, she was not interested in
every one being that one, in every one being the one she was interested in. She was not interested in any one being the one she was
interested in. She was not interested in that thing.

She was not interested in being one coming to perhaps not being
that one. She was not interested in that thing. She was not losing that
thing losing that she might perhaps be coming to not being that one.

She was one remembering something of any one being one believing that some meaning is existing. She was one not losing much
of remembering something of some such thing. She might have
been one being one not remembering any thing of any one believing that some meaning is existing. She might have been such a one,
she was not such a one. She was one remembering something of
any one believing that some meaning is existing.

She could lose anything, she did not lose remembering something of every one believing that some meaning is existing. She

might be losing anything. She did lose anything. She did remember something of believing that every one is believing anything of something being existing. She did lose anything.

Any one being any one is being one. Any one being that one is being that one. One being that one is one being that one and being then the one not losing anything of that thing not losing anything. That one, the one being that one and not losing anything is one completely clearly not losing anything. That one is one being one having a sudden feeling of having lost something and being then completely clearly searching and being then completely clearly not losing the thing, not losing anything. This one is one completely clearly not losing anything. This one is one not losing anything. This one is one completely clearly not losing anything.

Each one is one, there are many of them. Each one is one. Each one is that one the one that one is. Each one is one, there are many of them. Each one is one.

Each one is one. Each one might be one being like every other one if every one was one being like every other one. Each one is one. Each one is one not like every other one. Each one is one. Any one is like any one. Every one is like every one. Each one is one. There are very many of them. Each one is one.

Each one is one and is mentioning something of some such thing. Each one has been one and is mentioning something of some such thing. Each one is one and is mentioning something of being like any other one. Each one is one and is mentioning having been like any other one. Each one is one. Each one is one and is mentioning having been, is mentioning being that one. Each one is one. Each one is that one, the one that one is. Each one is one, each one is mentioning such a thing. Each one is mentioning something, each one is mentioning having been mentioning something. Each one is one. Each one is mentioning having been that one.

One was one and was mentioning something, mentioning having been that one and in a way that one was that one. That one was one, that one had been that one. That one had not been really mentioning quite that thing, had not been quite mentioning having been that one.

That one being that one had been that one. That one being that one was mentioning that thing was mentioning having been that one, was mentioning being that one.

That one being that one was one needing something, was one needing something to have been that one. That one being that one was needing something, was one needing something to be that one. That one was not that one. That one was mentioning that thing. That one was needing something to be that one. That one was mentioning that thing, was mentioning that that one was needing something to be that one.

That one had been one. The one that one had been was one who was not needing anything for being that one. The one that one had been was one not winning everything in being that one. The one that one had been was one doing everything and completing these things and not needing being that one. The one that one had been was one continuing being that one. The one that one had been was one willing to be needing something. The one that one had been was one almost willing to be giving anything to win that thing. The one that one had been was one not winning that thing. The one that one had been was one not needing winning that thing. The one that one had been was one not being one who could be living in having won that thing. The one that one had been was one not being able to live in winning that thing. The one that one had been was one not having been needing winning that thing. The one that one had been was one expressing that thing expressing having been the one that one had been. The one that one had been was one expressing having been willing to be winning what that one had not been winning. The one that one had been was one expressing being that one the one that one had been. The one that one had been was one expressing being completing being willing, being not willing to be winning what she had not been winning. The one that one had been was one expressing disillusion. The one that one had been was one expressing illusion. The one that one had been was one expressing having been such a one the one that one had been, was expressing having been completing willing the thing she had not been winning. The one that one had been was expressing some such thing, was quite mentioning every such thing. The one who had been that one the one quite mentioning everything of any such thing was one who went on being such a one one mentioning everything of any such thing.

Mentioning something was something this one was completely expressing. Having been loving and not having been then winning anything was something this one was mentioning. Having been marrying and not having been needing all of that thing was something this one was mentioning. Having been marrying and having been needing something of this thing was something this one was mentioning. Being married and not completely using that thing was something this one was mentioning. Being married and doing that thing, doing being married was something this one was mentioning. This one was one mentioning something. This one was one completely expressing that thing expressing mentioning something. This one was one having been mentioning everything. This one was one completely expressing that thing expressing having been mentioning everything.

In expressing mentioning anything, in expressing mentioning everything she was that one the one she was mentioning having been. In being one expressing mentioning any thing, in being one expressing mentioning everything she was that one the one she was mentioning.

She was mentioning anything. She was mentioning everything, she was expressing that thing expressing mentioning anything, expressing mentioning everything.

In being that one the one expressing mentioning anything, the one expressing mentioning everything, in being that one she was one being one being that thing being the one expressing mentioning everything, mentioning anything. In being that one, in expressing that thing in expressing mentioning anything, mentioning everything she was one going and always completing that thing completing and going on being one expressing mentioning anything, mentioning everything. In going on being that one, in completing that that thing she was going on being one expressing mentioning everything, mentioning anything.

In mentioning anything, in mentioning everything she was one expressing that mentioning anything, that mentioning everything is not anything as everything is something that is a thing that is not anything as everything is something that is just that thing. In mentioning anything, in mentioning everything she is one being one expressing that mentioning anything that mentioning everything is something that would be being mentioning anything mentioning everything if everything and anything were not being the thing she had been mentioning. In being one mentioning anything, in being one mentioning everything, in mentioning anything, in mentioning everything, she was mentioning everything, she was mentioning anything, in mentioning anything, in mentioning everything she was mentioning anything, she was mentioning everything. In mentioning everything, in mentioning anything she was mentioning that she was mentioning that in mentioning anything that in mentioning everything she was mentioning that not anything, that not everything was anything that she was not mentioning. In mentioning anything, in mentioning everything she was mentioning that in mentioning anything, in mentioning anything she was mentioning everything, she was mentioning anything.

Each one is one. Each one has been, each one is mentioning something. Each one is one. There are many of them. There are many mentioning something. There are many mentioning everything. Each one is one. There are many of them. Some are mentioning something, some are mentioning everything, some are mentioning anything. Each one is one. Each one is mentioning something.

Some one was mentioning something. She was not mentioning that thing, she was not mentioning that she was needing something. She was mentioning something. She was mentioning that she was not the one some one was needing. She could mention that she was not the one any one was admiring. She was one mentioning something. Any one can be one mentioning something. In mentioning something that one was mentioning that she had not been expressing anything of being one mentioning something. She was that one one mentioning something. She was that one not mentioning anything. She was that one one completely mentioning everything and mentioning it again and again and always then completing that thing completing mentioning everything. She was then that one one completing again and again and again mentioning everything. She was that one.

There are many who are telling anything in some way. Every one is one telling something in some way. One was one telling anything in one way. That one was one being that one. That one had been one loving in that way, loving in a way and telling something in a way, and telling anything in a way. The way she was telling anything was a way that was a way she was realising anything could be something. She was realising anything was something and the way she was telling about anything was the way she was one being surprised by the thing that was anything. She was surprised by anything being something. She was realising anything was something. She was telling about anything telling about it in the way anything surprised her by being something. She had been loving. She had not been surprised by everything of that thing. She had been surprised by something of that thing. She was telling everything in the way she had been surprised by something. She was telling anything in a way. She was telling everything in a way.

She was feeling something. She was feeling and she was remembering that feeling was existing. She was feeling something and she would be remembering that feeling had been existing. She was feeling something, she was then not certain that feeling was existing. She was feeling something. She would not be certain that feeling had been existing. She was feeling something, she was saying that feeling was existing, that she had not been certain that she had been feeling the feeling that was existing. She was feeling something. She was not certain that feeling was existing. She was saying that she was not certain she was feeling the feeling she was not certain was existing.

She was learning anything. She was liking knowing the thing she had come to be learning. She was surprised at the thing being existing the thing she had just learned was existing. She was surprised then. She was not surprised at everything. She was not surprised at anything. She was surprised at everything. She was surprised at anything. She was in a way saying she was being surprised at anything that she was knowing was being existing. She was saying in a way saying something. She was saying something and saying it in a way. She was saying being surprised at anything being existing and she was saying it in a way. She was saying that in a way she was not surprised at any thing being existing.

She was saying something in a way. In saying anything in a way she was saying that she was surprised at everything being existing. In saying everything she was in a way saying that she was surprised to be feeling that anything is existing. In saying anything, she was saying that she was knowing in a way that everything is existing.

She had been feeling something and she was remembering everything of what she had been knowing she had been feeling and she had been knowing she had not been certain she had been feeling what she had not been certain she was feeling. She had been feeling something, she had been feeling something, she had not been certain that she had been feeling something. She remembered everything of what she had been feeling. She remembered everything of feeling something. She remembered everything of the feeling she had been feeling if she had been feeling something. She remembered everything of that feeling of feeling something. She remembered everything, she went on remembering everything of the feeling she had been feeling if she had been feeling something. She had been feeling something. She remembered everything of that thing.

In saying anything she was saying that anything surprised her that surprised her and that anything surprised her because anything is existing. In saying that anything is existing she was saying that not anything surprised her because everything is existing and anything surprised her. In saying anything she said it in the way she had been feeling when anything surprised her and because anything surprised her she said everything in that way, she said everything in the way she said anything. She said everything in the way that she was feeling that she was not certain that she was feeling anything and was feeling that anything being something was something that was a thing that would be to her a surprising thing. She said everything in that way. She was saying something.

She was that one. There are many being living. Each one is one. There are many of them. Each one is one, each one in being one and saying something is saying something in a way, is saying anything in a way.

One was saying everything in a way. It was a very certain way. It was a very decided way. It was a very clear way. It was a quite long way. It was a completely clear way. It was a complete way. It was a delicate way. It was an entire way. It was a continuing way. It was a way that was a way that would come to be a thing that any one would know was a way that was that way.

There are very many being living. Some are being loving. Some are loving some one. Some are loving some. Some in loving some are loving very many of them. Some in loving are being one loving and being the one loving some and very many of them. Some in loving some and so loving very many are being such a one one loving very many seeing and loving, and hearing and loving, and loving and giving what any loving is meaning in having come to be existing.

One who was such a one was one seeing and loving and being then that one and was one hearing and loving and being then that one and was then that one the one being that one.

Some one was one living and hearing and seeing and being then all one loving, all one everything and everything then was being one completing again and again what is necessary to loving being existing. She was loving that is to say she was one being one in being the one giving what is necessary to loving being existing. She was hearing some one, she was giving then to that one everything that is needing for loving to have been existing. She was seeing some one, she was giving to that one the thing that being loving has been having. She was one who was one seeing some one. She was one who was one hearing some one. She was one seeing one and she was one being that one the one seeing that one and beginning then being the one who had seen that one. She came then to be the one who had completed that thing completed seeing that one and that one had been seen by her then and then it was all one her seeing that one, that one seeing her and everything had been done then and sometimes was then done again. She was one hearing one and she did then hear that one and she was then one being one who was coming to hear that one and she came then to have heard that one and that one came then to finishing that thing finishing her having been hearing that one and they finished that thing and it was then finished again. She was one being that one and that was not troubling one who was one seeing and hearing and being with that one and she was quite married to that one and they were both then married and living and they were then living and going on being living and they were then going on being married and being living.

Her voice, her pleasantness, her neurasthenia were expressing that she was being one who was all one hearing and loving, seeing and loving, hearing and seeing and loving. Her voice which was a pleasant thing was the voice of one who was one seeing and loving and hearing and loving and seeing and hearing and loving. Her pleasantness which was a present thing was expressing that she was one seeing and loving, hearing and loving, hearing and seeing and loving. Her neurasthenia which had been a pleasant thing was something that was expressing that she was one seeing and loving, hearing and loving, seeing and hearing and loving.

Her voice, her pleasantness, her neurasthenia were expressing that she was one hearing and loving, seeing and loving, hearing and seeing and loving. Her pleasantness which was a present thing was a pleasant thing. Her being one seeing and loving which was a pleasant thing was a pleasant thing. Her being one hearing and loving which was a pleasant thing was a pleasant thing. Her voice which was a pleasant thing was a pleasant thing.

She was one seeing and loving. She was one hearing and loving. She was one hearing and seeing and loving. She was that one. She was one loving.

She was loving. She was being one who was completing being loving. That was a pleasant thing. She was that one. She was loving. She was seeing and loving. She was hearing and loving. She was that one.

She was one completing what loving was needing, which was a pleasant thing. She was completing what loving was needing. She was that one.

In completing what loving was needing she was being that one. She was that one. She was one completing what loving was needing. She was that one. She was one which was a pleasant thing. She was that one. She was completing what loving was needing. She was completing what loving was needing which was that thing. She was seeing and loving. She was hearing and loving. She was hearing and seeing and loving. She was completing what loving was needing. She was completing loving, which was that thing. She was loving. She was seeing and loving. She was hearing and loving.

She was hearing, she had not then been hearing. She was seeing, she had not then been seeing. She had not then been hearing, which was a pleasant thing. She had not then been seeing, which was a pleasant thing. She was not hearing which was a pleasant thing. She was not seeing which was a pleasant thing. She was not hearing and seeing which was a pleasant thing.

Being one loving, being one, she being one, she was one.

She was one, she was one and being one she was one seeing and loving, hearing and loving, seeing and hearing and loving. She was one. She was one seeing and loving, hearing and loving.

She was one. She was loving. She was one. Being one she was one.

There are many being living. Each one is one. There are many of them. Each one is one. There are many of them.

One being one and being loving, one being one, being that one and being loving was being one being loving. This one being loving was being that one and that one was being in being loving. That one was loving and was that one one being loving. This one in loving was loving and she was loving. She was one and being loving and being loving she was one. She was being loving. She was being one. She was being being loving. She was one. She was being loving. She was loving. She was being one in being loving. She was being the one she was being. She was being loving.

She was loving. In being loving she was one. She was one in being loving. She was loving.

There are many living. There are many loving. There are many loving and marrying. There are many loving and completing that thing and are not marrying. There are many loving. Some are loving and are living in loving. Some are loving and are living. Some are loving and they are one. Some are being one and are loving some and are living and are being one loving and are being one living.

One who was loving and living was that one. She was loving and she was that one. She was loving and being one then living some. She was that one. She was loving some.

She was one living some and loving some. She was that one. She was one living some. She was one living some and she was loving some.

She was living. She was living and she was one being one living some. She was living some. She was one living some and she was that one.

In being one living some she was one sitting some. In being one living some she was one sitting some, she was one living some.

She was one living and she was one loving and in loving she was one sitting. She was one sitting and in being one sitting she was one being that one one living and loving, living and loving some, living and loving and being that one one loving and living some, one loving enough to be living enough, one loving enough to be sitting enough.

She was living enough, she was sitting enough. In being one living enough and sitting enough she was one doing enough loving. She was doing enough loving to be living enough and sitting enough.

She was one and that one the one she was was one who was living enough certainly living enough to be loving some. She was loving enough to be loving enough. She was loving enough to be sitting some. She was loving enough to be sitting enough.

She was one saying something saying that she was loving enough and living enough. She was one saying that she was loving enough and sitting enough. She was one saying that she was living enough and sitting. She was one saying that she was sitting enough.

She was one and being that one she was saying that she was that one enough. She was that one. She was that one enough.

She was one. She was enough needing being that thing, she was quite needing that thing, she was needing enough being that one.

She was one. She was one who was that one and was quite needing being that one. She was one. She was one who was one living enough. She was one. She was one who was sitting enough. She was one who was loving enough.

She was one and being one she was one being that one and she was being that one and being that one she was one going on being that one quite enough going on being that one. She was going on enough being that one. She was going on being one, she was one going on being the one she was.

In being that one she was one quite being one, she was one being enough one. In being that one she was being one who was one who was going on enough in being that one. In being that one she was going on being one loving enough, living enough, sitting enough.

She was large enough to be that one one sitting enough. She was large enough. She was giving enough of being one loving enough, living enough, sitting enough to be one living enough. She was giving enough of being one sitting enough, loving enough to be one going on living enough. She was large enough to be one living enough, sitting enough, loving enough. She was large enough. She was loving enough. She was sitting enough. She was living enough.

She was going on living and she was living enough. She was going on living. She was loving enough. She was going on living enough. She was going on living. She was sitting enough. She was going on living enough.

She was being one who did complete that thing quite complete that thing, quite complete sitting. She was one and she was being one not troubling that thing not troubling being the one being sitting. She was one and she was sitting and she was one and she was living enough. She was one giving that thing giving that thing enough giving being one not troubling being that one being the one sitting. She was one giving enough, she was one giving being one being one living enough, loving enough, sitting enough, she was one giving enough, she was one giving being one not troubling her being one being sitting. She was giving enough. She was loving enough. She was sitting enough. She was living enough.

She was one, she was one and she was different enough from any other one. She was different enough.

She was one. There are some. There are many being living. There are many being living. There are enough going on being living.

One going on being living, and she was going on being living, one going on being living was one telling quite telling, clearly telling that some who are ones being living are ones smelling and being living and smelling they are needing being ones using anything and being ones not having everything are ones taking what they are needing and being ones taking everything are ones smelling. Some one clearly telling everything is telling that such ones are ones being living, and is clearly telling that one listening is one being one coming to be one not having anything of that one being taken by any such a one.

Some are taking something, some are taking everything, some are not taking everything but would be taking anything. Some are taking what they expect to be taking.

There are many being living. There is one being living. This one had been being living. This one is one almost succeeding in not taking everything. This one is one taking anything. This one is one having been expecting to be taking everything. This one has been taking what she was taking. This one has been taking. She was expecting to be one any one would be expecting to have taken what she was expecting to take. She was one quite succeeding in taking what she was expecting to take. She might have been one succeeding in living. She might be one not succeeding in living. She was one not having everything. She was one not going on expecting anything. She was one being a quite sad enough one. She was one.

In being a sad enough one she was one who might have been one succeeding in living. She was a sad enough one.

In being one who might have been one succeeding in living she was one who had not been failing in living.

In being one who had not been failing in living she was one expecting and getting what she expected to be getting by asking.

She had been one loving. She was one loving children. She had been one loving. She married the one she was loving. Before she married the one she was loving she had had a child who had not been born living. In having had a child who had not been born living she had been one not needing that thing not needing having a child who had not been born living. In being one loving children she had not been one sorrowing. In being one loving the one she was loving she came to be one he was marrying.

She was married and she was expecting to be getting what she expected to get by asking and she was expecting to be one expecting getting what she was getting. She was one going on being one expecting to be getting what she was not completely asking and she came then to get something of that thing, she came to get more of the thing which she expected to be getting. She was succeeding in living. She expected to be getting what she expected to be getting. She went on being one getting what she had expected she would be getting. She was being a sad one. She was being a sad enough one.

She was one loving. She was one and she was one not expecting everything, she was one loving and not marrying. She was one loving and not marrying and then she was married by him. She married him and she was not expecting everything. She married him and they were living then in that thing and she expected to be having everything for which she expected to be asking.

She was one succeeding in living that is she expected to be having what she expected to be asking for. She did not expect everything. She expected to be one having what she was expecting.

She had this thing. She had loving children. She had one. He did not live to be going on being living. She was not expecting that thing, she was not expecting him to be one not going on being living. She was one not succeeding in living. She was a sad enough one. She was expecting to be expecting what she asked for. She was expecting what she was asking for. She went on expecting being one having that thing.

She was one liking children. She was a sad enough one. She was expecting being that one the one she was being. She was being one being that one. She was one expecting having what she was expecting.

Being that one she was creating remembering the thing remembering being that one. Remembering being that one she was one not remembering being one having been that one.

She was one loving children. She was one being one remembering having been one creating being a sad one. Being one loving children she was one refusing going on not creating being a sad one. Being one refusing something she was one loving children. Being one refusing anything she was one being a sad one. Being a sad one she was one going on creating having been that one. She was one refusing being one not coming because she was creating being a sad one. Being one being a sad one she was one creating coming because she was one going on loving children. Being one loving children she was one creating waiting to be going. Being one creating waiting to be going she was one being one having been the one she had been. Being that one the one she was she was creating being that one. Being the one she was she was a sad one. Being loving children she was one remembering she had been one being that one. Being that one she was waiting being one refusing to be waiting. Being one refusing to be waiting she was one having been one loving children.

Being one waiting to be refusing to be waiting is something. Being one creating that thing is something. There are many of them.

Being one expecting what they are expecting is something. Being one creating that thing is something. There are many of them.

Knowing everything is something. Knowing that in knowing everything one is leaving out something is something that some one expecting everything is expecting. Expecting to be not expecting anything is something.

One who was not expecting anything, that is to say one who was creating not expecting anything was one not expecting anything. This one not expecting anything was creating this thing. This one in creating that thing was one being one and that one being that one was creating not expecting anything. In creating that thing that one was creating something. That one then came to be one having something. That one then came to be needing everything. That one came then to be having everything. That one then had everything. That was something. That one went on completing that thing completing needing having everything, completing having everything.

That one is one. Another one is another one. Another one is one and she is one accepting what she is accepting to be having. She is one accepting and completing that thing creating acceptation.

She was one and doing something, doing everything in helping, going on helping, coming to be doing anything, she was that one she was married then and being one being that one she was doing what was needed and anything was needed, something was needed, she was doing that thing. She was married and was helping, she was coming in and remembering, remembering everything and reminding the one she had married what he needed to remember to be one completely telling how he had come to do what he had come to be doing. She was one doing everything, she was one doing anything, she was one doing something to be helping to be going on being that one the one helping. She was that one.

She came to remember everything. She had been remembering to be helping. She did remember everything. She was helping.

She was doing what she was doing, she was helping. She was remembering what she was remembering, she was helping. She was doing something to be that one, to be helping.

She was helping. She was moving anything that needed moving, she was leaving anything that needed leaving, she was preparing anything that needed preparing, she was waiting for anything that needed waiting, she was telling anything that needed telling, she was receiving anything that needed receiving, she was filling anything that needed filling, she was expecting anything that needed expecting. She was helping, she was that one, she did something to be that one, she went on being that one.

She was helping, she was giving helping to the one who was one being one and she was that one the one giving helping. She was that one. She was that one and she was one who came to be one having been that one. She was that one and she came to be that one and she was then one having been that one. She was that one.

In coming she was waiting, she had been loving and she was marrying and she was coming and she would be waiting and she would be proceeding to be completing having been one having continued helping. In coming she was remembering and starting and begging pardon and meaning to be continuing and completing having been believing. She had been one helping one who was one who was that one and in being that one was one who was that one. She one helping and was being one who was helping one who was one.

She helped and she was one who had been that one. She helped and she was one who was continuing being one who had been that one. She had helped and she was one who had been that one. She had helped and she was one continuing being the one who had been that one.

She was one, she had been helping in waiting, she had been completing waiting, she had been helping. She had been helping, she had been working, she had been moving, she had been waiting to be questioning, she had been completing having been waiting to be questioning.

She was one, being that one was everything that being that one she was one accomplishing. She was one completing in accomplishing being one being that one. She was one and being that one and accomplishing helping and waiting to be questioning she was one who could be one arranging in being that one to be one completing helping.

She was one moving and in moving she was not showing that in that thing she was that one coming to be that one. In moving she was moving and in moving she was moving. She was moving and in that thing she was that one and that one was one being one moving. She was that one.

She was one and in being one coming to be completing being that one she was one who was arranging that she would remember that in being that one she had arranged being that one. She was one having asked a question. She was one joining in being travelling. She had been travelling. She was then travelling again. She was then joining in travelling being existing. She had been one being one realising that she had been one completing helping. She had been one expressing that being that one she was one and being one she was one expressing that she was one. She had come to be one expressing being one, expressing having been one, she had been one completing helping.

She was married, she had children. She had children and she had a child and in being that one she was one completing arranging that she was one completing helping. She was one and she came to be one being one. She was one and she was being one. She was one and she came to be one being one and that one was one and being that one she was one who had been that one.

And being that one and having been that one she was one who in helping who in waiting to be questioning who in having been that one is one and she is one who in moving is one and she is one who in completing helping is one and she is one who in going on being one arranging having been that one is one, and she is one who in going on arranging something is one and she is one coming again to arrange something and in being that one in being one coming again to be arranging something she is one. She is one, she is that one, she has been one, she has been that one.

There are very many who being one are being the one helping some one. There are very many helping in being the one helping any one. There are very many helping in being the one helping some.

There are very many and helping is being existing. A little helping is being existing.

A little helping being existing some one helping, quite a little helping any one is one quite helping having some one quite helping her then. Some one having been quite a little helping some is one coming to be one having some one helping her in not helping, not helping any one.

Quite a little helping being existing some one having been being one helping quite a little helping is one being one helping one. Some one being one having been that one one having been quite a little helping every one is one being one quite a little helping some one. Some one being one having begun being one helping, quite a little helping any one is one being one helping some one and being one being helped then quite helped then, being one quite helped in being one not helping any one. A little helping has been existing. Helping is being existing.

If one is one and one being one that one is one, if one is one then one being one, and being one is being one suffering in being one, then that one being one and being suffering is being one, and being one and being suffering that one is one expressing anything. Being one being suffering, that is being one not suffering, being one having been coming to be suffering and having been one not having come to be doing that thing, being one being suffering that is being one being breathing in having been coming, being one sighing that is being one heavily breathing, being one suffering that is being one breathing in hurrying, being one suffering is something. Being one being one not having been one being the one any one would have been in being that one, being that one is something. Being one being one being the one being one coming from having been the one being with one who was suffering is something.

Being one telling something about each one and being one beginning from the beginning in telling that thing is being some one. Being one coming from having been hearing some one who was one having been telling that some one was some other one is something. Being one telling some from the beginning about some telling about any one being any other one is being some one.

She was one, she was enough one to be that one. She was that one. She was enough of that one in being that one.

She was one and was then one mentioning that she was that one and in mentioning that thing she was one expecting that she would be needing to be going on being that one. She was that one and again in mentioning anything she was mentioning that in being that one she had been one succeeding in expecting to be going on being that one. In being that one she was gathering in being expecting to be going on being that one. In being that one she was going on gathering in going on being that one.

If she was one and she was that one, if she was one she was not hearing everything. If she was one and she was that one if she was one she was hearing something. If she was one and she was that one, if she was one she was accepting anything. If she was one and she was that one she was angrily refusing something she had been hearing. If she was one and she was that one she was asking any one if she was one. If she was one and she was that one she was asking every one for something. If she was one she was remembering that every one had tried to give her that thing, or if she was one she was telling everything in telling that every one had been one the one trying to give her what every one knew she was certainly one not giving. If she was one she was that one.

She was one asking and giving and recommending and receiving and asking to be that one and helping to be getting and expressing any one knowing that she was that one and asking any one to be telling something of that thing and listening to any one having been not denying she was that one and remembering that any one was one having come to be denying she was that one and being one telling about such a thing and being one being one who might not have been that one if she had not been that one and being one remembering that any one was remembering that she was that one in being that one.

She was being one hearing, when she was hearing, hearing that she was that one. She was one hearing, when she was hearing, and was then hearing that some one was hearing that she was that one. She was one hearing, when she was hearing, she was one hearing that she was that one.

She was one hearing, when she was hearing, hearing that she might not be that one. She was one hearing, when she was hearing, she was one hearing that some one could be hearing that she was not that one. She was one telling what she was hearing, she was then quite telling every one.

She was one hearing, when she was hearing, she was hearing that being that one she was being that one. She was hearing, when she was hearing, she was hearing that then.

In being hearing she was hearing something. In being hearing something she was repeating. In being hearing something she was gasping. In being hearing something she was sighing. In being hearing something she was talking. In being hearing something she was remembering that she was one not offending. In being hearing something she was contenting in producing hearing that thing. In being hearing something she was confirming that she was hearing that thing. In being hearing something she was demonstrating that hearing that thing was an outrageous thing. In being hearing something she was breathing that any one could hear that thing. In being hearing something she was recounting that not any one would have heard that thing. In being hearing something she was pleasing in not having been hearing all of that thing. In being hearing something she was breathing in almost sleeping. In being hearing something she was feeling that being dressed is exhausting. In being hearing something she was being one who had been trembling. In being hearing something she was one who had been sighing. In being hearing something she was being one who had been gasping. In being hearing something she was one who would be completing telling. In being hearing something she was one expecting to not be hearing everything. In being hearing something she was one having been one not hearing any such thing.

In having been that one and being that one she was one and any one deciding that thing was certain, she was one who could have something from recommending anything. In having been that one and being that one she was one and any one was deciding that thing she was one having been helping becoming a lighter one. In having been that one and being that one some who were deciding were certain that she was one who was attracting. In having been that one and being that one very many were deciding very often that she had been helping any one to be one not helping her to be a completer one of a kind of a one. In having been that one and being that one every one was hearing, seeing and having her be one asking any one anything. In having been that one and being that one any one was having her having been doing anything to ask them to be one asking her to do anything. In having been one, in being one she was being one and some were deciding that not any one was suffering. She being one and having been one some were coming to deciding that they were certain that some one had come to be suffering. She being one and having been one some were deciding that she might have come to be destroying being that one. She being one and having been one some were coming to be knowing that she was coming again to be telling another thing. She being one and having been that one some might have been certain that in telling everything she was telling something.

How could she be one and be that one. How could she be one and not be that one. How could she be one and be that one, how could she be that one. How could she be one and be that one. How could she be one and not be that one.

Every one knowing she was continuing was laughing. Any one knowing she was continuing was laughing. Any one knowing she was continuing was certain was certain that she was continuing. Any one knowing she was continuing and being certain she was continuing was certain she was continuing being that one.

Being continuing is being continuing. She was continuing. Any one knowing she had been continuing was certain that she had done that thing was certain that she had been continuing. Being continuing she was being that one.

Any one continuing is continuing. Every one continuing every one is continuing. Any one continuing is continuing. Continuing is continuing.

Continuing and assisting assisting continuing is assisting continuing. Continuing is continuing. Assisting continuing is assisting continuing.

Some one who is continuing is assisting continuing. This one assisting continuing is assisting herself then is assisting herself to continue and in continuing is completely expressing what some one, what some are in being ones being existing. Some one continuing is quite continuing and in quite continuing is quite completely expressing what some are who are being existing.

This one continuing quite continuing and quite expressing quite continuing expressing what some are who are being living, this one is continuing quite continuing, this one is quite wonderfully continuing, quite completely, quite clearly, quite entirely, quite continuously continuing, quite expressing quite completely expressing what some are who are being living.

This one being one continuing and continuing being continuing this one being continuing is continuing expressing what some are who are being ones being living. This one is one continuing. Continuing is continuing.

Any one being one, every one being one, many being living, some being feeling, some being in having been going to be feeling, some being in wanting to be feeling, some being in expecting feeling, some being in feeling, some being in completing feeling by coming to be feeling, some being in continuing feeling in expecting to be feeling, some being in continuing going to be feeling, some being in feeling being coming, some being in feeling being existing, any one being one, every one being one, very many being living, there are some being living, there is one being living, there are very many being living.

One being living, one being feeling, this one is one having been expecting to be feeling, this one is one extending being feeling by not being feeling, this one is one completing being feeling by wanting being feeling, this one is one being feeling and this one is one including feeling by being one completely working.

In feeling in being feeling, in her feeling in her being feeling there is being existing that feeling is being existing, that is there is being existing that she is feeling and she feeling she is feeling something, and she feeling something she is working, and she working she is working to be one keeping being living and she being working to be one keeping being living and feeling something she is feeling that she is completing being feeling by being working to be one keeping being living.

She being one and being working and she feeling and feeling something and she expecting to be one always being one completing feeling she is one living in feeling being existing, she is one working in feeling being existing.

She is one working. She is one working and to be one working she is one feeling something, she is one feeling she is one living in feeling being existing and she being then one completely working.

She is one feeling and she is one working in feeling being existing, she is one working and she is one expecting to be one completely working and being one completely working she is one working in feeling being existing. She is one feeling something and she is one completing that thing in being one completely working.

She is not feeling that she is completing feeling being existing by being completely working, she is feeling that she has been having feeling something, she is feeling that she is having feeling something, she is feeling that she is completely working.

She is completely working, she is feeling something, she has been expecting to be feeling something, she is expecting to be feeling that thing, she is not feeling that she is completely working she is not completely feeling that thing.

She being one she is one remembering that other ones any other ones are ones having been, being ones and they are ones not understanding anything, not being ones being ones who are working in being ones, not working to be completing being ones. She being one she is feeling, she is feeling that every one, that any one is being one and is feeling that every one are ones being ones not feeling in working in completing anything. She being one she is one remembering that every one is feeling something. She being one she is feeling then something.

In being one she was married and being married she had a child and she could have had more then more children and being married then she could not have then more children.

In being one she was married. In being married she was completing that thing completing being working. In being working she was having that thing having being married to some one. In being married to some one she was continuing being one having expected to be one being one. In being married she was continuing having what she was expecting to want to be having.

In being a married one she was one expecting not to be needing being any other one. In being a married one she was one continuing to be expecting to continue being that one. In being a married one she was having what she was continuing to be expecting to be having. In being a married one she was a married one. In being a married one she was continuing being a married one. In being a married one she was continuing being one expecting to be continuing being that one. In being a married one she was a married one.

In being a married one she had a child. In having a child she was one continuing being one having that one. In having a child she was completing that thing by being one having that one having that child. In having that child she was remembering that children being existing she was having that child and in having that child she was one deciding not to be questioning about that child having been one and coming to be that one. In having that child and questioning about children being existing she was repeating that she could be deciding that the child she had was that one. She had a child. She had that one. She was repeating that thing. She was repeating that she had that child, that she had that one. She was repeating that that child was that one.

She was expressing that that child was that one. She was again and again expressing that thing. She was expressing that her child was that one. She was expressing that thing. She was that one the one expressing that thing.

She was one expressing that thing. She was one having that thing having expressing that her child was that one, was one, was the one that child was. She was remembering children were existing. She was completely remembering that her child was one, was that one, she was completely remembering that thing.

In remembering that children are existing she was mentioning that children being existing and her child being that one, her child was one and being one she was mentioning that thing. She mentioning that thing, mentioning that her child was that one, she mentioning that thing was mentioning that children are existing.

In being one she was completing, completing that she was doing what she was completely willing to be doing to be one completing going on being married and having the child that was the child she had. She was one completing going on being willing to be completing going on being that one and going on being married and going on having their child. She was one completing going on being living, she and the two of them.

She and the one of them, she and the two of them she was completing going on being living.

Any one living, every one living, very many living, one living. One living everything is existing. One existing, that is everything. There is one living. One living, that is everything. One is everything. One living is everything. One living is anything. One living, everything is existing. One living, that is everything.

That one, one is living, that is everything. That one is living.

That one is existing, that is everything, that one the one that is living is living and that one living that is everything. That one is everything. That one, that one existing, that, that is everything. That one existing, that is everything. One existing, that is everything. One living, that is everything.

Some are living. Several are living. She living, she being living is being one needing what she is taking. She is taking what she is needing. She is remembering not refusing what she was not taking. She is not remembering taking what she is not needing.

She was not taking everything. She was taking what she had taken. She was remembering taking what she had taken. She was remembering going on taking what she had taken. She did not refuse what she did not take. She was taking what she was taking. She remembered something which she had been taking. She remembered what she had taken. She remembered what she was taking.

She began being one and in beginning she was one and being one she was one needing to be taking what she had been taking. She began being one and in beginning being one she was one. In being one she was that one and in being that one she was using what she was taking. In using what she was taking she was not taking what she was not using. In using what she was taking she was needing to be using what she was using. In needing to be using what she was taking she was taking everything she was taking. In using what she was taking she was using anything she was taking. In taking anything she was not refusing what she was not taking. In refusing anything she was being one taking what she was taking. In taking anything she was using what she was taking. In using anything she had used that thing. In taking anything she had used that thing.

Why in taking something had she not taken everything, why in taking everything had she been asking for something, why in using anything had she refused that thing, why in telling everything has she stopped telling everything, why in remembering everything did she forget anything, why in forgetting everything did she continue telling something, why in telling something did she ask to remember everything, why in asking to remember everything did she give forgetting anything, why being that one is she being that one, being one being a careful one, being one using not being that one, being one asking to be using being that one, being one liking having been using that one, why not using being that one is she being that one, why using being that one is she one not having that thing not having using being that one, why being that one is she not being that one when she being that one is needing to be using what she is taking, is taking what she is using, is taking what she is needing, is needing what she is taking, why being that one is she one and she is one and she is that one, why then is she one carefully being that one if she is one not using being that one, why is she one not needing being that one when she being that one is one needing what she is using, why being that one is she one and she is one one being one who is taking what she is using, who is taking what she is needing, who is not refusing what she is not using, who is needing what she is taking, who is taking what she is needing, why is she that one, she is that one because such a one is one not being one who is being one but is being one in being one taking what she is needing.

This one is one who was one and being that one was one having taken one in being taken by that one and having taken that one in being taken by that one was leaving that one in being left by that one. In leaving that one in being left by that one she was one needing what she was taking. In being one coming to be taking what she was needing she was one being one using what she was needing. She was one then using what she was taking. She was then a married one and in being a married one she was one having been needing what she was taking and using what she was taking she was completing being one carefully taking and carefully using what she was needing.

She was one, she was a married one, she had children, she was a pleasant one and any one not being a pleasant one is not a pleasant one and this one was not a pleasant one and any one being a pleasant one is a pleasant one. This one was one. There are many of them. This one was one, there are quite a number of them. This one was one. This one and there are a number of them of this kind of them this one was one quite one of that kind of them. There are many of them. There are many of any kind of a one. There are many women, many being living.

There is one being living. There is one and that one being a pleasant one is one giving that thing giving being that one and in being that one and she is that one in being that one and giving she is that one and being that one that very one in being that one and she is that one she is that very one in being that one and in giving, in being that one and giving and she is that one and she is giving that thing, in being that one and giving that one she is giving that one giving all of that one and in giving all of that one she is giving all of that one and she is giving all of that one, she, that one, she is giving all of that one.

This one is one. She is that one. She is giving all of that one. She, that one, she is giving, giving all of that one.

She, that one, is giving is giving all of that one. She is giving all of that one. She is doing that thing. She is getting getting everything. She is getting everything that she is needing. She has to have what she has to have. She is getting what she has to have. She has what she has to have. She has that.

She has what she has. She has what she has to have. She has everything that she has to have. She has to have what she has to have. She has what she has to have.

She is one. She is that one. She is giving all of that one. She has to have what she has to have. She has what she has to have. She has everything.

This one is one. She is that one.

Some other ones who are ones are ones and being ones are ones wanting to have what they have to have and being such ones are ones and they are ones who if they had been ones having what they had to have would have been ones having what they had to have. They would have been ones having what they had to have if they had been ones coming to be ones having what they have to have. They are ones needing being ones giving what they are needing to be giving and being ones needing to be giving what they are needing to be giving they are ones not coming to be ones having been having giving what they are needing to be giving.

One is one and being that one is one being one having been one and being one needing to have what she is needing to have. She has this thing, she has needing to have what she is needing to have. She has been having this thing she has been needing to have what she has been needing to have. She is being one and she is one having been receiving that thing having been receiving needing to have what she has to have. She is one who would have been such a one needing to have what she has to have if she were such a one if she were one needing to have what she has to have. She is one. She has to have what she has to have and she would be such a one if she were such a one.

She was one who in beginning was nicely that one. She was one who in completing that beginning was beautifully that one. She was one continuing and being that one and was then a pleasant one in going on succeeding in being that one. She was then that one and was then going on being that one. She was then one, she was then quite that one.

She was that one and being that one and having that thing having needing being receiving having what she was needing having she was one being one being that one and being that one she was one refusing something and refusing that thing she was refusing what she was not needing to be having. Refusing that thing she was laughing, refusing that thing she was persisting, refusing that thing she was refusing what she was not needing to be having.

She was one and she was needing what she was needing to be having. She was one and she was one going on being one that one the one needing to be having what she was needing to be having. She was that one.

She had a feeling and she was saying something she was saying that being one she was being that one. She had a feeling and being then walking she walked very much and walking very much she was feeling that being one she was that one.

She was one and telling something she was certain that she had been telling that she being one she was that one. She being one and deciding that in walking she would not be running she running was liking that she was running and liking that, she was knowing that she would be agreeing that she being one she was that one.

She knowing that she could be agreeing that being one she was that one she was feeling in being one receiving encouraging in being one. She being one receiving encouraging in being one was certain that she could be telling that in being one she was that one.

In being certain that she could be telling that in being one she was that one she was feeling in being one who was certain to be gently denying something.

She was that one and certainly if she could be one having what she was needing to be having she could have been one asking for everything. She was that one and if she was one certain to be gently denying something she was one feeling in being one who was coming not to have been having what she had been needing to be having. In being one feeling in being one who was one not having what she was needing to be having she was being one deciding in telling anything. In being one deciding in telling anything she was defining that in being one she was being that one.

She was that one and she was one who deciding that being that one she was hearing something was one deciding that if she was one having what she was needing to be having could be one hearing something that she being that one had been deciding that she was not hearing.

She being that one she was one deciding that being that one she might go on being that one. She being that one, she was one deciding and being one deciding she was deciding that she might be that one. She was deciding that she might be that one and she was then being one deciding that she would be deciding about going on being one who was one hearing what she would be hearing. In deciding about hearing what she would be hearing she was deciding that she could be one who would be deciding to be expecting to be having what she was needing to be having. In being one who was deciding to be expecting to be having what she was needing to be having she was deciding that being that one she was one expecting anything. In deciding that she being that one she was one expecting anything she was deciding that she was going on being that one. In going on being that one she was quite deciding that she was needing what she was needing to be having. In deciding to be that one she was being one expecting anything. In expecting anything she was expecting to be going on being that one. In going on being that one she was deciding to be deciding what she was going to be hearing. In being that one she went on being one.

She was one. There was another one. Another one was one and being one was one who in studying was learning learning what she had been studying. In studying she was one going on working and in going on working she had been learning and in having been learning she was that one the one she was.

In being that one the one she was she was deciding that she was not needing being one having any other thing. In deciding that thing she was agreeing that she was one and she was agreeing that she was quite that one and she was agreeing that some needed something that they needed to be having.

She was one and in being that one and she was that one she needed enough of being that one to be needing being studying and being studying she was one having been learning what she had been studying.

She was that one, she was needing that thing needing being that one, she was studying, she was needing that thing needing studying, she had been learning what she had been studying, she was needing that thing she was needing having been learning what she had been studying. She was this one. She was an older one. She was knowing what she had been studying and learning. She was quite that one. She was that one and she was enough that one to be one being one and she was enough one to go on being one and she was enough one to be an older one.

There are then some. There are many of them. Any of them being living are going on being living and when they are dead ones and all of them sometime are not living, there are then some of them, there are then many of them.

There is one. She is one being one and being one she is one creating that thing creating that there is one. In creating that thing creating that she is one she is not creating anything. In not creating anything she is being that one she is being the one not creating anything and in being that one she is one and in being one she is creating that thing creating being one. She is one. She is that one. What a tender thing it is to be one. What a one she is the one that is one. She is one and being one she is a tender one and being a tender one she is one. She is one. She is a tender one. She is that one. She is the one that is one. She is a tender one. She is that one the one that is a tender one. She is one. She being one she is one. She is one and being that one she is being creating being one. She creating being one she is a tender one. She being a tender one she is quite one, she is one. She is one. She is that one. She is that one who is one who is a tender one.

There are many very many. Any of the very many being that one is one who if she is a tender one is in a way a tender one. If she is in a way a tender one she is in some way a tender one.

If she is in a way a tender one and there are very many and any of them who are tender ones are in a way tender ones, if she is in a way a tender one and some one is in a way a tender one, if she is in a way a tender one she is one who being a tender one is telling something is telling something of having been loving. If she is in a way a tender one and she is in a way a tender one, if she is in a way a tender one she is telling about being loving. If she is a tender one and in a way she is a tender one, if she is in a way a tender one then when she is in a way a tender one she is telling that she could have been needing having loving.

She was needing having loving. She was being a tender one in telling that she had been needing having loving. She was a tender one in telling that she would have been needing having loving.

In being a tender one she was one being one who being loving was telling that she would have been needing having loving. In being a tender one she was one giving being that one.

In being a tender one she was one telling about having been loving and not having been a tender one. In being a tender one she was telling that she had been loving, that she had been having loving, that she had not been a tender one.

If she were telling everything she was telling she would have been an honest one. She was not telling everything she was telling.

She was not an honest one that is some were certain that she was an honest one. She was an honest one that is some were certain that she was an honest one.

In being an honest one she was a good one. In being an honest one she was telling what she was telling. In being an honest one, in telling what she was telling, she was needing being one being an honest one in being a good one in being one being telling what she was telling.

In being one succeeding she was one helping any one to be certain that in being succeeding she was not having that thing she was not having being succeeding. In being succeeding she was helping any one to be certain that in being succeeding she was being one being succeeding.

In coming again she was being one who might be one not coming again. She might be one not coming again and if she was one not coming again she was then one being one who might be coming again. If she might be coming again she was one who in coming again was one who might not have come again.

In coming again she was one who in coming again was one who might not have been coming again. She was one and in not coming again she was receiving that if she would be one coming again she would be one who was one who might not have been coming again.

She was not coming again. In not coming again she was being one who was one who would not be coming again. In being that one she was receiving that she was being one who would not be coming again. In being that one she was one who being one receiving something was receiving that she was one who might be one coming again.

In coming again she came and in coming she was one continuing to be receiving that she was one who might have been one who would not be coming again, she was one continuing to be receiving that she was one who might have been one who would be coming again.

She had not come, she did come, in coming she came and in having come she had been one who had been one who would come. In having been one who had been one who would come she was one who could have been one who would not come. She came.

In coming she was one coming and in being one coming she was one who had come and in being one who had come she was one who was one not coming if she had been one who had not come. If she had been one who had not come she would have been that one the one who had come.

She would not go on remembering that she had not been using anything. She would go on remembering that she had been using something. In remembering that she had been using something she was being that one the one who had been coming. In remembering that she had been using something she was being that one the one who might not have been coming.

In being one she was one who if it took courage to be one being living could be one being living. In being one being living she was living in being one having courage and in being one having courage being one being living. If it took courage to do something and she did that thing she was one being one who had done that thing. If it took courage to do something she having done that thing she was being one who had courage. If something was done and she had not done that thing she was being one who had not done that thing. If something was done and it needed courage to do that thing and she had not done that thing she was then one who had not done that thing.

In doing everything in being one doing something she was being one who was doing what she did for every one. In doing what she did for every one she was one doing anything for any one. In doing anything for any one she was doing everything.

She did everything, she did anything, she did something for any one and in doing something for any one she was being one who was not needing that anything was being done. In not needing that anything was being done she was being one and being one she was one whom anybody accepting was realising as being one who was one who not needing that anything was being done was one doing anything.

In being one doing anything she was one remembering that she was not needing that anything was done. In being one remembering that she was not needing that anything is done she was one reminding any one of something they should be doing. In reminding any one of something they should be doing she was being one doing anything. In doing anything she was being one being that one and being that one and not needing that anything be done she was one coming. And in coming and in going and in staying and in waiting and in running and in asking and in buying and in loving she was one doing that thing doing anything and being that one one not needing that anything be done. She was being that one and in being that one she was one who if she could be one telling everything was telling that if she were doing a thing and it took courage to do that thing she had done that thing. She was one and if she could be one telling anything she was one who would be one telling that if she did not do something and it would take courage to do that thing she not having done that thing would be telling every one everything.

She being one she was not needing that anything was done. She being that one and doing everything was doing anything.

She was one and being loving and having been that thing and being one who, something needing courage to be done, had done that thing and being one not having done something and being that one, she being that one and being loving had been loving and having been loving and having been doing that thing and having been doing everything in doing that thing she was one and being one she was doing anything and being one she was that one the one who not needing that anything is done is loving and having done that thing has been one having been loving.

She in living continued being living and this being what was happening she was continuing being that one. In continuing being that one she, doing everything, was continuing and in continuing she was one being one steadying that continuing is existing. Continuing is existing, she was being one and being one, continuing not being existing, she would not be one. She was one and she would be one if she was one. If she was one and she was one, if she was one she was one continuing. She was one. She was continuing.

She was one and being one and doing anything she was one continuing and continuing she was being one who in being one was one who if in doing something she was needing courage was if she was doing that thing being that one. She was that one and being one and continuing, continuing being existing, she was that one, she was that one and doing everything and not needing that everything, not needing that something, not needing that anything was done, she was continuing in being one, she was doing anything, she was continuing she was therefor certainly being one.

She was that one. There are many of them. Why are there many of them. There are many of them because there are many of each kind there are and she was of one kind. There are many of them.

Why are there many of such a kind of them. There are many of such a kind of them because that kind is a kind. That kind is a kind. There are many kinds. That kind is a kind and any one of that kind of them is one that is being one living in being living the way that kind of them live in being living. There are very many of any kind.

There are kinds in women. There are enough kinds and being enough kinds there are enough of each kind. There are very many of them. Each one is living. Any one is living. Any one living is in living coming to be going on living.

One who is one and is an especial one, one who is one and that one is one and is an especial one, in being one and certainly being a kind of a one is creating that thing is creating not being a kind of a one is quite creating that thing. Creating that thing is something. Creating not being a kind of a one is something. This one being one creating not being a kind of a one is one and having been creating that thing this one has been creating everything and creating everything this one is that one. This one is not a kind of a one. This one is one. She is that one. She is that one and being one being creative she is creating being one who is not a kind of a one.

There are many being living who if they were being what they would be being if they had been created to be creating would have been creating being one who is not a kind of a one. One who would if she had been creative would have been creating that she was not a kind of a one was one who was resisting quite resisting being certain that she was one who was a kind of a one. She was one who was creating that she would be resisting being certain that she was a kind of a one. She was one who being a kind of a one was not listening in creating that she would not be certain that she was a kind of a one.

She being loving and she was loving, she being loving and not succeeding not succeeding in being loving, she being loving was feeling that she was not creating being that one.

She was loving. She being a loving one and being certain that she was not listening to being a kind of a one and feeling that she was not completing creating being one was one who not troubling every one in being one was one feeling any one feeling that she was one as any one was one feeling that she was one.

Any one was one feeling that she was one and she was that one she was the one whom any one was feeling was that one. In being that one she was one deciding that she was not succeeding in being loving. In deciding that thing she was developing that she was being one who had been one coming to be one deciding what she would be deciding.

She was one and being one being loving and being one deciding that she had been one who would be coming to decide what she would decide and being one expecting to be developing being one who would express that thing express developing and being one who would be one earning needing to be expecting to be completing being one, being that one and being one being loving and being one who was not one succeeding in being loving she was one who was succeeding. She was succeeding, she was giving that thing, she was giving that to some.

In understanding anything she was being that one the that one who if she was feeling would be deciding that the thing she was understanding was a thing that she should be rejecting and being one accepting what she was understanding she was being one who was accepting something very often. In being one she was one accepting something very often and being that one she was being one feeling in understanding anything, feeling in understanding and being then that one being one feeling, she was one who understanding something was deciding that she was one accepting and rejecting something. In being one understanding anything she would be one feeling. In understanding anything she was one feeling. In understanding anything she was one being one who was feeling in being one who was one who being that one was one having decision in being one who in understanding anything was rejecting and accepting something. She being one and having feeling she was one and in understanding anything she was that one the one understanding something and accepting and rejecting something. In being that one she was one and in being one she was feeling and in being one rejecting and accepting something she was one being one understanding something and having feeling. In being one having feeling she was being that one and being that one she was one feeling in understanding something and being that one and accepting and rejecting something she was one and being that one she was feeling. In being that one and accepting and rejecting something she was feeling that in understanding something she was accepting and rejecting something. In being one she was that one, she was feeling that thing.

In coming and going she was being one expressing enthusiasm and in expressing enthusiasm she was expressing needing enjoying and in expressing needing enjoying she was expressing feeling everything and in expressing feeling everything she was expressing being one coming. In expressing being one coming she was being one who in being coming was continuing enthusiasm. In continuing enthusiasm she was one being loving. In being loving she was being one being feeling. In being feeling she was one coming and going. In being feeling she was one coming. In being feeling and going she was one being feeling. In being feeling she was coming, in being feeling she was going.

She was feeling and coming. She was feeling and going. She was feeling and coming and going. She was feeling, she was moving, in being feeling she would be exciting if she were not being so excited in not coming, in not going, in moving, in feeling, in coming, in going, in enthusiasm. She was being excited and in being excited and in being one who would be exciting if she were excited she was feeling and in feeling she had enthusiasm and in enthusiasm she was being that one the one who was excited, the one who would be exciting in feeling, in moving, in coming, in going, in enthusiasm. She would be exciting, she would be exciting if being excited in enthusiasm, in coming, in going, in moving, in feeling would be exciting. She was exciting if being excited in feeling, in enthusiasm, in coming, in going, in moving, in staying is exciting. She was excited in enthusiasm. She was feeling in staying, in coming, in going, in feeling, in enthusiasm, in moving. She was enthusiastic in being one who could be exciting if feeling in enthusiasm, in staying, in coming, in going, in moving, in listening, in walking were exciting. She was one feeling, she was one walking and listening and going and staying and coming and moving, she was one having enthusiasm, she was one being exciting if one were being exciting in feeling, in walking, in listening, in staying, in moving, in coming, in going, in having enthusiasm.

She was one and being one and being that one she was the one who was the one who in listening, in talking, in walking, in moving, in going, in coming, in staying, in having enthusiasm was one who was completely one being one having the enthusiasm in being one who being excited would be exciting if being that one was being exciting and in being that one she was the one being all of that one being quite all of that one, being everything and in being everything and she was being that one she was one feeling and being one feeling and she being that one and being one having enthusiasm and she being that one she was being one and she was all of that one, she was everything, she was that one and being that one she was one who was one and being one and being the one who was one she was all of that one and being all of that one she was everything everything of being one who would be exciting if being all of being the one who was feeling in enthusiasm, in moving, in staying, in coming, in going, in listening, in talking, in moving were being one who was exciting. She was all of that one. She was every bit of that one. In being every bit of that one she was one and being one she was all of that one.

This was one who was all of that one. There are many. All of them are all of the one they are. There are many all of them are not all of the one they are. There are many. There are very many women. There are very many living. There are many of them.

One of them and being all of that one is everything and being everything is exciting. She is not exciting because she is all of that one. She is not exciting because she is everything. She is exciting. She is everything. She is all of that one. This one and she is exciting, this one is feeling and being feeling she is completely exciting and being completely exciting she is everything and being everything she is all of that one. She is all of that one. She is every bit of everything. She is that one the one she is and being that one she is such a one, such a wonderful one, and being such a wonderful one she is that one and she being that one she is every bit that one. She is a wonderful one, she is exciting, she is everything, she is every bit that one. She is the one who is everything. She is the one who is exciting.

She being exciting and being a wonderful one she is exciting, she being the one who is exciting is one being feeling and being feeling she is everything and being everything she is every bit that one.

There is this one. This one is. She is every bit that one.

Any one who is one who is a woman and very many who are ones are being such ones, all of them are ones who being ones and being ones who are certainly being careful to go on not doing what they might be doing are ones who could come to be certain that if they would they could and if they would they could not do what they might be doing. There are very many being living. There are some being living. There are some who are living. There are some.

One was living. She was moving some. She was not going when she was moving she was moving so as to be where she could see the place where she had been. She was not moving so as to do that thing. She was not moving because she wanted to see the place she had been. She was moving because if she could have what she was needing she would not be having anything. She was moving and she was not going. She could see the place where she had been.

She was one. Any one mentioning that thing was mentioning that she was that one. She was one. In feeling that thing she was not mentioning that thing she was not mentioning that she was that one.

In moving she was one coming to be mentioning something to every one. In mentioning something to every one she was mentioning that she had been moving and had not been going. In mentioning that thing she was mentioning that she was interesting any one who was interested in that thing. In mentioning this thing she was being one. She was not mentioning that thing she was not mentioning that she was one.

In not mentioning that she was one she was being one mentioning everything. In mentioning everything she was mentioning that she was telling any one that she was loving some one. In mentioning that she was telling any one that she was loving some one she was mentioning that she had come to be certain that loving is existing. In mentioning that she had come to be certain that loving is existing she was being one who mentioning everything to every one was one not expecting everything. In not expecting everything she was one helping any one. In helping any one she was moving and in moving she was not coming she was not going, she was moving and she could see from where she was she could see where she had been, she could see that place then, she could move so as to see any place where she had been.

In being where she could see any place where she had been she was not looking. She was moving then. In moving she was moving to where she could have seen every place where she had been.

In working and she could be working in the evening or in the morning or in the early part of the afternoon or towards evening, in working and she could be working and in being one she was working, in working she was teaching and in teaching she was telling that in working she was teaching and in teaching she was helping every one, she was helping herself, she was helping some, she was helping some one.

In being one and having been living she had been one and had not been telling everything of that thing, she had been one and had been intending to be one who had not but who would be telling everything of that thing. In being that one and being living she was one coming to be telling everything and in telling everything she was one not completing expecting everything. In not completing expecting everything she was telling that being one telling something she was continuing being one telling everything. In continuing telling everything she was not completing expecting something. In not completing expecting something she was expecting and expecting she was moving and moving she was where she could see where she had been and being there she was moving and moving she was being where she could see where she had been. In being there she was working. She could work in the evening. She could work in the morning. She could work in the afternoon. She did work and working she was teaching and teaching she was telling that she was expecting everything and expecting everything she was loving and loving she was telling every one everything.

Being one and that was that thing, being one and helping she was one expecting to be helping that thing. In expecting to be helping that thing she was helping anything and helping anything she was being one teaching and being teaching she was telling something to some.

In telling something to some she was telling that thing again. In telling that thing again she was telling it again and in telling it again she was again telling it again and in again telling it again she was telling it again.

In telling it again she was one being one expecting everything expecting to be telling it again. In being one expecting to be telling it again she was being one and being that one she was one expecting everything. In expecting everything she was being one and being one she was loving some one and loving some one she was expecting, that one being loving, she was expecting everything and she was then telling every one that she was that one she was one, who loving some one and that one loving, was expecting everything. In telling every one that she was expecting everything she was telling every one that she was teaching and in telling every one that she was teaching she was asking every one if any one was not one who could be one expecting everything.

She was one moving. She was one moving again. If she had been one looking she could have been seeing from there where she was she could have been seeing where she had been in being moving. She was not one looking between moving. In not looking between moving she was hearing herself asking any one if she would be moving. In asking any one this thing she was disturbing the one and disturbing the one she had moved and having moved she moved to where she could look if she did look and see where she had been. She being that one she was teaching, she being teaching she was telling something, she being telling something, she was telling that thing again, she telling that thing again was asking if any one telling that thing was not one teaching and if any one telling that thing was teaching was not being one teaching being a thing having the meaning that in doing anything one was meaning that in helping anything one was loving. In asking everything she was helping everything, in helping everything she was asking that she was telling that she was teaching and doing that thing. In helping everything she was asking if she was not telling everything. In telling everything she was asking if she was not teaching. In being teaching she was asking if she was not loving. In loving she was asking if she was teaching everything. In teaching everything she was asking if any one needed any helping. In asking if any one needed any helping she was asking everything. In asking everything she was asking it again. In asking it again she was teaching. In teaching she was telling anything. In telling anything she was telling it again and in telling it again she was asking that thing and in asking that thing she was asking it again.

She was that one, she was that one and being that one and telling something and telling it again she was that one and being that one she was all of that one and being all of that one she was being one who was that one.

There are many being living, there are enough of them so that any one who is wanting to meet all of them can meet very many of them. There are very many of them. There are enough of them so that every one who can be taught something by any of them can be one being taught something. There are very many being living. There are very many.

One who can teach some one everything in teaching that one everything is teaching that one that everything being something that one can learn everything from that one. That one being one teaching is one teaching some one everything. That one being one learning everything is being one being taught everything by the one that can teach that one everything. That one the one that can teach some one everything is that one and being that one and understanding that thing clearly understanding that thing clearly understanding that she teach some one everything is telling that thing quite telling that thing and completely often is beginning to go on teaching teaching everything. Being that one and being one teaching some one everything that one is that one completely that one the one teaching to the one learning everything. These then are two then who are knowing that one can teach everything. These two then are two mentioning that thing that one can teach one everything. That one the one teaching is one mentioning quite often mentioning that thing.

There are many being living. There are enough of them so that every one can meet some. There is one being living. She is one telling that she being one being living she is being living enough so that every one wanting to meet her can ask her if she is the one they are wanting to have tell them that she being living is living enough to explain all of that thing.

She being living enough is knowing that any one meeting her is knowing her enough to know that she being living can explain enough that she is the one living enough. In being the one knowing that she can explain enough to any one that she being living enough is that one she is one knowing that any one she is knowing is knowing her enough to know that she can explain enough that she is the one who is living enough.

She being one knowing that any one knowing her is knowing her enough to know that she can explain what she can explain enough she being one knowing this thing is being one explaining everything enough and in explaining everything enough she is explaining that she being living she is living enough to be explaining everything that she explaining enough is explaining.

She is one explaining enough, she is explaining that thing enough, she is explaining enough that she is explaining enough. In being that one she is one telling something. In being one telling something she can be one telling everything. In being one who can be telling everything she is telling that she is telling what she is telling.

She could come and coming she would not come again if she were not certain that in coming again she was feeling and in feeling she was being that one the one doing all of the right thing that she would have been deciding to do if she had already come to a decision.

In coming again she would be one telling something and being one telling something she could come to be one telling everything.

She was one feeling and in feeling she was one going and in going she was knowing that she would not be explaining enough that she had been going. In going she was being one and in being that one she was not telling all of everything and in not telling everything she was knowing that she could not be explaining enough that she could not tell all of everything.

In telling anything she was telling something and in telling something she was telling that that thing was more something than some other thing and in telling that what she was telling was more something than some other thing she was telling that she could explain enough that she was knowing that she could tell something.

In being that one and she was that one, in being that one she was one explaining enough in explaining enough that she was living enough and that in living enough any one knowing her was knowing her enough so that they could know that she was living enough to explain enough.

She being that one and she was that one she was one and any one knowing her enough was knowing enough that she was that one and knowing enough that she was that one was knowing that in telling something she was telling enough to be one who could be enough one telling everything. She was that one and being that one she was the one who was being that one and being the one who was being that one she was one who was enough one and being enough one she was the one who being that one was being one who was that one. In being one who was that one she was the one who was one who was being that one.

In talking and any one talking could be one knowing that she was one talking, in talking and she was talking in telling anything that was needing that talking is existing, in talking she was one deciding that not deciding is something and not deciding being something she was one and could be one who was deciding and deciding was just such a thing.

She was one who had been one and she could remember everything of all of that thing.

In telling she was telling that it was happening that she could remember all of everything.

She was telling that if she had not been one remembering everything she would not be one being the one telling what she was telling. She was telling that being the one telling what she was telling she had been one carefully chosen in choosing to be the one she was being.

She was telling that in developing she had not been changing and this was something that was a curious thing as she was coming to be one deciding to choose to be changing enough to be telling that which she was going on telling.

If she had been doing what would be frightening she would have been one exercising everything. She was one who could be one being an uneasy one and being one then not remaining interesting. She was not interesting in not being loving. She was never loving. If she had been loving she would have liked marrying. In almost following some one she came to be one who was not a married one. She was not loving. She was not marrying.

She was not at all marrying. If she had been one continuing to be one staying when she was an uneasy one she might have been one coming to be marrying. She was an uneasy one and that was a strange thing, she was an uneasy one in being an ordinary enough one. She was not interesting in being one not loving. She would not have been loving if she had followed when she almost followed one. She was not loving when she was being one being living. She was not loving.

She did what she did, she said that she would do what she did when she said what she said and she said that she said what she said.

If in remembering everything she followed everything she would remember very much and she did remember very much, she followed everything she remembered and she remembered everything.

She could do what she did. In doing what she did she could do everything she did and in doing everything she did she did everything. In doing everything she was being that one the one saying that she did everything she did when she said what she said and she said what she said.

In doing everything she was being one being one attacking and in being one being attacking she was being one saying that she was only being one attacking when she was saying what she said and she said what she said.

In being one saying what she said she was being one saying that she was not saying what she said to be one being the one attacking, she said that she was one feeling in being one saying what she said and she said what she said.

In being one saying what she said she said she was being one saying what she said and having been one saying what she said she was one feeling and being one feeling she could be one feeling and being one feeling she was saying that saying what she said was not feeling and feeling was not what she said when she said she said and she did say what she said and she was feeling and saying what she said and she had said what she said she had been feeling.

She could say that she knew some thing. She could say that thing.

Some one knowing something could say something. She said that thing, she said some one knowing something could say something.

Some did say something. Any one said something. Any one knowing something and saying something and she saying something she was saying that having been coming to know what the one knowing something and saying something was knowing she could say something and saying that, she could say something that the one saying something had not been knowing and not been saying. She could say something. Knowing something she could say something.

Feeling that she had been enjoying she was saying that she had been enjoying what she had been enjoying and saying that thing she could be saying that being that one and enjoying something she could say that she had been enjoying what she had been enjoying.

She said that she would be enjoying something, in saying that thing she was saying that she would not be enjoying that thing if she would not be enjoying that thing and she would be saying that she had not enjoyed that thing if she had not enjoyed that thing.

In helping any one and in being one helping any one she was helping any one, in helping any one she was saying that she was continuing and being the one continuing she would be helping any one if she was the one being the one she was and she was that one and in helping any one she was helping any one.

Being that one she was the one planning that in continuing she would be arranging to have something. In arranging to have something, she was not being one. In being one she was telling something and in telling something she was hearing that she was one telling something and hearing that she was one telling something she was telling that in telling something she was telling what she was telling.

In expecting to be continuing she was feeling and feeling that she needed something and she was arranging so that she would have something and in arranging that she would have something she was feeling what she was telling.

In succeeding she was one who would be the one succeeding in doing what she was doing. In succeeding she was the one telling what she was telling, she being one having been hearing what she had been hearing when she was telling what she was telling.

She was that one. She was the one who was the one that was that one.

Knowing that any one is doing what that one is doing, suspecting that any one is the one that one is, is what some one, who is one and is all of the one who is what she is, is completely doing. This one the one who is all of what she is, is one suspecting that any one is what they are, is knowing that any one is doing what they are doing. She is all of that one and being all of that one is knowing everything, is suspecting everything. She is suspecting anything and in suspecting anything is deciding to be suspecting something and in suspecting that thing is suspecting that every one is doing what every one is doing. She is knowing anything and knowing anything of any one is one deciding that something she is knowing of every one is what every one is and she is knowing everything. She is that one. She is all of that one. She being all of that one and suspecting everything and knowing everything is all of one.

There are some suspecting something. There are some knowing something. There are some knowing and suspecting something.

One was knowing that some one should not continue to show to some one something. She was suspecting that the one looking at what some one was continuing to show him was saying what would discourage the one showing something. She was one knowing something and suspecting something. She was one.

She was one and being that one there were very many little ones. She was one and being that one and there being another one she was one feeling that she would not be continuing to live long.

She was living and in living she was exercising that living is existing. She was living and she was exhausting continuing being living. She was living and being that one she was living.

She could be one. In being one she was not saying that she was that one the one she was being, she was not saying anything.

She could be one. She was saying something. She was saying that she liked some things.

She could be one. She was one. She was not saying anything. She could be one. She was not saying anything.

She could be one. In not saying anything she was not saying anything of that thing. She was not saying anything of not saying anything.

She could be one. She was one. She was saying something. She was saying that anything is something. She was saying that something which is something is everything and that everything is not something and not being something she would be suspecting that in continuing it was not everything. She was not saying anything of this thing.

She could be one accompanying some one and always accompanying some one she could always have been listening. In being one who could always have been listening she was one not saying anything. In being one not saying anything she was one suspecting what she was suspecting. In being one suspecting she was one deciding and in deciding she was arranging and in arranging she was continuing that the one she was accompanying was not showing what he might have been showing.

In being one she was one and in being one she was one who accompanying and could be listening and suspecting and deciding and arranging and continuing and being that one was one living long enough in being that one to have been one being one expecting enough of not continuing being living.

There are many living and any of them can be one being that one be one being living and any of them being one being living can be one saying something and deciding anything.

One and one was one, one and she was a woman would have been a younger one in being a woman if she had not been an older one in being a woman. In being an older one in being a woman she was one being a younger one, she was one being an old one, a young one, an older one, a younger one, she was one being a woman and being that one was one being one. In being one she was being living and being living she was that one that woman and being that woman she was always all of that one a young one, an old one, a younger one, an older one. She was that one. She was that woman. Being that one she was all of that one and being all of that one she was that woman and being that woman she was all of that one.

There are many being living. One being living and saying something and deciding anything was an older one and being an older one was remembering enough of having been a younger one and was remembering enough of going to be an older one. She was one remembering enough.

She was one feeling in remembering enough. She was one talking in remembering enough. She was one explaining that she was being living and that she was remembering enough.

In being living she was one remembering enough that she had been a younger woman, that she would be an older woman. In being living she was remembering enough that in being living she could have what she was having and that she had been remembering enough of what she had been having, what she was having.

She was one, and being living was enough that thing to be a thing that she could remember enough. She was living and she could remember enough of having been a younger woman, of being an older woman, of coming to be an older woman, of coming to be an old woman.

She being one was remembering that she was that one. She remembering that she was that one was remembering it enough to be one having done what she had done and being that one. She having done what she had done and being that one she was one living and remembering enough that she was that one and she was one arranging what she was intending to continue to be arranging and she was one remembering enough.

That is the end of that and she was one being one. Any being one is one some are describing. Any one being one is one that one is describing.

Some one being one and being the one being beautifully described as completely beautiful one, that one being the one being beautifully described and being beautifully described very often as being beautifully that one, as being a beautiful one, that one being one is one some describe, that one being one is one that one describes. That one being one and being described beautifully as a beautiful one is one that that one describes and that one describing that one is describing everything of that one and describing everything of that one is describing anything of that one and describing anything of that one is describing that one and describing that one is something that some can do in beautifully describing that one as beautiful one.

Any one being one is one some are describing. One being one is one some are describing. One being one is one some are describing and they are describing that one as a pretty one and describing that one as a pretty one they are describing that one to be a pretty one and describing that one to be a pretty one and describing that one they are describing that one. In describing that one they are describing something and describing something they are succeeding in describing and succeeding in describing they are describing that one a pretty one.

She was one that one, she was one being one having come to be that one in having been one who had been one and always would be one having come to be that one and having come to be that one she was being that one and being that one she was describing herself as being one having been one and having come to be that one and having come to be that one to be one then being one describing herself as being that one.

She having been one she was remembering that she was not being one having been one. She was being one being one and being one expressing that being one is expressing everything.

She was one and she was one hoping that being one and expressing conviction she was one remembering everything.

If she was a pretty one and she was a pretty one if she was a pretty one she was expressing that being that one she was hoping that she was completing hoping everything.

She was that one. She was hoping that she was completing hoping everything. She was that one she was expressing that she was being one remembering that she was not being one having been one. She was that one, she was expressing that hearing that she was that one she was succeeding in expressing that continuing is succeeding in hoping everything.

She was one and being that one and continuing she had happen what did happen and that was something that could not happen to every one and that was something that she being one was not continuing to be accepting. In not continuing to be accepting that thing she was not completing anything and in being one succeeding in hoping everything that thing was continuing.

She did say what she did say. She did say she was continuing. She did say that she was succeeding in hoping everything. She did say that she was feeling what she was feeling about any one being one and hoping everything. She did what she did say. She did do all of that thing.

She was one and being one and being one remembering what she could remember she was remembering she was being one and being one enough were certain that she being that one she was quite being one and quite being one she was a pretty one and being a pretty one she was one and was not being that one in being that one.

In not being that one in being that one she was being that one and being that one and being the one who did say what she did say she was being the one being that one and being the one being that one she was not the one being that one in being the one being that one.

She did say what she did say. She did say what she did say when she did say what she did say and she did say what she did say.

She did say that succeeding in hoping everything is all of that thing and saying this thing she did say this thing and she did say this thing in saying this thing. She did say what she did say. She did say that she did say that succeeding in hoping everything is what any one succeeding in hoping everything is succeeding in. She did say what she did say. She did say this thing in saying this thing. She did say what she did say. She did say that she was one being one who was one succeeding in hoping everything. She did say what she did say. She did say this thing in saying this thing. She did say that any one succeeding in hoping everything is succeeding in hoping everything. She did say this thing in saying this thing.

A little one who is little enough to be a big one and who is big enough to be a little one is that one and being that one is one and that one is that one and that one is one and she is one who does not say what she does not say and saying everything is saying something every day of not saying what she does not say. This one is one. She is a big one and a little one and she is one and she says she does not say what she does not say. In saying that she does not say what she does not say she says everything. She is the one. She is one satisfying one.

In being one satisfying every one that that one is some one some one is satisfying every one that she is some one. She is that one. She is one and satisfying any one that she is some one. She is one. She is some one. She is satisfying, she is satisfying every one that she is some one.

She, she could feel in being that one, was feeling in being that some one who was satisfying every one that she was some one. Feeling was delivering that she was giving everything that she was getting.

Effecting that she had been learning she completed keeping what she had been getting. She was and is one restraining what she could see moving. She was one feeling. She is one feeling.

She was continuing and was not burying what was not growing. She is continuing and what is growing is filling and what is filling is burrowing and what is burrowing is what is moving and what is moving is showing that moving is not steadying. She is one and she is convincing any one that she was that one. She is one and satisfying every one that she is some one is something.

She, she was expecting what she had been saying, she was attacking what she was expecting, was one satisfying every one of being one, she being one, believing what attacking, what expecting, what believing, what saying is meaning. She had begun and what she had begun was what was meaning to be what she, satisfying every one that she was some one, was expressing in believing that attacking, that believing, that expecting, that giving what she would be receiving was meaning.

She satisfying every one that she was some one in saying what was coming was saying what she was expecting to be saying in attacking what she was attacking in believing what she was believing in meaning meaning what was winning in giving what she would be receiving.

She satisfying every one that she was some one was satisfying herself then that she was saying what expecting to be saying was attacking whom she was attacking in subduing what she was subduing in believing that she was meaning what she was meaning in giving what she would be receiving and in giving what she was giving. She satisfying every one that she was some one was satisfying herself that saying what she was expecting to be saying was subduing what she was expecting to be subduing, and she being one satisfying every one that she was some one was one feeling what she was feeling in giving what she would be receiving, and she being one satisfying every one that she was some one was believing what she was believing in giving what she was giving, and she being one satisfying every one that she was some one was one being one being one not having moving what was not moving and being one feeling that what was not moving was being what it was being and she being one satisfying every one that she was one feeling that she was not burying what she was not burying, and she being one satisfying every one that she was some one was being what she was being she being one satisfying every one that she was some one.

She, she working was arranging that having teaching was what she had not been burying in not burying what she was not burying, cleaning was continuing that she was arranging what she would be arranging in being one satisfying what she was satisfying in being one and satisfying every one that being one she was some one who was some one.

She in satisfying every one was satisfying every one that she was some one and in satisfying every one in satisfying every one that she was some one was satisfying every one that she was someone and in satisfying every one that she was some one she was one who was, in satisfying every one that she was some one, was satisfying every one that she was some one.

She, she was expecting what she was arranging and was arranging to be saving what she was saving, giving what she would be receiving was feeling what she was receiving in giving what she was receiving. She was believing what she was giving in receiving, and giving what she was receiving and receiving what she was giving she was feeling what she was believing. Feeling what she was believing she was not burying what she was not burying, she was not feeling what she was not feeling, she was believing what she was believing, she was expecting what she was arranging, she was satisfying in satisfying and in satisfying she was satisfying every one that she was some one.

In developing, and she had been developing that she developing was developing, in developing, and she had been developing in continuing believing and she was believing, in developing she had developed and having developed she was being what in being is meaning that she is being. She being and meaning being in being she was being and she being being was meaning and she being was meaning what she being was meaning. She being she was meaning. She was meaning and she was being. She was being what in being is meaning that she is being.

She, she was being and being was meaning that she was being and meaning what she was being, she continuing was remaining and having been remaining something was not coming and something not coming she was being and she being she was meaning and meaning she was meaning what she was being. She was satisfying every one that she was some one.

When she came to having been and being and continuing being that one she was one and being that one was meaning to be that one and was meaning being that one and was satisfying and satisfying was satisfying every one and satisfying every one was satisfying every one that she was some one. In having come to be that one and continuing and being that one and not burying anything in not burying anything and being that one in meaning that thing in meaning being that one and being one satisfying in meaning, in being that one who was one who was satisfying every one that she was some one in continuing having come to be that one she was one coming to be expecting to not bury what she was not burying and in expecting that thing she was not expecting what she was not expecting, she was not expecting and not expecting she was not expecting and she was not expecting and not expecting and giving what she was receiving she was not burying what she was not burying and she was not expecting and she was satisfying every one that she was some one and satisfying every one that she was some one and being one and meaning and believing she was satisfying every one that she was some one and she was not expecting and she was giving what she was receiving and she was being what in being is meaning that she is being and she is being meaning what she is meaning in being and she is being and being she is satisfying every one that she is some one.

In coming to be one needing to be burying what she would be burying she was one coming to not burying what she was uncovering. That being uncovered was being what she would be burying if she could come to be burying what she was not coming to be burying. She was changing, that is in satisfying every one that she was some one she was satisfying every one that she was continuing being some one and in satisfying every one that she was continuing being some one she was satisfying herself that she was satisfying every one that she was some one. She was some one, she was satisfying herself in satisfying every one that she was some one. She was satisfying herself that she was continuing satisfying every one that she was some one. She was satisfying every one that she was some one.

In arranging, and she was arranging in believing what she was believing, in arranging she was continuing arranging what she was arranging in believing what she was believing. In arranging she was continuing in arranging and in continuing in arranging she was believing what she was believing. She was believing what she was believing. She was arranging in arranging and she was continuing in arranging and she was believing what she was believing and she was arranging in arranging. She was satisfying every one that she was some one. She was satisfying herself that she was satisfying every one that she was some one. She was believing what she was believing. She was arranging and believing what she was believing. She was believing what she was believing.

If she was one satisfying every one that she was some one, and she was one satisfying every one that she was one, she was one and she was satisfying every one that she was some one, if she was that one she would be changing in coming to be the one she was being when she was being the one she was being in being one who was being that one. In being the one she was being in being the one she was when she was the one she was she was being one and looking she was feeling what being that one she was feeling. She was showing all of this thing and showing all of this thing and showing anything she was showing all of being the one being the one she was and being that one. In showing all of being that one she was looking and looking she was feeling that being one showing anything she was being the one having what she was having, and having what she was having she was one to be continuing, if showing anything is meaning nothing, she was one to be continuing having what she was having, she being one believing what she was believing and being one satisfying every one that she was some one.

If any one continuing is coming to be a dead one they could then have come to be what they had come to be but if they had not come to be a dead one they had not come to be what they had come to be. She had not come to be a dead one. She had not come to be what she would come to be.

Each one is one, there are many of them. Each one, every one, all of them, any of them, one of them, one of them, each one being, every one being, any one is the one and the one is the one and any history is the meaning of the one not meaning what any meaning is meaning.

One is one. Why is one one. One is one because one being one is sweetly telling that thing and sweetly telling that thing is sweetly telling that that one being one is meaning, and not meaning what any meaning is meaning, is being the one sweetly telling that that one is hearing that that one sweetly telling that, that that one, is one is sweetly telling.

One is one if one were one and sweetly telling something that one would be telling something sweetly. Any one can be telling that that one is not sweetly telling anything. This one is one. She is one and is telling that she has been telling delicately telling what she would have been sweetly telling if she had not been telling what she has been telling. She is telling what she is telling and telling that she is telling that thing as she would be telling that thing if she were sweetly telling that thing.

She is one and telling is what she is doing in telling what she is telling, and that telling is what she is excelling in telling she is telling, in the way she would be telling what she is telling if she were sweetly telling what she is telling. She is convincing, she is convincing in telling that she is telling what she is telling in the way she would be telling what she is telling if she were sweetly telling what she is telling.

She is that one. She was the one telling that she is feeling that some one is telling what that one is telling and is sweetly telling what that one is telling. The one the one who is telling what she is telling sweetly, so some one telling is telling, that one is telling what she is telling and she is remembering that she has not been telling what she could have been telling and that she is telling what she is telling. She is remembering that she is telling what she is telling. She is feeling that being that one the one she is is fatiguing, she is telling that she soon will be continuing to be being the one she will be and telling is what any one expecting anything will not then be expecting. She is one living in remembering that she is being one who could be one continuing being one remembering that she was telling what she was telling. She was one being one expecting to be continuing to be resting, having come to be one who can be continuing to be telling what she is remembering she is telling. She is one remaining where she is remaining in continuing to be remembering that she is telling what she is telling. She is one remembering that telling what she has been telling has been continuing to be fatiguing. She is one expecting some one and the one she is expecting is one telling that she is not needing to be telling what she is telling, she is just needing to be talking and needing to be talking she is not needing anything. The one expected is the one not needing anything and being talking is telling that she has been needing something and has been needing talking. She has been talking and not needing anything has been getting what she was needing being getting so that when she is talking some one can be listening, when she is walking some one can be looking, when she is fixing something some one can be stopping. She is that one. She has returned and is telling that she has come and telling that she has come she is telling that needing talking is not being needing anything. She is not telling what she is remembering of having been needing talking as she is remembering that she has not been needing anything. She is that one.

When any one is gone and is not coming again that one is gone and is not coming again and being gone and being not coming again some one saying something is saying that not any one is saying that thing. That is all that is said by that one.

One who is saying what is clearly said, one who is saying anything that is clearly said, that one is saying that saying something is not at all exhausting and that one clearly saying everything is not being exhausted and not being exhausted and being clearly having clear things coming is for that reason just then so clearly that one that any one can see enough to look again and again. That one is that one. That one is then for that reason that one and one looking is looking. That one is clearly that one. That one is always so clearly that one that one looking is looking and looking.

Some one is one. Some one being one is expecting what not having been one she would not have been expecting and being one she was one completing expecting, she came to be completing expecting. She came to be that one. She came to be one.

Being one and completing expecting she had what she had and she kept all that and was completing expecting. She had come to receive what she could keep and she had come to be one and was completing expecting.

In coming to receive what she could keep, she did keep what she could receive, and she was one and she was completing expecting. She was one and she was completing expecting and she had been one having all she was having. In having been one having all she was having she had been one being that one.

In suffering she was bewildering, and in losing what she had been having she had been suffering, and in having been suffering and in continuing she was completing having been expecting completing that thing. She was expecting completing that thing completing continuing she having been one suffering and continuing. She was one continuing, she was one expecting completing, she was one expecting to be completing.

In being one she could be bewildering and she was one continuing and expecting completing. In suffering she was bewildering and she was one continuing and she was one expecting to be completing and being one. In continuing she could be bewildering and she was one expecting completing being that one and she was one expecting completing and she was one having all she was having and she was one having expecting completing in that thing.

In being that one and she had come to be that one and she was having what she was having and she was expecting completing, in being that one she was one, and being one, and deciding she was one having what she was having, and she was expecting completing, and she was having receiving that she was expecting completing and being continuing in deciding continuing bewildering in having been losing and in having what she was having. She had come to continuing coming to being that one, and being that one she was expecting completing, and having what she was having and continuing in deciding being continuing in bewildering in having what she was having. She was deciding that she was continuing and having what she was having and deciding and continuing bewildering and having lost what she had lost. She was continuing, she was having what she was having, she was deciding to be continuing and having what she was having and having lost what she had lost. She was deciding to be continuing and she was bewildering and deciding to be continuing and she was having what she was having.

She did say that she was that one and was deciding to be expecting to be that one. She was continuing and was expecting to be that one and she was that one and she did say that she was that one.

When she continued saying that she was that one she was having what she was having and was continuing expecting to be that one and she was not denying that being one having lost what she had lost she was bewildering in being one expecting to be that one. In expecting to be that one she did say that she was that one and that she deciding was completely deciding that she was continuing being that one.

She might have arranged that thing arranged deciding to be that one if she had not been one being that one and having what she was having and being one deciding to be expecting that she was continuing being that one.

She did decide that she was expecting continuing being that one, she did have what she did have, she did decide to continue deciding to be that one, she did not arrange to be that one, she did not decide to arrange to be that one, she did not decide to expect to be that one, she did have what she did have, she did continue to be that one, she did lose what she had lost and she did decide to continue to be that one. She did not ask what she did not ask, she did decide, and not asking what she did not ask and having what she did have she did decide to continue to be that one. In not asking what she did not ask she did not refuse what she did not refuse and in not refusing what she did not refuse she did decide to continue to decide what she did decide in continuing to be that one. She did decide to continue to be expecting to be that one and continuing to be that one she did say that she was expecting to be continuing being that one. Having what she had she was not arranging to decide what in deciding to be continuing expecting to be that one she was continuing to decide.

If any one needing loving is being one and being loving could be doing what that one is doing then that one giving loving is giving what that one the one loving could be giving if that one were giving what that one is giving. Such a one is one. Any one who is such a one is such a one.

One who is one and is not such a one is one who is one is one who giving and loving and needing is giving and loving and needing and could not have been giving without loving and could not have been loving without needing and could not have been needing without giving and could not have been giving and loving and needing without having been giving and needing and loving. One who is loving and giving and needing is one completely giving and completely loving and completing needing.

That one is one. That one the one who is one is one. That one the one who is the one that is that one is one, is the one who is that one.

One who is one giving is one who would be one giving if that one were one who was loving. That one is one being certain that she being one who is giving would be one giving if she were one who was loving. She being one is certain that she could be one needing. She is one giving, she could be certain that she could be one needing. She being one being giving might be believing that she could be one being loving. She being one being giving might be feeling that she might have been one who being loving in being needing. She was one and she could be one being giving and she might be one being needing and she was being one loving. She was one and loving and giving and needing was not loving and giving and needing it was that she being one and giving was one intending needing, was one arranging expecting loving. She was that one. She was one giving, she was one who could be one continuing, she was one who might be loving, she was one expecting needing. She was one.

If she had been continuing being a young one she would have been one having what she was having. She was continuing being a young one. In having what she was having she was one not loving. In giving what she was giving she was being that one and being that one if she were continuing being a young one she was one who had been giving what she had been giving. She was continuing being a young one, she had been giving what she had been giving, if she were not continuing being a young one she would be being giving what she was giving. She was giving what she was giving, she was continuing being a young one.

She was having what she was having, she was giving what she was giving, she could be loving in loving, she could be needing in needing, she could be giving in giving, she could be having in having, she could be continuing being a young one.

Continuing being a young one is something if being a young one is anything and being a young one is something if continuing being a young one is anything. Continuing being a young one is something.

One who was a young one and was continuing being a young one was one who being a young one was being that one and continuing being a young one was being that one and being that one and being a young one that one was one and anything is something and that one is a young one and that one continuing is a young one and something is something.

Any one having been listening and having been gently not being delicately listening that one is one expressing something of succeeding in living. One expressing something of succeeding in living is such a one.

She is such a one and she is one continuing when continuing is not everything and when not continuing is not anything. She is such a one and she is living and she is expressing something of succeeding in living.

She came and there were others and they all of them lost something and she expressed something of succeeding in living. She came and was one continuing to coming to being one who was one gently not delicately listening. She was one gently doing what she was doing not delicately listening. She was filling more of expressing something of succeeding in living.

She did resist something and that was not anything and she did resist that thing and she was not expressing not quite expressing that she was continuing resisting what she was resisting. She was continuing and could be expressing that what she was resisting was not anything and she would then be expressing that had she been resisting she would have been resisting what she had been resisting and she had been resisting what she had been resisting. She was expressing something of succeeding in living. She was continuing. She was filling being expressing something of succeeding in living.

She was not delicately listening. She was gently not delicately listening. She was continuing to be hearing what she was hearing. She had been hearing she was hearing something of some succeeding in living. She was gently not delicately listening. She was expressing something of succeeding in living. She was continuing. She was filling expressing something of succeeding in living.

One who was clearly and happily agreeing that she was amiably feeling in wanting to be winning was one resisting what she was resisting was deciding was not opposing. She was happily and clearly feeling that she was explaining that she was having in amiable feeling a way of being of amiable feeling and she was happily and clearly deciding and deciding she was correcting and correcting she was convincing and convincing she was not regretting. She was happily and clearly being. She was happily and clearly feeling. She was one who was clearly the one amiably feeling. She was one who was happily the one amiably feeling. She was clearly one who was an amiable one. She was happily one who was an amiable one. She was happily and clearly the one who clearly was amiably one. She was clearly and happily the one who happily was amiably one. One who was clearly, one who was happily amiably one was happily, was clearly an amiable one, the amiable clearly, happily, clearly amiable one. One who was one was one clearly. One who was one was one happily. One who was one was one amiably. One who was the one was an amiable one.

However it came to be that so very many were living it did come to be that some of them continuing were living. Many of them were living, and continuing, some of them came together and continued that way then. One of them was one who if she had been an amiable one would have been continuing being an amiable one and she was continuing and was being an amiable one and she had been one being an amiable one. She was not needing that thing needing being an amiable one. Not any of them were needing that thing needing being amiable ones. All of them who were being together then were continuing and she was the one who was one of them and she was continuing. She was one. She could be, she was, she would be an amiable one.

She was one. She was that one. She was continuing. She was living. She was being. She was meaning. She was remaining. She was counting. She was planning. She was having. She was pleasing. She was giving. She was keeping. She was feeling. She was worrying. She was continuing.

She was not needing to be wearing what she was not giving and getting. She was not needing to be changing what she had arranged to be changing. She was feeling in having what she was deciding to be having. She did have children. She did have a married living. She did have many living and living she was living with many and many were living. She was continuing to be counting what she was arranging. She was having what she would be doing. She was quieting what she could be feeling. She was resting what she had been feeling. She was continuing regretting what she could have been saying. She was filling everything she was arranging to be filling when she was counting.

She did have what she was being. She did give what she was offering. She did feel what she was filling. She did please in being occupying. She did do what was continuing. She did satisfy in having children. She did arrange in doing counting. She did turn in being wounding. She did consider in being forgiving. She did thank in receiving attention. She did distribute in being enjoying. She did continue in being yielding. She did remain in being sweetening. She did resist in being accepting. She did enjoy in being satisfying. She did receive in having marrying. She did continue in being affectionate in having, in giving, in receiving, in marrying, in resisting in spoiling in expecting in attending in deploring in obeying in enjoying her children. She did continue in expecting weakening. She did continue in hoping strengthening. She did continue in worrying eating. She did continue in rounding fading. She did continue in attending living. She did continue in enjoying feeling not being denying. She did continue in having been arranging to be counting worrying. She did continue in being affectionate in weakening. She did continue pleasing in declining. She did continue receiving what she would be having. She did continue having what was being. She did continue being what all of them were being who were living. She did continue being as she was being living. She did say all of enough of that thing. She did say what she said of being living. She did feel what she felt of continuing. She was what she had been in being. She was what she was and she was all there was and that was all of that one. She was continuing in arriving where she would be fading. She was weakening in aging where she would be ceasing.

She was giving what she had for giving. She was feeling what she had in being. She was receiving what she used in living. She was paying in every day arranging.

She was filling what was not needing emptying. She was deciding what would not have been changing. She was keeping what was not gathering. She was renewing what was continuing.

She was being and she was living. She was having what was enjoying. She was doing what was collecting. She was giving what was continuing. She was receiving what was gathering. She was hearing what was sounding. She was losing what was fading. She was saying which was enjoying and conditioning. She was accepting which was pleasing. She was resenting which was resisting. She was suffering which was accusing. She was worrying which was counting. She was reflecting which was grieving. She was being which was accepting. She was laughing which was completing.

If there were many and there are many, if there were many then some of them would be satisfying any one and some of them are not satisfying any one and some of them are satisfying any one. And any one who is satisfied by some of them is satisfied because they are satisfactory the ones that satisfy them.

One to be satisfying must be satisfying. One is satisfying. That one being satisfying and not deceiving and not beguiling and not resisting only detaining is one completing being that one being satisfying. That one being one and being satisfying is being the one being completely satisfying. Completing satisfaction is completely being that one.

There are some being living, there are those and those all of them are doing what they are doing. One of them is one being an old one and having come then to be receiving worrying about coming to be a sick one. She has been one who has come to something.

She and she herself had come to something and was succeeding in having had what she had given to be needing to be receiving what she was receiving, she was not asking what any one could be answering she was asking that she should continue to give what she gave and get what she got.

If she were quietly doing what she was doing she would be receiving what she was receiving but she would not be having what she was having and she would not have been asking what she had been asking.

She did give every one she was needing what she was needing to give to them. She was feeling what she came to be feeling when she came to have what she was having.

She came to want to be enjoying what she was feeling in doing what she was doing. She came to feel that she was having what she was having and she might be doing what she was doing.

She was feeling what she was feeling in loving what she was loving in having what she was having. She came to feel that she was feeling what she was feeling in needing to be having what she was having. She came to feel that she was feeling that she was having what she was having and that she might be doing what she was doing in feeling what she was feeling.

When she was succeeding she was succeeding in living and when she was succeeding in living she was feeling what she was feeling and she was doing what she was doing. She was feeling what she was feeling and she was doing what she was doing.

Succeeding in living she was placing what she was placing and helping what she was helping and following what she was following and doing what she was doing and feeling what she was feeling.

She was continuing in expecting to be placing what she was placing. She was continuing in expecting to have been having what she had been having.

She was coming to continuing fearing what she could be fearing. She was continuing having been feeling what she had been feeling.

She had been asking what she had been asking. She was continuing to be receiving what she had been asking. She was willing to be changing what she was seeing when she was looking. She was willing to be seeing what she was seeing when she was looking. She was willing to be having what she was asking. She was needing to be doing what she was doing in asking what she was asking in receiving what she was receiving. She was willing to be feeling what she was feeling. She was coming to be doing what she was not needing to be doing to be having what she was having.

To direct everything so that what comes is coming is doing what one knowing what everything is and being directing can be doing. Succeeding in directing is something.

One who is one and is knowing what everything is could be directing and she is directing that is she is reasoning and being reasonably understanding what everything is can be directing so that what comes is coming. She being that one is rightly judging everything. She being that one and saying that to be always right she must be wrong quite often, she being that one and always being correct in judging and complete in knowing what everything is and reasonable in telling and firm in directing she is one and what comes is coming. She is one and knowing what everything is and being one clearly expressing that thing and firmly directing she is one curing what would need curing if she were not being the one directing that which she is directing which is certainly all of the two of them. She is the one knowing all of what everything is and directing what she is directing, and she is that one of the two of them and what comes is coming and she is directing, and she is correcting what is to be coming and she is knowing what everything is and reasonably telling and quite curing what might be needing curing if curing were needing to be continuing. She is quite that one. She is a lovely one. She is a directing one. She is a one knowing what everything is.

There are some who are succeeding in placing what they are placing, there are some who are marshalling all of what they are placing. There is one and she is directing all she is directing and she is succeeding in being and any of that being everything she is everything in failing.

She is that one. She had seven and she arranged that all of them would be all of them and that she was placing what she was placing.

She was sitting and sitting was not everything. She was sitting and she would be placing what she was placing when all of them had been all of them.

All of them were all of them. All of them had been all of them. They were coming all of them were coming, some of them were coming that all of them were not all of them. All of them were not coming. All of them were all of them.

She was sitting and when she was not leaving she was not remembering everything. When she did remember everything she was sitting and keeping what she had had when she was sitting.

In succeeding in continuing she had been succeeding in living and all of them were all of them and she was placing what she was placing and she was not coming to what she was coming and all of them were not coming to be all of them and they were then what they were then when not any of them were all of them and some of them might have been all of them.

She was one and she had what she had when she was coming to having been placing what she would have been placing if all of them being all of them all of them had been all and some of them had been all of them.

In not having what she was having and sitting she was receiving what she would be having if she had been having what she was having in placing what she was placing.

She placing what she was placing and all of them being all of them she sitting was not standing and not standing she was receiving what she would be receiving in placing what she was placing, all of them being all of them. She was placing what she was placing. She was receiving what she would be receiving. In remembering what she was remembering she was receiving what she would be receiving.

She could be intending. She was placing what she was placing. She was saying what she was saying when she was sitting.

She was intending that all of them were all of them. Some of them were intending that all of them were all of them.

She could be intending. She had been, she was intending that all of them were all of them. She was continuing, she could be intending.

All of them could be all of them and they were all of them and she was continuing and she could be intending. She could be intending. She was intending that all of them were all of them and some of them were intending that all of them were all of them. Some were hoping to be intending that all of them were some of them. Some were intending that some of them were enough of them. They all could be intending. All of them were all of them.

She was placing what she was placing. In placing what she was placing she was showing what she was having. In showing what she was having she was placing all of them so that all of them were all of them. In placing all of them so that all of them were all of them she was using what she was having. In using what she was having she was showing that all of them were all of them. She was placing what she was placing.

She was saying what she was saying when she was sitting. She was sitting. She was saying what she was saying when she was sitting. In sitting and saying what she was saying when she was sitting she was intending to be saying that she was saying what she was saying. She was sitting and all of them were all of them.

Anything being together and there being pieces that are being used and all the pieces are being used and all of them had placed on them what was placed for them and they being where they had been again and again, all of them being there then and they could be there and nothing was anything and there was there not anything she was placing what she was placing and all of them were all of them and that was too much of that thing in all of them having been continuing and all of them not coming to use anything, and she was placing what she was placing and all of them all of them being all of them all of them all of them were coming to intending and all of them coming to intending she was sitting and sitting was that thing. All of them intending all of them a piece being on all of them, a piece being on all of them some of them, anything being together all of them were all of them. All of them were all of them. She was placing what she was placing. All of them were all of them.

She sitting and sitting being that thing, she sitting and all of them being all of them and she having not been completing that thing completing sitting she was not completing that something would not be together if a piece was on each one of them. All of them were all of them. They were losing in using what they were using in a piece not being on each one of them. They were not losing in all of them coming to be intending. They were losing in coming and they were coming to be intending. She did sit and she did not do that thing, she did place what she placed and she did not do that thing. She was sitting.

If she had the way of sitting and she did not have a way of sitting she would keep in being what she did have in sitting. She did not have a way of sitting. In sitting she did have in being what she was not losing and not losing she did not give anything of sitting. She did not give anything of sitting. She did not have a way of sitting.

She did not have a way of sitting. She was not being in continuing sitting. She did not lose being sitting. She did not lose sitting. She did not keep in sitting. She had sitting. She was having sitting. In having sitting she did change what she did not change in placing what she was not placing. In continuing she did not change when she was remaining in having been moving being sitting. In having been sitting she was not sitting. She was not sitting in the way of sitting. She was sitting in having been continuing remaining in having moved in sitting. She was not being in not sitting. She was not being sitting. She was not being, not sitting, sitting. She was intending in sitting, in saying what she could be saying.

A little one who could not push did push and pushing was telling that pushing was not succeeding. A little one pushing is a little one pushing.

She could tell all about pushing. She could tell and she did tell all about not pushing. She did tell and she could tell that having had what she had had she would have what she would have, and she did have what she did have and she did tell what she did tell.

Some are some. Some being some and one telling them that that one is one not telling what she might be telling if she had been listening, when she was listening they are hearing that she is not telling what she is not telling and all of them she and they are all continuing in friendly living. She is telling that hearing is something. She is telling that listening is something. She is telling that telling is something. She is telling that she is hearing, that she is not listening, that she is not telling.

In living and in repeating she was determining in being exciting. In being exciting she was not living and in living she was not continuing and she was being the one conveying being exciting.

She did feel that which feeling she did have as being. She did begin what she was finishing and she did not continue hearing when she was listening.

In having been feeling she was saying that she had been giving up what she could be needing and in giving it up she had been doing without it. She was saying that she had been feeling in being living, and being living and continuing she was being not having given up everything.

In being married and feeling she was married and was conveying that thing that she was continuing. In having children and she had two children she was feeling what she feeling. She was feeling what she was feeling. She was feeling something. She was saying what she was saying. She was saying what she was feeling. She was saying that she could determine not coming to be exciting. She was saying that she could say what had meaning.

In having children and arranging she was conveying that arranging can be something and that she was not arranging what would be arranged.

She had two children. She was feeling what she was feeling. She felt that she had had two children and having two children one of them was one and the other one was the other one.

She had them and she needed being living to be feeling what she was feeling in having them. She needed being living and being living she was not needing what she was needing in conveying being exciting and having the one child and the other child.

One was one and was like that one, was one being that one and being completely like that one in being one. She had that thing having that one and having that one she was needing being living to be feeling what she was feeling in that one being that one and being living.

The other one was that one and being that one was being any one being living and winning intending some winning of continuing being one. That one was having intending some continuing. She had that one and having that one was one saying what she was saying about having that one, about that one. And saying what she was saying about having that one, about that one, she said all she said about having that one, about that one, and saying all she said about having that one, about that one, she was one conveying intending in not saying, in not feeling, in saying, in needing all she was saying in feeling, in remembering in needing what she could be saying in having that one, of that one.

She was needing being one living to be feeling what she was feeling in having the one, in having the other one.

In feeling what she was feeling in having the one, and she had the one, she was not compelling what she was saying in telling that if she was living she was living. She had him and feeling what she was feeling she was telling that she was not compelling being one being living, and being living she could be feeling what she was feeling in having the one who was that one one being one she had.

Like that very much like that and like that she did what beginning and ending she was continuing not compelling saying in saying what she said and feeling what she felt in feeling what if she were feeling she would have to be living. She was feeling and coming in not continuing she was in beginning and ending continuing and she was saying what she was saying in feeling what she was feeling if she was feeling what to be feeling she would have to be one being living. She was not compelling saying, she was not compelling not continuing, she was beginning and ending in continuing, she was saying what she was feeling and to be feeling what she was feeling she was to be being living and being living was not compelling living being continuing and she beginning and ending was continuing and not compelling saying, and not compelling continuing.

She was continuing. She was saying in beginning and ending she was continuing. She was continuing. She had one. In continuing she was saying that anything, anything that was beginning and ending was like continuing. She was saying that beginning and ending was not like continuing she being living and having one and not compelling saying. She was saying that not compelling continuing

214

she being one and having one and feeling what was like not continuing, she was not feeling like compelling continuing, she was continuing if beginning and ending is continuing and beginning and ending is and is not like continuing.

She had one and like that one, that one, and she was one, was one saying what he was saying in feeling what he was feeling in feeling what to be feeling was needing being one being living. That one, and she was one, that one was having been saying what feeling was enlivening, feeling beginning and ending and not compelling having been continuing.

She, and she had one he, she and he saying what they were saying, and they were saying what they were saying were repeating what they were feeling beginning and ending being continuing and it was continuing and they were feeling and saying they were saying what was like what they were saying. They were saying what was like what they were saying. She had him, he was like what he was feeling, she was like what she was feeling, he was saying what was like what he was saying, she was saying what was like what she was saying, she was feeling, he was feeling.

She had one. He was one. They were feeling. They were saying. She was feeling and was not compelling saying. She was saying and not compelling feeling. He was saying and was not compelling feeling. He was feeling and not compelling saying. He was feeling. He was saying. He was like what he was. He was saying.

She had another one. Having another one she was like that one like one having that other one. She had not been like that one like the one having another one. She had that other one. She was saying. She was saying and was not compelling feeling.

She went on being one and went on being the one being so like that one that feeling, that saying, that being that one and being that one she was saying, she was feeling, she was saying that she was not compelling saying, she was feeling that she was not compelling feeling. She had feeling vivid feeling she had feeling like that one. She had saying much saying all saying like that one.

She had feeling vivid feeling. She had saying, much saying.

All, and very much is all. All is what very much is and very much that is all is so decisively all that very much is so very much that it is everything and everything being all and all being all how wonderfully beautifully sweetly clearly all can be everything.

All is all. All being all and being all, always all that is all being comp[l]etely all if a little thing is a little thing and a little thing can be a little thing a little thing is so decisively expressing all that expressing is expressing that completely all is being all and always all being all all is everything.

To begin what is not begun is not to begin everything. What is all is deciding that having been expressed it is that and being that why should not that have what it has and it certainly has what it has, it naturally has what it has because it is what it is and it is everything and everything is all. It is not begun and that is not puzzling in feeling. It is not begun and that is not mentioned in loving. It is not begun and that is completely expressed in telling. It is not begun and that is why each one and there is only one is decisively adjusting all that is interesting. One, how can that one not be that one when that one being that one is that one. That one that very one, that one like that one is not enough like that one so any one not that one can remember all of that one. That one enough of that one is all compelling. That one all of that one is all there can be of remembering. That one, that one and only that one and quite that one and not translating, that one quite that one and never translating, that one always that one and not having begun and that one and that one who is that one, all, everything, why not certain that only that one that that one. Being certain is not anything. Being begun is not being begun. Being the one the decisively adjusting, the completely not translating, the not having been begun one, being the one, that one how that one how very that one is everything. All is everything.

That is the way when that way is a way that is the way that way is the way.

There can be some. There can be some quite often. There can be a great many quite often. There can be very many very often.

There can be one who having lost her husband and having four children and having a great deal of money and saving it for the children and spending it for the children can not do what children can do, there can be one who continuing living and looking as if she were being living is being living and is continuing being living.

She is in a way not an old one being quite an old one and she is in a way not an old one as she has had taken a photograph of herself her daughter and her daughter's daughter and in the picture is also her mother. There are four generations of them. She in a way being an old one is not an old one and that is not startling not at all startling she having four children and being rich and having lost her husband and having been lonesome and having been saving for her children and having been spending because she was feeling something of what she was being feeling.

She had lost her husband. She knew that. She had four children. She knew that of all four of them.

In meeting and she was always meeting what she was having in meeting she said that what she asked she would have had, having what she had and she could have all she had and she knew all she knew knowing all the children she had and knowing that she had the four.

She did feel that she had given what she had given and that having given all she had given in giving what she had given all was not what it might have been if her children could have come to be what they came to be and her husband had gone on living to die before she died so that she would be living and not dying.

That was what was and she had grand-children. She had been being living and being married and buying what she was buying and feeling in having what she was having.

Being married and having children, having all four of them and there were not any more of them, she was saying what she was saying in all of them moving to where they were moving. Some one living with them was knowing all all of them were knowing. Some one staying with them was arranging not to be telling what any one of them was not telling. They moved and having moved and having built what they built and having feeling in being living as they had feeling in being living she was having all she was having when she was giving what she was giving and continuing buying what she was continuing buying in arranging what had come to be an arranged thing.

She did do all of it and doing all of it she was married and having two of three children coming to marrying if marrying was all of something. Marrying was all of something and being married and the two children came to marry, being married was not all of something. She did say all she would say she had said.

Having what she was having and being married and there being four children she was continuing buying what, that being arranged which was arranged, she was buying. She was married. She was giving what she was giving in there being all in the house that there was in the house. She had what she was having.

She did say all she came to believe. She did come to believe all she did say. The natural way of ending being dying she did not come to believe that she would be feeling that dying was existing. In not believing everything she was having all she could be needing.

She knew that ending being existing and dying being existing those who were not dead were left and being left they felt what they felt and they said what they said.

She said that she being left felt what she felt and said what she said. She said that having what she had she knew what she knew and knowing what she knew she gave what she gave and giving what she gave she was not expecting what she was not expecting in continuing what she was continuing and continuing what she was continuing she did have what she could have in she being the one she was being and having the children all four that she was having and having lost the husband the husband who died and she had been a wife who was living.

In keeping what she was keeping she was not keeping all she was keeping as she was giving something that she was giving. She was liking what she was liking and saying what she was saying and asking everything she was asking and supplying all she was supplying.

She said and did that which in needing all she could have she would say and do. She repeated that in liking what she had been liking she had, in giving what she had been giving, been having what she had. She was not repeating in feeling. She was not repeating in dying. She was not repeating in not dying. She was repeating in giving. She was repeating in asking everything. She was repeating in being living.

In being living she was introducing something she was introducing what she was asking. In introducing what she was asking she said what she said. She said what she said and when she said what she said she left what she left when she had what she had and she gave what she gave when she left what she left.

She said that she did not leave anything and saying that she attended to what she attended. Attending to what she was attending she said all she said. She did not say that she felt anything that she was not asking. She did not say that she liked more than she liked. She said that what she saw was what was left when she gave what she gave. She said that she said what she said. She said that she had said what she said. She said what she saw and she saw what there was when she had what she had.

She was not the one who did come to have what she had. If she had come to have what she had she would have lived when she lived and she would have died when she had had what she had had. She was not the one who was all in having what she had and she did not have what she had having four children and each of them being the one of the four of them that each one was and her husband being succeeding and being living and she being living so that he was dead before she was dying, she was not the one having what she had. She was the one saying what she saw and she was seeing what she had.

She was not leaving being that one in being one continuing and she did not leave being that one because she was seeing what she had and she was saying what she saw. She was not leaving being that one.

It could be that she was that one. It could quite be that she was that one. It was that she was that one.

She said what she saw and she saw what she had and she said what she said and she had what she had.

If she saw what she had and she said what she saw she had being living and a husband and children and succeeding in not having been using in feeling that she had not died and left her husband living with the four who were being living and being living being existing. She did say that she could be using all that she could say in saying what she saw and seeing what she had. She did say that she could not be using what she did say in seeing what she had. She did say that having what she had she did not use what she would use if she saw what she had when she said what she saw.

All that there is of what there is when there is what there is is that which in the beginning and the middle and the ending is coming and going and having and expecting. All that there is of what there is is that all that is that. Four or five or six and there are six and there are five and there are four and five and six all that there are are then all there and being all there how can they not be there when they are there and they are all there when they are there, when they are all there. They are, they are there.

One and if not why not one and if one why not the one who is one. The one who is one is there when she is there.

Thanking that one is not all of everything. Not thanking that one is not all of everything. Thanking can be something.

If saying that thanking is existing is convincing then saying that thanking is existing is saying that thanking is thanking. If all the thanking is existing and if completing thanking is existing then thanking is thanking. Thanking is enough.

All of that all of thanking is all of thanking and all of thanking and thanking is thanking, all of thanking is thanking. That is quite thanking.

If she was beautiful one day she was beautiful that day because she was beautiful that day.

She was doing more than she intended and she liked it.

If she was beautiful one day she was beautiful that day because she was beautiful that day. She was beautiful any day.

If she was beautiful every day she was beautiful because of the way that she was beautiful that day. She did more than she intended and she liked it.

To begin then. She was beautiful one day. She was beautiful that day because she was beautiful that day. She was beautiful that day as that day was the day that she was beautiful that day. She did more than she intended and she liked it. She was beautiful that day.

She was beautiful that day and that day the day she was beautiful she was beautiful and being beautiful that day because that day she was beautiful she was beautiful on that day because she was beautiful that day. She was beautiful that day.

She was beautiful one day. She was beautiful that day because being beautiful that day she was beautiful that day. That day she was beautiful.

All one day she was beautiful. She was beautiful that day. That day she was beautiful and being beautiful that day that was the day that day was the day that she was beautiful and so she was beautiful that day.

One day she was beautiful. She was beautiful that day.

A day being a day and day being the day that she was being beautiful because she was beautiful that day, a day being a day and she being beautiful that day she was beautiful and being beautiful that day that was the day she was beautiful, she being beautiful that day. A day was that day the day that she being beautiful that day was beautiful that day.

Why if a day was a day and she was beautiful that day why if a day is a day and a day is a day and a day she is beautiful and she is beautiful a day why if a day was a day and she was beautiful that day why is she beautiful every day. If she is beautiful every day she is beautiful every day. She is beautiful every day and each day she is beautiful she is beautiful because that day she is beautiful and she is beautiful that day because that day she is beautiful.

That is not a reason and that is not a day, any day is a day, she is beautiful every day, there is not a day that there is not a reason that she is beautiful that day and there being days and there being reasons and she being beautiful every day every day is a day and she is beautiful that day and she is beautiful the day she is beautiful because she is beautiful that day. Any day is a day.

Having what in the beginning is all of ending is being what in being living is existing. Any one, all of them, any one is what any one liking any one not liking is liking is not liking, any one liking, any one not liking is any one not liking, is any one liking.

Any one liking is intending is not intending. Any one not liking is intending is not intending. Any one liking, any one not liking is not intending, is intending.

Any one and any one, one and one and two, and one and one and one, and one and many, and one and some, and one and any one, and any one and any one, any one and any one is one and one is one and one is some one and some one is some one, any one and one and one and one, any one is that one and that one is that one and any one and one, and one and one, any one is the one and the one who is the one is that one. The one who is the one who is that one, any one and any one is one, one is one, one is that one, and any one, any one is one and one is one, and one and one, and one and one and one and one.

WHEREIN IOWA DIFFERS
FROM KANSAS AND INDIANA

With a title suggesting a rigorously expository essay, this turns out to be a dis-associated meditation, which is a typical Steinian form.—R. K.

Otherwise seen and otherwise see and otherwise seen to see, to see otherwise.

Otherwise seen. The difference to be seen the difference and otherwise seen, the difference and otherwise seen the difference seen otherwise.

In Iowa, in there, in Iowa and in there in there and in Iowa it is noticeable the difference in there the difference in Iowa and in there.

Iowa means much.

Much much much.

For so much.

Iowa means much.

Indiana means more.

More more more.

Indiana means more. As more.

From *Useful Knowledge* (1928).

223

Kansas means most and most and most and most. Kansas means most merely.

This is the difference between those three.

Samples.

Have examples.

Add examples.

Added examples.

Every one has heard it said.

Iowa in Iowa and in Iowa no one had heard it said in Iowa.

In Indiana and in Indiana and they heard it said in Indiana.

In Iowa heard it said in Iowa.

In Indiana and heard it said.

In Kansas and in Kansas how it was heard how it was said how it was heard and said and in Kansas how was it heard as said.

And in Iowa held it.

And in Kansas hold it so as to hold it for it. In Indiana held it to hold it, hold it to hold it. In Iowa held it, in Kansas hold it, in Indiana to hold it.

Do you see what I mean.

As a question.

A question is made to state something that has not been replied to there.

Is Iowa up or down.

Is Indiana down and why.

Is Kansas up and down and where is it.

There are questions only because no one thinks of three things at one time.

Iowa plans for Iowa these are not the plans for Iowa.

Kansas and Indiana the plans for Kansas and Indiana are these.

There are the plans for Indiana.

Iowa for four more for four more and four more. Iowa for more. For more and Iowa. Changed four to for, changed for to four.

Indiana four. Indiana for.

For Kansas.

Fortunately for and as fortunately for and fortunately for Iowa. Indiana and four and leave it alone and all.

Kansas and not to leave it all alone and so forth.

Iowa and so forth.

Iowa evidences, there are evidences that Iowa, there is evidence that in Iowa or in evidence, for instance as an instance and in Iowa.

More than an instance and in evidence and in Indiana and for instance. The instance and as evidence and Indiana and evident and as Indiana and as evident.

And Kansas and as evident and as an instance and for instance and in Kansas for instance and as evident as Kansas and as evident and as an instance and as for instance and as for instance for instance as Kansas and as for instance next to it.

As next to it nearly as next to it nearly in Iowa next to it.

In Indiana for four more next to it four more next to it and Indiana and Indiana for four.

In Kansas and not next to it and so so.

Next foremost and a plan, a plan and next to it and foremost foremost and next to it and a plan and planned as planned as foremost and next to it and a plan. Consider Iowa as considerably as so.

In Indiana next to it and foremost and a plan and also and foremost and also and consider it and also and as considerably and also as Indiana and foremost and considerably and also and next to it, and next to it and also and considerably and foremost and a plan and next to it and foremost and considerably and also, and also and considerably and plan it and next to it and considerably. And Kansas and considerably and also and foremost, and foremost and considerably and also and also and Kansas and considerably and foremost and also and Kansas and a plan and Kansas and considerably and Kansas and foremost and Kansas and next to it and foremost and Kansas and considerably and foremost and Kansas and a plan and Kansas and considerably.

Iowa and not another difference, Indiana and if and not if another difference and if another difference if a difference if a difference in Kansas, if Kansas is different.

If Iowa or so if Iowa has if Iowa has had if Iowa has to have, if Iowa is to have to have, and if in Indiana and if it has to have if Indiana has to have it and if Kansas has had has to have has it, if Iowa Indiana Kansas if Kansas Iowa Indiana, if Indiana Kansas Iowa has it has it, if Iowa has it if Kansas has it if Indiana has it has to have it had it, if Iowa had it, if Kansas had to have it or what nest.

Not continued as Iowa, not continued as as continued as Iowa, as continued Iowa as continued and Indiana as continued as Indiana and as Kansas as Kansas as continued.

The next makes a meeting between Iowa, to notice, the next makes a meeting between Indiana a notice the next makes a meeting between Kansas or makes a between Kansas or makes a meeting, Indiana makes a meeting, Iowa a meeting, Iowa a meeting, makes a meeting Indiana, makes a meeting Kansas. Meeting Kansas meeting Indiana meeting Iowa, next meeting Iowa next meeting Indiana next meeting Kansas.

Next.

Meeting.

Next meeting as if they had to have parties Kansas, as if they had to have parties. Indiana and as if they had parties as if that had to have parties and Iowa has to have a part and parties.

Iowa Iowa and this to see Iowa Iowa in a little while, formally. Iowa Iowa and next and next Iowa Iowa in a minute. So much for that. Indiana as Indiana or outwardly more so Indiana for Indiana more than a half, Indiana in the meantime reflected again. As for Kansas purely as for Kansas surely as for Kansas hourly as for Kansas, as for Kansas hourly as for Kansas as for Kansas fairly as for Kansas and as for Kansas, for favourably as for Kansas for for it.

Iowa forty-four Indiana forty-four fifty, Kansas fifty-four forty and so forth.

Iowa has made it, Indiana has it and has it made it, Kansas and has it made it as it has it.

Iowa for fourteen, Iowa four fourteen, Indiana fourteen, fourteen for all, Kansas as fourteen are four more than ten exactly.

The next question has an answer.

Iowa and the next question has an answer.

Indiana has the next question and has the next answer.

Kansas question and answer.

Has the next question an answer, is the answer is this answer is this the answer to the next question.

The next question and the next answer.

The next question.

Iowa and the next question.

Indiana and the next question.

Iowa and the next question.

Indiana and the next question. Iowa and the next question or the next question or Iowa. Indiana and the next question and the next question Indiana and the next question, the next question left the next question Kansas and the next question, Indiana Iowa Kansas and the next question.

FRANCE

"France" appears to be a series of paragraphs with no apparent relation to its predecessors and successors, thus suggesting arbitrary ordering, cohering perhaps in the quality of Stein's highest prose style.—R. K.

Likely and more than evenly, unevenly and not unlikely, very much that and anyway more, this is the left over method. There is nothing left because if it were left it would be left over. This does not make music. The time to state that is in reading. There is a beginning in a lesson in smiling.

What is up is not down and what is down is not reversing and what is refused is not a section and what is silenced is not speaking. This does not make the rude ones murmur, this does not make a penny smaller, this does not make religion.

All the time there is a melodrama there is monopoly and all the time there is more there is no excuse.

A luck in breaths is more to be denied than music, much more. The only long string is that which is not twisted. All the same there is no excuse.

From *Geography and Plays* (1922).

A sight is not a shadow and a whole rise in a cry is not more piercing than danger of being mixed into an affair where there are witnesses. If writing is in little pieces and little places and a little door is open, many little doors are not open and writing is not surreptitious, it is not even obliging.

To show the difference between an occasion and merit and a button it is necessary to recognise that an honor is not forced so that there is no question of taste. To exchange a single statue for a coat of silk and a coat of wool is not necessary as there are appliances. A somber day is one when there is no pleading.

Made in haste, not made in haste, made in darkness, not made in darkness, made in a place, made in a place. The whole stretched out is not part of the whole block, the whole stretched out is so arranged that there is not stumbling but what is just as remarkable, pushing. An easy expression of being willing, of being hunting, of being so stupid that there is no question of not selling, all these things cause more discussion than a resolution and this is so astonishing when there is nothing to do and an excellent reason for an exchange, and yet the practice of it makes such an example that any day is a season.

To be sure that the trees have winter and the plants have summer and the houses painting, to be sure of this engages some attention. The time to place this in the way is not what is expected from a diner. The whole thing that shows the result is the little way that the balls and the pieces that are with them which are not birds as they are older do not measure the distance between a cover and a calendar. This which is not a question is not reverse and the question which is a question is at noon.

To question a special date is not mercenary. To answer a single servant is not obligatory. To be afraid is not nearsighted. An exclamation does not connect more grass than there is with any more trees than have branches. The special scenery which makes the blameless see and the solitary resemble a conversation is not that which resembles that memory. There is no necessity for furthering the regulation of the understanding. One special absence does not make any place empty. The dampness which is not covered by a cloth is not mingled with color. And it comes. There is no astonishment nor width.

Education, education, apprenticeship, and all the meeting of nephews and trains and changing papers and remaining when there is no chance to go there, all this occupied a whole sentence. It is a shame that there is not such an only use for that, it is a shame and there is no indignation more indignant. Everything is an indication of the simple remedy that is applied when there is no refusal and no application. Every thing which shows that is not tied with a string or any little string. All the same there is not much of a remedy.

Alarm over the action of the one who when he sees the light rise and the sun set and the stars shine and the water flow alarm is the same alarm as any alarm.

In all the same ways that pieces are separated in all these ways there are those placed things which are not pieces. They are not pieces and there is reason, there is reason in it because the whole thing shows such dissociation that all doing it for that purpose and together there can be no question but that they succeed.

A tobacco habit is one that a leaf does not enlighten and yet carelessness is so extraordinary. Supposing that the arrangement had been made and that it was agreed that no separation between any one being one and being another one could be established, supposing this were agreed and there was no conversation, would this enlighten any one, if it would why is the result so ambiguous. It is not ambiguous because the authority which does not authorise washing does supply soap. This does not make any change.

It is sensible to be around it is very sensible, it is so sensible that there is every way of stopping a selection, and then there is selection, there is a respect for resignation, there is no disturbance in a disappointment. The question is is there more urging than satisfaction, is there more distribution than renewal. This is not a question, it is a relaxing. And then the time comes for more noise. Is there then more noise. There is then reestablishment. Does that mean return of a price which is plentiful. Nobody knows. All this shows something it shows that there can be suspicion.

There is no separation in majesty. Terms, lines, sections, extra packing, nothing shows that confidence. All the same there is news. The time to stay away is in vacation. Why is there no place chosen. The answer is simple it consists in explaining that there has been given the use of all that will be used. This does not show feeling.

A curtain is not crazy, it has no way of being crazy, it has hardly a way of enraging a resemblance, it has no resurrection. Indeed the chances are that when there is seen more astonishment than anything that is placed it is very likely that the whole system will be not so much estranged as devastated and yet supposing they do not mean that, supposing they do say that it will be a success, supposing they do say does that mean that oration is contradiction, it does not.

Just a word to show a kite that clouds are higher than a thing that is smaller, just that word and no single silence is closer.

Suggest that the passage is filled with feathers, suggest that there are all together, suggest that using boxes is heavy, suggest that there is no feather, suggest all these things and what is result the result is that everything gets put away.

All the silence is adequate to a rumble and all the silliness is adequate to a procession and all the recitation is equal to the hammer and all the paving is equal to summer. All the same the detaining most is the reason that there is a pillar and mostly what is shocking is a rooster. This is not so easily said. There is no occasion for a red result.

Laugh, to laugh, all the same the tittle is inclinable. What a change from any yesterday.

A period of singular results and no gloom such a period shows such a rapid approach that there is no search in silence and yet not a sound, not any sound is searching, no sound is an occasion.

A fine fan and a fine closet and a very fine handkerchief and quite a fine article all these together shows where there has been plenty of rebuke and plenty of expectation and plenty, plentifully reduction of suspension, and so the season is the same and there is every corner.

No chance shows the rapidity of exchange, no chance and this which means one is the same as any two halves and this is not outrageous, not a bit outrageous it is simply the sign of splendor.

All the tempting and the chewing and the cloth all of it shows no sign and no symbol it does not and that is no disgrace.

If standing is an illusion is it necessary to be pressed to bend in that direction is it necessary and if it is necessary is it polite and if it is polite is it urgent and if it is not urgent is it an impulse.

No question has so much disturbance as the principal reunion. This is not so distinguished when there are no ties in the window. This is completely changed, once there were none and now there are none. There are no rebukes. A privilege is not painful. A recurrence is not artificial.

It is not separating that which satisfies no finger, it is not fading. What was it that was not wished. The reason is that the section is there and no reflection makes abundance. The only tangle is when there is abundance and there is abundance when there is pulling and piling. Does this seem to scream, it does not there is not even clustering and yet not hampering not singling everything does not make sorrow, it makes no plant grander, it does make a plant slender, it does not make it so slender that there is every size. All privilege and all practice, all suspicion and grandeur, all the timber and a little wood all this makes silver, paper is chosen and gold is cheap, does this make a little salt, it does not, it makes copper.

Little frame if it is cheaper than a big one is a different size. There is no use disputing as memory is a reminder.

Not to pay for a conversation, not to pay anything for any conversation, not to throw away paying, not to pass paying, not to pay anything this is not being a victim. What is victory, victory is that which eschewing liberation and a girdle and gratitude and resignation and a choice display and more flavor shows a strange reluctance to have a maritime connection. This is victory.

A license, what is a license, what is a license.

An angry coat, a very angry coat shines.

Butter is not frozen, this does not mean that there is no bravery and no mistake. This does show a conclusion.

Difference is no excuse, grain is no excuse, even the remains of a pear is an excuse and yet is there graciousness, there is if there is generosity. There is so much fruit. This is kindly a mistake. No misunderstanding is insurmountable.

Cage no lion, not to cage a lion is not dirty, it is not even merciless, it is not malodorous, it is not virtue.

To surround a giraffe, what does that mean. To surround a mixture, that means something.

Solid, what is solid, is more solid than everything, it is not doubtful because there is no necessity.

Haughtiness, there is haughtiness when there is no tape and no billiard rooms and no need to be secured from wet. There is certainly some selected obstacles.

The certainty of a change in the parts that speak, this uncertainty does not show as it does not fashion speech. All union is in the widow and all menace is in the band.

Any way to bend the hat is the way to encourage vice. Virtue all virtue is resolved and some and any hat, every hat is identical. A shadow a white shadow is a mountain.

Kindness what is kindness, kindness is the necessity of preserving of really preserving all the parts of speech and teaching, not music so much as trimming and a costume, and sincerely most sincerely shoving regions together.

Notice a room, in noticing a room what is there to notice, the first thing to notice is the room and the windows and the door and the table and the place where there are divisions and the center of the room and the rest of the people. All this is necessary and then there is finance.

Heavy where heaviness is and no mistake plentifully, heavy where the breeze is and no darkness plentifully, heavy where there is a voice and a noise and singling out a company, heavy where there is a sale of accents and raisins and possibly more ways of not being heavy. Certainly there is no peril and yet think, think often, is daintiness and a collar heavy is it and what is the disturbance, is there not more registration.

So there is not coming anything. There certainly is no single space useful and betrothed and vulgar and not pretty. There is a sign in placing nothing. This changes from day to day any day. Surely no change is a blessing. All the search is in violation and yet a single search is a single search willing. It is cautious. There is riot.

The likelihood of dipping and drawing and digesting and drinking and dirtying not dirtying smoking, the likelihood of all this makes such an order that every discussion is simultaneous. A large increase in beer, any large increase is here, some large increase is clear, no large increase is dear. A lily a very lily lily is accurate and described and surrounded and so venturesome that there is risk and writing, there is even inlaying.

Darkness, there is no darkness in extremity and in mixing and in originating scattering religion. There is no darkness in designing.

A group a single group proceeding show the necessity of the distribution of the same organization as there is if there is, assuming that there is, if there is reorganization.

Flower, flower and water and even more even a gram of grain and a single little blister, very likely the chance is not perfect and the exquisite arrangement has lace, very likely there are no stains and more likely there are ruffles. In all of this there is no use in practicing medicine. Quinine any quinine is useful and more there is more, there can be more, there is an apartment.

A sign of saving consists in spending the late morning in the morning and in urging in certainly not urging a calculation. A sign of saving is so simple if there is enough handed about, and surely no pains in piling are more shown than when everything is in dishes. This does not happen in an asylum, it does not even happen in the hay and in the double shapes that shelter cooking.

A top a tiny little top that sits and spits and shows the courage calmly, this this is so soon an exasperation and a piece of lightning, it is so ordinarily just that occasion, it is so kindly dispiriting, it is so haughty if there is pushing. There is pushing, this is what makes it repetition.

A long, what is a log to do when it floats, it is to do nothing as it floats but certainly it would be best that it should adjust that to itself certainly. This alone does not make an explanation.

A degree of resorts and a shining wave all this together does not make a regulation and it does not make that irregular, it sustains mischief and an order and it even enforces the likelihood of the season and some color. So sustained is a paragraph that a sentence shows no staring and some noise. This is so simple in the size that is medium and is medium sized sentinel. There is no kilometer. That does not make a sample.

Keep the place that is not open, close the place that has one door, shut the place that has a cellar, suffer where all suffer more, argue, and shelter the understanding orphan, and silence that is silence is not sufficient there must even be sleep.

Puzzle is more than a speck and a soiled collar. A pound is more than oat meal and a new institution. A silence is no more than occasional. It respects understanding and salt and even a rope. It respect a newsstand and it also it very also respects desert. All the ice can descend together.

Was there freedom, was there enchaining, was there even a height rising from higher. If there was what is a coat worth and by whom was it made when.

A lining any lining is a trimming. More trimming is extra.

A sort of arranging, a kindling of paying a shilling, does that mean another extravagance and more candles, no more candles. It does not show.

A famous single candle has a chance to shine so that glaring meant that no more would be reversed by lightning. The safe lamp and the bright lamp and the dirty lamp and the long lamp were all not the lamps that were attending baptism. Why is the baptism patient, baptism is patient in the first place because there is no coarse cloth, in the second place because when there is nothing taken enough is left to give every reason. A practice which engaged more attention than the rest was that which shaved a tame stopper and did not even end that. Supposing crossing a street is necessary, supposing it is, does that show more of such occasion. It does and it does.

A lime is in labor, a lemon is cooler, a citron is larger, a currant is redder, a strawberry is more vexed, a banana is straighter.

A little thing is a little thing, a single point is bigger, a bigger thing is a bigger thing, an older thing is older, an older thing is an older thing, a station is a station, a station is a station and a station is a thing and stationary only that is a stationary thing.

A blind being blind and deaf and deaf being deaf and blind and blind and deaf and a coat with a cape and more use in all than in any shape all this makes a reason for criticising the use of machinery and paper and even a pen and even a stamp and even more flags than ever.

In the pin in the picking of a pin, in sewing a little feather and avoiding deserting a pin, in retaining the feather and arranging to rank the pin as a pin and to hold it there where if it is seen it is found and if it is found it is seen, to not mark a pin and select a pin all this is a reason for using that way of waiting.

A standard blessed is a standard that is blue if it is blue and blue and white when it is blue and white. Supposing there is no money, supposing there is no dress and no skirt, supposing there is no window and no bed, supposing there is no more distribution and not any more violence, supposing there is not even arithmetic and intelligence, supposing there is a light and round hole, does that mean that there is no success suggested. It does not. A little bit of choice makes a color regular. A little bit of black makes dinner necessary.

If there is a shape a real shape prettily, if there is and there is no wonder does it happen all the time, if it does not is there a certainty that there is collusion. These interesting questions crowd the house, they crowd, they do not crowd everywhere. They crowd separately.

All there is of more chances is in a book, all there is of any more chances is in a list, all there is of chances is in an address, all there is is what is the best place not to remain sitting and suggesting that there is no title for relieving rising.

An excursion, what is an excursion, an excursion is a picnic if it is recurrent, it is a picnic if there is no absence, it is a picnic and not necessarily, it is a picnic.

Black horses, very black horses are not peculiar, very large horses are not peculiar, very splendid horses are not peculiar, horses are peculiar regularly and with an awake resemblance to the best the very best description and regret. The kindness of this is mentioned and very often quite often the same rebuke is outrageous.

Not allowed, not only allowed to eat, to ache, to resemble, to project, to make a motion, to study preaching, to stumble on anything, to stretch audibly.

Not allowed a prize or a couch or even what is not necessary a searching, not allowed more formerly, not allowed more entirely, not allowed a dispensary.

It is a custom, it is a custom when it is not undue, when it is not undue, when it is not. It is a custom. It is a custom when it is more due, when it is, when it is an angle, it is not a custom, it is a custom altogether.

In cross and across, in that show and wide there is the sensory statement that there is night rule and a winter rule and even the chamber is empty and watches why are watches lighted.

What a day to pay to stay, what a day. When the work is done too soon and there is a crossing of hands and even of heads entirely when there is and when the rest is so awake, is there any slept out sleeping, there is not gradually, there is more chance than there would be in a colored collection. There is more chance certainly.

What is the resolution between a cutlet and an ingredient. It is mentioned and made in paper and floating.

What is the example of a miner. A single example is in the best of cups and also in the rest of the places and also in the show that is there.

After a mixed cloud is there any use in a trimming, there is, there is. There is a trimming behind in. There in no use. There is the case.

Calm, a calm, that calm, along the calm. This which is in the ell is so much are so. When and when and when is there. When the rail is the passage to. Through and so and much orderly.

Beginning to twining and sudden girls what is mended in a street, what is a rut in finnish. What is it in a market.

A considerable engagement, a considerable engagement.

Excuse the point that makes a division between the right and left that which is in the middle in between. Surprise an engagement, surprise it so that an agreement is all the time.

This is a way, this is a trout, this is the succession.

To linger in the pale way and not to show spots to be greener to do this means that all the references are what they are.

A pedal a pedal is that which when examined is made and this is no mistake in regularity it is a splendid thing.

Covering in and covering, covering with inside covering. Covering a lion with the same shape as the bear and yet what is the best measure for a tiger, what is the measure steadily.

A half safe wife and a whole safe wife and a half safe wife and a half safe wife.

A bet and sugar and a bet and within, a bet and within and a bet in within.

Cut a slice to show a pear, cut a slice to show a row, cut a slice and there is visiting. An angel is in the exchange.

Suppose that there is a cost, suppose that there is a beggar, suppose that there is a powder and a powder suppose there is a real gold mine.

A curly fate and a household fact and a gloom too soon, and a couple of necessary pockets.

Explain, explain why there is a shell fish and an oyster.

A pleasant little spot to have gold. The same spot is used for silver. The gold is the best way to keep it. The silver is the way to keep silver.

A cloud of white and a chorus of all bright birds and a sweet a very sweet cherry and a thick miss, a thick and a dark and a clean clerk, a whole succession of mantle pieces.

Conceal a nose and climb, counsel a name and shudder, believe a glass and relate, cool a pound and put in that.

Wednesday is a day and a closed begging is reasonable, reasonable, is reasonable, reasonable is reasonable.

Piston and clothes, consider the wet sack, coal hack, hack a piece of gum.

WHEREIN THE SOUTH
DIFFERS FROM THE NORTH

Did she answer the proposition posed by her title? The literary steps are nonetheless rich.—R. K.

An agreement in it.
    As the north.
    As the north in agreement with it.
    Are they ready yet.
    Not yet.
    In the north in agreement with it.
    North in agreement with it.
    North is a name all the same.
    North in agreement with it.
    And the north in agreement with it.
    As the South in an agreement with it.
    And an agreement with the South.
    South is not a name.
    And the same.

From *Useful Knowledge* (1928).

The south is not a name.

And in the same way the south is not in agreement. An in agreement. An agreement. And an agreement. As an agreement. The South is not in agreement with it.

Not as useful it is not as useful.

Used to used to, used to the same used to it and used to the same. Used to it used to the same. To see the same. Used to see the same. Used to the same.

North used to the same. The north used to see the same.

The north used to see the same, the north used to see the same the north used to used to see the same.

The north used to see the same.

Or the south. The south or the south or the south did did the south ordinarily the south ordinarily did do did it usefully. It did it usefully. The south ordinarily did it usefully.

As fat as that.

In this way.

North has north what has north thought about it.

And in this way.

What has the north and what has the north what has the north finished. What has that made what has made that, what is made and what is it that it has made. It has made the fact that in this way not only is there an interruption and no interruption recedes not only has there been no interruption but as to being careful, carefully now.

And so forth.

It is perfectly useless to entertain.

So much so much so much.

It is why to change, it is why it is necessary to change. It is in change.

Numbers do it.

North and south negroes.

No one means that.

South and north settle.

No one means that.

No one means that south and north settle, South and north settle no one means that.

Furthermore.

What would it do, how would it do, would it do as it is.

It is a very extraordinary phenomena, that it has always been a habit to remark that seasons have ceased to exist and in this way it is the intention to express that seasons have lost their identity.

Not at all in this way.

A pleasure.

Baby pearls.

S for south and n for north s and n for south and north.

No not kneeling.

It is certainly a conclusion which has been come to that there is no reason why if in the midst of the two in their midst, if in their midst if in their midst, collectively. As many.

North water, south water, south water, north water. No difference.

All at once as soon, all at once so soon all at once and all at once and all at once and soon. To say so soon. Can ask.

They can ask which way they can go. They can ask and they can ask if they can ask.

An interruption and in between.

As an interruption can it be different.

As an interruption can it be differently.

And as an interruption.

North as an interruption.

The north as an interruption. It did not interrupt.

As in interruption. The North was not interrupted. North was not interrupted. Uninterrupted. Not interrupted. Uninterrupted. As uninterrupted as the south. As uninterrupted as North is uninterrupted as South is uninterrupted as north and south and as uninterrupted. Nobody shares pears.

The second time.

Too busy to say so.

First along.

Dislike choosing.

Second along.
Going to choose.
First choice.
North.
Second choice.
South.
Third choice[.]
South.
Fourth choice.
North.
First choice.
North.
Second choice.
South.
Third choice.
South.
Fourth choice.
North.
Fourth choice and first choice.
North.
Third choice and second choice.
South.
Second choice.
South.
Third choice.
South.
Fourth choice.
North.
First choice.
North.
First choice.
North.
First choice.
North.
First choice.

North.

First choice and fourth choice.

North.

Third choice and second choice.

South.

Third choice and second choice.

Fourth choice and first choice.

First choice and fourth choice and second choice and third choice.

South and north.

Next.

South and north.

To dislike sending.

To dislike sending it.

To dislike sending it there.

Where.

Partly north.

Partly north and partly north.

Not partly south.

Partly north and not partly south.

No more capital. Capitals are so worth while.

North what north. What north. What north and which North. Which is north. Which is north. Where is north.

Where is the north. North of it.

North of it. The north a north, it is north it is north of the south it is as south of the north it is as south it is as south of the north. It is as south of the north as that.

When it is anticipated, when they are anticipated, when they anticipate what is to happen as if it were to be arranged and more often indeed made responsible for it, if it is equally and gradually if they are gradually persuaded that they need not and they have to be they have not to be refused then in that case there is no need for opposition.

Candidly say so. And so forth.

More than opinion. More than that opinion. And more than that as that opinion. To say so.

Refusing and under and under refusing and refusing and under refusing have it and have it so and to have it so.

One and two, sound as around as around as round as the well and as very well. Very well sir.

The North shall be satisfied and the South also.

All the elements of an introduction and now to proceed to debate. A debate does mean that as antedate and as rebate and as restate and as rightfully as they can.

The first martyr.

Martyrology as understood.

How suddenly they succeed one another and as suddenly.

As at first a martyr.

As at first a martyr all the time.

As at first a martyr.

The martyr.

Martyrology understood and carefully annotated as observed and not withdrawn from.

May we if we please.

Not as north as as south.

Not as north.

Now north.

Acceptably.

Cunningly say so.

They cunningly said so.

As nice and so forth.

They led them to it.

They led them away from it.

As nice and so forth.

As the north.

As nice and so forth.

Believe them and so forth.

And believe them and and believe them.

If when and more nearly fairly well nearly very well, very well nearly accustomed to coming as they had formerly energetically countenanced exchanging, exchanging bundles for bundles. Not at all. Not exchanging bundles for bundles. Why not at all. Why not at all why not at all because if new since is more nearly replaced not every day but methods, supposing for instance that there are preparations, preparations enough.

Think it is right, and necessary. Think it is necessary. They think it is necessary as that.

What do you think.

What do you think what do you think when each one has a name. Do you think that it indicates the place a place.

Place it.

Do they think do they think in case of. North. Go north. South. As south.

Do they think do they think in case of it. In case of it do they think. Prepare to astonish everybody.

Make it more north than south do make it more north than south to make it more north than south, make it north and make it south. Up or down, down or up, as up or up, up or down or up. Europe.

Not covered up as much or much, not covered or as much or much. Much covered up, much covered or much covered up. Is it much covered up.

North and south needlessly.

North and south considerably and for this, this makes it.

North. This makes it north as much as south. This makes it south as much as north. A struggle to say so. Say so. As say so. Could it be a custom to select fish because they are flatter than they were. Could it be a custom. Could they become accustomed to it. As much as that.

Not north.

Not the north.

Not too north.

Not easily south.

Not ordered south.

South and North mentioned the south and north mentioned.

North did you say.

And north did you say.

In that direction.

North did you say.

As north did you say.

As in that direction.

As you say.

When it is more nearly come again when is it more nearly and come again and south as south as that. Suppose you were used to it, suppose you meant by that something else, supposing in that specialty supposing as that reminded by it, reminded by it and reminded and not as she shuts it, shuts it, not as she shuts it. As she shuts it and reminded, remind her of it, to remind her that it is as that it is as particularly, it is particularly wanted, and remind to remind can remind how do you remind them that once in a while very much as that is. See there. It was changeable. See there it was changeable.

If at a time and a time is more if in time and in time to hear, if in the rest particularly scared, scared of it, afraid to say so, all the time any time and plentifully, currents plentifully, chances plenty of chances, extensively.

This breaks up a union.

Remember to get up. To remember and to remember and get up. Get up.

How many countries can you count.

Count count count.

How many countries can you have counted.

How many countries have you counted in this count.

How many countries have you counted.

North by north.

Counted.

Lost it up lost it as up, lost it up, happily lost it as up and lost it as up. You don't say so.

Lost it up. Lost it as up. And happily lost it as up. Lost it up.

Lost it as up.
That is done.
One run. Say so.
One run that is done say so.
Say so that is done one run that is done.
Not not hot.
Not not as what.
Not and not.
Not as hot.
Not as what.
Not.
North.
South.
Plenty of time.
North and south as we say plenty of time.
Not north for nothing.
Not for nothing.
Not north and not for nothing.
Not north and not for nothing. North not for nothing.
For nothing.
South for nothing.
Not South.
Not for the South and not for nothing.
Next.
Not next.
Not next to north.
Not annexed.
Not next to it.
And not next to it.
Next to it.
North and south for nothing.
Not deceived by the moon, not deceived and at noon not deceived very soon not deceived just as soon not deceived and not deceived any more.

Not deceived any more about the sun and Sunday she was not deceived any more about the sun and Sunday.

Not deceived any more she was not deceived any more in the north. Not deceived any more as to the north and as to the south not deceived any more as to the South and not deceived any more as to the south.

She was not deceived any more in the north she was not deceived any more as to the south.

Any more as to the South.

In the middle of attention.

Any more as to the north.

In the middle of inattention.

Any more as to the north.

Any more as to the north.

In the middle as an attention.

Any more as to the north.

In the middle as in attention.

Any more as to the north.

In the middle of an intention.

Any more as to the north.

And any more as to the north.

Settled is it.

Is it settled.

Settled is it.

In attention as to the south.

Settled is it.

In attention as to the north.

It is settled is.

In attention as to the south.

In attention in intention.

It is settled.

As to the south.

Come again come again.

Up.

Come again come again down.

Not so easily.

Come again come again up.

As come again up.

Feeling an attraction the or center center of course.

To please furnish to please and furnish to please and to furnish, to please and to furnish and to furnish please.

North and south nestles.

North and south nestles north and south.

South and north nestles south and north.

South and north nestles.

South and north nestles south and north. And north and south and south and north and not in as much. Nestles.

If it was meant that all the same when it was it came back again.

Another instance.

He would and he would and he would and he would.

Around it.

Not around it.

If if if we, if if if they, if if if he if if if he if we if we if he anyway, if he. So much so.

Plenty of violence.

Made of papers made of papers it is made of papers to be made of papers it is to be made of papers. It is to be made of paper. It is to be made of papers.

If if anyway. It is anyway. If it is anyway.

Was he big or was he.

He was large.

In there in the meantime.

A chance to notice.

Now a new way.

If in the meantime if and in the way and as they say, said.

In union there is strength.

Right and left.

No.

Left and right.
No.
Left and right.
No.
Right and left.
No.
Oh no.
Right and left.
Left and right.
No.
No.
Left and right.
Right and left.
No not right and left, no not left and right.
No not right and left.
Not left and right.
Left and right.
No.
Right and left.
No.
Not left and right.
Not right and left.
Other changes.
North as is best.
South as is best.
Not as is best.
North not as is best.
South not as is best.
Rid of it.
To be rid of it.
To be rid of it and not south.
To be rid of it.

To be rid of it and not so south. To be rid of it and not as south as to be rid of it as to be rid of it and not as south and not to be rid of it.

Many additions. There are as many additions to it as there were. Coming in as before.

Are they coming as they were before. Yes and no and they say so, can say so and can say so.

Yes and no.

Instantly.

For instance.

A little observation as to the impression made upon one by observing the difference in the light and heat made by artificial light and the sun, also the difference made by the impression as to how it all had happened. And was he as satisfied, and was he, as he was satisfied. A little observation of the difference made by all the difference experienced as nearly as can be exactly. Not to be exactly careful. This can be taught.

Once more.

Restitution.

Bargains bear up bear up bargains, bargains and it is bargains. To bargain into the bargain.

Not only but also the explorer should be able to know how to and also to recognise the spots he has seen before and which he will recognise again as he occupies as he successively occupies as he occupies successively the places he recognises and not only that he occupies them successively but also that he will later be able to make maps of the region which he has traversed. Such is the duty of an explorer. In short it depends upon him in short he is to realise that he is to acquire knowledge of the directions of the direction of a direction of previous visits and successive visits. It becomes necessary therefor that he indulges in active plans and map drawing and also in constant observation and relative comparisons. In this way he easily finds his way.

Where is it is it there there it is. North there it is and there it is once more and yet and again, once more to resist attacking a new fashion of remodeling and so much more.

As so much more. Fancy it, fancy that a nuisance fancy that it is a nuisance. That it is a nuisance to consider that up and north and up and doing and up and south and up and doing and across and all of it. Expectantly shining, as is easier than that and not always fairly presentable. An entirely new type of ship and an entirely new type of ship and an entirely new type of ship.

Choose it. Choose it as carefully as the north choose it as carefully as the south choose it as carefully or the north choose it as carefully or the south or the south or the north or choose it as carefully.

Share and share, if a share of it if a share of it is there there where in the meantime all day long as it is. Joined immediately. It was joined immediately it was joined to it immediately.

When there is more or or less when there is more or less in the meantime when there is more or less when there is more or less in the meantime. In the meantime when there is more or less.

The north manages it very well, as the south manages it very well as the south manages it very well as the north manages it very well.

Ninety-two, as well as ninety-two.

Ready and ready enough and very ready and readily, readily stated stated intervals intervals come.

Come some, some come, come come, come some some some come. Intervals stated stated intervals, readily stated stated intervals and very readily, stated intervals as some come at stated intervals. Plant and planted. In the north planted and plant it in the south plant it and planted. In the north planted and plant it in the south plant it and planted. In the north in the south in the north planted in the south plant it in the south planted in the north plant it, plant it planted in the north planted in the south plant it in the north plant it in the north plant it. In the south planted, in the south planted, in the south planted in the south planted, in the south plant it in the north planted. Planted in the north. Next to it usually. Usually next to it. In the south usually next to it in the north usually next to it, in the the north usually in the south usually in the south usually in the north usually next to it in the south usually next to it in the north usually next to it in the south usually next to it, in the south usually next to it in the north usually next to it.

Does it was it was it does it does it go was it gone was it does it does it have was it far was it does it does it come was it for it was it was it for it does it do it does it does it do it was it for it was it for it does it do it.

Was it as far was it as far as that, was it was it as far as that and was it.

To to be too to be to be north to be north to be north to be south to be south to be north to be to be south to be it is to be north it is to be it is to be south it is to be south and north it is to be north and south. It is to be.

The rush south was over as the rush south was over. The rush north was over or the rush north was over. Over and over. As the rush north was over as the rush south was over the rush north and the rush south were over.

Plenty of instances are needed to explain that if in the interests of telling in the interest of telling this is told there are plenty of instances of this being told to explain that in the interests that in those interests in the interest it is in their interest it is to the interest of the north that it is told it is because it is to the best interests of the south that it is told it is told to explain the best interests that there are interests that there is interest in the north that there is this interest in the south that there is interest for the south that there is interest that there is enough interest to interest the north and that there is enough to interest the south just enough to interest and enough explanation of the interest and of the south and enough explanation of the north and enough interest. There enough interest.

North and south expected, north and south it is expected, north and south expected, expected, north and south, expected. Expect, what to expect. Expected what is it that is expected. North and south expected, what is expected north and south expect, expect north and south. To expect north and south, to expect, expected, expected north and south, expect north and south expect. Expect north and south.

Next time.

Expect north and south next time. Next time expected north and south. Expected north and south next time.

What is seen in between in between as the north in between what is seen what is seen in between. What is it what is seen in between what is it. What is it what is seen in between. What is seen in between the south what is seen, what is it what is seen in between. In between has the reason, flowers please as much as gloves, gloves do not please any more. Gloves please flowers please if you please. As much as gloves if you please. Not any more if you please. Please as please. What is it. And so as it is nearly as much of an advantage as ever.

North north it, it is not an advantage as it were. South south by it it is not an advantage as it were. As if it were, as if it were as an assembly.

Mainly able meanly able to mainly able to put through mainly able to go through mainly able to go through to the north mainly able to go through to mainly able also to go through to the south and to the north. Mainly able to.

Stretches and stretches if it stretches as it stretches as stretches. Stretches and stretches.

Mainly able to as it stretches toward the south mainly able to and it stretches to the north. As it stretches mainly able to go through to the south as south. Mainly able to. As many as are able to as much as there is to do.

As much as there is to do just as much as there is to do, to do just as much as there is to do, to do, just as much, to do just as much, to do, just as much, as there is, to do just as much as there is, to do, just as much, as there is, to do, to do, just, to do just as much, to do just as much as there is, to do just as much as there is to do.

Have it as we have it. An authority, formerly and favourable as favourable as that.

Two makes two two makes two too, two makes too as for instance. Two makes too, nicely. Two makes too, two and two and nicely. Two makes too nicely.

It happened again as it happened again as it happened again and sustained too as it happened again and it was sustained too as it happened again. As it happened again, when, as it happened again and was sustained too. Fairly speaking. Find it up find it up, find it up and find it up. All up. Find it all up, find it all up and find it up. Up as up, upper as upper, find it up, finding if finding find and upper makes a difference, it does not matter very much. Very much a difference upper finding up, finding out, if it makes very much difference if it makes a difference and more so in the case as constituted. It is very likely to be very well arranged. Very well arranged.

In plenty of time there can be, in plenty of time they can be there in plenty of time, they can be there they can be there in plenty of time. They can be there in plenty of time and not as well as they all know it. As well as they all know it and there is no effort in it. There is no effort for it and as well as they all know it. And as well as they all know it and there is no effort in it. There is an effort for it and as well as they all know it. And as well as they all know it and there is an effort for it. There is an effort for it and as well as they all know it.

As well as they all know it would if it could would if it could be avoided would it if it could be avoided would it be if it could be avoided. And north. North of it. Would it if it could be avoided would it south of it. Would it north of it. Would it south of it. Would it if it could be avoided north of it. Would it if it could be avoided south of it.

Would it if it could be avoided south of it in the meantime.

Would it if it could be avoided in the meantime north of it.

Would it if it could be avoided in the meantime north of it.

Would it north of it in the meantime would it if it could be avoided in the meantime would it in the meantime north of it would it in the meantime if it could be avoided south of it. In the meantime.

Plenty of plants there are plenty of plants planted here and there those plants. There are plenty of those plants planted. North here and there. South here and there. Planted here and there. Come to Mary, a name. North a name come to Mary. North. Come to Mary. South. A name. Here and there. Come to Mary. South. A name. Come to Mary. South here and there a name. Come to Mary here and there a name. North here and there a name. North, Mary here and there a name. Here and there a name south, Mary here and there a name. Here and there a name Mary, north, here and there a name. Here and there a name Mary. Here and there a name. Here and there a name Mary a name. Here and there a name North a name. Here and there Mary a name. Here and there Mary a name South a name. Here and there a name North a name. Here and there a name south a name. Here and there a name.

AMERICANS

"Americans" contrasts with "France" in more ways than can be noted here.—R. K.

Eating and paper.

A laugh in a loop is not dinner. There is so much to pray.

A slight price is a potatoe. A slimness is in length and even in strength.

A capable extravagance that is that which shows no provision is that which when necessity is mild shows a certain distribution of anger. This is no sign of sin.

Five, five are more wonderful than a million. Five million, five million, five million, five are more wonderful than two together. Two together, two together.

A song, if a sad song is in unison and is sung, a sad song is singing. A sign of singing.

A gap what is a gap when there is not any meaning in a slice with a hole in it. What is the exchange between the whole and no more witnesses.

From *Geography and Plays* (1922).

Press juice from a button, press it carelessly, press it with care, press it in a storm. A storm is so waiting and awful and moreover so much the worse for being where there is a storm that the use the whole use of more realization comes out of a narrow bridge and water faucets. This is no plain evidence of disaster. The point of it is that there is a strange straw being in any strange ice-cream.

A legal pencil a really legal pencil is incredible, it fastens the whole strong iron wire calender.

An inherent investigation, does that mean murder or does it only mean a railroad track with plenty of cinders.

Words that cumber nothing and call exceptionally tall people from very far away are those that have the same center as those used by them frequently.

Bale, bale is a thing that surrounding largely means hay, no hay has any more food than it needs to weigh that way henceforward and not more that most likely.

A soap, a whole soap, any piece of a whole soap, more whole soap and not mistily, all this is no outrage and no blessing. A precious thing is an oily thing. In that there is no sugar and silence.

A reason is that a curly house an ordinary curly house is exactly that, it is exactly more than that, it is so exactly no more than more than that.

Waiter, when is a waiter passive and expressed, a waiter is so when there is no more selection and really no more buckets altogether. This is what remains. It does. It is kindly exacted, it is pleased, it is anxious, it is even worthy when a material is like it. It is.

What is a hinge. A hinge is a location. What is a hinge necessarily.

When the butter cup is limited and there are radishes, when radishes are clean and a whole school, a real school is outrageous and more incensed, really more incensed and inclined, when the single satisfaction is so perfect and the pearl is so demure when all this is changed then there is no rattle there is hardly any rattle.

A and B and also nothing of the same direction is the best personal division there is between any laughing. The climate, the whole thing is surrounded, it is not pressed, it is not a vessel, it is not all there is of joining, it is a real anxious needful and it is so seldom circular, so more so than any article in the wire. The cluster is just the same ordinarily.

Supposing a movement is segregated and there is a piece of staging, suppose there is and the present is melted does that mean that any salt is bitter, would it change an investigation suddenly, when it would would it mean a long wide and not particular eddy. Would it and if it did would there be a change. A kind of exercise is hardest and the best excellence is sweet.

Finding a best hat with a hearty hat pin in mid-summer is a reason for being blindly. A smell is not in earth.

A wonder to chew and to eat and to mind and to set into the very tiny glass that is tall. This is that when there is a tenement. All weights are scales.

No put in a closet, no skirt in a closet, no lily, no lily not a lime lily. A solving and learned, awake and highing and a throat and a throat and a short set color, a short set color and a collar and a color. A last degree in the kink in a glove the rest.

A letter to press, a letter to press is not rowdy, it is not sliding, it is not a measure of the increasing swindling of elastic and breaking.

The thread, the thread, the thread is the language of yesterday, it is the resolution of today, it is no pain.

What is pain, pain is so changing the climate and the best ever that it is a time, it is really only a time, it is so winding. It is even.

A warm banana is warm naturally and this makes an ingredient in a mixture which has banana in it.

Cooling in the chasing void, cooling more than milder.

Hold that ho, that is hold the hold.

Pow word, a pow word is organic and sectional and an old man's company.

Win, win, a little bit chickeny, wet, wet, a long last hollow chucking jam, gather, a last butter in a cheese, a lasting surrounding action.

White green, a white green. A looking like that is a most connected piece of example of what it is where there is no choking, no choking in any sign.

Pin in and pin in and point clear and point where.

Breakfast, breakfast is the arrangement that beggars corn, that shows the habit of fishes, that powders aches and stumblings, and any useful thing. The way to say it is to say it.

No counting, no counting in not cousins, no counting for that example and that number of thirty and thirteen and thirty six and thirty.

A blind hobble which makes distress. A place not to put in a foot, a place so called and in close color, a place best and more shape and really a thought.

Cousin why is there no cousin, because it is an article to be preparatory.

Was it green told, was it a pill, was it chased awake, will it sale per, peas are fish, chicken, cold ups, nail poppers, nail pack in hers extra. Look past per. Look past per. Look past per. Look past fer. Look past fer. Look past fer.

No end in yours, knock puzzler palers, no beast in papers, no bird.

Icer cream, ice her steam, ice her icer ice sea excellent, excel gone in front excel sent.

Leaves of wet perfect sharpen setters, leaves of wet purr feet shape for seal weight for shirters.

Leaves of wet for ear pole ache sold hers, ears for sake heat purse change to meeters, change to be a sunk leave to see wet hers, but to why in that peace so not. Knot lot.

Please bell room please bell room fasten a character fasten a care in apter buttons fasten a care in such, in such. Fasten a care in, in in a in.

A lovely life in the center makes a mine in found a lovely pond in the water makes it just a space. A lovely seat in a day lump makes a set to collapse, a lovely light in a grass field makes it see just the early day in when there is a sight of please please please.

Due tie due to die due show the never less more way less. Do, weigh the more do way less.

Let us call a boat, let us call a boat.

Leave little grace to be. Leave little grace to bea, live little grace to bee.

Leave little grace. Leave little.

Leave little grace to be.

Near red reserve leave lavender acre bat.

Shout us, shout horse curve less.

Least bee, least bay alter, alter the sat pan and left all, rest in, resafe in article so fur.

A cannon ball a cigar and a dress in suits, a cannon ball a cigar and a dress suit case, a cannon ball a cigar and a dress suit case, a head a hand a little above, a shake in my and mines.

Let us leaves, moor itch. Bars touch.

Nap old in town inch chair, nap on in term on chain, do deal sack file in for, do bale send on and for, reset the pan old in for same and chew get that all baste for, nice nor call churches, meet by and boot send for in, last when with and by that which for with all do sign call, meet with like shall what shirs not by bought lest, not by bought lest in own see certain, in own so same excellent, excellent hairy, hairy, excellent not excellent not knot excellent, excellent knot.

B r, brute says. A hole, a hole is a true, a true, a true.

Little paper and dolls, little paper and row why, little paper and a thin opera extra.

No use to age mother, no whole wide able recent mouth parcel, no relief farther, no relief in loosens no relief abler, no relief, no relief pie pepper nights, no relief poor no relief or, no relief, or no relief.

America a merica, a merica the go leading s the go leading s cans, cans be forgot and nigh nigh is a niecer a niecer to bit, a niecer to bit.

It was a peach, it was a long suit, it was heavy harsh singes.

Leave crack his leave crack his eats, all guest all guest a stove. Like bit.

Nuts, when and if the bloom is on next and really really really, it is a team, it is a left and all it cut, it is a so like that between and a shun a shun with a believer, a believer in the extra, extra not, extra a rechange for it more. No sir.

No it sir.

It was a tame in, it was a tame in and a a little vent made a whole simmer simmer a wish.

What is it not to say reach house. Coal mill. Coal mill well. It to lease house. Coal mill tell. Coal in meal tell.

A pill shape with a round center.

Color Cook color him with ready bbs and neat show pole glass and nearly be seen every day more see what all a pearly little not shut, no rail see her.

No peter no rot.

Poles poles are seeds and near the change the change pets are swimming swimming and a plate all a plate is reed pour for the grammar grammar of lake.

Lake in a sad old chimney last and needs needs needs needs needs needs needs, in the mutton and the meat there is a change to pork walk, with a walk mean clean and butter and does it show the feather bench does it mean the actual and not or does it light the cylinder. It is in choice and chosen, it is in choice and knee and knee and knee and just the same two bay.

To irregulate to irregulate gums.

America key america key.

It is too nestle by the pin grove shirr, all agree to the counting ate ate pall. Paul is better.

Vest in restraint in repute.

Shown land in constate.

I am sorry I am awfully sorry, I am so sorry, I am so sorry.

No fry shall it see c bough it.

Nibbling bit, nibbling bit, may the land in awe for.

It is not a particular lamp lights which absolutely so far pull sizes and near by in the change with it not in the behoof.

It was a singe, it was a scene in the in, it was a singe in.

Never sink, never sink sinker, never sink sinker sunk, sink sink sinker sink.

A cattle sheep.

By the white white white white, by the white white white white white white, by the white white white white by the white by the white white white white.

Needless in pins.

In the fence in the for instance, in the fence or how, hold chirp, hold chirp her, hold your paper, hope hop in hit it.

Extra successive.

Little beats of long saturday tileing.

No neck leg ticking.

Peel more such wake next stir day.

Peel heaps pork seldom.

Coiled or red bench.

A soled in a light is not waver. There is for much ash so.

In the second, in the second second second.

Pour were whose has. Pole sack sirs.

A neat not necklace neglect.

A neat not neglect. A neat.

A neat not neglect.

Put a sun in sunday. Sunday.

AMERICAN BIOGRAPHY
AND WHY WASTE IT

Do you see any connection between yes and yesterday, I will repeat this, do you see any connection between yes and yesterday.

There is a way of recording an arbitrary collision but in inventing barbed wire and in inventing puzzles there is no arbitrary collision. Not at all.

They murmured about excess not about excess not about exceeding their limit. They murmured about success. Be brief.

I found a way of saying arrange for many more. And then they went away.

Second to none and have you been interfered with, I ask you again have you ever been interfered with either in there or where. Where have you been interfered with and where have you been when you have been interfered with there.

Now understand.

In the future, in the past because there has been really a previous occasion, in the future and then why does it matter. Why does it matter particularly.

_____

From *Useful Knowledge* (1928).

Now tell us about their principles. The principal thing is that contracts why do contracts come along. Why do they.

Why do they include all brushes. All brushes are alright.

When you have seen the result of reflection reflection does result in this when you have seen the result of reflection reflection does result in this.

And narrowly in cream.

Satisfy the spectacle.

I satisfy all the places. In place of this place me.

Once more we come to inventions.

Did he say he wished me to relieve rolls.

What was it he said about reminding. I never remind them.

Can you think and listen can you think and listen can you think and listen.

Can you think of them and listen to me.

This is why we stay in their way.

What did the first one say. They say they are endowed with memory circumstance occasion and reconstruction. Can you call it reconstruction to add, to begin or to acquit.

Can you.

He smiled and I smiled. Then there is coercion, cohesion and administration, then there are authentic dispatches, then there is recognition. I recognise him, he recognises me, they recognise us, and when we hear them say what are your branches, I wonder if they mean stems.

The introducers are highly educated.

Not wishing to begin.

One little Indian two little Indian three little Indian boys, four little five little six little seven little eight little Indian boys. To an American an Indian means a red skin not an inhabitant of the east or west Indies or of India.

When we are astounded astonished concerned received or intimidated we do not recount roses.

Roses grow and rhododendrons and woods and woods, the poor man's overcoat.

Woods the poor man's overcoat and I'll say so.

Now then begin again, begin with Adam the Adams and then pour easily pour out. Do you easily pour out. Do you easily pour out about their cold, this was told. This was what they hold to be the return of the collection.

Let me see.

To begin with what did he say. What did he say.

To begin with what they remember.

They remembered that very much and they were nickled and embroidered. To be nickeled, how do you reveal how do you dare to presume everything.

Goodness knows.

I can feel that.

They were met by themselves, and suggestions, how easily they parody suggestions, how easily they parry suggestions.

Cover me they care for me. They care, they do care.

They and they do care.

I do not freely recollect speaking.

When they were there when they were in there he said he he said of them he did not say this to them, he said to them come and be able to remember everything. He remembers why they fasten trees to trees. In our country they do not fasten trees to trees.

What do you do. We commence to supplant, we supplant fruit and oranges, and how often do you prune, a great many make verbs. This will surprise you.

This will surprise you.

I remember that some one said that one should arrange for a longer term, twenty-five years roll around so quickly.

Now what is the difference between age and ages.

What is the difference and why do you marry.

What do you exchange for directions. He directs me to come and to go. He directs me to go and to come.

Did you hear what she said, they are going to have summer time in April in New York city and Chicago.

You were pleased not to hear them. I was very pleased not to hear them.

I did not hear them at all.

And now I wish to tell exactly how I have been impressed, I have been very well impressed. For instance memory and then discussion, analysis and then barter, and did you feel that when they went further they adventured. To me it really does not seem so. And to them it does not seem so. They were not at all elevated to this degree.

They said that they would say so and they said nothing at all about it they did not carry this there in their favour. Indeed one might say that they were blameless. They were more readily not altered. An altar is made by the rest of their stay. All stay. They stay anyway.

And now to attribute. I attribute this to this. To what do you attribute this.

There is no flattery in this.

Do you remember how often we had cake. Do you remember how often we had butter. Do you remember how often we had what we needed. Do you remember how often we thought about it and how often a great many people circled.

We know about blame and circles and now we know about considerably added currents. The currents that come come there. Where. Where did you say.

Call me louder.

Do you remember how you affected her. And when did you state this.

When did you state this.

And now be able to state what I find to relate.

Distributed.

We can praise that verb. We distribute all of the same letters to make the letters. A great many say what letters.

Do a great many say what letters.

It is a reminder. Call it a reminder. Let me glory in messages.

Let me.

Now then they do not press hurriedly. And this is not asser-
tion. Not at all. Not at all. Not that at all.

He arouses him.

Not that way.

He arouses the land you mean that he does not only use that
he does not abuse. Do I mean religion, do I mean men women and
their children. Do I mean that there is a third.

Do you mean what you have heard. Do you mean. What do you
mean.

And now then as to appetite. We have a very good appetite.

Almost any one can think faster than another man can talk, I
wonder if that was so yesterday.

I gently feel. You do not mean that you feel gentle, I gently feel
of it. That before this.

And now we know we are rescinded.

The cannon of Australia makes a noise and we say and they
say we are telling how we found our country to be the land of liberty of which we sing. The cannon of the Indian makes that noise
and they do not say that they know the difference between that
and everything. Everything else is opposed to that. I see why they
do not like noise and make a noise. I know. The reason is this
when they went they were still and still when they were there they
were there, where there, and they knew they heard that, they hear
that they hear that, they do not hear that they have come there,
this they do not hear there, they do not listen to hear, nor do they
hear by ear, listen and you do not hear, but they they were there
and they met to declare, what, the air, to the air and by the air.
Here here is not there. Everywhere is not there nor is it here nor
there. I declare and they declare. And the air. We do not recognise an heir.

So there.

Responsibilities are all there, and they are not to be followed by
prayer there, they are to be followed by the songs as sung. Responsibilities are not to be followed there, they ought not to be followed

there by prayer but they ought to be followed by the songs as sung, they ought not to be flung there they ought not to be followed by prayer there.

I know the result I know that result. A responsibility followed by another is plenty good enough.

I do not think that all of this is very unpleasant and not very affable. Do you not feel that way about it. I do come to think of it. I do come to think of it and there are three men and one man. We know that together three men and one man make four men. We know this of them and knowing this we can mean that there is one man and that there are three men and together the three men and the one man together there are four men and when they say we have a remarkable opportunity they mean by this an imagination just as has the president.

He knows everything but the third, third what, but the third congratulation. Do not mention it by yesterday. Do not measure by chairs. You know how they sign. They sign by chairs. And how are hours changed. Hours are changed by settling this and they say we knew when we came. And they say the same. In this way we weigh the same. Do you remember me for this. I do not want to be persistent. I do not want to have the blame. We can claim that we do nothing for fame.

We can claim we do claim we shall claim shall you claim what we claim. No. I told you so.

Now then to liberate adequate.

A responsibility will be followed by another.

Thank you.

Recall, do you recall this at all. They made and they made it they made it all, they made it and they made it for them and they made all of it for them they made all that was made.

What was it that was said. How does he say it. Who are you to say how does he say it and why and why does he say it, because he had it. No one caresses you. Do you hear. No one caresses you.

Now to finance lumps.

We do not know about clouds and lumps. We do not know where to go. He said I will tell you this to move you.

And now not the same.

I said I would not measure for them, I would not measure more than that for them. I said I would not measure more for them than that.

Soldiers. How do you mean soldiers.

Come to think of pillows. He does not know the meaning of harassed and yet they are all there.

They said, we do not see that this is of any use. He said, I came and I was born there. And they said, we are born to surprise. And he said. Do they surprise beside. And they all say that they have all preserved their cinches. Now listen to this. Inches. Now again, all are not elbowed again.

We say they are not heavier than they say.

Not heavier than that, they say.

In Spain there is no rain.

When this you see remember me.

There is no rain in Spain.

When this you see remember me.

Do not repeat this as formerly.

In learning in learning to feed, we feed the same number and with what, I ask you and with what.

We feed the same number and we feed them here.

I have endangered no one more than that. They have endangered no one more than that. And they have said it successively and do they frolic about.

Words do.

Do they frolic about.

What do they frolic about.

This brings me to another collision. I feel you are sincere.

How many heads are there ahead.

How many are there ahead.

How many are there at the head.

I would like a photograph of that said Captain Dyer.

What he saw of them made him see that.

Now then tell me why can you at your discretion tell them that you can tell them apart.

Now what do you mean by this.

I can deliver crowns, you mean those that kings wore. We never mention that as rain. I can deliver them from there.

I can deliver these from them. You are not here again and again. Nor for mounting.

Recall having sent articles.

I know exactly how to receive their weight.

Do you read.

Thank all who thank me.

Other races.

I do and you do too you do conceal clouds. Clouds shine and you shine. All of it, do, do all of it. Do do all of it.

There is not going to be much more of that.

A biography.

Eugene George Herald was refused because of his accentuation. We do not accentuate, we increase in regard to measure sound and sections. In this way we are united to stand.

LEND A HAND
OR FOUR RELIGIONS

Look up and not down look right and not left look forward and
not back and lend a hand.
We lend you lend they lend he lends they lend you lend we lend he
lends.
And then they tell to-day they tell it to-day they tell it to-day and
yesterday and to-morrow.

First religion	My sister
Second religion	My sister and her sister
Third religion	My sister or my sister
Fourth religion	Your sister.

First religion advances and then sees some one she advances and
then she sees some one.

Second religion   Second religion they advance and they
see some one, they advance and they see some one as they advance.

Third religion   She advances and she sees some one,
she see some one or she advances.

Fourth religion   As she advances she sees some one.
Some one is seen by her as she advances.

Fourth religion   As she advances.

From *Useful Knowledge* (1928).

Fourth religion | As she advances she is led.
Third religion | As she advances or as she advances
or is she led.
Second religion | As they advance they are led.
First religion | Is she led.
First religion | As she advances is she led.
First religion | Is she led as she advances.
That is the name of a house isn't it.
And a well.
First religion as she advances. Furnish a house as well.
Second religion as they advance. They furnish a house as well.
Third religion as she has advanced. Has she furnished a house as well or has she furnished a house as well as she has furnished a house.
Fourth religion as she is advancing and she will furnish a house as well.
Fourth religion | Very well to advance to see some one then and to furnish a house as well.
Third religion, third religion to advance and to see some one or to furnish a house as well or to advance and furnish a house as well or to see some one or furnish a house as well.
Second religion | They advance and as they advance they see some one and they furnish a house as well.
As well furnish a house. They might furnish a house as well.
First religion | She might furnish a house as well she might see some one and furnish a house as well, she might advance and she might see some one as she advanced and she might furnish a house as well.
First religion | First religion attaches it first religion attaches it.
Second religion | They attach it, they attach it to that and which ever water, kneeling, in a kneeling posture.
Third religion | She attaches it or in that way kneeling in a way in that way, in that way kneeling and being a chinese Christian meditatively. And there where there is water flowing there

274

where she attaches it she attaches to it or she attaches it to it there where the water is flowing or kneeling there or beside it in a way of kneeling.

Fourth religion   Does fatigue make a sensitive alliance and reliance. She attaches it and as she attaches she is kneeling there and she is kneeling there where she is kneeling in a box there where the water is flowing there where she attaches it there. Where she attaches there where she is where she is as she is kneeling there in a box and the water is flowing there beside the water where it is flowing there she attaches it there.

Fourth religion   I am not losing it too.

Third religion   I am not losing it too or I am not losing it too or I am not losing it.

Second religion   They are not losing it they are not losing it too. They are not and they are not losing it too.

First religion   She is not losing it too.

First religion   They will furnish a house as well. As she advances she see some one and she kneeling in a box beside the water where it is flowing and she will furnish a house as well is she losing as being kneeling beside the water where it is flowing in being a christian will she furnish a house as well. In losing it as she is advancing and she sees some one as she is advancing will she furnish a house as well.

Second religion   Will they furnish a house as well. In being kneeling beside the water where it is flowing will they furnish a house as well. In advancing and seeing some one as they are advancing and in kneeling beside the water where the water is flowing will they love will they love it they are kneeling beside the water where it is flowing and will they furnish a house as well.

Third religion   Will she furnish a house as well or will she be kneeling beside the water where the water is flowing or will she be advancing and as she is advancing will she see some one or will she furnish a house as well. Will she furnish a house as well or will she be furnishing a house as well.

Fourth religion   Will she be kneeling beside the water where the water is flowing and will she be losing it and will she furnish a house as well and will she see some one as she is advancing and will she be a christian and will she furnish a house as well. Will she be kneeling beside the water. Will she advance and will she furnish the house as well. Will she be kneeling there where the water is flowing. She attaches to it this, she attaches to it.
Fourth religion   The sky is blue.
The hills are green.
She is green too.
And her eyes are blue.
She attaches something. As she advances she sees some one.
She kneels beside the water there where the water is flowing. She is a chinese christian. She is losing it. Does she furnish a house as well.
Fourth religion   Does she furnish a house as well.
Fourth religion   Are grasses grown and does she observe that the others remove them. Are grasses grown four times yearly. Does she see the grasses that are grown four times yearly. Does she very nearly remove them. Does she remove them and do they very nearly grow four times yearly. Does she as she sees some one does she advance and does she very nearly remove the green grasses that grow nearly four times yearly. In this country they do.
Third religion   Does she very nearly or does she see the green grasses grow four times yearly. Does she remove them or does she know that they do grow four times yearly. Does she see some one as she advances or does she kneel there where the water is flowing or does she furnish a house as well. Does she nearly remove them.
Second religion   Do they see the grasses grow four times yearly and do they remove them and do they advance and see some one and do they touch it and do they lose it and do they see them grow almost four times yearly nearly four times nearly.
First religion   Does she almost see the grasses grow four times yearly does she see the green grasses grow four

times yearly and is she nearly kneeling beside the water where the water is flowing. Does she touch it and does she remove it and does she see the green grasses grow nearly four times yearly. Does she see some one as she advances and does she kneel by the water is she kneeling by the water where the water is flowing. I do not think so. She is feeling that the green grasses grow nearly four times yearly.

First religion   She is feeling that the grasses grow four times yearly and does she furnish a house as well. Let her think of a stable man and a stable can be a place where they care for the Italians every day. And a mission of kneeling there where the water is flowing kneeling, a chinese christian, and let her think of a stable man and wandering and a repetition of counting. Count to ten. He did. He did not. Count to ten. And did she gather the food as well. Did she gather the food as well. Did she separate the green grasses from one another. They grow four times yearly. Did she see some one as she was advancing and did she remove what she had and did she lose what she touched and did she touch it and the water there where she was kneeling where it was flowing. And are stables a place where they care for them as well.

Second religion   Did they think of stables as well and did they see the grasses grow four times yearly and did they kneel by the water where the water was flowing and did they as they advanced did they see some one and did they touch it and did they lose it and did they furnish a house as well.

Third religion   Did she think a stable was for a stableman or for the caring for Italians or did she see some one as she was advancing or did she kneel beside the water where the water was flowing or did she see grasses grow four times yearly.

Fourth religion   Did she see the stables and did she know that stables are used to take care of Italians and did she know that green grasses grow four times yearly and did she kneel by the water there where the water was flowing and did she kneel there a chinese christian and did she see some one as she advanced and did she touch it and did she lose it and did she furnish a house as well.

Fourth religion   Did he count, count ten. If you count count ten, do you count with your lips moving. If she counts, counts ten does she count with her lips moving. If she kneels and if she kneels does she kneel by the water there where the water is flowing and does she see the green grasses grow four times yearly. Does she count ten and does she count ten with her lips moving. And does she as she advances does she see some one and does she know that a stable is a place to care for Italians. And does she count ten and as she counts ten are her lips moving.

Third religion   As she counts ten or as she counts ten, as she counts ten are her lips moving. If she counts ten does she count ten and are her lips moving. Are her lips moving as she counts ten. On Thursday actors and actresses are arriving. As she counts ten are her lips moving or is it Thursday and are actors and actresses arriving.

Second religion   As they count ten are their lips moving. Do they as they count do they have to have their lips moving. On Thursday do they have to have actors and actresses arriving and do they nearly see green grass growing four times yearly and do they kneel there where the water is flowing. As they count are their lips moving, do they count ten and when they count do their lips move are there lips moving.

First religion   On Thursday when Thursday comes and actors and actresses are coming when she counts ten does she move her lips while she is counting. When she is moving her lips is she counting and does she count ten and does she very nearly kneel there where the water is flowing and does she furnish a house as well and as she advances does she see some one and does she nearly see the green grass growing four times yearly and does she know that a stable is a place where Italians are taken care of and does she choose and refuse and lose and does she nearly see her lips moving as she counts ten and does she nearly believe that she can clearly count to ten. Does she count to ten when her lips are moving. Does she know that a stable is to take care of Italians and does she furnish a house as well.

Very well.

First religion   Not even hardly. When there was a settled plan and sleep.

She sleeps, she keeps, she keeps she sleeps.

Not even hardly.

I plan to satisfy their blessing.

In this way she can say that they were not in her way, in her way she does say that they are not in her way in their way she can say they were there in their way. Explain it to me.

They understood everything.

She needed that and this and in there. Did she say that they were expected to-day.

Second religion   Did they say that they had expected to stay that they had expected to come to-day.

Third religion   Did she or did she not stay. Did she say that they were expected to-day or did she say that she keeps them there or are they coming to stay. Or are they coming to stay.

Fourth religion   She keeps them and they share what they have with what they have. She stays there and did she say that she had been in the way. It sweetens volume to stay. Do you understand how they feel how Italians feel how chinese Christians a stableman, grasses, houses and water actors and actresses and men who are men then how how do they feel when they see separate volumes. Separate volumes.

Fourth religion   I pass I surpass she passes she surpasses, she passes and passes and she surpasses the folded roses. They fold roses and she surpasses them. She surpasses them in this way. And this is the way to fold roses. She says this is their way of folding. And she does kneel there. Where. Where does she kneel. Where did she kneel. When did she kneel and why did she pass and surpass pass and surpass them.

Second religion   Mix it, in mixing them you can always say one three four two. In mixing them and surpassing them they can always say one three four two one three four two one three four two. And can they fold their roses too.

Third religion   If she folded roses or if she folded roses for them, if she folded roses for them did she pass them or did she pass them and fold roses for them or did she surpass them in folding roses for them. Did she or did she not surpass them.

First religion   Melons melons what did she say choosing melons is the difficulty. And did she pass them, did she surpass did she surpass them in this way. Do not choose them in this way, choose them and use them choose them and stay and put folded roses away in this way.

First religion   Did they gather their excellent father. Did they gather their excellent mother. Did they gather. Did they gather that their excellent mother did they gather that their excellent father, did they gather. Did she gather. Did she gather that she did gather and did she gather this from them, did she gather this from her did she gather this. Who says this. Who said that. Did she gather that.

Second religion   Did they gather that their excellent father went to the winning of their excellent mother and to the winning of one another and to widening of every other one. Did they gather that they saw that in this way there where there was a plan to succeed when and where there was sawing. We hear it.

Third religion   Did she or did they, did they or did she gather that their excellent that their excellent mother were father and mother or did she hear that the sawing was there where they were sent unaware. They were sent there or were they sent there. Were they sent where they went and did they go or did they go where the sawing was meant to be done without sun. We know that the sawing is done in the sun or without the sun when the sun has been seen or has been seen.

Fourth religion   And did she know and did she go and did she know that they gather that they can gather an excellent father and an excellent mother and she needs to know that the fourth also says so.

Fourth religion   Merely whether it is their celebration that makes their pleasure so prepared. She is prepared. When is she prepared. She prepared them for this. The fourth says so, and we say it is the third.

The third religion   If the third, we criticise the third, if the third and the third is prepared or if she is prepared and the celebration is prepared. If the third is prepared or if the celebration is prepared, to please her.

Second religion   If they are prepared, have they shared the preparation of their celebration. Glasses share, they prepare to keep an orange tree protected out there. Not glasses nor glass. Nor glass nor glasses. She passes in and out and she leaves no roses about.

First religion   We prepared what she had to say. I was not indifferent, nor was she indifferent nor was she more indifferent. We must state this to be here. She prepares the celebration, she prepares the celebration. She prepares the glass to protect the orange trees as they pass. The orange trees pass. The orange trees do not pass us.

First religion   First religion can be added. First religion the first religion can be added it can be added to the one and that one and it can be added.

Second religion   The second religion can be added. They can be added. In this instance they can be added.

Third religion   The third religion or is it added to the third religion or is the third religion. If the third religion is added then she adds it. She has added it.

Fourth religion   She is adding to the fourth religion. She is adding to the fourth religion. She is adding this and to the fourth religion. The fourth religion is added to this. The fourth Religion.

Fourth religion   Meadows for men and more meadows then. We know how they lie and where they lie. The meadows lie in between.

Third religion   Meadows are seen to lie in between and she or what was it in case it was there. Four of them, there were three of them. In three of them there was one in each of the three of them.

Second religion Does she remember the scene and there with the glare of the sun shut out there is no need indeed there is no need we know how the sides are made. They are made indeed they are made.

First religion By no means by their means by her means she saw seven of them lean. They lean as if they were inclosed and we refused them. Not ardently. Remember that the meadows are there.

First religion First for a religion. At first for a religion. They were for a religion. She was the first for the religion.

First religion At first she had always thought she had always fought for the religion and she was kneeling there where the water was flowing and she was a chinese christian and she could furnish a house as well and the meadows were for men and the orange trees pass and are inclosed with glass.

Second religion They were second to religion they were to second and they were to second all the second religion was the same as the first. They were kneeling there where the water was flowing and they were seeing green grasses growing four times yearly and they can gather an excellent father and an excellent mother and they surpass and they pass.

Third religion The third of the third or the third, the third was at first the third and then the third was there or was she kneeling there where the water was flowing and did she furnish a house as well. Indeed as well.

Fourth religion Did she furnish a house as well as a fourth religion as a fourth religion as a fourth religion did she know that stables are made and stablemen to take care of Italians and did she know that meadows are made for men and did she know and did she say so did she know the fourth religion.

Fourth religion The shepherds spend the summer in the mountains and the winter in the plains in this way they and the sheep are cool in summer and warm in winter and what do their families do. They do not always accompany them. She was the one who said how do you do, I forgive you everything and there is nothing to forgive. She was the one who said, how do you do I forgive you everything and there is nothing to forgive.

Third religion   They carried their happiness there and they meant to meet with the shepherds and their sheep. How do you bleat. Shepherds have animals too. They advance before the sheep and they carry the baskets and in this way they act as leaders. Who can lead them.

Second religion   Question the question is who can prefer them. Can they use a drum can they use a fair can they use a road and can they use it or have they measured or have they forgotten that they or they or they that they can convince them.

First religion   She saw me and she said two will stay and two will go away, two will go away and two will stay and two will stay and two will go away. Can you go away so soon.

First religion   First religion here.

Second religion   Second religion here.

Third religion   Third religion here.

Fourth religion   Fourth religion here.

Fourth religion   Fourth religion being here and having her and she having been and she is perfection.

Third religion   Third religion being here or is she perfection third religion is here and she is perfection. Third religion or is she perfection.

Second religion   Second religion and they are here and they are perfection and they are here and perfection.

First religion   She is here and perfection.

First religion   In the way in her way in her way in that way in that way in my way in my way in her way in her way in our way in our way in her way she can say and she can say, she can say I spend it and intend it. She can say that sheep give way when they do not stray. They do not stray, they do not stray at all.

Second religion   In their way they are there to stay in their way not in their way no not in their way not at all in their way and not at all in the way not at all in the way. They have an intention and we hear it now they have an intention and they hear it now, they have an intention. In the midst in the midst we know what sun is. This is their hope and there are leaves to cover and caress. So there are.

Third religion   In her way who mentions Saturday, or in her way who mentions Monday or in her way who mentions that they are in her way or in her way, away in a way, and in any way she bows to please. Does it please or does it betray that abundance is on the way.

Fourth religion   I mean that she can mean that she can mean to stay. That she can mean to stay.

More religion

Fourth religion   More religion fourth religion. More religion or third religion. More religion and second religion. More religion first religion.

First religion   I feel that here I feel that here they seem to lie and grow and feel and are tall and dark and large and delicate and there they are full and soft and rich and delicate. I feel that here they are full and rich and tall and there they are not small they are large and full and rich and tall and delicate.

I describe. You describe. What do you describe. What do I describe.

Second religion   I feel that the difference is this. There the colour is of a splendour and rich and full and delicate and here it is high and strong and rich and delicate.

Third religion   Here it is delicate and there it is delicate.

Fourth religion   I describe it as different there than it is here. Here it is rich and full and large and delicate there it is full and rich and warm and delicate.

Fourth religion   If she can gather together and then settle whether the land is found how do you find land readily. She did. How do you find land readily.

Third religion   If she can be found and she can gather it together and she can find land readily is it land that is to be found. Land is found and sold by the pound. Land is found and sold by the pound.

Second religion   Or if they can gather it together and can find it readily is it land that they have found. Where is land. Land is at hand. When they gather it together they can sell it readily.

First religion   If she gathered it altogether and found that the land was entirely gathered together would she be bound to gather it together entirely and would it be land. Would it be that land.

First religion   Very well.

Second religion   Very very well.

Third religion   Very well very well.

Fourth religion   Very well.

Fourth religion   If she had returned if she had re-turned would she advance and as she advanced would she have seen some one.

Third religion   If she had returned if she had re-turned and if she had then advanced would she have seen some one as she advanced[.]

Second religion   If they were returned and they then advanced would they see some one as they advanced.

First religion   When she returned and when she advanced would she see some one as she advanced.

First religion   If she is a stone breaker and has a rope attached to a mountain she would not be a wife for Michael. If she had a rope attached to the mountain she would be a stone breaker and would she see some one as she advanced and would the green grass grow four times yearly. If she had a rope attached to the mountain a stone breaker uses her arms from the elbows and it looks mechanical and she furnishes a house as well. She does not use the rope which is attached to the mountain. That is used by those who roll the stones down to her. She does not kneel there where the water is running.

Second religion   If they had been the ones having the rope attached to the mountain they would be the ones who did stone breaking and they would be kneeling there where the water is flowing and where the green grasses grow four times yearly and they would furnish the house as well.

Third religion   There where the rope is attached to the mountain or as she was repeating, is she kneeling there where the water is flowing or as she was saying is there any grass growing four times yearly or does she furnish a house as well.

Fourth religion   The rope attached to the mountain is for the benefit of those who roll the rocks down the mountain and the umbrella and the mechanical motion is hers who is breaking the rocks open and she is observing that the grass is growing nearly four times yearly. She can establish this very well.

Fourth religion   She would not wonder if this were not thunder it should not thunder and she would not wonder. She would not wonder if this were not thunder. And what would they see if the sheep did not come to be seen where it was dry and where it was green.

Second religion   They would not wonder if there was no thunder they would know that if wool is wet it weighs more than when it is dry.

Third religion   If she needed to amend what she said if she needed to mend thread if she needed more than she said she needed, if she needed more than she said she needed, why does she kneel there where she said she was kneeling, why does she prepare to prepare what they need for feeding. In this way this can stay and I can take it away in this way.

First religion   If she should hear and wonder would she wonder if she heard and there was thunder. If there was thunder would she wonder. She would.

First religion   Not round all around but orange and brown and smaller than the second the third and the fourth.

Second religion   Not round all around but yellow
and redder and not round altogether but larger than the first and
not so large as the third and the fourth.

The third   More round all around but not
round altogether or rather not round all around and more orange than yellow and larger than the first or than any of the two
others.

Fourth religion   Quite round all around not quite
round all around not larger than the second and more yellow.

Fourth religion   They have it there and warmer and
if at night it is warmer in the day time it is warmer. They have it
there it is warmer.

Third religion   They have it there and it is warmer.
If it is warmer in the day time and they have it there they have it
there and it is warmer.

The second   They have it there. They have it
there because it is warmer there.

First religion   They have it there and it is warmer
there and it is warmer there in the daytime and it is warmer there.
In the night time it is warm there.

First religion   Can you refuse me can you confuse
me can you amuse me can you use me. She said can you. Sweet neat
complete tender mender defend her joy alloy and then say that.

Second religion   Can you not confuse this while and
that. Can you not refuse this length and that. Can you not amuse
this height and that. Can you mention sweet neat complete. Tender
mender defender, joy alloy and toy, and more of this.

Third religion   If you did refuse or if you did confuse if you did confuse or if you did refuse and if you mentioned
neat sweet complete joy toy alloy, tender mender defender, if you
did or if you did scatter them why do you not stay.

Fourth religion   If you did not refuse and confuse
and use, if you did not mention sweet neat complete tender
mender defender, joy alloy if you did not what would you do instead.

Fourth religion   Very nearly a present and I thank
you.

Third religion   Very nearly at present.

Third religion   Very nearly for a present and I
thank you.

Second religion   Very nearly and a present and I
thank you.

They thank me.

First religion   Very nearly a present and I thank
you.

First religion   Indirectly and directly directly and
indirectly and do oblige do not oblige them to lead, we know that
flocks of sheep can go ahead and to be mentioned. In this way
roads smile and roads smile every mile and they advance and pray.
Pray here. She can suggest there and there.

Second religion   They can suggest there and there.
They have been and they have been here and they say flocks can
pray and roads can smile and they can stay and smile and pray and
they can say that as they advance they see some one.

Third religion   As she advances she sees some one.
She sees here and there. She hears here and she hears there and she
can say or does she hesitate in any way that flocks can lead the way
and pray and that roads can all that while in that way come to go
that way and they may. She can advance and as she advances she can
see some one.

Fourth religion   Can she can she betray her care that
she can care to lead and she cannot lead and pray because flocks
can lead and can pray and they can see the roads in that way and
the roads can stay.

Fourth religion   If she did advance and if she did see
some one as she advanced and if she said that there were stablemen
there do we hear of stables every where. Is there a stable there and
are there chinese christians not to stare but to kneel in prayer there
where the water is flowing and there where if she were standing and

mechanically moving and a rope was tied to a mountain would she know that the flock was leading and that the flock was leading here was leading them to be here and there. Would she come and would she see the flock as well.

Third religion   If she or the flock were seen to be surrounding the road which was not what was to be told. They surrounded the road. Indeed she can believe it to be she can believe it to be surrounded there.

Second religion   They were mentioned as fairly small and they were mentioned as fairly small. And they were there where they knew that they stood and could they see that they were there and that was the day when they were there and they could they furnish the house as well when they were well and they were very well.

First religion   First religion who knows how to say what can be said when questions are asked and flocks have lead and flocks have lead and ropes have been tied and roads have been wide and been surrounded beside. Thank you.

First religion   I thank you.
Second religion   We thank you.
Third religion   I can thank you.
Fourth religion   I do thank you.
Fourth religion   Thank you.
Fourth religion   She can believe and receive and believe she can receive and she goes where she goes and do they believe and receive they believe and receive they receive and they go where they go.

Third religion   Does she believe does she receive does she go, do they go does she go do they receive does she receive does she believe do they believe do they believe and receive.

Second religion   Do they believe and receive and do they go. Do they go and do they believe and do they receive.
First religion   Does she go.
First religion   No and not yes.
Second religion   Yes and not no.

Third religion   Yes and not no and no and not yes.
Fourth religion   No and not yes.
Fourth religion   No and not no and not yes.
Fourth religion   The fourth religion is the religion
of which we have spoken.
Third religion   The third religion is the religion of
which we have spoken.
The second religion   Is that religion is it the religion of
which we have spoken.
The first religion   Is it the religion of which we have
spoken.
First religion   She has spoken.
Second religion   They have spoken.
Third religion   She spoke.
Fourth religion   She has spoken.
Fourth religion   I can see the sea.
Third religion   I can see that sea.
Second religion   I can see to the sea.
First religion   I see the sea.
First religion   And she should see to it.
Second religion   And they should see to it and she
should see to it.
Third religion   She should see to it.
Fourth religion   She sees to it.
Fourth religion   A fifth only of the bananas were
shown.
Fourth religion   If he surprised if he was surprised
if a fifth only of the bananas were shown, if all the bananas were
grown if she was surprised if they were surprised and in their surprise are they wise.
Third religion   If they are wise, if all the bananas
are grown if a fifth of the bananas are shown are they surprised,
were they surprised.

Second religion   If only a fifth of the bananas were shown, if it were known that all the bananas were grown, if they were surprised if she was surprised, is she wise if all the bananas are grown.

First religion   If all the bananas are grown. If a fifth of the bananas are shown. If they are wise. If she feels surprise if a fifth of all the bananas are shown.

First religion   They look and see and so they know that they do not share in their attention. And why does she show that she does share in their attention.

Second religion   And why do they share in their attention and why do they show that they know that they share in their attention. They share in their attention.

Third religion   And why does she share in their attention. Why does she show that she knows that she shares in attention. Shares in their attention. Share in attention. Why does she show that she does that she knows that she shares the attention so that she does know that she does share in their attention.

Fourth religion   She could know that she could share in their attention.

Fourth religion   If they stop it if they say they have received it indeed they have received it and they have stopped they have stopped it indeed they have received it they find that they need to receive it. Indeed they do. Compare what there is to say with where they stay. Compare. I find that they are kneeling there where the water is flowing.

Third religion   If she is to receive and to stop if indeed she is to stop it if indeed she is to receive if indeed can she need it can she receive it, need she stop it, can she furnish a house as well.

Second religion   Can she find that she is kind can she receive it can she need it can she stop, can they need it can they stop it can they receive and and can they need it.

First religion   Does she see the grass grown four times yearly can she receive it can she stop can she need it can she receive can she need it can she receive it.

First religion   I can appoint I can point out this way.

Second religion   She can point out that way she can appoint the delay.

Third religion   Can they appoint, can I say can they point in this way.

Fourth religion   She can be disappointed at their delay and she can point this way in this way.

Fourth religion   Can you prepare the house so that she can furnish the house as well.

Third religion   Can you prepare the earth so that the grass can grow nearly four times yearly.

Second religion   Is the water flowing so that they kneel there where the water is flowing.

First religion   Can she prepare the way so that one fifth of the bananas are shown when all the bananas are grown.

First religion   She can be cherished.

First religion   She can prepare in that way.

First religion   How can the first be the first. And the second be the second. And the third be the third. And the fourth be the fourth. How can the fourth be the fourth.

Fourth religion   She made them stay.

Third religion   She came in this way.

Second religion   They came and they were there where there was place for them.

First religion   She came in the same way.

First religion   At first they came to stay. At first they care when they go away. At first they stare and in this way they stay. At first they go away.

At first she can go away. At first she can go away or she can be sent away. At first she can be sent in this way. At first she can stay. At first what may she do at first. At first what can she do.

What they can do she can do.

She can do what they do. What do they do.

How do you do.

Second religion   What can they say. What can be said the second day. And how can you say a second and not stay. How can you how can they second them in that way. Secondly they stay. Secondly they do know when they stay.

Secondly they go away. If they go away and stay do they stay away. Every second of the day.

Third religion   The third makes one third, one third and she may stay. One third and if she may begin in that way she can go or she may even be sent away.

One third stay. Indeed one third do stay. Or do they stay. Or do they stay away. Or do they stay. Or does she stay. Or is she sent away. Or is she away. Or is she to stay.

Fourth religion   Four and no more. Did you say four. Did she say four. Are there more. If she stays and a fourth more. Two fourths more. She will stay, she will not leave she will say she will stay.

Fourth religion   More and more every day.

Third religion   In this way.

Second religion   Because they may.

First religion   She easily may.

First religion   She may not easily stay. If she does go away will she take with her where will she take her with her.

Second religion   If they stay if they go away will they go away there where we remember to have seen that there were no difficulties.

Third religion   If she does not or if she does not go away, or if she goes away or if she comes to stay, I do not think so. I do not think so. Or I do not think so.

Fourth religion   If she does go away, yes, if she does go away, yes if she does go away, if she does stay if she stays yes if she does stay.

Fourth religion   To send, to pretend to offend, to descend and to descend, to contend, to defend, to mend, to descend to defend to contend to tend, to attend, yes I will say so.

Third religion   To receive and to believe, to believe and to deceive to establish and to blemish to arrange and not to change and please how can she come to please and how can she not come and how can she not please, how can she especially please very especially please.

Second religion   Can they rejoice, who can rejoice, have they the choice, who can choose, can they exchange, who can exchange, can they prepare with whom can they share what they prepare.

First religion   She has brought it here, she has brought it to bear on that, she has brought it there and she has brought to bear there on that. She has brought it to bear on this. She has brought it here she has brought it here to bear on this.

First religion   Now I call out, call out and she calls out and I hear and she calls out and she hears what is said. Now I call out and I hear what is said. Now she calls out and I hear what is said.

Second religion   If in walking they hear what is said if they hear what is said and if they are walking when they hear what is said they said no they said we are not prepared they are not to prepare for it. They are not ready to prepare. They prepare it. They say prepare it.

Third religion   If either of them or if either one of them, if she sees to it that she walks and prepares, that she prepares and that she cares, that she cares and prepares if she sees to it that she cares, if she sees to it that she prepares that it is prepared if she sees to it that it is prepared.

Fourth religion   Does she hear it does she hear them does she walk and does she hear them does she hear them as she walks and does she care to prepare does she prepare to care does she care and does she prepare.

Fourth religion   A fourth religion and what not and a figure with sheep with a cock and with a flower.

Third religion   And if not why not and a figure with a cock a figure with a sheep, a figure with a flower.

Second religion   And indeed why not if there are figures and if the figures have sheep and if the figures have cocks and if the figures have flowers.

First religion   If the figure is the one that has the sheep, if the figure is the one that has the cock if the figure is the one that has the flower if the figure and there is no other need for it.

First religion   If you can see accidents birds and messages, if you can see that you are not young and had better remain so, as you are, remain so as you are, if you can see accidents birds and messages if you can remain so as you are, count less count eight or nine. To count less brings her back to their finding that she was kneeling there where the water was flowing and the glass if it is prepared abundantly covers it all. It is made to roll and cover easily spring vegetables.

Second religion   If you can see leaves wood and disturbances if they can see disturbances leaves and wood if they can see green grass growing nearly four times yearly if they have felt that it will all be covered by wool made in the North from sheep who feed in the south if they know that it will all be covered here where the grass can grow nearly four times yearly then they have their land.

Third religion   If she can see melons and smoke and violence, if she can feel that no one kneels there where the stable is built by an Italian who has not built it but is the stableman in it. If she can feel that she can see smoke and disturbances and she can see melons and smoke and disturbances can she see me. If you see me God bless the moon and God bless me.

Fourth religion   Will she see to it that she can see a reader a pleasure and an alarm. Will she see to it that there is no harm in that that she can furnish a house as well. Very well. She can furnish a house as well.

Fourth religion   Sixteen fifty four and seven, all good children can even see to it that they meant to be told what was not wonderfully told. Are they bold then.

Third religion   Fifty four

Sixty seven

One hundred and nine and nearly every time they fasten it back.

Second religion   Eighty four and eighty four did they ever before have such an opportunity of colouring bananas. No one colours bananas I say no one colours bananas.

First religion   Nine and seven do not make fifty four any more, nor did they ever.

First religion   To continue.

Second religion   We continue.

Third religion   They can continue.

Fourth religion   We can continue.

Fourth religion   We do continue.

Third religion   We continue too.

Second religion   We continue to continue.

First religion   We do continue.

First religion   Climb a wall all climb a wall. All climb a wall. All can climb a wall. They all can climb a wall. What is a wall. A wall is not a well. Very well and was she satisfied with water.

Second religion   Very prettily. She very prettily makes three of them, one of them and another of them and two of them. Three of them actually see the tree. I see the tree and the tree sees me. Very prettily too. Very prettily.

Third religion   And was there a place called a plan, and was the plan a place w[h]ere there were four roads and were four roads only two roads and are two roads four roads. And a plan. We do not plan grain. By grain we mean seeds and by seeds we mean flowers. Plan and four roads and two roads are four roads.

Fourth religion   I do believe in warming water. I do believe in warming water I do believe in warming water I do believe in warming water.

Fourth religion   An extra account.

Third religion   On account.

Second religion   On their account.

First religion   To count.

First religion   In a way a false winter they say. In a way.

Second religion   A false winter if a winter is false does it mean that it is warm and seems cold, that it is cold and seems warm, is there any harm in a false winter is there any charm in a false winter.

Third religion   If a false winter seems warm if a false winter is warm, if a winter is false is there any reason for alarm, is there any reason for alarm if a winter seems warm, if a winter is warm if there is a false winter in winter.

Fourth religion   If there is an opening which leads to a street does that mean that there can be or can there seem to be as there does seem to be a false winter and not so greatly not very gently and yet a false winter if it is warm would it not be so gently, it would not be so it would not be gently so it would not be so gently.

Fourth religion   And now she will see that she says that she can see and looking she can see that she saw it rightly. It was a green frog and very much such as it would be if it had been painted.

Third religion   It was a necessity it was necessarily a decision it was necessary to decide if it was a blade and if it was a frog and beside it was necessary to decide.

Second religion   It was more than necessary to decide if there was beside anything beside that which she saw there. She saw there what was there.

First religion   If she looked and if she sighed she did not sigh she did decide, she decided that she saw what was there and beside that there was nothing to see there.

First religion   Feathers and first religion. She feels
the first religion freely, she feels it freely and she does not need security for it. She does not need security and security is scarcely seen
while no one scatters out of her way in this way.

Second religion   She surrenders herself there and selections are easily made, indeed selections are easily made. Select
me. I select you. Select her. I select her. Select them I select them.
In this way not by her delay, she does not delay them.

Third religion   To be thirty, thoroughly to be thirty
and then to be satisfied beside who is satisfied when she is satisfied
and if she is satisfied who is satisfied beside. Who is it that is satisfied beside.

Fourth religion   From religion for there are four religions, and for religion what is there for religion, what is there and
what is it that there is for religion. What is for religion. Four religions and she and she is needed for religion. For four religions.
For the fourth religion.

Fourth religion   Furnish the religion.

Third religion   There is a third religion.

Second religion   Sending a religion sending the second religion. And two. Sending the second religion and two. In
every language there is second and two.

First religion   One and one and one and the won,
this I have begun. First and one one and then one we do not feel
that in every language there is a first and one and really there is not
a first and one not in every language. Not in every language is there
a one, is there a first is there a first and one. First one and then another one. First one. The very first is one. One and one.

First religion   Did she earnestly pursue did she
earnestly pursue this for that.

Second religion   Did she determine to do this and
that.

Third religion   Did she repeatedly renew this in
that.

Fourth religion this for that. — Did they undertake anew to give

Fourth religion — Did they.

Third religion — She did.

Second religion — She did realise this.

First religion — She did realise it.

First religion — What did happen.

Second religion — And what has happened.

Third religion — What is happening.

Fourth religion — What is happening to her.

Fourth religion — Are they our roses.

Third religion — Is it our dew.

Second religion — Is it our water.

First religion — Is it our garden.

Fourth religion — Is it in our garden.

Third religion — Are they on our roses.

Second religion — Is it for our water.

First religion — Is it frost or dew.

First religion — And they remain few.

Second religion — Are they there anew.

Third religion — Are these for you.

Fourth religion — And can you.

Fourth religion — Many words mention this.

Third religion say this. — And are there any words in which to

Second religion — Why do they say that there.

First religion here. — Why do they say this when they are

First religion — Alphabets are a way of say a b c.

Second religion love for you and for me. — Alphabets are a way of expressing

Third religion — Alphabets are in the way.

Fourth religion bets to-day. — Alphabets are as one may say alpha-

Fourth religion given away.

Mutterings begin when roses are

Third religion.

Roses are not given away in this way.

Second religion

No roses are given away.

First religion given away in this way.

Roses are necessary and they are

First religion

And now for an address.

Second religion

And for redress.

Third religion

And for excess.

Fourth religion

And for authority.

Fourth religion

I have neglected I have not neg-
lected she has not neglected nor has she been neglected nor indeed does she neglect it.

Third religion

Extra pieces here and there, extra
pieces are here and extra pieces are there and she can care for the extra pieces.

Second religion

Can there be really flowers here
when sisters strangers and they themselves need it.

First religion

And naturally when, when do they
naturally arrange for this and for that and when do they nearly arrange for it and for them to be near.

First religion

First a religion.

Second religion

Second a religion.

Third religion

Third a religion.

Fourth religion

Fourth a religion.

Fourth religion

Fourth in religion.

Third in religion.

Third in religion.

Second religion

Second in religion.

First religion

First in religion.

First religion

First in religion what do you say
when a sheep thrusts a lamb out of her way and a lamb is in the way when the lamb is thrust out of the way.

Second religion

Second in religion when you say
that it is needful to ripen pumpkins in this way.

Third religion   Third in religion when they say that
in this way they are gay.
Fourth religion   Fourth religion when they spread
out there where oranges are not rare.
Fourth religion   Do not despair.
Third religion   Do please care.
Second religion   Do do share.
First religion   Do they dedicate themselves to this
preparation.
First religion   I know how to play hide and seek.
And so does he, and so does she and so do they and so do the
others.
First religion   Mention this to them at the same
time.
First religion   No no she says no and I clap my
hands and say no no too.
First religion   Do you appear to be interested in
the south and its cultivation. Are you as you appear to be interested
in the development of the cultivation of the south and of vegetables and animals and trees and shrubs and climates. Are you as you
appear to be humanly free. Are you as you appear to be deeply interested in the cultivation of the earth and in the growth of vegetables trees flowers shrubs and climate. Are you as you seem to be.
Are you humanly free as you seem to me to be. Are you free to be
interested in the cultivation of vegetables flowers trees and shrubs.
Second religion   Is she rarely seen to be between the
houses. Is she very rarely seen to be between the houses and in this
way is she very rarely seen to mean to all of them, to mean to
be to all of them what all of them seem to all of them to mean to
any of them. Does she rarely mean to be seen between the houses
by all of them. Does she rarely mean to seem to be seen by all of
them between the houses of all of them. Does she rarely mean does
she mean very rarely to be between the houses and does she mean
not to be seen to be between the houses. She does not mean to be
between the houses.

Third religion   In this way we cannot find this to say.

Fourth religion   In their houses if their houses meet, houses do meet the street, if their houses meet, if between their houses it as it were houses meet, and houses are on the street, how can she seem to be between the houses. How can she seem not to mean to be between the houses. As between houses. How can she mean not to be between houses. I wonder how she can mean not to seem to be between houses. I can wonder how she can mean this about not being in between houses.

Fourth religion   Rapidly prepare for days.

Third religion   Rapidly prepare this for days.

Second religion   To rapidly prepare days.

First religion   To rapidly prepare for days.

Fourth religion   To repair here and to repair there.

Third religion   To repair.

Second religion   When can you repair this.

First religion   Where can you repair.

First religion   We have two wishes.

Second religion   We have to wish.

Third religion   We have two wishes and we have to wish.

Fourth religion   We have to wish and we have two wishes.

Fourth religion   May she be eager.

Third religion   If she were more eager may she be more eager might she be more eager.

Second religion   If she were more than eager she might be more eager.

First religion   If she were eager and she was eager, she was eager and she might be eager. She might be more eager. She might be more than eager. She might be more eager.

First religion   He does not hesitate to leave and to come she does not hesitate to leave and to come. She does not hesitate to leave and to come.

Second religion   She does not hesitate to leave. She does not hesitate and if she did hesitate she would not hesitate to leave nor would she hesitate to come. She would not hesitate either to leave nor to come.

Third religion   Come then.

Fourth religion   To come then.

Fourth religion   She did not hesitate to come.

Third religion   She did not hesitate nor did she hesitate to come.

Second religion   She did not leave she did not come she did not leave to come.

First religion   Neither did she leave nor did she come.

First religion   We said. He said it certainly.

Second religion   If she was discovered being very able to say that.

Third religion   If she meant to be absolutely rever-berating.

Fourth religion   If they were excelled altogether.

Fourth religion   I know that you do know.

Third religion   This and that and more.

Second religion   She had it as if she had made it.

Third religion   Who has said it who has had it who has had it who has heard it, who has heard it, who has hid it, who has hid it, who has held it, who has held it, who has it.

First religion   Steadily to colour stockings, very steadily indeed and steaming it there any steam I wonder and do you plan to add this here.

Second religion   Do you plan to add to this and do you fairly furnish a reason for it or do you doubt the use of horses here.

Third religion   Do you doubt that houses are to be used at all and are you not silenced by lack of sound. He sounds as if he heard it.

Fourth religion   He sounds as if he heard it as readily as if he had been able to furnish it to himself as well.

Fourth religion   And then and then very well then.

Third religion   When do you intend to send it again.

Second religion   It is far easier to realise that she is able to sing.

First religion   Not really for very far for them to hear a motor horn.

First religion   For them to hear theirs.

Second religion   For them not to hear it.

Third religion   For them when they do hurry it.

Fourth religion   For them then.

Fourth religion   And for them then.

Third religion   I have heard water and negroes and children and electricity.

Second religion   And they need furs and wax and light and rapidity.

First religion   And do they inhabit the houses.

First religion   Excellently this time.

Second religion   And very well for rice.

Third religion   And do they please her enough.

Fourth religion   Excellent fires which burn bamboos in trees.

Fourth religion   And now for this there.

Third religion   Is it nearly so situated is it nearly so nearly situated.

Second religion   He had found it to be there.

First religion   Where.

First religion   As to burning bamboos.

Second religion   She might easily think that there was no reason for their being richer there.

Third religion   Where.

Fourth religion   Where they grow vegetables so plentifully.

Fourth religion	If you courtesy.
Second religion	If you hold a hat on your head.
Third religion	If they are not told.
Fourth religion	Across to me.
Fourth religion	She walked across to me.
Third religion	And what did she see.
Second religion	What did she say to me.
First religion	When she walked across to me.

First religion   I need not tell you that I see the moon and the moon sees me God bless the moon and God bless me which is you.

Second religion   She need not tell me star light star bright I wish I may I wish I might have the wish I wish to-night. And I have not told you what it was.

Third religion   I wish I was a fish with a great big tail. A polly wolly doodle a lobster or a whale. And I am certain no one is deceived.

Fourth religion   Very well.

Fourth religion   If you know that a town is small that the houses are enormous and tall that every one is very rich and you do not see any one fall nor indeed do you see any one at all tell me what is the name of the town.

First religion   Cavaillon.

Second religion   If you find narrow streets and wonderful trees and plenty of seclusion and very little ease.

First religion   What is the name of this town.

First religion   Cavaillon.

Second religion   If you can describe sacks. How do you describe Romans.

Third religion	And Paulines.
Fourth religion	We rode into this.
Fourth religion	To-day.
Third religion	When.
Second religion	Morning or afternoon.

First religion   Before or afterwards.
First religion   To very nearly please.
Second religion   To very nearly please me.
Third religion   To very nearly please me here.
Fourth religion   To please me.

FINIS

THREE SISTERS WHO ARE NOT SISTERS

A Melodrama

JENNY, HELEN *and* ELLEN
SAMUEL *and* SYLVESTER

We are three sisters who are not sisters, not sisters. We are three sisters who are orphans.

We are three sisters who are not sisters because we have not had the same mother or the same father, but because we are all three orphans we are three sisters who are not sisters.

Enter two brothers.

We are two brothers who are brothers, we have the same father and the same mother and as they are alive and kicking we are not orphans not at all, we are not even tall, we are not brave we are not strong but we never do wrong, that is the kind of brothers we are.

JENNY: And now that everybody knows just what we are what each one of us is, what are we going to do.

From *The Gertrude Stein First Reader and Three Plays* (1946).

307

SYLVESTER: What are we going to do about it.

JENNY (*impatiently*): No not what are we going to do about it there is nothing to do about it, we are three sisters who are not sisters, and we are three orphans and you two are not, there is nothing to do about that. No what I want to know is what are we going to do now. Now what are we going to do.

SAMUEL: I have an idea a beautiful idea, a fine idea, let us play a play and let it be a murder.

JENNY:

HELEN: Oh yes let's.

ELLEN:

SYLVESTER: I won't be murdered or be a murderer. I am not that kind of a brother.

SAMUEL: Well nobody says you are, all you have to do is to be a witness to my murdering somebody.

HELEN: And who are you going to murder.

SAMUEL: You for choice. Let's begin.

ELLEN: Oh I am so glad I am not a twin, I would not like to be murdered just because I had a sister who was a twin.

JENNY: Oh don't be silly, twins do not have to get murdered together, let's begin.

Scene 2

A room slightly darkened, a couch, and a chair and a glass of water, the three sisters sitting on the couch together, the light suddenly goes out.

JENNY: Look at the chair.

HELEN: Which chair.

JENNY: The only chair.

ELLEN: I can't see the only chair.

JENNY (*with a shriek*): Look at the only chair.

All three together: There is no chair there.

SAMUEL: No there is no chair there because I am sitting on it.

SYLVESTER: And there is no him there because I am sitting on him.

JENNY: Which one is going to murder which one.

SAMUEL: Wait and see.

Suddenly the light goes up there is nobody in the room and Sylvester is on the floor dead.

[CURTAIN]

ACT II

Scene I

The light is on.

Sylvester is on the floor dead.

Jenny is asleep on the couch.

She wakes up and she sees Sylvester on the floor dead.

Oh he is dead Sylvester is dead somebody has murdered him, I wish I had a sister a real sister oh it is awful to be an orphan and to see him dead, Samuel killed him, perhaps Helen killed him, perhaps Ellen but it should be Helen who is dead and where is Helen.

She looks under the bed and she bursts out crying.

There there is Helen and she is dead, Sylvester killed her and she killed him. Oh the police the police.

There is a knock at the door and Samuel comes in dressed like a policeman and Jenny does not know him.

JENNY: Yes Mr. Policeman I did kill them I did kill both of them.

SAMUEL: Aha I am a policeman but I killed both of them and now I am going to do some more killing.

JENNY (*screaming*): Ah ah.

And the lights go out and then the lights go up again and Jenny is all alone, there are no corpses there and no policeman.

JENNY: I killed them but where are they, he killed them but where is he. There is a knock at the door I had better hide.

She hides under the bed.

Scene 2

SAMUEL (*as a policeman comes in*): Aha there is nobody dead and I have to kill somebody kill somebody dead. Where is somebody so that I can kill them dead.

He begins to hunt around and he hears a sound, and he is just about to look under the bed when Ellen comes in.

ELLEN: I am looking for Helen who is not my twin so I do not have to be murdered to please her but I am looking for her.

Samuel the policeman comes out of the corner where he has been hiding.

SAMUEL: Aha you killed her or aha you killed him, it does not make any difference because now I am going to do some killing.

ELLEN: Not me dear kind policeman not me.

SAMUEL: I am not a policeman I am a murderer, look out here I come.

The light goes out. When it comes on again, the policeman is gone and Ellen murdered is on the floor.

Jenny looks out timidly from under the bed and gives a shriek:

Oh another one and now I am only one and now I will be the murdered one.

And timidly she creeps back under the bed.

[CURTAIN]

ACT III

Jenny under the bed. Samuel this time not like a policeman but like an apache comes creeping in.

SAMUEL: Aha I am killing some one.

JENNY (*under the bed*): He can't see me no he can't, and anyway I will kill him first, yes I will.

Suddenly the room darkens and voices are heard.

I am Sylvester and I am dead, she killed me, every one thinks it was Samuel who killed me but it was not it was she.

HELEN'S VOICE: I am Helen and I am dead and everybody thinks it was Samuel who killed me but not at all not all not at all it was she.

A THIRD VOICE: I am Ellen and I am dead, oh so dead, so very very dead, and everybody thinks it was Samuel but it was not it was not Samuel it was she oh yes it was she.

The light goes up and Jenny alone looks out fearfully into the room from under the bed.

JENNY: Oh it was not Samuel who killed them it was not, it was she and who can she be, can she be me. Oh horrible horrible me if I killed all three. It cannot be but perhaps it is, (*and she stretches up very tall*) well if it is then I will finish up with him I will kill him Samuel and then they will all be dead yes all dead but I will not be dead not yet.

The light lowers and Samuel creeps in like an apache.

SAMUEL: They say I did not kill them they say it was she but I know it was me and the only way I can prove that I murdered them all is by killing her, aha I will find her I will kill her and when I am the only one the only one left alive they will know it was I that killed them all, I Samuel the apache.

He begins to look around and suddenly he sees a leg of Jenny sticking out under the bed. He pulls at it.

SAMUEL: Aha it is she and I will kill her and then they will know that I Samuel am the only murderer.

He pulls at her leg and she gives a fearful kick which hits him on the temple. He falls back and as he dies,

SAMUEL: Oh it is so, she is the one that kills every one, and that must be so because she has killed me, and that is what they meant, I killed them each one, but as she was to kill me, she has killed all of them all of them. And she has all the glory, Oh Ciel.

And he dies.

Jenny creeps out from under the bed.

JENNY: I killed him yes I did and he killed them yes he did and now they are all dead, no brothers no sisters no orphans no nothing, nothing but me, well there is no use living alone, with nobody to kill so I will kill myself.

And she sees the glass of water.

JENNY: Aha that is poison.

She drinks it and with a convulsion she falls down dead. The lights darken and the voices of all of them are heard.

We are dead she killed us, he killed us sisters and brothers orphans and all he killed us she killed us she killed us he killed us and we are dead, dead dead.

The lights go up and there they all are as in the first scene.

JENNY: Did we act it are we dead, are we sisters, are we orphans, do we feel funny, are we dead.

SYLVESTER: Of course we are not dead, of course we never were dead.

SAMUEL: Of course we are dead, can't you see we are dead, of course we are dead.

HELEN (*indignantly*): I am not dead, I am an orphan and a sister who is not a sister but I am not dead.

ELLEN: Well if she is not dead then I am not dead. It is very nice very nice indeed not to be dead.

JENNY: Oh shut up everybody, shut up, let's all go to bed, it is time to go to bed orphans and all and brothers too.

And they do.

[FINIS]

ARE THERE SIX
OR ANOTHER QUESTION

One—Are there six.
Two—Or another question.
One—Are there six.
Two—Or another question.
Two—Are there six.
One—Or another question.
Two—Are there six.
Two—Or another question.

From *Useful Knowledge* (1928).

OBJECTS LIE ON A TABLE

A Play

*Because Stein used the epithet "play" to subtitle texts that initially resembled con-
tinuous prose, the first impression was that her "plays" were meant only to be read.
Only after her death were some of them performed.*—R. K.

Nuns ask for them for recreation.

First a nun. Have you meant to have fun and funny things. Do
you like to see funny things for fun.

Objects lie on a table.

We live beside them and look at them and then they are on the
table then.

Objects on a table and the explanation.

Who says glasses.

Who says salt in Savoy.

Who does say pots of porcelain.

And who does say that earthen ware is richer than copper, glass,
enamel, or cooking. We have the very best celery salad and selec-

---

From *Operas and Plays* (1932).

314

tion. Now then read for me to me what you can and will see. I see what there is to see.

You want to show more effort than that.

And now how do you do.

I have done very well.

The objects on the table have been equal to the occasion. We can decorate walls with pots and pans and flowers. I question the flowers. And bananas. Card board colored as bananas are colored. And cabbages. Cabbages are green and if one should not happen to be there what would happen, the green would unhappily unhappily result in hardness and we could only regret that the result was unfortunate and so we astonish no one nor did we regret riches. Riches are not begun. They have a welcome in oceans. Oceans can not spread to the shore. They began description and so we relish seas. Over seas objects are on the table that is a wooden table and has not a marble top necessarily. So thank every one and let us begin faintly.

As to houses certainly houses have not the same restfulness as objects on the table which mean to us an arrangement. You do not arrange houses nor do you fancy them very much. I have a fancy for a house.

When I appeal I appeal to their relation. What is a relation. A British Dominion. And will there ever be no memory will there even not be a memory. I remember you. And you. Yes you remember you remember me. And I say to you you do remember do not you and you you feel as I do. I remember you, and you are certainly aroused by the apple the descent from the cross and the dog and the squirrel. You do please when you please.

Combining everything with everything.

This is their flour.

I find that milk salt flour and apples and the pleasant respective places of each one in the picture make a picture.

Esther.

I prefer a merry go round.

And I a street.

And I nothing at all says Rose as she decides to stay away. But she comes again repeatedly.

Have you hesitated about singing.

Have you hesitated about singing.

He said he had met her there.

And now we have explained the interest a cellist can show in a sculptor. She does not play the cello any more but she does continue to cover the wood the stone and the wood and color the wood. She does not color the wood.

And now houses and buildings and houses and the buildings containing houses. I live in a house here and there is a house there. Do not bother to remember about the other place of worship. See to it that you have an equal respect for all who are all together.

And then when you mean to see me.

Call to me.

Come to me readily and prepare in that way.

What do you know about fields and table-cloths.

Objects are on the table when I am there. And when you are not there.

Let me explain this to you.

About ten pages.

And what are their ages.

Their ages are you know, you know what their ages are and their weights and their measures.

And you know how very soon we can be up before noon.

Yes. To-morrow and then we will buy we will buy we will not buy, yes we will not buy all that we need to buy because we will not be able to agree about them. You agree with me.

And so we will see just what we need to gladden their Christmas tree.

Objects on the table do not imitate a house and we do not mean Esther.

How does Esther be named Esther and not take cognisance of Ahasuerus but only of Olga she is a Russian how dare she.

Does he shine when he means to whine. Of course he does and now speak connectedly.

He said that he respected the expression of opinion and she said, I believe in looking facts in the face. And he said and what do you see when you do as you say you do and she said I see but you and he said the same to you. And then they said they greatly appreciate the painting of houses and objects on a table.

Come up out of there is very well said when the instinct which has lead to the introduction of words and music not pictures and music, not pictures and words not pictures and music and words, not pictures not music not words when the instinct which has lead to the spread of rubbing has been shed then we will invite each one to sign himself Yours sincerely Herman G. Read and very quickly I include everything in that new name.

We will now consider an ancient quadrille we will.

Ladies change.

How can you neglect admissions.

And she was seated and she said I am not pledged to much retribution.

Come again.

Forward and back.

Look right and not left.

And lend a hand.

The lend a hand society.

Calming.

Pocket the watch.

Can soldiers surround a chinaman.

Pray then.

Pray then why do you wish for this thing.

Providing.

Providing you need strengthening why do you reiterate that you are coming.

Going and coming.

Was he willing.

Has he been willing.

When is he willing to vary everything.

He says he invents nothing and then I say do not invent a table cloth to-day do not let the table table that you invented stay. And he says I am very willing but I have had to invent something to fill in and I say to him you had better really have it and he said I am not able to get it and I say to him I am sorry I have not one to lend you and he says oh that is quite alright I will realize that I can replace it and I say I am willing to address you and he replied, I do not doubt that you will be of great assistance to me and as for the result that is still in question.

What is the difference between houses and a table. What is the difference between objects on a table and furniture in houses. Had you ever thought of that. Objects on a table make a standpoint of recompense and result, furniture in houses do decide matters.

Very well let us come to that decision.

No they come together.

Scotchmen, frenchman chinamen negro and the black races. When will you adopt. You or me, when this you see remember me.

Chinamen are cautious with negroes with frenchmen with scotchmen and with candles. They are cautious with oil and impoverishment.

No one is easily impoverished then.

And now compare them with these.

They have instincts they cook and turn and apples and salt. These have their way, they are not wretched with wood and gold nor are they eager with riots. And so many people appeal. They appeal to flushing. They flush when they have no rapid silence there. And they do not despise arrangements. Who can be merciless to the best armament. And do they like poise. I like the noise. I do not like the noise. How can you forget riches. Riches can mean prejudice. Can riches mean that. Yes in a crew. How can you cut a fish. Babies look, boys look and we look.

We look there.

Believe the future that he tells her.

Really though she told him. He was not disappointed because I had warned him. Objects have been recognised as a knife, a pot, a pan, a cover, a ladle, carrots, apples and a salt cellar. These all have been recognised which really is not so astonishing as his aunt is a farmer and cultivates her own ground and has cows and sheep and a sheep dog. His mother is an exceedingly capable manager and his father has been connected with the government. He is now over age and has been retired on a pension. His sister and brother-in-law have a hard ware store and do a successful business although in their part of the country it is exceedingly difficult to get payment. You can see that it is not astonishing that the objects are easily recognised. They are a chair, table, tea cup, tea pot, a pot, a ladle, a bottle a pan, a cover carrots, salt-cellar with salt in it, apples and a pitcher.

It would appear that she is near, it would appear that he is near he is nearly he is merely delayed.

And so he will come.

And so he will come.

And so he will come.

And so he will come.

He will be welcome.

He will come when he has time.

And what will he do then.

He will say that objects are to-day recognised as something with which to play. And we will reply this is not why we like them here but the real reason is that we have not displaced them for a violin simply because of this reasoning. We have displaced them because we have replaced them.

Thank you so very much for this explanation.

Please tell Mr. Edmund Holt that if he will understand I will be delighted.

And houses with their hooks upon which in the country they still do need to hoist furniture and water and other hooks that support the lights. It is very interesting that a light or a house is sometimes on the side and sometimes at a corner and in either case it compares very nicely with the house even in the day time when the light is not lit and the house is not necessarily ready to be recognised. A house readily recognised is no longer necessary and yet can we deny recognition can we deny that yesterday we were certainly not displeased with our residence.

How lovelily the wall how lovelily all of the wall and we do not necessarily hesitate he did not, he found it thin. The wall is thick and not heavy and has a support and when you look at it again they have not changed anything and yet it is to be painted red and a lemon yellow and pretty soon every ten years they will again oblige every one to do something, to paint the houses and arrange a wall which is crumbling. This is the law that they are reinforcing. And where did his mother get her ration. She did not she had copper and earthen ware pots and so she found then when he went away she had nothing to say. How neatly a man and woman who go away every day come home to stay. They are very neat in their washing and ironing and in their eating and drinking and in their sleeping and waking. Can you believe that he uses their room all day. Can you believe this I say to you and he has said to me that he was under no obligation to them for anything. He was not satiated with eating how could he be in choosing bananas or a persimmon. How can he be violently radiating when ordinarily he was visiting and when visiting they had said to him, listen while we are talking. He talked readily while he was listening. Objects on a table are hazardous.

Imitate a cheese if you please. We are very well pleased with gold coin and ribbons.

Imitate a cheese very well if you please, and readily reflect how can you be credulous of more than the assumption of imitating ham. We were not pleased with the imitation of the lamb.

I have a special taste in feeling. I can feel very well. I can feel that some resemblances the resemblance between a sausage made of sugar and a sausage made of meat is not as great as the resemblance between an object made of almonds and an object made of wood.

How often do we see what we have not readily recognised. I readily recognise the object that has the most perfect quality of imitation. Then can you be astonished by a meal. How easily you had rather blame him and blame them and how easily she had rather fly than swim. We have discouraged her together we have discouraged her altogether. Dogs are good for photography and recoil. Do please at the rate that you do please how can you be so anxious.

She was told to be measured and she said assuredly I shall be there. How often do you mean to remain. Remain to me the culminating tender tree. And how can a woodbine twine.

And now how do you feel what you hear.

I come back to expecting a house and a farm and not a farmhouse and a southern climate in the north. We do not go very far north. Mountains are just the same, very nearly the same. I have had a special taste in rivers. And now remember to see me.

Objects on a table are all there and I do not care to say that they have been studied. Study again and again and leave me to my wishes I wish that they could copy all of it as well as they do copy it. No one can say yes again. Have I forgotten that fruits do not remember flowers, that flowers contain what they contain and that together with fruit they do not possibly force me to be round and innocent. I am prepared to share fruits and at the same time know that I have wished to be queen. How can she stay there very easily. She gets up and she says very well this is quite what I mean.

So we consider flowers masculine. We have not mentioned the resemblance between trees and streets and all of the things that have not been constructed. How can you prejudice him.

We are not only patient but satisfied, we are not only satisfied but more than satisfied. Do we suppose that a rose is a rose. Do we suppose that all she knows is that a rose is a rose is a rose is a rose. He knows and she knows that a rose is a rose and when she can make a song as to which can belong as to what can belong to a song. Now let us pray that a table may that a table may very well stay, that a table may that a table very well may stay to be settled for in that way. And when the objects may be disposed in this way upon the table upon which they will not permanently be put away. We had a wish and the wish was that when rose colored ribbons and no roses because of course after all roses are supposed to be of the color of imitation trees. How can you imitate trees so prettily. I find I have changed my meaning. I find I have changed my meaning in changing my meaning from the meaning I had to this meaning. I mean to do right. I do not mean to settle the clamor by reiterating have you met one another and do you care to ask a question. I ask the question I say have you succeeded, you succeed. Can you succeed and do you succeed. I succeed in recalling this to their mind. I do not fall behind.

CIVILIZATION

A Play
In Three Acts

This play is so abstract that any company performing it deserves a reward.—R. K.

Characters in Act I

George Couleur and his mother Marietta.
Therese Manner and her nephew John and her niece Pauline and
her sister Ivy.
Therese Manner and her mother and her father.
Therese Manner and her brother John and her brother Frank.
Jenny Henry and her husband William Henry.
Then the landscape. And the animals.
An old woman from the mountains who should sell raspberries but
sells mushrooms and her brother. The nephews are not seen.

ACT I

They speak of it. As is natural. Not that they are very interested. As is natural. But they do not say. Exactly. What. Makes it.
And therefor. They are. Not interested in it.

From *Operas and Plays* (1932).

No one speaks of George Couleur and his mother any more. Than they speak of his mother and George Couleur, except those who have been interested, or else those who have something to do with it. One may say. That some one with whom. Some of them. Are very pleasantly. One may say. They are friendly. Say she is very well. At least. Not very far. From very well.

These may not connect these with others.

After all the only thing he says is. That he would be glad to see him. Even then. Though. Actually. It is undoubted. That getting richer. And therefor working harder. Does not happen to interfere. With. Coming. When. They do not come. And so. They are finally. Not ready. Not to come. After all. They have been. Not without. A wish.

ACT I

George Couleur and his mother.
Marietta Couleur and her son.

ACT I

Therese Manner may be. Without hope.

She may. Or she may not be. Without hope. She has no obligation. And no obligations. To be of aid. To her nephew John and her niece Pauline because they have a father and a mother, a mother and a father, industrious, painstaking. And probably. Not richer than they have been. But as rich. As they will have been. And everybody is prospering.

Therese Manner. Is thinking of everything. And no one. Has been beguiled. By anything. But every one. She has a brother John, he is a man tall and thin and he likes hunting and is successfully. Incidentally, the best shot. Never shot. This was surprising. We asked him why. He said he did not. He never had.

Therese Manner is not avoided. By women. Or by men. She is devoted. To her mother and her brother John and her nephew John and her niece Pauline and her brother Frank and her sister Ivy. She is not older than all of them. One may say she is not extravagant.

324

Jenny Henry and her husband William Henry. She has lost her husband William Henry and has been seduced by a man working. This made no difference as she was serenely prosperous and could like sheep. And always be pleasantly prepared. In no way was there any interference. And now Act I.

George Couleur. One and one.

ACT I

Therese will be. Credited with devotion. To her family. By those. Who follow her. She will. Not be denied. Hope and resistance.

ACT I

Therese will amount. To a belief. In their respect. She will not know. That they say so. Either to go there or here.

ACT I

George Couleur. May never have met her. Nor will he yet and again.

ACT I

George Couleur will not trouble to wonder but he has a mother. No mother has a mother nor has any mother more than their mother. George Couleur had a father and they resemble their mother and one another. She may not be selfish if they say it. She may be prosperous. And a good manager. She may be lonesome with the company and accompanied later. Indeed. They may say that it is selfish. No one need know who knows. It is all who have hopes. Of wholesome. And a wedding. And they will be willing. To be helping. If a milliner or either a dressmaker or either a helper or either forbidding. Who means whom. They must be at once.

George Couleur is no misanthrope and he manages well, that is industriously and twice they have seasons of seeding clover, that is it is better.

ACT I

It is in land. May they. May they indeed. For. If they should be only with. The riches. Of it. Always. Not having been. Very lately. Acquired.

How can riches have been very lately acquired.

Nor may they have been acquired if he listens.

Which may they do. In not turning.

All of which. They feel.

A marriage can come to mean anything.

And so. They will influence them to their hurt.

In which they deprive them of obligation.

Nor need they mind. What they deprive.

Of what they are deprived.

ACT I

In meditation. Florence Descotes. Is not resting. Nor indeed. Is she working. Nor preparing. And so they. Witness it.

ACT I

A brother can replace a mother. Or not.

If the mother is faithful to. The brother.

They may be more particularly. With. One.

After all. Who may account. For their. Denial.

And they were eager. And they were.

She may be seen to have coats.

ACT I

Florence Descotes. Has not been one.

CIVILIZATION

ACT I

It is very well known that they are not happy.
It is very well known that. They are not happy.
Each one is content in unison.

ACT I

A father and a mother. May make either parent.
A mother and her father.
A sister and her mother and a brother.
Nor may they.

ACT I

George Couleur has his mother. She is living. They will have an attraction. But they may be. Said as yet.

ACT I

She may be without doubt allowed.

ACT I

Marrying. Or. Religion.

ACT I

Would they could they. Or cause. Or rest because.

ACT I

They were marrying and he came with her.

ACT I

Florence Descotes is fairly busy. With her farming.

ACT I

Could all who call call them to come.

ACT I

Be men. Or be. Men. Be men or be men. And so George Couleur knew when to go. He had a very good reputation. And he. Had a very good reputation. George Couleur and his mother were prospering. They were rich. And they were buying.

George Couleur was rich. His mother was rich. They were rich. And they were buying. Land and a house. A house and land. And they already had some. And they were buying. Land. And a house. And they already had one. George Couleur and his mother was prospering and he was marrying. And this. Was lengthening. And so they meant to be women. That is. Women meant to be women.

ACT I

Therese would not marry any one and no one had wanted to marry any one. She had not known George Couleur. And never knew him. She had met his mother. But that was natural. As she went to market. And saw her. And why. Should she see her. She never answered any question. That is to say. She never asked any question. She always answered every one. And this makes no connection. Naturally not. Any connection.

ACT I

George Couleur and his mother were prospering.

ACT I

Have no have no help to know. That they have no one to know, that they have no one.

Therese is one and one.

ACT I

She may be wedded. With one. And no one. With. No one.

She may be added. With one. With. Any one. She may be added. In adding any more than any one. And so they have a pleasure in their ending adding one.

ACT I

Therese having one. Begun.

She may be added. As. Any one.

And so they may be of use. And she may be of use and they. May be of use. In one. As. In one.

ACT I

Therese may be the necessary one.

ACT I

No err Couleur, she never knew one.

There was no reason not to know some one.

She did not she did not know any one. She had met one. One of one of the two of them. And there is no connection. They live there and they live there.

ACT I

George Couleur is married to his wife he has a mother, she is a mother and he is married to his wife and his mother they will be ready with. Any one. And they live as they may say one and one. And not narrowly. And any one. Working in the fields works hard with grain and corn and nuts and wine and oxen and help and any one.

ACT I

It was a chance that she looked well.
It was a chance that she looked well spoken rapidly.

ACT I

It was a chance that she looked well. She did not mind the cold although she appeared to suffer from it. This was not because she said she minded it. She said she did not mind it.

ACT I

She said. She was ready to stay in order not to go away but she wanted to go away rather as she wanted to go away and she wanted to be there. Where. She was. Where she was. When she. Was. She wanted to go away where. She was. She wanted. Where she was to stay. And so. They say. Timidity won the day. Timidity. Won the day.

ACT I

George Couleur and his mother and his wife he had no sister never knew her. There are a great many who do not know every one. One and one. Everywhere they eat they eat with some one. Some eat with some and some eat with some one one and one.

ACT I

Therese was easily pleased by forgetting no one. Easily pleased. By not. Forgetting any one. Therese was easily pleased by not forgetting not any one of any of them.

CIVILIZATION

ACT I

No one does know any one of them because although they do not come together there are not very many. There. At any one time. At any one time. There are. All of them who are there there but not to know them. This is easy to understand. By them. Of them. And not. Of everybody. Who does not know any of all or one of them.

ACT I

Therese may make a mountain out of a molehill.

ACT I

Molehill. May be. A whole. May be.

ACT I

May be. A pleasure. Or may be. A pleasure. But. She met her. And aided her. That is they asked her.

ACT I

George Couleur was never to be an orphan. He had had a father and he had a mother. And they had one another. And he worked very often. And whenever. He gathered the harvest later and earlier. It is very well to work well. George Couleur and his mother worked well. And his wife worked as well.

ACT I

No one. Places. Faces. As having been met.

ACT I

Very well met.

ACT I

Therese will not leave often. May be she will not.

ACT I

Who may they be. They may be.

ACT I

May be they will be. Ready. To end. Act one.

ACT II

All out but you.
Therese has taken pains.

ACT II

Therese. Is not ruled by you. She is influenced by you. She will be ready to be through. And come to be. Ready for whoever should be better than ever.

Therese. May be inclined to be thoughtful and older any one could meet and collect them in their clover. That is the seed need be filled. With what. They need when they sweep. A road. And so. Which may be. That they will. A third. They have a third more or two thirds less than are needed.

Therese. She may be able to come too.

ACT II

No or one more. Because they will not question. Nor need they. As they. Do not. Ever think. Of George Couleur. Who had a mother. Who heard her.

ACT II

May she be three. Or readily free. Or made a mother. One two three. Who needs wishes.

ACT II

George Couleur has a hope of a mother who is a mother to her father which may call mother mother may they help with them as farther. They may exist. May they. With warning. Or may they. Be equal. In with. Farming. Farming is a station with out shaping their destinies. She may be thought. That. She may be. In. Amount. And would a brother and a mother desert her.

ACT II

It may be heard to be hard. To leave them. For two.

ACT II

Therese never comes as a witness.

ACT II

Because she never had been in that place.

ACT II

And that was natural. As it was not in that way that she went when she went to her home.

When she went. To any place. Where. She went. No one allows them. To have been.

ACT II

Thinking. Of winking.

ACT II

Many could be one or two.

ACT II

George Couleur had a mother and she could press a pigeon to be or rather. They could be there with her. She had a husband and a father. She was a mother and a sister and a daughter. Her son had a mother. They may be outlined.

More which. Is it. As made. With which. They call. That it is. Well. To be. Very often present. As well. When they will. Arrange. For it. As well. Which they may. When they. Are ready. As well. As when they are thought. They were married.

ACT II

She might like. Seeing at a distance. And like. She might like. Which she will see. At a distance and like. She might not like and seeing at a distance she might not like. To see at a distance.

Therese. May be attached to the children of men and women and women and men. And she does say so in not seeing them.

Therese may be an advantage for them to have them come with them to have them coming. May she be. Men and women. And it is early. To have them follow them. She does stay at home not precisely. As she does not move about with them. They never leave them. She does not leave them.

ACT II

She will stay to be useful too. They do not need to need two.

ACT II

Therese. Could she smile. Awhile. If she was met by two. Or yet. Not new. Therese. Could she think as well. As if there were more than a few. But not two. She is not very happy as well. Therese will be well met by three and two. And not by seeing through four or two. As much. Therese will be joined by them. This makes it useful. She may not be imagining. Therese will not be hurt. By questioning nor wait as she is waiting. She will come again. They may be ready yet. And she is waiting. It might that they might not might be there but might be here. She might be here.

ACT II

Could anybody know through George Couleur leaving anybody who is with which without a complaint as they mean will they touch which they yield for themselves in and on around and they might include. George Couleur and his mother or. Might they have another than the mother than their mother. Than any than a mother. George Couleur.

ACT II

It is easy to think that Therese. May be in place. Of her half sister. Ivy. Who after all. May be not at all. The child of her mother or of her older brother or of her older sister or not at all. Just the youngest of all. And therefor tall.

Therese.   I am going away.
Question.   To stay.
Therese.   No not to stay away.
Therese.   I am not only going away.
Therese.   I am not going to stay away.
Therese.   I am not going away.
Therese.   I am not going away.
Therese.   I am going away not to-day.
Therese.   But she went.
Therese.   Went away the day that is two days for four days anyway. And there is a survival.

ACT II

Of many which. They may be rich. To think of which. They will be selfish. They may be where. They will not care. They may be there. They may be selfish. She may be there. She may be where. She may have come. She may be won. She may not think. She may not blink. The facts.
Therese. Is not away.

ACT II

George Couleur, fastens a rabbit, that is he does not shoot, nor does he wish nor does his brother-in-law, nor does his brother-in-law shoot although both of them are capable.

ACT II

One two one two. They leave two.

ACT II

Not as much as they were.
With care.

ACT II

New who. Who can be through. Who means to.
Be better there than two. And though two.
May make it easy for two. Two may not.
Make it easy for two. Or more. Or through.

ACT II

Therese.   May not be. Attracted either.
            By a mountain. Nor. By a big city.

ACT II

Therese.   May wish. That walking. At a distance.
Therese.   That walking a considerable distance.
Therese.   That walking a very considerable distance.
Therese.   May or may not be walking.
Therese.   A very considerable distance.
Therese.   In either case.
Therese.   It makes no difference in either case.
Therese.   Nor will they be a pleasure.
Therese.   Nor will they be without pleasure.
Therese.   Whether. They will. Or whether.
Therese.   They will be. With pleasure.
Therese.   Will in any case. Be a pleasure.
Therese.   Will return. As a pleasure.
Therese.   In any case.

ACT II

George Couleur. Has whether. It may be. In.
May have been. Not in. A suit. Of clothing.
Because it could. Not have been.

He could not have been. It could not have been.
It could not have been. Him.

ACT II

Not finely because of one or two.
George Couleur, could be. As if. He.
She his mother could be. As if indeed.
They could be as if they were more.
Than if indeed. They were. Remembered.
Than if. One or two. They were.
Could everybody. Be a mother and son.
One two.

ACT II

Otherwise are you through. Practically.

ACT II

Therese.   When they will dwindle and have one.
Therese.   When they may. Or better one.
Therese.   Let us see certainly. They ask to see.
Therese.   And whether they may. They ask. To say.
Therese.   That she will move around. In moving away.

ACT II

A button. Or a fire. Or a sheep. Or a sound.
Therese.   She will be present. When they are around.
Therese.   And strangely. The hearing is acute.
Therese.   Because they will not be selfish.
Therese.   And so they hope so.

ACT II

Therese makes three more useful.

ACT II

It is not there. But here.
They will be here. And there. And may they sell.
Or give with them. None can give them.
Or plainly.

ACT II

Three words are selfish. Fish. The same. And meant.
Therese.   She may have a sister.
Therese.   And indeed many.
Therese.   And they may count.
Therese.   As one more.

ACT II

Therese.   May she be meant. For you.

ACT II

Therese.   But that has been her wish.
Therese.   Ever since she was a little girl.

ACT II

May George Couleur never be deceived. In having been as well known. As his mother with him. Not without a father with him, nor indeed marrying with him and no father with him. A mother and a mother without with him.

Act II

They need two to be two.

Act II

Therese.   Will be they may be indeed they will be.
          It is well to be able to be of avail.
Therese.   She may be naturally without fail.
Therese.   There without fail.
Therese.   Not very likely.
Therese.   That she may be.
Therese.   Be able to disregard a sister.
Therese.   Or likely to place at a disadvantage.
Therese.   Who missed her.

Act II

Therese.   What is the difference.
Therese.   Nor might they go.
Therese.   For which they will change.

Act II

Or through. Do not disturb. Nor hesitate to detain. Those who might.

Act II

Therese.   For them it is a choice as well as a chance.

Act II

Therese.   She may be equal to gratitude or gratefully.

ACT II

George Couleur may be with her. That is may be with her. He was made to a purpose and believe. Or need it. She may or need it or deceive.

George Couleur regret very much to having forced it to give him a meal.

George Couleur. Or should. May they be when they come or carry out their intention for which they disturb no one. George Couleur is a tiller, of the soil and owner of very many who have not added to being [lent] or given. No one lends anything. And they are careful to be left to mine. May they carry as they call. Or either be thorough carefully.

ACT II

Therese.   Has not arrived in her place.
Therese.   Nor will she know him.
Therese.   Nor indeed might any one.
Therese.   For this is as safe as natural.

ACT II

Therese.   May be easily an older woman older.

ACT II

No one need think of anything.

ACT II

Therese.   Yvonne is agreeable and condescending but it is very nice that it is you.
Therese.   Because in any case it is very nice that it is you.

Therese.   Because Yvonne who is very pleasant one by one it is very nice that it is you.

Therese.   Because of them that is they are as old as they were to become when they were to go with them.

Therese.   They may be lent to be made then to come for them.

Therese.   It is why and they will wish.

Therese.   For which they mean as well as meant them.

Therese.   Any little while they will go as they did when they will go and part.

Therese.   May not be pleasant as a witness but she is pleasant as a witness.

Therese.   For them or more than for them.

Therese.   She will be more as a witness that they went there with and without and for them.

Therese.   Should she be better able to be asking more for them than she would if she were by them with them. And so they married. Certainly not they. Or more with them. It is very strange how many in the country are not willing to be married although it is necessary and yet is it necessary not if they have house with a window and they may have them.

Therese.   She may be mentioned with them or she may be not mentioned she may not be with them.

Therese.   Which she mentioned with them.

ACT II

Therese.   May be and may be mentioned with them.

Therese.   Is here with them.

Therese.   Is here is here with them.

Therese.   Could it be easily found that she was happy without and with them as she was happy without them as she was happy with them.

ACT II

George Couleur may dream of the mother of a sister or either of the sister of the mother or either of a father of a mother as a mother and a sister and a mother. George Couleur may dream of one another.

ACT II

Civilization follows every season.

ACT II

George Couleur said that he still expects guests. Nor need he. Trouble to be questioned. Nor left alone. He will be able to be advised. And they will. Never apply what had been devised. For their entertainment or their pleasure. George Couleur would willingly wait. He speaks as if he were silent or out loud.

ACT II

Therese.   Has really heard. That they were more than a third.
Not there. Or nearly there. Or not behind.
Therese.   It is strange to see her anxious.
Therese.   No one need know any one.
Therese.   She might be left to have been or to leave it to be left.
Therese.   May listen if they mean after or before then.
She has heard what they are saying.

ACT II

There is no door they have no door therefor they have no floor. Therefor they are near the door therefor they do have to clean the floor and open the door. This may be for them.

ACT II

They will please whoever they will have seen known them.

ACT II

Civilization all through.

George Couleur known to have had a mother too and still they are to blame. Who is to blame because. After a pause. They will satisfy any one.

ACT II

Will they come George Couleur and not his mother. Naturally not he will come George Couleur will come and not his mother or naturally not. Neither will come as a sister ought or a mother ought or a mother or a brother. Ought.

ACT II

It may be true that if it is stronger there is no comfort and if it is not stronger there is no use.

Therese.   Dwell evenly upon it. Be proud of a sister and be a comfort to a mother.

Therese.   They be capable of obtaining more than they gave them.

Therese.   For which they will wish not to thank them but to see them.

Therese.   Because they will include that they went there with them.

Therese.   Many do not mention who went there with them.

Therese.   But they will remember whether they went there and not without them.

Therese.   For them in asking them anything.

Therese.   And they will answer as they like them.

Therese.   But all of it for all of it for them.

Therese.   They should have been allowed to see them with them.

Therese.   They may be all of it for more of more without them.

Therese.   May be they may have been with them before they may be out side near them.

Therese.   It is plainly just what they would like as they do like them to have it as it is given to them to keep for them.

Therese.   It is very well for all of them.

Therese.   Just as she will.

Therese.   They may in the way.

Therese.   Come if they can.

Therese.   Which is why they are able to come.

Therese.   In no trouble.

Therese.   Without any difficulty.

Therese.   And when they go away again.

Therese.   They will have it there for them.

Therese.   It is very easy to be there with them.

Therese.   If they are not there again.

Therese.   When they have not gone away with them.

Therese.   Just yet.

Therese.   All may be.

Therese.   Just here when they left.

Therese.   May she be missed or left.

Therese.   By once in a while fairly.

Therese.   When they knew.

Therese.   It makes no difference in coming.

Therese.   They come just the same to go away.

Therese.   About this time.

Therese.   Will willows fall.

Therese.   By them they will be here by then.

Therese.   They and by them they will be finished by then.

Therese.   Accurately or registered.

Therese.   Just when will they like.

Therese.   Even if they are not alone.

ACT III

George Couleur saw a door and they stood and they were oxen. More than if they were alone.

Act III

George Couleur there is a difference between scissors and a thimble between oxen and wool and between various ways of welcoming. George Couleur. They change.

Act III

George Couleur.   May be for. For which it is better. That it is for. For them. Would he be. That they had may may she be spoiled or not be better for. For them.

George Couleur may not be asking any or for them. In eclipse or brown or a starry night or and. It may be called collection or collecting. For with them.

Act III

There may or they may be no mission nor or mention or motion nor no mention of nor or. For them.

Act III

George Couleur.   Which a wish or oxen.

Act III

Each which may or did not mind or in a mid or manage he with she. Three. May they motion or mention with them. George Couleur could or was with or with oxen.

George Couleur is young with or without or waiting with a wedding or adding oxen to adding mention or adding mention with without wedding or nor with oxen.

Act III

It is often with or without a or without or waiting. If. Visiting.

ACT III

They may call girls girlish. With or with or without mention or nor no adding waiting. Could they carry a that they may.

ACT III

George Couleur.   May or may be or or has not to do with or or oxen.

ACT III

George Couleur.   She meant to be very careful with reading the paper. Which it did matter. This was no need of knowing her or Therese. He was older that is younger and so he would not know the family beside did they live there.

ACT III

Therese.   She is properly proud of her sister.

ACT III

George Couleur, I love my love with a d because she is a darling I love her with a y because she is beautiful.

ACT III

George Couleur may be with a large or larger not hesitation or eagerness but made nor indeed may eagerness.

Fill feel or ought a color be white or felt a fail. George Couleur is not as avoided as within hail.

He meant to be. And no attendant to her attend for her could be fail. George Couleur has a mother his wife has a mother George Couleur has a mother a mother has a wife that is George Couleur has a wife and mother he has a mother George Couleur and a father he is not faded. A father is faded not a mother. George Couleur and a mother the mother which is his mother. To the mother.

ACT III

Therese.   Has nothing to do with leaving or demeaning. It is called early or brother. One sister and a brother or a sister and a brother and a brother and there may be three.

ACT III

Civilization suggests enters.

ACT III

A moon. They need to have good weather.

ACT III

George Couleur.   May share. And he may wear. Or nearly. A suit of clothes. And they. May be. With which they will relish. That he is more than leave it. As a pleasure. It is a wife who has joined with a mother and they need not be neat because or gather that they will add neither. A father.
The grandfather having been dead.

ACT III

Should no one. Shown.

ACT III

Therese.   Shone. Or wood. Or would she. Be fond of leaving. Open. But not after night fall. The entrance as a door.

ACT III

Therese.   There is no care to have them share anything with her as her sister will be longer in not adding more or longer. Can you see that they are not the members of the family.

ACT III

She may be easily heard to be. One of four or of three.

ACT III

Therese.   May more quietly and noisily. This may be not only is not the habit of the country.

ACT III

Therese.   Ours and hours in their country.

ACT III

Therese.   If they will remember one another.
If the father and her brother.
Come back as they shall.
With less or more than ever.
But best because there is no doubt.
She will need when. They had.
Better come to eight.

ACT III

It is strange not to be timid but not to go alone. Because. He is timid. And he does not go nor go not go without them.

ACT III

Therese.   May be well and not willing.
She may be well and willing.
She may be well and she may be willing.
They will go with some some go.
They go and it is as well.
That they are well.
They are well and they are willing.
Some go and some are willing.
Some go and some are well.

ACT III

It is very easily forgotten. Who was going.
As easily forgotten. Who was well.
As easily forgotten Jenny William.
And as easily forgotten. Jenny. William.

ACT III

It is as easily forgotten. Jenny William.
It is as easily forgotten. Any money.
It is as easily forgotten. Mushrooms.
It is as easily forgotten and Jenny William.

ACT III

George Couleur.   She may be often told less. Anybody may be an
orphan. That is with women. With a mother and a wife and any
other. Anybody may be an aid to any. Be women. Two may. Be.
Women. Anybody may aid any orphan to be of women. He had a
mother and a wife living.
George Couleur.   If they did. Stay and nobody went away. Which
one went with them. He went with oxen and they went with and

with him. He stayed with oxen and did not they did not they went with them. It is easy to resemble men and women and oxen with them.

ACT III

Therese.   Two many twos whose. Which went with them. She had a mother and a father and two brothers with them. Very often as much.

Therese.   All who are timid with them.
May be they will for them.
As many as stay with them.
They will be ready with them.
They add it with them for them.
It ought to be eight or them.
And so with any for them.

ACT III

It takes several weeks for it to pass away.

ACT III

Therese.   She shall be certainly sharing her quarter. And they will like blankets.

ACT III

I have decided that only the timid.
Are eating. Only the timid are eating.

ACT III

Therese.   Either whether. They will. Gather.
Therese.   Will not tell whether he is very well.

Therese.   Because he will have heard it heard that he is very well.

Therese.   Should they be careful or with them cautioning or with them caution.

Therese.   If they are leaving or not leaving as well.

Therese.   Will. Tell.

ACT III

Therese.   May need no as a distinction and she will come as well. She will not need no not need no as a distinction she will come as well.

Therese.   And now do I need my life.

ACT III

Therese.   Any day or any day I may stay with them all of every day. And so gradually.

ACT III

George Couleur needs more to be obeyed or as they are more. To be obeyed.

George Couleur.   Leaves no one to add more to each one. To leave more with each one. To come one.

George Couleur.   Feels often healthier.

George Couleur.   May join exactly always in their way as never, or indeed.

George Couleur may think and have as need. May be they do require a wife and mother.

George Couleur or one another.

ACT III

George Couleur.   Will work with his oxen as hard will work with his oxen as hard. Will work with his oxen as hard.

George Couleur.   May they be there for her with her.

And still waiting for a visit to her.
To them to her.
George Couleur. May be they do.

ACT III

George Couleur. For when her. For the love of for when her.

ACT III

Therese. Has been thought very even may even have come.

ACT III

No one knowing any one or Jenny and William. They may be many of them and they will who will be going by then or marry William. Not as Jenny.

ACT III

Therese. May have added coming to women.
She herself with any feeling.
Or nearly when they were needing.
It is easy to remember them with angry feeling.

ACT III

She chews gently at her food.

ACT III

Therese. If asked would it be a gain.
It would be very plain.
That they meant to remain.

And it would not be a pleasure to remain.
But to remain. All the same.

ACT III

Therese.	It will or they must with their care be very busy.
Therese.	She may be often left to be aware.
Therese.	She may be often there.
Therese.	Or with them they may be not often.
Therese.	They may not be as often there.
Therese.	But which with them. They will not be.
Therese.	They will not be often there.
Therese.	Just at one time.
Therese.	They may not be as often not there.
Therese.	They may be not as often and not there.
Therese.	They may be there.
Therese.	Would they have heard.
Therese.	That they would go again.
Therese.	Only one.
Therese.	They would be there.
Therese.	Just when they were as well there.
Therese.	As often there.
Therese.	They were there.
Therese.	Which was not but it was by the time there.

ACT III

Therese.	In consequence.
Therese.	They were there.
Therese.	As they were not there.
Therese.	In answer to not there.
Therese.	But which in answer.
Therese.	With it is it is.

ACT III

George Couleur. Mountains and might then.

George Couleur. If a mountain is covered with snow I have not seen it.

George Couleur. Nor with them in wedding.

George Couleur. In summer.

George Couleur. May in the middle.

George Couleur. Of winter.

George Couleur. Nor what is winter or weather.

George Couleur. How many acres can be as a mother. Nor any father.

George Couleur. They never think together.

George Couleur. Or any other.

George Couleur. Please think of it with it.

George Couleur. A great many read a mother for a father.

George Couleur. With one a mother.

George Couleur. Or as or father.

George Couleur. With as or mother.

George Couleur is married and resumes well, being well he resumes being well.

George Couleur is married and he resumes being made very well by winter and by summer.

George Couleur has no use for a difference in oxen he knows very well well.

George Couleur for they may take pains.

ACT III

At last they change, they may be made to change red to blue all out but you, and so they think well, of resting. They may be feeble with pleasure and excellent at most.

ACT III

Anxiously for their investigation in order to please and be pleased with more there. With which. They may plan. With which. They may plan with. More there. Or for it. And so anybody which may as pleases.

ACT III

If George Couleur married to her may be with her married to her or rather her married to her or rather a mother who rather no brother or rather a brother with whoever or other which they may have as a care.

ACT III

Come welcome or most which when they can rest with all as they may in guidance.

And now contentedly eat slowly as often as more.

ACT III

They may be meant not be meant to be restless.

ACT III

George Couleur.   Please be without pleasure for three.

ACT III

Therese.   Having gone and stayed may remain and in neatly and frame.

ACT III

Therese.   Would never know that there had been. George Couleur. Nor would Therese leave when they went investigating.

ACT III

Therese.   They may be religious or met at once.
Therese.   For will they be met or may they be met or may they be met at once.
Therese.   They may not ease be met at once.

ACT III

George Couleur.   It is as easy to be cold with when they will be a plain chain of well or rather not as much as left. To have a fire. They will speak loudly. And not mutter.
George Couleur.   Be met very often as a name.
George Couleur.   It is hopeless to be cold and warm.

ACT III

George Couleur.   Is rather.
George Couleur.   That they disturb is rather.
George Couleur.   He had no brother not even a brother Henry nor a sister not even a brother Henry a sister Clara or a father not even a brother a sister Clara or a father William Couleur.
George Couleur.   He had a mother and a father.
George Couleur.   He had a wife her name is Florence and she may be rested or eating not with or without not with or without them.

ACT III

George Couleur.   More startling.
George Couleur.   Or interesting.

George Couleur.   Or breathing.
George Couleur.   Or explaining.
George Couleur.   Or planning.
George Couleur.   Or laying.
George Couleur.   May they be three in occasion.

ACT III

Therese.   May or may not have heard.
Therese.   Any Therese may or may have heard.
Therese.   She may be with them.
Therese.   As alone.
Therese.   Or a little.
Therese.   Just when.
Therese.   Timid in the scope.
Therese.   Would they wait.

ACT III

Therese may inhabit any two or village.
Therese.   May inhabit two. A village.
Therese.   In not moving from one she.
Therese.   In inhabit one.
Therese.   Therese can inhabit two a village.
Therese.   In visiting a third.
Therese.   Not two and a third.
Therese.   A third village.
Therese.   Two a village.
Therese.   Can inhabit two. Village.

ACT III

George Couleur has been. A street car conductor he has not been. Because he is rich he has been. And had a wife and he has been. Not left to grow more than they have been. His brother that is wedding a wedding.

No more will George Couleur try to cry.

It is easy not to have a fire in autumn.

ACT III

Therese.   She will be older in case.

ACT III

She will not in place.
She will be older in case.
She will not be older.

ACT III

When you will be with me still.
In which way they will.
Which they may.
Will or stay.
Which they will be which or will.
Will they.
Will they stay.
Or will they must.
Stay.
Which way.
A. Thousand.

FINIS

AT PRESENT

A Play

"At Present" is perhaps more clearly a conceptual play that is meant to be read only; perhaps not.—R. K.

Nothing But Contemporaries Allowed

THEY BRING AND SOME.

George Hugnet.   It is felt wish which are they they might be wonderfully and a wish might men. A woman is wire or more.

Virgil T.   A spring like eye lashes which is released. They think their mother with mother.

Pierre de Massot.   Made is a vainly useful lowered with a repeal. He makes it. Made is why they wean herds.

Bébé B.   Five win baby.

Anita & Basket.   A train or pure purely with all.

Maurice G.   We hope to.

From *Operas and Plays* (1932).

Scene II

They come in and they make it is in reason that make and wake made Mary seen.

Scene II

Charlotte comes in and makes women.

Eugene Berman.　　　　Have hatters had a show.

Pablo Picasso.　　　　So all dogs show their tail they mind a part
　　of yesterday they lay.

Alice B.　　　　　　When this you see remember me.

Ralph and Elizabeth.　They are radicals to the core.

Scene III

Virgil T.　　　　　　He makes a mistake in time.

　　In time is reasonably meant let it left it for them to be accurate it is nicely whenever they are around.

George Hugnet.　　　Bewilder or fill there he filled it for Satur-
　　day in two.

　　In the midst of this action two come in everybody keeps guessing they cannot guess. It takes patience to guess I guess yes.

　　What is there needed in a dictionary this is a question they ask.

Henry Levinsky.　　　He comes in.

Bernard Fay.　　　　They who are farther with them.

Mildred Sitwell.　　　It is well all well all very well. How are
　　Howard to-night Howard and Ursuline.

　　Tonny and Anita come in they are not welcome.

Scene II

The door of the house is the same as part. Now when you say part you mean that it is very pleasant.

Tonny and Genia Berman. They repeat what they say.

Ours and ours.

A wandering brook with them to look as well as with a bay.

Andre Masson fastens a choice he makes day no delay.

Andre Masson Eugene Berman and Kristians Tonny sing with a ribbon.

Virgil Thomson.   Buy or by a blind to put horses or a care.

They will wish it for them for or to me.

Scene III

Avery Hopwood.   Is dead.

Scene IV

Pablo Picasso.   Has his hair made his hair has his hair on his head has his hair. So they or there.

Bravig Imbs.   May remain George as three men may re-member George as three men.

ACT II

At present Bernard Fay.

Rene Crevel Pierre de Massot Yves de Longuevialle Herbert Milton and Eric Hauleville and George Neveux and Arthur Acton and William Cook and George Hugnet know Nelly apart.

Act I of a middle act.

At dinner Singria does not sing. After dinner Genia does not disturb a song. Afterwards they will welcome in a direction a correction of well and giving.

Ralph Church was a mother in singing.

Who has translated Ralph Church. Bravig Imbs.

Back to Act II as an ending.

Alice B. tenderly she asks is and are guessing and grading. Mrs. Hugnet makes it be indifferent.

Nobody leaves Maurice for me.

Now we can added Madame L.

Scene II

Bernard Fay and P. Picasso and Christian Berard and William Cook also Robert Graves.
Who has made it do will with them three times in singing.
Women as women.

Scene III

Genia Berman sends a message to George Hugnet.
George Hugnet sends a message to Pierre de Massot.
Pierre de Massot receives a message from me when this you see.

Scene IV

Shut the door.
Two and two make four.
Pablo Picasso mentions that he came.
Singria wakes them up as they go away. He is left a little.
Andreas Walzer is dead.

Scene V

I love my love with an l because she is little I love her with a p because she is pretty.

Scene VI

An antagonism is a flaw an antagonism made of shore a shore is a sea a sample of he with Lee Sherman. He was not invited because it was not certain that it was suitable.
Henry Horwood and McBride. They made speeches in English.
A blonde a blonde can be a Spaniard a blonde can be merrily a Spaniard. Basket and Anita. He squeaks regularly so does Eugenia.
Eugenia who married a postman.

P. Picasso.   I may go and stay.

P. Picasso.   I am younger.

P. Picasso.   I may go and be here.

B. Berard.   I am not acquainted with George who may
although many are my cousin.

George Hugnet. Met is meant and mistaken.

  George Hugnet plans a festival.

  George Gris could come if he wanted to say, Meyer is a name.

  She is bathed in sunshine and flowers.

Scene VI

  Will he break the basket. Or let it fall.

Henry Romeike. Henry Romeike.

Virgil Thomson. Virgil Thomson.

Pierre de Massot. Pierre de Massot.

Alice Toklas.   Alice Toklas.

Jenny Chicken. Jenny Chicken.

Pablo Picasso. Marie Laurencin.

Helena Guggenheim.

Humbert Griggs.

Bravig Imbs and organisation.

Scene VII

  They pardoned the two.

  Kristians Tonney and a tall Pole.

  Polish who has a pretty manner.

Pavelik.   May be very well.

       But I doubt it.

Jenny Lind.   Sang a song.

Marthe Martine. Singing.

Cliquet Pleyel. Makes twenty five a woman.

Virgil Thomson. By by fifty by.

AT PRESENT

George Hugnet.	Knows Juando.
George Hugnet.	Knows Maurice.
George Hugnet.	Knows me.

ACT III

Ralph Church and Bernard Fay and wealth and questions. There are no questions to answer. There are relatively no answers to questions.

It is frightfully in doubt not the dinner but back of it.

Bernard.	Will
Ralph.	Do
Edward Sept.	It.
Bernard and Ralph.	Will Edward Sept do it.

A very tall gentleman came in and said he was very good friends with his equally as tall sister who wrote a book about a general. These were Poles from Poland.

Pierre de Massot, Patrick McIver junior and Andre Masson were invited.

Andre Masson's sister.

Pierre de Massot's wife.

Patrick McIver's mother.

They were not the ones known first.

Scene II

Marguerite in case of all.

Scene III

They made weddings. It is all of it as any of it with a parallel. All who can come can say parallel.

Busy as wooing.

Mr. William Bird has a shop a shop with canaries canaries are red Mr. William Bird has painted his shop a canary red.

Scene III

William Maciver is married to a woman. She is a woman who knows women. Mrs. Maciver is a woman.

Scene III

P. Picasso.   Met a Pole. They invited him to an invitation.
Mr. Pierre Massot.   Came in and he asked.
Mr. William Virgil Thomson said let it by them.
Mr. Maurice Grosset. Liked it as a wire.
Mrs. Emanuel Kant.   Needed to be certain that there is a bloom. To a rose.
Mr. George Hugnet.   Was not to blame. That Marguerite was displeased.
Tonney.   Has come.
Basket.   Has been painted.
Mr. William Erving has died of tuberculosis.

Scene IV

They may be measured for their hats but Basket needs a new collar. The last one did more than wear his hair the last one tore out his hair.

Scene V

Picasso and Tonny.   Have no conversation.

Scene VI

It is very rare to have a scene six.

Scene VI

Harry H. enters and sings. Ellen does.

Scene VII

And what is your name.

T. Thoma.	I have no name in short have no name.
B. Barker.	What is the name of this I adore names.

Scene VII

P. Picasso.	Come and go.
G. Tonny.	Love her so.
Henry McBride.	Leave matches be.
V. Thomson.	They are all to me.
V. Bernardine.	She will compel.
P. Tchelitcheff.	Very well after all it is what I like.
B. Berard.	They make classes.

Baby windows resemble bay windows
When you think of it.
Mrs. Margaret and Mrs. Jacqueline.
May end a scene.

Scene VIII

Pablo Picasso hears Alice talk to a dog.

Pierre de Massot has not come when invited.

Tristan Tzara has found that dogs foundered which is mentioned. He returns horses.

Mrs. Tristan Tzara is very gracious.

Mr. Guevara has married. His mother. Without them.

William Charles Lamb. Have milk with their toast.

Jacqueline is Jacqueline without hesitation. In spelling.

May waltzes. Have sisters. In imitation. Of Hyacinths.

ACT IV

Le Corbusier and Jeanneret
        and   Fasten it namely.
Maurice Darantiere
    Laura has a library.
    The play is to be now adagio. Will it be andante or adagio and
save Laura.
    Save Laura they went there they all went there save Laura.
Me. This would never go into grammar.
Alice and Sarah.   They would never go and save Laurie.
          A hymn of praise.

Scene II

Father who made a pleasure.
Tonny Basket and So.   How will they be an ally.
    Not by laying it as much there.
    It is difficult to make candy their fall.
    There believe it or not.

Scene III

Three Poles. One of them bought a picture that is gave it. It is a
former.
    They went away.
    Two Russians and two a poles made a Russian pole, russian
pole. We said we did not like we prefer the Russian or the Pole.
    To come back to the present.

Scene IV

    It is awfully easy to not be thinking not at all awfully easy.
Virgin Ophelia.   She is a dog named Cleo.

A candle.   They will say. They have been successful
for a protestant named Ralph.
Bibliography.   They have been successful for a protestant
named Jane.
Churches.   They have been successfully this is an effort.

    Jack always has difficulty.

    Lena always has always difficulty.
Birdie.   They made difficulty with them.
James Bush.   He was not dead.

Scene V

George Hugnet.   Can shave.
                         Beards.
George Hugnet.   Can kiss birds.
George Neveux.   Can love hers.
George Maratier.   Can nestle.
George Prunet.   Can fish.

Scene VI

There is no doubt that I in believe names.

Scene VI

How many names are there in it.

ACT V

    Predict pray so that they cross it out.
Herald Lean.   She made a cake.
Betty Jenny.   She is a mistress of a cook.
Helen Avocat.   Was an old looker on.

Jenny Chicken.   Was an individual.

Henry Thomson. Was in his youth very short sighted and now is not a famous lawyer.

Scene II

In which they tell it to them.

Scene III

Bernard Fay.   Managed to close his ears.

William Cook.   Managed to doubt if any one had heard that he had an accident.

Why should she ring a bell three times. Why should she ring a bell three times. Because dinner was ready.

      Continuation afterwards.

Herman and Elliot Paul. And Bravig Imbs. They came and stated.

Scene IV

It is very pretty to have wishes.

Maurice Darantiere have never seen Pierre de Massot.

With them.

Virgil Thomson has met Kristians Tonny and gone there with them.

George Hugnet has not neglected to attend to something that was missing with them.

And then it is lifeless.

P. Picasso is married and is made interesting with them.

All of it.

They have an allowance.

Geraldine Bonner is not the same as Grace Llwyllen Jones nor David William McIver with them.

They are sweet eaters with them.

Scene I

Bridget Gibb. Who is a wife of genius. She is a wife of genius. Now realise a genius or genius.

Scene II

Virgil Thomson. Measures scenes in sitting. A sitting room is where they sit.

FINIS

THE FIRST READER

This includes the phrase that became the title of the first Stein biography—When This You See Remember Me *(1948).*—R. K.

To Carl Van Vechten

Who did ask for a First Reader

Lesson One

A dog said that he was going to learn to read. The other dogs said he could learn to bark but he could not learn to read. They did not know that dog, if he said he was going to learn to read, he would learn to read. He might be drowned dead in water but if he said that he was going to learn to read he was going to learn to read.

From *The Gertrude Stein First Reader and Three Plays* (1946).

He never was drowned in water not dead drowned and he never did learn to read. Are there any children like that. One two three. Are there any children like that. Four five six. Are there any children like that. Seven eight nine are there any children like that.

Ten. Yes there are ten children like that and each one of the ten had a dog like that. Ten dogs like that and ten children like that, and the dogs and the children played tit for tat but there was no learning to read in that, not even if they each one of them was fat, fat just like that.

Next to this was a hare and next to the hare was a bird a daily bird. A daily bird is just a third of an ordinary bird, a daily bird being just a third was very likely heard and when he was heard well was it reading he heard, yes he heard them trying to learn to read the ten dogs and the ten children and as he the bird was a daily bird, and a daily bird is a third of a bird, he heard them every day trying to do less than a third of what they heard, so he said said the bird, I will get together ten daily birds and see who learns to read first ten children ten dogs or ten daily birds.

The first dog who tried to learn to read not the one who said he was going to learn to read that one did not need to have ten dogs to learn to read, he was the one dog who had it as a great need to learn to read. But would he learn to read. Who can tell, a bell learns to read, why not a dog, why not, the dog had tears in his eyes why not. A dog. But the first dog who really tried to learn to read he was a Saint Bernard a big dog so big that if he opened his mouth it was just the same as any word and when he said a word it was a big word. Saying a word even a big word is not the same as reading that word. Oh no said the daily bird no indeed it is not, not, not knot.

Just notice that if you say not knot, how do you know if you do not know how to read, which knot has a knot, and which not has not a knot. So you see you have to learn to read. The daily bird knew what was what.

The daily bird was all excited. He had heard a word. It might have been worm the word he heard but it was not. The word he heard was po-ta-toe. Sweet po-ta-toe, a lovely word, a sweet word, that was the word the daily bird heard. And he said hoe, no they mean hoe or ho and he said ha no they mean tea and he said toe oh yes toe, toe is that so. And then he said no it is not so it is potatoe and he smiled and smiled and said oh potatoe sweet potatoe that is so.

Daily birds like sweet potatoes that grow and if he could not read he could hear it said that they would hoe sweet potatoes in that bed.

Bed Bed, of course a bed when all is said is where you sleep, where any little boy or girl is put to sleep in a bed. But a bed when all is said is where they put potatoes to grow, and the daily bird knew that was so. Bed bed when any dog says bed bed, he means a cushion a basket a kennel or straw but when any child says bed he means a bed stead where he can lay himself down without a frown and with a pillow made of down he sleeps sweetly until he wakes up and comes down, down the stairs. Who cares which way down is spelt but it is spelt the same whether it is in the bed or out, remember all the little ten children were stout, but even so they did go in and out. But to the daily bird a bed when all is said is where the seeds are said to be in bed because they plant them so and so the daily bird when he heard po-ta-toe knew that that was a bed and so he said sweet potatoe bed, when all is said so sweet is a sweet potatoe bed and he heard the daily bird heard that word. Potatoe is what he heard and he read well he could not read but he read that they would plant potatoe seed in that bed and so he said oh how he said potatoe sweet oh sweet sweet sweet potatoe bed. And he was so pleased he was not dead, he was not in bed, and so he said, yes so he said, this the daily bird said.

Remember they plant sweet potatoes in the spring and eat them in the fall and that is all over when children are not fat but tall.

Oh dear yes that is all.

Think about spelling without yelling spell oh spell potatoe and know it is so. Potatoe, even if so has no e and potatoe has an e on toe. Potatoe.

So, now sew and so, so is so and sew is not so, you see to know whether sew is so or so is sew how necessary it is so that is to read is so necessary so it is. And read just think of read if red is read, and read is read, you see when all is said, just now read just then read, do you see even if a little boy or a little girl is very well fed if they do not read how can they know whether red is read and read is red. How can they know, oh no how can they know.

Dogs barking is different they bark louder that says so and so and they bark lower and that says and so and they make a little noise and that says so and so but well even if one dog said he would learn to read there was really no need and so well no, he would not learn to read, what did a dog care to know whether know is no, whether sew is so, whether read is red, what indeed did any little dog need to know, but a daily bird well a daily bird does not sing he twitters so, it is always just so, and so if he reads red or sees sew, even sow or even so so, even if it is printed on a shed and the daily bird sits upon the shed, no it is not for him to know the difference between so and sew and sow.

But a little boy and a little girl with or without a curl or a little boy with or without a toy, it would annoy a little boy oh surely it would annoy a little boy not to know that no is know that knot is not that sew is so and a little girl just even without a curl could not allow that if she saw a cow she would not bow because she did not know how to read a cow when she saw it said on a paper or on a shed that a cow is red. Think of the little girl with or without a curl who could not allow a cow to be a cow because she did not know how to read a cow. Think, oh think of that little girl now.

And so the daily bird was asleep on the bough and that is how it came to be now just now.

All alone a daily bird, it is a daily bird you can tell it is a daily bird because it is never heard. Daily daily daily bird.

Now the ten children who were stout were beginning to move about, and one said and another said and another said and another said and another said and another and another said and another said and another and another and they all ten said now if we count will we like it better that we see a bird a dog a cow or a hen, and when

when they said a hen, they all began to cry and say no not I, I want to see a daily bird, a daily bird and that was all that was heard all the ten little children who were fat, they were just that, and being fat, they were afraid and being afraid they were not layed where they had seen a dog or cow oh dear not now, they would rather than read than weed, so that was what they knew, now remember about knew and new. Just remember, it makes one think of a cat just like that, it makes one think of a dog or a frog it makes one think of a man or a can it makes one think of also ran. Just think of that, a bird can twitter and sing and fly like anything, but a daily bird well a daily bird is a third of a bird, and eating is not everything, there is reading and writing, there is running and walking, there is sitting and hitting, there is barking and talking, there is white and black. Oh dear to read white and black. It looks very funny indeed it does. White And Black. It does look very funny indeed indeed it does.

PART TWO

The daily bird might be right.

Halve biscuits and have biscuits. Have to have biscuits. Have to halve biscuits. And have to have half a biscuit. Just think how to drink lemonade and have payed to have a biscuit or to have bread. When all is said. So you see said the daily bird, I like crumbs said the daily bird, crumbs of biscuits and crumbs of bread, but if the ten could not sleep in bed and when all is said could not read what is read, would I and the Daily Bird gave a sigh would I have crumbs of biscuits and bread and if I had not any crumbs then I would be dead, that is what the Daily Bird said. Dogs bark, it is dark and dogs bark and the Daily Bird well the Daily Bird had a friend, there were ten daily birds and three of them just three of them preferred the dark even if dogs the ten dogs did bark.

Bark, do you know what bark is, bark is what a dog does in the day time and in the dark and bark do you know what bark is, bark is what surrounds the wood on a tree and makes the wood all lovely for you and for me because all the ten little children quite stout could mount on a chair, perhaps the chair might break and feel like an earthquake because the ten little children were stout and if they were stout and the chair fell about then of course the stout ten little children would shout, and if and if not then what, they would carve their names on the bark, not the bark of a dog not even the bark of their dog, the dog who said he would read not even on that dog's bark would they carve their names but on the bark of the tree, dear me.

Lesson Two

A little boy said I read a new word to-day.

What did you say.

The little boy said I read a new word to-day.

What word they said.

You guess he said.

Guess that's a new word.

No said the little boy no not that.

That they said, that is a word you never heard.

Oh no said the little boy don't I know that.

Well they said is it know.

No said the little boy no it is not know cant you guess he said.

Is it guess they said.

No he said no it is not guess not at all guess and not yes not at all yes, please guess.

Is it please they said no he said, not please, you are just anxious to please.

Is it anxious they said is anxious the new word you just read.

Yes said the little boy anxious it is, that is the new word I read. Yes they all said.

And they were so pleased that they had guessed.

Fortunately, fortunately is a long word, they would never have guessed fortunately, fortunately they were already to go and so it was yesterday.

Yesterday was a long word they would never have guessed yesterday, they might have guessed Wednesday or to-day but they would never have guessed yesterday.

One little boy said, I do not remember yesterday. Then the other little boy said I do I remember yesterday, yesterday is to-morrow. And they all laughed. They thought that was very funny.

By the time they had stopped laughing one little girl said, I was very wide awake yesterday.

Yesterday they all said.

And she began to cry. Yes she said I was very wide awake yesterday.

And then they all began to sing like anything.

I was very wide awake yesterday and they sang it and they sang and then the little girl said I said it, she was the one who had said it and they all said, yes she said it and then they all sang yes she said and they all laughed and laughed like anything.

By this time it was time to go home and they all said who said, and they all said I said and then some one said who was not a little boy or a little girl it is time to go home and they never said it is time to go home no little girl no little boy ever said it is time to go home. They can never have said it that way, you just try to say it that way any little boy any little girl, you have to learn to read before you can say it that way, it is time to go home.

There is something about that, no little boy no little girl who cannot read can say that.

Lesson Three

Willie Caesar was a wild boy. Whether he went or whether he would not go he always saw a w. Counting ws was a way for Willie Caesar to pass a whole day.

When he went away it made him wish that it was better weather. Which was why it was as well for him not to win whatever there was to be won. If he won well then he was one and in one there is no w.

But and butter is always but, but what. Now no one would ever think that Willie Caesar was attached to butter but he was. He ought to have been attached to cream because that would go with Caesar but no Willie was like that. Cream made him feel funny but butter, he did love butter, he loved butter better even than counting ws, and that is why he was so thin.

It seems funny that Willie Caesar was like that.

Willie Caesar loved to sit on a wall. He loved to wait for a wind, that is when he was flying kites and he was wonderfully well, and he was Willie Caesar and he would always wind up any piece of string and he was white with delight when the wind was whistling which is the way wind has. He liked the wind to be from the West which was his wish. Oh Willie said the West Wind, if your name was only Willie and not Caesar.

But Willy would not listen to the wind, his name was Willy Caesar and no matter even if the wind was from the west and was nice and windy he would not not have his name Caesar, he just would not.

Willy said that the wind from the West was welcome to go away if it only wanted Willy to be Willy and not Willy Caesar. Willy Caesar was what he was. He was a wild boy and he was called Willy Caesar because Willy Caesar was his name.

When he sat on a wall he was awake wide awake. Which was not a mistake.

When he sat on the wall and was wide awake he Willy Caesar said a wall will fall. Well will it.

If said Willie the wall will fall then unless I am as soft as butter I will be wounded by the stones and the clatter. And it will, it will fall, the wall will fall and Willy Caesar not being as soft as butter but only as thin as a pin was wounded by the stones and the clatter.

As he was falling off the wall he counted the last ws of all and that made how many? Wall, Well, Wall, Willy.

Lesson Four

Benjamin Baby.
Baby Benjamin.
Borrowing Baby Benjamin.
Benjamin was his name and he was not a baby. Little by little he was not a baby.
Saturday he was not a baby and Friday he was not a baby.
He was a baby Tuesday and Thursday.
He skipped Wednesday and Sunday. Wednesday and Sunday was when they borrowed Benjamin Baby.
So it was easy to notice which day it was. Was Benjamin a baby and you knew which two days it was. Was he not a baby then you knew which two days it was. Was he a borrowed baby then you knew which two it was.
And then there was Monday. Nobody ever knew there was a Monday, and yet they might know because on Monday there was no Benjamin Baby at all. There just was none.
How do you do said everybody on Monday and there was nobody to say how do you to because there was no Benjamin Baby at all.
More than that, Baby Benjamin had very little to say, he talked all the time but he had very little to say.
It does sometimes happen like that and when it does happen like that then Baby Benjamin has to wear a hat.
By all means when Baby Benjamin has to wear a hat and he always has to wear a hat, everybody wondered what day of the week it was. Was it a day of the week. You know sometimes a week has no days, when that happens joy abounds. But later well later they see Baby Benjamin and they know that a week has days nothing but

days. So it was very easy to know Monday, no baby Benjamin, Tuesday Baby Benjamin was a baby Wednesday, Baby Benjamin was borrowed, Thursday Baby Benjamin was a baby Friday Baby Benjamin was not a baby Saturday Baby Benjamin was not a baby. Sunday they borrowed baby Benjamin. And so the week was over and everybody knew what day of the week every day had been, it was not necessary to read or write all they had to do was to watch Baby Benjamin, and nobody had anything else to do than to watch Baby Benjamin too and so everybody knew what day any day could be. Which was a pleasure too, and a trouble too but what else could they do. Baby Benjamin boo hoo.

Lesson Five

Wild flowers.
Is Ivy on a tower a wild flower.
If white violets come out before blue
If they do.
Then it is true.
That the dew
Likes white better than blue.
If they knew.
White shows more than blue.
And then spring,
Spring makes water
Water makes spring,
And that makes everything
Just like anything.
If you see a yellow butterfly before a white one,
If you do
That means that the white one is coming too.
If you see two white butterflies before you see two yellow ones,
That means that everything is coming true.

Just for me and for you.
Believe it or not but you do.
That is what makes flowers come through
Yes they do.

Lesson Six

Just why Johnnie was Jimmie.
Just why Jimmie was Johnny.
Johnnie liked to measure everything, he liked to measure from here to there.

He liked to measure more than he liked to read yes indeed.

He measured his hair, he measured his share of a pear, he measured his feet he measured to where he would meet he measured his mother and his brother and he measured Jimmie.

And that was why Johnnie was Jimmie. Because Jimmie was measured by Johnnie, so that when Johnnie measured Jimmie they were back to back and when they were back to back because Johnnie was measuring Jimmie, Jimmie began to measure Johnnie and they were so back to back that neither Johnnie nor Jimmie could back. They were just back to back. Which was Johnnie and which was Jimmie or was Johnnie just Jimmie and was Jimmie just Johnny and just back to back.

Nobody knew if it was true that Jimmie was measuring Johnny or if Johnny was measuring Jimmie, nobody knew and this is true, that measuring everything from there to there makes it that nobody could tell whose hair was being measured there, was it Johnny or was it Jimmie or was Jimmie just Johnny or was Johnny just Jimmie.

It is better to read than to measure even a treasure. If you read it is true just like me and like you but if you measure well how can you be so together that it is true that Johnny is just Jimmie and Jimmie is just Johnny and they both are through.

Better much better to read than to measure, measure from there to there, very much better.

Lesson Seven

By the time dates are ripe, by the time bananas are yellow, by the time olives are green by the time there is no in between, by the time it is time to get up and be sleepy by the time all the words are written by the time chocolate is sweet and sugar is eaten by the time oranges grow and they all say so, by the time it is hot in summer and cold in winter by the time everything grows and everything shows by the time any boy sees by the time any girl knows by the time one is one and two is two by the time three and three make six, by the time shells have no fishes by the time water is blue by the time children are lost by the time too they are found through having been put to, work and play too, by the time it is not easy to have to do what they do by the time they are through by that time they two can read one and two and you and true, so they do.

Lesson Eight

The thirteenth of March was a day when it was dangerous to play.

The moon was full that is to say the moon was full of moon.

The water tide came in and out and everywhere all about it was dangerous to go in and out.

A little boy said he would all the same, the little boy had a name. But nobody said his name. It was just better not to say the same.

And so when everybody stayed at home because the thirteenth of March is a day like that, this little boy accompanied only by a cat and without a hat went out, the round of the moon was just turning about and he began to shout. And just th[e]n a fat hen saw a trout. It was a little trout who was just getting to go about, and the fat hen said when I see that trout I will be a duck and go about in the water and eat that trout. This was a mistake the fat hen would not have thought of doing so if it had not been that it was March the thirteenth a day when it is dangerous to be out, so the hen thinking she was a duck in a theatre and that the water was not real went after the baby trout and the fat hen was drowned dead before she could get out when she had found out that she was not a duck in a theatre but a hen in the water.

So the little boy who had a name saw that so he put on his hat and tried to go home again. But and that is why it is dangerous to be out on the thirteenth of March, the rain came again and before the little boy who had a name could say when he was drowned like the hen. This is what happens on the thirteenth of March, no little boy should say when then.

Lesson Nine

The sun is very full of sunshine which is very pleasant just at nine, when the wash is hanging out on the line. Turkeys are wild and turkeys are tame which is a shame. Peacocks too and they are blue and if all this is true who are you.

This is what the sun said when after having been up since nine he thought of setting time after time, but they said no, what is there to show that the sun has sunshine if he is setting all the time. So the sun said he would shine even if it was nine and he did just as if he was a lid which he was because there was a cover which did cover all around the sun cover the sun all up and after that there was no bother nobody had to get up even at nine. Anyway there was no sunshine, not yesterday. It is different to-day. Thank you very much for such.

Lesson Ten

This is the way they talked. Who said which first. If he said which first, which which did he say first. He scratched his head and he said, for me just for me I like which first. Well that was very funny not just for money but that was very funny, very very funny. Then they began to think well not really to think, you know what thinking is, you look up and you look down and you think and when you think well when you think you know which says which first. Each one who thinks thinks he said which first. Not to be neglected they think again. And when they think again, well now it is extraordinary, but when they think again which is extraordinary then better and better and more and more they know which one said which first. Now which one did. That is the question. Which one said which first.

Almost at once each one said which first. Almost at once. And then it was very kind, it was very kind of each one very kind of each one to think that they said which first. Very kind indeed, yes indeed, very kind. It was very kind very kind indeed, of each one of them very kind indeed of each one of them to think that each one of them said which first. Very kind, indeed very kind, indeed very kind indeed.

Yes very very kind.

Lesson Eleven

Now when butter is careless, and milk is anxious, and potatoes are mournful and spinach is angry and carrots are sudden and cabbage is morose and eggs are polite well then when that happy time has come it is very necessary that every little boy and every little girl says how do you do, and when every little girl and every little boy has said how do you do, how does every little boy and how does every little girl do. They just say very well I thank you that is if they know how to say that but if they do not know how to say that they just say well they just do not say, they do not say how they are. Imagine that when every little boy and every little girl when every little girl and every little boy says how do you do, well then nobody sometimes just nobody does know how they do do. Do first think about that.

It is almost quite almost necessary, almost quite necessary to think about that.

By this time they are all there, believe it or not as you like but it is true, by this time they are all there, all there by this time.

It is very likely that they prefer peas to spinach, it is very likely and it is very likely that they prefer water to daisies very likely, it is even more likely that if they walk and there is mud, that there is mud where they walk. What is more likely. Well really nothing is more likely. Nothing is as much likely as that. Nothing. Just think of that.

Lesson Twelve

Some sheep are loving and some sheep are not.
What what.
Can canaries cry.
Not if four pansy buds can try
To be better and better.
Better than butter
Butter what
Butter cups
Butter cups are yellow
So can pansies be
Which make pansies come to see
That butterflies come sooner than a bee.

Butterflies butter cups
Butter butter nuts
Butter Butter
If sheep are loving
What does it matter,
Cows make butter
Sheep can try
But it makes them cry,
Butter butter,
So they stamp their feet,
Which are neat,
But not better than butter.
Oh butter oh butter,
A sheep can butt her
Yes she can yes she does
Loving as she is,
A sheep can butt her
Which she does
When a little dog is yellow
Yes she does
She does butt her.
Butter.
For which we say any day butter is better.

Lesson Thirteen

Jenny is a little girl with blue eyes. She was fond of flowers but she was discouraged about picking them. Whenever she picked them pretty blue flowers or rosy flowers or pink flowers or white flowers and she held them in her hand or she tied them up in a handkerchief, by the time she got home they were all gone, there were none left and she never knew what had become of them. She thought it was very funny but it was so all the same. She thought it had to do with her hands and so she was always comparing her hands with the hands of little girls who brought home flowers but her hands and the hands of the other little girls looked just the same. She did not know what it was but there it was, it was just like that, no matter how often she picked flowers and however carefully she held them in her hand or her hands when she came home her hands were empty, there were no flowers in them.

Now why was it.

If anybody could tell her would it help her or would it not.

Lesson Fourteen

Once upon a time there was a farm on a hill, and there was a tower there, and there was a large farmer's wife there and as she stood there she saw a soldier passing. He looked at her and she said to him young soldier what are you doing. I am just passing said the soldier. And she said to him and why are you all alone. I am all alone said the young soldier because I am lonesome. Why are you lonesome said the farmer's wife. Because said the soldier I come from a place where they have been bombarding. And are your people dead, she asked. Oh no, said the soldier, they are alive but they have no homes, all their homes have been bombarded to nothing and the church where I went to see a friend married just before I left home, that too is all bombarded to nothing. Just then the farmer came along and he said to the soldier come in. And they sat him down at the table and they talked together until evening and the young soldier went back to his garrison. He was still alone but was he less lonesome. No he was still lonesome.

Lesson Fifteen

Believe it or not it is true.

They need what they need which is blue.

And the wind blew and they blew and they whistled for you and then well almost always it was true that just as much as ever they could they would just as much as ever they could and by the time it was often well just by the time it was often they began to soften and much as they liked it they went away twice. Now going away once is not often but going away twice just going away twice makes them not like mice. They think very carefully whether mice or in the house or out of doors they do think very carefully twice about mice.

You know it does get to be a habit to do everything twice. If you do it in private you will do it in public, but it works the other way so they say, if you do it in public you will do it in private so you have to be awfully careful just most awfully careful about that word twice. You do whether you do or whether you do not like mice. You do have to be careful about twice. Twice is one of the things one of the things about which you have to be careful.

Twice. You have to be careful twice, once and then twice. How nice.

Lesson Sixteen

A Play

Act One

A little boy was standing in front of a house and opposite him was a blackberry vine. The blackberry vine had a very pleasant expression.

How do you do little boy, it said.

Very well I thank you said the little boy only I am all alone.

Not like me said the blackberry vine I am never alone.

No said the little boy not even in winter.

No said the blackberry vine, not even in winter, I am never alone come and see said the blackberry vine always with the pleasant expression.

Just then a little girl came along and she saw the little boy and she said to him how do you do little boy.

The little boy said very well I thank you only I am all alone.

Not when I am here said the little girl if I am here then you are not alone.

Yes said the blackberry vine and it had a pleasant expression yes he is a stupid little boy he does not understand anything.

Act Two

The little girl took the little boy's hand, she said now let us go away and play.

Not at all said the little boy I cannot go away and play because I am all alone.

Beside said the blackberry vine still with its pleasant expression if you went away I could not go along, a blackberry vine is never alone so it cannot roam.

Well said the little girl I see no reason why the little boy and I should stay with the blackberry vine.

But said the little boy I do not stay with the blackberry vine, because if I stayed with the blackberry vine I would not be alone and I am said the little boy I am all alone.

He is said the blackberry vine he is a stupid little boy he just does not understand anything.

The little girl was not pleased with the blackberry vine, she did not like his pleasant expression not at all, but since the little boy would not come at her call she had to stay with the little boy and the blackberry vine.

ACT THREE

The little boy sighed, he said it is bad to be all alone.

But said the little girl and the blackberry vine, not at all little boy not at all, you are not all alone not at all alone, you stupid little boy, stupid stupid little boy.

I wonder said the little girl I wonder is he all alone I wonder.

And the blackberry vine began to cry, it still had the same pleasant expression but it began to cry. Oh my, it said perhaps I am all alone perhaps if I try I might only sigh and not have anybody else be by. Perhaps the little boy knows why.

And the little girl said not at all not at all not at all. The little boy is not alone, about the blackberry vine well it can do as it likes but the little boy no I will show the little boy until he knows it is so, and if the blackberry vine scratches, and I put on ashes on the scratches the little boy will know I am I and so he will not cry because he is all alone.

And so that is what the little girl did, she gave the little boy a shove, and the blackberry vine still with its pleasant expression made the little boy whine, oh my he said it scratches, of course it scratches said the little girl, it has torn my dress oh yes.

Oh yes said the little boy well then I guess I am not alone so let us go and play.

That is what I say said the little girl.

And the blackberry still with the same pleasant expression said go away or stay it is all the same to me, I am never alone and it is true, no matter what you can say winter or summer night or day a blackberry vine is never alone and it always has the same pleasant expression.

The little boy and the little girl had gone away to play.

Lesson Seventeen

Cups and saucers. Tables and chairs.

It was no credit to Johnny and Emma no credit to them not to break the cups and saucers not to cut the tables nor themselves with the knives. No credit to them.

They were very careful to sit down on chairs, they might have sat on the stairs but they did not, they were very careful to sit on chairs.

Noises were heard.

When they heard the noises they though the noises were on the stairs so they got off their chairs and they took the knives and they went behind the tables and they waited.

If they waited long enough they would hear the noises again but they did not wait long enough they began to make noises of their own. Johnny made his and Emma made hers and together they made each others. They thought they were waiting but they were really making noises.

And so even if the noises came again they would not know their knives clattered so, their chairs moved so their tables wiggled so.

And so just when it was all so, the noises came and they did not hear them come.

The noises were on the stairs one by one, and one by one the stairs were run, they were run by the noises that came one by one.

Nothing is so bad as noises that come one by one.

Johnny and Emma were two and so they thought that two would stop noises coming one by one. But no, the noises said no, the noises said just so, we will come from below said the noises and we will come one by one, one by one.

So they came one by one the noises did and as they came one by one Johnny began to run and Emma began to run and they began to run one by one, and as the noises came one by one and as they began to run one by one it might have been fun, but dear me no, it was not so it all came from below, and how could Johnny and Emma run, because the stairs were there and there was no other where where they could run.

Noises coming one by one. And so it was awful and just then well just then the door was opening and in came hopping well not a dog and not a bear, it was a hen and she had something to do she had an egg to put before you, which she did. Johnny and Emma were ashamed, yes they were, they dropped their knives yes they did, they sat upon their chairs yes they sat and that was all of that.

Lesson Eighteen

A Ballad

A big bird flying high
In the sky
Makes little birds sitting by
Know that they must do or die.
It was in the woods and it was dark,
And dogs bark,
But little birds know that dogs are there
There where they cannot stare
Into the nests where birdies are,
But a big bird that flies on high
Even when leaves are everywhere
He can see right down from the sky
And see even nests hidden with care
And so they do not dare
The little birds do not dare
To let the big bird fly too low
Because he will take their little ones so
Right in his claws and away will go
To give them to eat to his own big birds which need to eat and
have a treat of littler birds which are so sweet.
And so.

As I said.
And as you have read
When a big bird flies high
The little birds know they must do or die.
And so they do
And to be true
It is not the little birds that die but the big bird that flies high
in the sky.
The big bird is there,
The little birds with all care all together fly over there.
They fly higher and higher.
And higher and higher,
And they come nearer and nearer
One after the other
Until the big bird begins to feel queer
And wonder what is all the bother.
And so the little birds in a big number,
Come on hitting the big bird on the head
And hoping he is dead.
And another comes down and another comes down.
And the big bird begins to frown,
And he tries to get away
But no there is no way,
The little birds say,
If he gets away he will come back another day,
And so one after the other so
Quickly that they seem like bees,
Come down and hit the big bird on the crown,
And slowly the big bird sinks lower down,
And down and down,
And the little birds begin to frown
And they begin to know
The big bird will go down,
And down and down,

And at last no more,
The big bird can soar,
And he falls down and down
And the little birds keeping hitting at him down down and the big bird at last has fallen down and the lake is there and he will drown.

And all the little birds fly away to tell their little birds to stay all the danger has gone away.

And this does happen any day just like I say.

Lesson Nineteen

Which is, said a wild pen.
Which is,
A wild pen is different from a pencil,
and it is even different from a slate pencil.

A wild pen is a pen that makes blots that makes dots that makes spots.

That is what a wild pen is.

And a wild pen is a pen that can get wilder and wilder and when it gets wilder and wilder it does get wilder and wilder and instead of saying how do you do it says you had better not have said how do you do because if you have said how do you do how do you know what a wild pen will do.

A wild pen will do anything it just will do anything, it will go round and around, it will run away, it will give ink away, it will change its name, it will fasten a stain on a finger so strong that the stain will not go away for ever so long. A wild pen is wilder than anything, it is wilder than a cat or a cow or a bat or a tiger or an eagle or a rat, it is wilder than anything and anybody knows how wild is that.

That is what a pen is when it is wild and so a pen should be told that a pen is a thing to be sold, that a pen should never be bold that a pen should never be cold.

A pen is naturally a pen, and so anyone who has a pen should
be firm with that pen and never let that pen be bold never let that
pen be wild because that is awful for a child to have a pen that is
wild awful for a child, just awful for a child.

Lesson Twenty

Be very careful of how do you do.
Be very careful of when this you see remember me.
Be very careful of very well I thank you
Be very careful of please can I go out.
Be very careful of what do you want.
Be very careful of how many eggs are there in it.
Be very careful of what have you in your pocket.
Be very careful of how can you hear me,
Be very careful of one two three
Be very careful of how old are you
Very careful.
Be very careful of Many many can tickle you
Be very careful again be very careful of how do you do.
Very careful of How do you do.
By this time they were all tired of being careful,
And so
They were told so
they were told to be very careful they were told so.
Be very careful of can you guess.
Be very careful of never the less
Be very careful of it is hot it is cold
Be very careful of I want to be told
Be very careful of next time
Be very careful of at once
But be most careful of all of how to fall when running away.

Be very careful I say all night and all day,

Be very careful of at work or in play,

Be very careful, yes I say be very careful very very careful, just as careful, as careful can be, when this you see be as careful as you can be.

And all the little girls and all the little boys said yes we will be you will see we will be as careful as careful can be.

ARE THERE ARITHMETICS

Are there arithmetics. In part are there arithmetics. There are in part, there are arithmetics in part.

Are there arithmetics.

In part.

Another example.

Are there arithmetics.

In part.

As there are arithmetics. In part.

As a part.

Under.

As apart.

Under.

This makes.

Irresistible.

Resisted.

This makes irresistible resisted. Resisted as it makes.

First one to be noticed.

Another one noticed.

From *Oxford 1927* (May 28, 1927).

To be noticed.

The first one to be noticed.

First one to have been noticed.

Are there arithmetics, irresistible, a part.

Are there arithmetics irresistible resisted a part.

Are there arithmetics irresistible apart.

Ever say ever see, as ever see, ever say.

Notably.

Arithmetics.

Are there arithmetics, a part.

Bowing and if finished.

Are there arithmetics a part.

Ever say.

Are there arithmetics if finished, bowing if finished are there arithmetics ever say, are there arithmetics apart.

Not four.

No sense in no sense innocence of what of not and what of delight. In no sense innocence in no sense and what in delight and not, in no sense innocence in no sense no sense what, in no sense and delight, and in no sense and delight and not in no sense and delight and not, no sense in no sense innocence and delight.

Alright.

Don't you think it would go into arithmetic nicely.

If and intend if and intend, if and to attend, if and if to attend if to attend if and intend, or and nearly equal, two ahead and four behind, two ahead and two behind, two ahead as two, and two, and two ahead and have to, and have it or in needles in case of.

I am not sure I like that one there are arithmetic one day.

If in it as if in it as as has if in it as it has if in it as it has been, if it has been as if it had had as if it had had it as it was, as it were if it were to be captivated, if it were in this and that way very fairly stated, state it. To state it.

Gradually in counting as gradually as counting. If there are more.

Now see here.

Plain plain plain. To be plain, it is plain it is made very plain, plainly. And arithmetic and more so, and more or so. Grapes and chocolate. Name it flourish to flourish to flower, name it as flower or flourish or name it as flourish as flower or flower.

How large is a field when fenced. How many are there of hats and hats, how many are there of cows and cows how many are there how many are there are there many and how many and who says so, so and so.

Now repeat it. Can I repeat it. I can repeat it. As I repeat it, as I repeat it, they and they do, do and do do, do and do too, do and do do. As to a shot, and as to a shot and as to and as as to a shot, a shot or anyway they and to-day very industriously the nearly finished.

It had no intention, it as it had it and it it had no intention, Dora Katorza and it had no intention it had no intention.

Or or or will they plunge us into or, or or or will they will they will they or, or or or will they plunge or will they, they will not. What, rice, what rice or what pears or or what rice or what or not, pears rice, will they or will they not. And what do they mean. They mean to keep by this they mean to keep it or by this means by this means they mean to keep it. Or or or do they mean to bring some more.

Double cover and a double cover. Double cover a double cover. Double cover. A double cover. Double cover. A double cover is used when the one and the double cover is used not used up. The double cover. A double cover and a double cover. Cover.

Shove her.

Not a knee not a knee, see knee. Not a knee not a knee see me. Knot a knee not knot a knee to me.

So Mike did.

In funny too funny, too funny for funny for funny as funny as funny is funny. Is funny. It is funny.

Be can be back, be can be back. For this because of this reduplication.

Arithmetic or more. Cora Moore. They cannot forget interesting days.

Nice little new little new little nice little nice little new little three. New little nice little nice little new little new little new little as three. Three. Three. Then seated. Then sit as if to be seated. I newly carried I carried it away.

Why and why, why and why, not nearly astonished enough.

A BOUQUET. THEIR WILLS.

This is obscure and abstract, as well as unique, as only Stein can be.—R. K.

The Art of Making a Bouquet

The way to make a bouquet or to receive flowers the way to make drawings acceptable or a needle make points of different additional distances which result in a man and a basket at an advantage in consequence of which drawings of calla lilies and green trees and plums all in white and a plan of realising the fancifulness of adaptability when having made azaleas prominent they were more delightful than ever before both as to cherubims and isthmus and alas plenty of time planted in dispersal of the unification of their maligning it by penetrating without a doubt that it was an elaboration of their without having divided what was not only not sent but meanwhile in their enlargement a quarter of it this is what she had when they were entitled to have domes domes and better than ever it is not which when in and

---

From *Operas and Plays* (1932).

letting it have fairly thought making it be with joining it prevailing that it is a chance of a balance by reason of their contradiction inespecial reconciling it more with having introduced not because of prevailing theirs in genuine consideration of it pointedly more than it is made hearts be black upon a brick in color that without doubt and lines made it in straining it from without that most of it coming letting it be seen not with but in the reason for this in said to be made into another purse and language because maidenly can be on account of when willing should it be theirs as an indication of delight that they were fountain of iniquity to change this with aside next to be near that without some to have triumphant netting it more precariously need it for this when is it in appointing that two things made making it from there to have a cactus blend behind in a night with when it is made of which that two make four mainly behind the never have it make it see which can when whether in and altogether they will be beside beside in kings kings have been known as horses and more which can there in place the change of have it for the most of it left to them that is whether it is no account of fed to them in rectifying it by the employment of when a dromedary could be lasting made it have it nor is it considerably named more than come to the persuasion of not more which is confessed at most than there sweetness in allowance because within remained may be as soon as when became left to the undivided elaboration of vindication to be unabridged continuation of whether it is precarious as they single charms as larger than as lambs make it to do unduly in the welcome that is not justified by justifiable inauguration of their will it be not for this and for that alone in the collection of their most and whether if when it is what is what they had which is that the beside and the closest in the main which whenever as they like it is when they do wish to wish what they what they wish that they wish which is what they wish what is the wish which is what which they wish to be a date is when retrospectively in an avoidance of their meteor meteorologically in forbearance that is in no exacting identification of the readily to be not because of the five fifty that it is without it choosing to be so. And so and so. What is it. It is what they wish which is which is which is it.

THEIR WILLS, A BOUQUET.

IN SIX ACTS

Pauline and Charles Daniel and Dolene Chorus of Baltimoreans.
Food fusses me as blowing wind fusses you.
Chorus of Baltimoreans.
Have not had a habit of wills. Let us make wills. He and she
hurried.
Not Saturday but Thursday.
If Charles had no children and only a half brother and half sister and Pauline had two children one of them a daughter and the
other one a daughter and they had not a child of one another and
Charles left his money to Pauline and Pauline left her money to
him and they were both killed together who would inherit everything the half brother and half sister and this was what was as un-
expected as it was startling and she Pauline had done that thinking.
This makes no account of anything of accomplishing and exami-
nation this is finally predicting that if two are killed it is assumed
that the husband will outlive everything and so nothing goes to the
daughters and this is surprising. Let it be changed so that thing will
not be happening and it was done but it took a long time.
Chorus of Baltimoreans had heard nothing.
Pauline. Authorise made easy with a care for them. It is a very welcome for the thing which can that it is plain in conspicuous management of demean in estuary as can fairly make sensibly fortunes
consist in conclusion for the main management. It is all call that a
home is what is can contemplate not be for which in coupled to be
made might with fortune in conclusion.
Charles may be a banker he has heard vainly of a candidly com-
pelled in collection of reconsider in partly that a chicken country
has one kind of architecture and wine country has one kind of architecture and fall of the year that which when makes it a claim.
Chorus of Baltimoreans are distinguished by their management.

In Baltimore there is traffic management in spite of of every country prefer the United States of America of every state prefer the state of Maryland of every city prefer the city of Baltimore of every house prefer his house of every wife prefer his wife and their use.

Chorus of Baltimoreans do not see either the brilliance or the necessity.

Bouquet of rose very tiny daisies made to fit in a receptacle.

Who has pressure to bear.

Dolene and Henry, Amy and Simon Hilda and RoseEllen Nimrod and Caesar. They call classes.

It is a bit whether they go or stay.

Dolene and Charles.

Dol[e]ne detained and undecided.

Charles made courteous by hovering and detaining Helen and RoseEllen.

Caesar respected by a sophistication in memory of reputed roses. John and Albert married to Amy and Hilda.

Who has been thoughtful.

Very well I thank you. Coupled to clauses.

In every hand on any hand in every hand hand in hand.

It is very certain that if they had been killed together they would have if they had made their wills in favor of each other that the half sister and half brother of the husband would have altogether succeeded to all that either of them had had and that the children of the mother would have had no inheritance and rather it would have been an extraordinary pleasure in a way for the half sister and the half brother because there had been some question that had nothing to do with either either or the father who was not their father and the mother who was their mother.

Chorus of Baltimoreans have not been rather have not been induced matter that it does not follow mortgage in a picnic for the summer with fur gloves which have been won one before the other in a way made much after either altogether.

It is not well to think about what they want when they want it.

Charles and Helen are happily married in spite of the fact that Helen has headaches. Helen and RoseEllen Nimrod and C[ae]sar Charles and Hilda Dol[e]ne and Simon Ida and Llewelen Eglantine and Kleber withstand and made much of as they were. As they were in circumstance.

The lawyer of Helen is Herbert Walter.

They had different lawyers but neither of the lawyers had realised the matter and when their attention was called to it they were able to remedy it after a sufficiently long time.

Chorus of Baltimoreans have indefinable resignation and insist[e]nce and they may be never the less susceptible to the symbol of recovery.

How many Baltimoreans have flushes and may be they do and may be they may be may be forsooth.

Charles and Helen may have a little son named Julian.

They will be careful to have it and hurried with every afternoon a nap.

May or may be not.

May be they will if they are to go about it.

A scene in which they are to learn the art of arranging a bouquet.

Find flowers which grow and mix them with grasses known as the bread of birds.

Charles and Helen make banking a profession not because of succeeding but because of Llewelen.

Stones and streams make a change in house and home.

Chorus of Baltimoreans have meant very much to them.

Susan, Who is known as the mother of Elizabeth one at a time.

They have no hope.

Hope and no hope.

They have no hand in hope.

They have not held out any hope.

Who has heard of hours and they meant.

It happens that men's hats are made.

ACT TWO

Simon is a brother of a banker. He is very well off.

Simons a bouquet will be an interlude.

After the third act.

Charles and Helen who are the father and the mother of Julian and Helen is the mother of Kate and RoseEllen.

Claribel and Etta are relations. There is intermarriage. There are plenty of pleasant circumstances. There have been names such as Hortense Louis Caesar Clarence Jonas Henry and Bernard. Any rule is made for Baltimoreans.

A blonde boy can be appointed and maltreated by West Point Cadets. There is no need of probably searching for abbreviation. Chorus of Baltimoreans in allowance.

Nobody likes a bargain.

If one were in a desert and wanted a glass of water and there was no possibility of having it what would they do.

Baltimore integrally.

Do please do do please do please do do please.

Baltimore Chorus of Baltimore Baltimoreans.

If Charles and Helen were married and Helen had had two daughters and their son Julian was not yet born and they had made wills in favor of each other and Charles had a half brother and a half sister and if Charles and Helen should be killed while they were together nothing would be left to any daughter even if they the daughters were the half sisters of the boy Julian who had not yet been born. Nobody had thought that it would happen as it would happen if they were killed together because altogether the presumption is that the man will live longer. How do they like their two per cent they would not even have this sent. Come Thursday not Saturday because of thinking. Thinking one one one one one makes two and San Francisco is made miles of soften.

She sleeps by day day by day she says day by day she says day by day she says day by day to-day now to-day day to day. Which one is it the one that is doing that is to doing to sleep to-day sleep in the day. Bertha Helen Simon Julian RoseEllen Caesar Nimrod Bernard Hilda and Constance and Llewelen.

A list can be filling. They all say.
Chorus of Baltimoreans which is it in forsooth interlude.

They did not matter to a mother who has arranged it differently. Could stocks see.
Chorus of Baltimoreans. Never sing flowers as they are not fond of flowers, they prefer oysters with widening areas. They leave out which is way amount.

A will which is in a reason that it was not brought about may be that two brothers and their half brother and half sister if they have a mother two and mother they will unless it is promised refuse to do so even so.

Might it be for rain.

They like food on the table and screens in the window even when it is necessary.

Think about which came first.

Their wills in forget-me-nots.

Forget-me-nots a bouquet.

Not Charles and not Helen not Julian and not RoseEllen.

When this we see two see one see he sees further than that.

A very little clouded withdrawn.

Charles and Helen who has misnamed Helen. Helen is a nightingale with petals of which with plenty of copper balls of noises in a gather with when speckled of finery. She dresses simply.

Charles and Helen Belle and Belles which could have been pressed with a leaf like a wild pansy is an herb.

A scene in which willows turned into poplars and olives into willows.

Without their having made a will they would not have left their money to each other. Having made a will each of them with their own lawyer they left it to one another and if they should be killed together the assumption would be that the man had lived longer and so if their son had not yet been born their property would not be left to her two daughters but to his half brother and half sister. Thinking of this and laughing is not only what might have happened but would have happened if they had been killed together presuming that the husband lived the longer and their son then had not been born and her two daughters would have been left with nothing and his half brother and his half sister would have had everything.

Simon and William were not half brothers Simon was a brother think of Simons a bouquet think of Simons a bouquet think of everything to say think of a boat rocking made of earthenware and signed and numbered. This is an exact pressure of their widening in the hope of a president.

A scene in which they have dinner quietly.

Chorus of Baltimoreans have no detail which is missing it is not missing because Charles street avenue extended is not any longer.

Means made to go.

If in an auction there are places where they do not hear one another bronzes are pictures and pictures are boats and boats are nets and nets are doves and doves are do and dove tailed.

Chorus of Baltimoreans consist of men and women.

The sergeant said fire fire while you can.

They were not perturbed.

A collection of excellencies.

There are many excellencies in definite delight in handling formally which is without a pleasant time with which to plan to prey upon the saturday in practically for this with the sown of which it is the happy way of dangling in between the four leaf clover a heart and is it well to see it to to see it.

They made miles.

One two and three.

The last time is the worst. Chorus of Baltimoreans consist in men and women.

Have had across.

Consecrated to leaves of wheat.
Made miles in very much that they knew.
Do you know why he thought.
Because he flushed.
Do you know why he smiled.
Because he flushed.
Do you know why he went.
Because he was bent upon it.

ACT III

After Act three there will be an interlude Simons a bouquet.
Helen and Simon.
Would Helen be considered wrong if she was a leader.
Would Helen be considered wrongly not to have been a leader.
Their wills a bouquet.
Would Helen have been considered to have been wrong in not being a leader.
Charles is a banker and he is not cautious he says that one state follows another and he leaves out which one.
They are thoughtful.
If they had made a will in which they left everything to one another and their son had not been born and they had been killed together it would be assumed that the man lived longer so all would have been inherited by his half brother and his half sister and not by her daughter and her own daughter not even what she had inherited she her mother from the father who had been her husband and was the father while she was the mother of the daughter. Thursday not Saturday. Thursday instead of Saturday. She said come out Thursday instead of Saturday, she had been thinking she said come out Thursday come out Thursday which is a little before Saturday. She had been thinking and had thought out his matter.
There is no difference between one daughter and another except that one of them is older.

Chorus of Baltimoreans are all very quiet in the home although they are gay and talk in laughing and laugh in talking. Chorus of Baltimoreans can be slowly tangible.

There is no need for half indeed when they make honey suckles consist in various colors. There is a great deal of happiness in might is right.

Having forgotten every name how can they count when they see the fame that they have earned.

Charles and Helen now.

Simon and Julian and Horace and Hattie and Hilda and Caesar and Nathan and Claribel and Hortense Hortense is her name and Carrie and Eveline. Jonas makes many. It is delightful. They are after all at peace.

Plainly sanctioning.

A scene wherein they have decided to be very certain that they have decided correctly.

They are leaving everything to them.

This is in that amount.

They are not without doubt. Without doubt. A readily felt very well.

A baker should always have a school teacher as his wife.

This is not included in Baltimore.

Does my baby love blue or who. Does that look like a hundred and ten. Stitches when counted silk and wool on tortoiseshell nearer a hundred and ten than a hundred and fifty. A hundred and fifty means four persons.

My baby loves blue and so do you.

Connection between beneath and above. Regularly envisage.

If a million is two hundred and three how many Michaels make a Simon and how many RoseEllens make a melon. Three ages in three.

It is a meadow which makes cake.

It is no matter whether grain has been given or taken. Give and take.

RoseEllen and Julian are travelling they have nothing to do before leaving. They are not going to die. They are fairly certain and there is not hesitation.

Julian. How many days are there in April. How many days are there in May.

RoseEllen. How many days are there in April May and either June or July.

If you are comfortable you had better stay where you are.

Chorus of Baltimoreans. An appreciable difference between hotter in the sun and cooler in the shade and the heat off of a sunny field the more or less hot shade under the trees tree shade is never permanent the only shade that is permanent is a wall of a house or a wall which is a wall, prominent like the, y in Byrne.

END OF ACT THREE

AN INTERLUDE

Simons a Bouquet

Necessary.
Necessary said light, necessary.
Necessary.

Needles in pins.
Pains not knits. Knits necessary.
Necessary. Needles and inns.
In ins, necessary. Needles and necessary.

Celluloid.
Suppose b, c, meant you and he would that shut up. In the best way I will say that there is a short gate. Another wine. Yes. Ick Icktoburns.

A lease.

Clean susans with pallor and a rude cross rude across a smother with a little lang and old chest up. The belief is pain. Yes I died.

Too ducks what. A little suse susianah. It is hutch. All pine.

A sheating.

Poor light, make a mixed stall, show the illuminating lantern and whether not, it was a question. When I came again I come to fastener. This is a good please. Show what shut. Entirely when. It is come in. All the same let.

A cool bay.

What please. If it is near why let the center sound her. This is a little new sense. A bean is arched a little left. All the same Sunday.

A cool bag.

A cool bag has a goal hole.

A bud book lay.

A bud by lay saw if soon to shed a looking sight a tremendous soon. This got out. A left was rest ladled. This made a key soon.

Not necessary.

Simons

A Bouquet

Go in deer. Dear what. A saleing soon. This was a boat.

In. Knows. Necessary.

Noes necessary.

No s necessary.

Knows. Necessary.

No necessary.

No. Necessary.

In climbs and gopher sheds and little keys, large boats wore shells.

Bull put perspire.

No c in me. A last tinned.

Put loud.

Nest oh where cut it spell. Lean more show white. A violin in in.

A walk.

Lay lea a little green. Let it be horses. Horses and a practice, a called practice. Practice not. A least excrescence into the foreseen hillside with two waters not show height. No such peas neglect.

Not walk.

Not walk pot. A pot is a loud sized pea with a nail thimble and a join knot.

Break fast.

Breaking fast so that glasses, glasses, are nets and a thin tongue is glowed glowed with sand and hammer and a noise nail.

A bouquet.

All the bank old dinners are shouted and little cools little cools fishes and big negroes big negroes cigars.

Paid red.

Paid red is a sash not a sash on but a little atlantic. Atlantic what atlantic sit the and lever when, when it is a mother. A mother and a sister. All tracks and leaf leaf of why more should extend so sew more.

Any shade.

Sharp not necessary for a stool. A maid a made where. All this to be boat and a cat less not it necessary not it occasion.

Window, brother, leave call. This is the rate of the road. It makes heavy. It makes what, not carrying this is pass.

Each bone.

Each bone care and a change heat, a change and heat, heat is heat.

A care less.

Suppose it came that by a reason which is beside the shock it happens that sisters are wives, very neatly then mothers are calling. This is disgrace at least in a fashion which makes it necessary that there is a disagreement. Take herd, take it so that there is a kind candle and little blight moon and it is nearly so, it comes to be winter, not winter it has rust and little seizes of the same sam sand stone and hole pieces. This is a bother. Then came to see saturday. All the rest is in the hose. Real bean is oblique.

Neglect of gorge.

A real smell, a real smell is tight, it is stout too and nearly painted.

A real smell is a sticked not so after chandelier. It is a page of birds and little little were trimmed corsets. Nearly all.

This is the mean, meaning in and a question a question of ladling of ladling is ill.

No old clothes make a sash, wet.

Simon.

A bouquet.

(Necessary)

Necessary be when, a violin.

Simons.

Be necessary.

A, follow that with sprain. A leave a rain.

Suppose a cute a cute flute. Be quaver, that is getter.

Simons, not boo.

Simons not bouquet.

Simons a boot quay.

Please claque claque pen, pen with hogs, sticks and stacks.

Simons not bouquet.

Simons tickle.

Simons be such lay.

Simons seat sir.

Simons say nickle.

Simons say.

Simons in why mow. Simons set set let, set, let.

Simons not re leaving.

Simons sit in go shade by a sit so.

Simon.

Simon.

Simon is Simon is Simon is is.

Simons

(A bouquet)

Pleasanting the language of the hat makes tobacco makes it a green shutter. Lively and leaves and let us sundries, sundries is what is.

Suppose a wooden a wooden nickle, suppose it so carried that fruit and vegetables are jewelry. Is this a heard case and it is necessary to keep a pencil in books. Is it neglected.

So that fourteen ninety two makes percent. So that there is a violin.

Perspire. What is perspire. Perspire is not not moon on a light and needs a hundred needs a 100 mills needs a little sandy lea and row needs a sandy needs a lea and row needs a sandy land row.

All gall is dealt with in and much. It is to gay.

Simons, a sin to say.

Simons, grief. Simons dishes. Simons a real little oil and lard stir. A real little steal.

Suppose Simons a bucket to pay. Suppose Simons a real advertiser. See it in furls and in a house paint and a proof a proof of roof. It is a such such touch, touch tough thick pealed oysters and a blessing a blessing is money, money, mealed money, a silent pea season.

Sup in a cap and show it show it farther. A little turn a stage plenty plenty full of going back to [break] fast break fast dinner. This is the time. No use, no use in spots.

Simons, a bouquet.

Re lease a little large prod, prod of what, pave in, between, select bin.

A cool large, a loan, a seed bread, a bolt a bolt a bolt of black brown all brown, all pulled brown all cut.

Leak bet with sheds, sheds roof let net. Limb own seen no limb no own no seen no, limb own seen know, limb know seen know, own no seen limb own seen.

Nick naked and a bloat a bloat hammer a shuckle a shuckle thing a limb own a limb seen own. Go last. Wetness. Go last witness, wit, wit chest wit wit.

A bouquet of Simons.

Leak leak mut, leak a stool a graduated glass, a poison a pill a little grange, a moat, a pile a change, a salt fat, a grain fight, a change bust, a laugh whet, a chill chapper, a chill chapper, a kind horse back, a loaf best, a vexed sugar, a share, a share pony, a pile a put sand, a counsel.

Bouquet of Simons.

Necessarily, not, necessarily not, not not.

A bouquet.

Simons.

Simes whens, siming, siming no song, sung, sung sung sung.

Sing sing sing, singing. Sing sing sing, sing sing sing, sing a sing sing, sing sing sing, sing sing, sing.

A bold bat, bat in batting.

Little wolves hen, hen and hen, lead wolves when, hin and hin, hin up, hinder hinder a peach a peach.

Little wolves.

A roll a roll of pasting with heaven snatches and sups sups and apples.

It makes a baker's pie.

Lead colored light the bouquet has no buttons, not buttons and not limb buttons, a chance leg, a followed piece with little pots, pots of pull, pull, tell.

Please set, set up cold, cold choice beef steak, beef steak not blind, blind not to be all, not a paid egg, six eggs ten.

Not a but.

Part of three, blue black. Part of one, Simon, simoon, must mutter, blue black.

Blue Black.

Blue Black.

Part of one, must mutter.

Part of one.

Must mutter, sitter, sitter in on weighed water, water is weighed black. Sitter in weighed water. [Water] is weighed, sitter in.

Weighed Water.

Weighed water not weighing water, not weighing paint and coal and excellent cream, not weighing a turkey, weighing ducks, weighed breath and bale water, weighed in weight.

Part in one. Part in one excellent exceedingly managed by a returned train that has an omnibus that is to say wheels. Wheels are betired. This is a spin a spin in, a spin in in.

Here is a shed to beef.

In beef. Here is a shed in beef.

Supper in a call. Call in and pass a button a little button with a size of a cap and nearly, nearly. To be all.

Leaf in a hand.

A leaf in a hand and much vegetables much vegetable capable.

Much vegetable capable.

Leave a gold pipe leave a gold pipe in a glass fitting strange older be wired arranger with a neglected pocket case such which is a comb.

Not a nursery, not a nursery and a place and a piece of water and careless, able to guess pleasant cutters, cutters with. Not a coloring beetle not nearly so exhausted.

This is a little higher than that higher than sugar or birds or molasses or real gates or the selected radishes which have tons, tons share. A whole eighty and it sent is an inclined day, a day behind more than fertile in inches. More bellowing.

Boots are not polite blessings. They easily pack in.

Please get let sentences so sunk. A collected extra pin is not what makes sham and pain, it is lordly, lard what it is, come in, come in, come in. Come in. Come in.

Nor a bouquet.

Nor a bouquet, not to lay not to lay. Nor in a bouquet.

A blank gall.

Least Mays seventy nine.

A piece of May warm cream warm cream shutter smash late bycicle jest custard and a sweater, really oats and lark trees and twins in quails, twins and barns and all mice and a kind of stick lantern, really all a joint a joint of eggs more eggs in a wagon in a wagon in.

This is both.

Both what both soup soup late.

Suppose a done can boat and place a right station in a meadow, does grass wind in to fat, does it. Come in.

Leaves of chest, best water rusher, animal eleven dotters and leg late not served in state, more shoes is. Rest or quiet or pale gold or real little water green or a chatter later or a grand and exchanged word room and nearly please and nearly please nervous. What are eye glasses in winter, there are in thin, golden go, go at shoe full and nice screens on tables and mended water. All of it drink, drink a pleased tough reasonable and altogether a travel and more suits. Pale gall with a yellow ribbon and clothes, james clothes. Be go stupid wake land in a house where if a door is a relief a whole door is better than next. Come to dista[s]te that coincidence new bell in. On ease sit with bales.

Six and simons and a birth plate and a loaf of leather.

One and Simons and a back sheet and a last cape and a dog gold cellar.

Three and Simons and real egged black gold and more stress more stress why linked beads guess.

Go shame a glad and garfield season and beds and bakers and let a horse know, let in by spots spots glued and mounted and nervous and really what, why meals are poked and a gallon a gallon is forever forever what, pickles, salt water stranger, beer. No glass is wooden and more deeper collided and a violin a violin is in in a smell.

What is a son, a son is a careful concealed revolving autograph with little saddles and mounted may blossoms and real pay poodles and more selections.

No such walk.

What is a day stake. A day stake is a direct dark dimple and a real question is there talk, is there white siphons, are there pieces of beet sugar placed cups, curls.

What is a careful extinction. A careful extinction is no supper and twelve eggs and really that really that something.

A bouquet of Simons.

In Simons, A bouquet of Simons, Simons. In Simons.

A bouquet in Simons.

Simons. A bouquet, A bouquet. Simons, A bouquet. Simons.

Color in lobsters, release vegetables, please ripe pears, keep a flannel, flannel, keep a kind dog, keep a place for a cigar a cigar green, a green stand, a stand crackers, crackers and crackers.

A bouquet of Simons, all and bellow, all and below, all and, all and and and, all and and and, all and and and.

All call it with a spoon a, all call it with a with a spoon, with a, with a stepper, in a stepper and a rain a rain clearly a clearly startle, a noise soon, a girl beef, a slept height, a real round and a piggle a piggle in between dinner. No bow, no bow caution, not a grease bottle and ache house, not a little light arctic, not a please old carry all in buds and oysters, not in it.

No coat is a pew.

Failing pearl ground and little lilacs and never mentioned in the hand when left in that she by the right long, in the sea shine and search preceeded and little oregon left by separation and more buttons any more indicated more is a baked key a key with an eye glass and fine any fine lap, lap full of of eaten lasts and really old fired reread moistness with a second in plain and much in the collect.

Collect what, it is not edible, not be for and more grown more grown by between and left in the piece of valise which is a case, all in a trunk which is where there is that date that date to be ate sweet. Sweet. Sweet.

Many tickle some one thin, many tickle many tickle with a fellow fat, fat with a pecked old bank stake which means a house. Many tickle some one in. Many tickle some in. Some in bouquet, bouquet of Simons, some in Simons, some in Simons.

Necessary.

Necessary pick out chairs.

Necessary called photographs.

Necessary give gas lamps electric gas lamps.

Necessary go chambers, left in chins and gowns.

Necessary bind cups with lots of dotted dark little poodles and not any dogs.

Necessary read ss.

Necessary put in legs.

Necessary leave on it.

Necessary.

Simons a bouquet. A bouquet of Simons.

Necessary.

Not necessary to be an owl with eggs and sashes. Not necessary. Not necessary to be old and candy. Not necessary to be like like. Not necessary to show oh be wasted. Not necessary to please simple chimneys. Not necessary to have useful bold and between cases. Not necessary to rechange more glasses than to be a ribbon and an inclined hand. Not necessary to be an only wide sheet. Not necessary to be in a seat. Not necessary to relieve old watches and new boats and wide sleeves and old oysters and real butter and extra pears and left over apricots and more white bites and nearly outer with draws. Not necessary to double roosters. Not necessary to see in grate. Not necessary to make nils nils and sheds sheds and brown brown. Not necessary to under re-liver moisture. Not necessary to breathe baths and real paste steps and more shapes. Not necessary to reconsider purchases. Not necessary to miss stems. Not necessary to have it to be set. Not necessary. Simons a bouquet.

If they will all they have to one another and they are killed together the man is supposed to live longer and his relatives will have everything that they had before they had it together if her children have had another father who has not been killed but who has died altogether. Altogether is better than country bread. Bread which not been eaten but which has dried and when it is refreshed is sweeter and eaten.

One two three. Swim.

Do they doubt that they are hurt if they are not cakeless. Can those who said they would sell suffer.

Arthur and almonds.

Give and take.

SCENE II

Red white and blue all about you.
Remy.

SCENE III

Establishment.

If they were pleased that they were white would they like it.

Julian and RoseEllen and fifty million speaking of oxen as pears.

Not in maiden aid in Reagan.

RoseEllen Reagan Joseph Philip and as a wedding. It is very difficult to be unalloyed.

RoseEllen Helen Margaret Lewis and Francine.

If they had made their wills in each others favor and nobody had been there and they would have been accidentally killed it would be presumed that the man had lasted longer.

Who makes chocolate cake out of cocoa once in a while but when they were resigned to having it it had not been made.

Gaston is a name that goes with Berard.

Gaston Berard.

Live and learn.

Chorus of Baltimoreans are exchanged for chorus of Washington and Kansas cities.

Not a cherry a cherry not a cherry not a cherry not a cherry a strawberry.

Chorus of Washington city district of Columbia exchanged for chorus of Baltimoreans state of Maryland.

Chorus of Kansas city changed for chorus of Independence chorus of Independence Iowa changed for chorus of Grant Virginia. And so all day.

If they had made a will come earlier Thursday not Saturday they have been thinking.

SCENE III

Did you my precious pet say not yet.

Interlude
Simons a bouquet.

ACT IV

Anybody with a wife has to have and in a couple of lending lamps lamp a jacket with a cause because do be noon at a day. A day calls caterpillars.

Julian RoseEllen Dorothy Robert Remy Winthrop a little reason for a name and two syllables.

If a man and his wife and she and he had made a will each one in favor of the other and they had thought about it they would have known that if she had children and he had none and he was fond of them and then they have had that if they could she did think that if they were to be alike and came to an accident accidentally and she would be known that is the concurrence that it is presumed that he lives longer not by the time that and she were killed. So that they would be pronounced identical in after all. Perhaps they would not be be left yet.

RoseEllen and Julian. Mother is a mother of one or two and father father is a father of one or two one or two.

The little pasture which has not given place given place.

They made a made a made a wailing down.

Remy. Fastens flowers in broken badly in account for the waiting that it had blown away.

Just as at a finally they must do.

Dorothy. Dorothy had three brothers Etienne John and Ernest. She was known as Annabel and he was known as Hannibal. They had not been doubled in collusion.

Anybody can print a will.

SCENE II

Bother ably dislike amiable with a key stone held handle may be. May be they do but do doubt it.

Elsa more head with italic.

RoseEllen had a pretty very much held by and wall.

He made her think oxen were tall and all if they come down hill will.

They made a lake betake better take a lake.

With wishes and crosses and shawls and alls alls bells balls cover how do you do deniably.

Singing RoseEllen as Ellen.

Playful with a take be mine monkey shine lay low have a shadow of realise wise.

Ernest Wise Henry Wise and Edgar Wise. They were all three three of five brothers.

It is by luck and not by management that Julian was a man.

Their wills made in favor and for shade not for shadow because it is likely supposing that there was an accident and they were found and he was alive and she was not the presumption would correctly be that he had lived longer and so to believe so to do so and it was so.

Everything which is not lost is brought in and very often even if it is lost it is brought in. Bring in.

What do they do when nothing happens.

SCENE III

When this you see remember me to them.

There is no use in saying so in saying so in saying so there is no use in saying so if he does not move in then. There is no use in saying so in saying so in saying so there is no use in saying so in looking as well then.

There is no use in saying so in saying so in saying so. There is no use in saying so in hearing it in them.

Wills are a curious subject. When they are made she can say come to-day.

Wills are a curious subject he can say when he has heard her say come to-day he can say I am coming in a day.

Wills are a curious subject they can say that after all she was right.

Wills are a curious subject they can say that it is told at once.

Wills are a curious subject it may be that her lawyer for her and his lawyer for him were mistaken.

Wills are a curious subject they can be very careful after she was thinking.

Wills are a curious subject it is very easy to move from one side of a sunny tree to another side of a sunny tree and still be in the sun even if it is a hot day and they which is may be they are separately avoiding being in the sun.

Chorus of Baltimoreans are very reserved they tell nothing about pictures photographs fortunes rays of lanterns and dress. They are terrified if any one is beckoning they also feed upon their very delicious food.

Chorus of amiability.

Very many changed Howards for Birds and Freds for Henriettas and Julians for Claribels and RoseEllens for abruptly and belike for forsooth and predict predicate Julia for Joellen and Booth for beside. This is made Rose.

Chorus of Baltimoreans are intermediary and intimidated.

A voice natural to Godiva.

Heard in the distance when made in succession.

RoseEllen and Julian have arranged with their lawyers that their wills are as they should be.

They think of everything.

No interest in do very well very well I thank you.

SCENE IV

Chorus of Baltimoreans have a mixture of their seeing religion.
Chorus of Baltimoreans. Have a conscience about sun on Sunday.

425

Baby might baby might baby baby baby baby baby baby baby might baby might baby baby baby might.

Very near to tears.

SCENE V

Judith and Judy and wildly and sell.

Better very well.

If they were cautioned that they had to wait and they had waited waited with them.

Julian Mary Bernard and soothing.

Would they call the process of elimination that they had inherited. Socially yes.

Chorus of Baltimoreans are mentioned before.

They make satellites in market tamely and sundries.

One one in a single with a stretched as they may be out with them in ferocious conceptions of amalgamated does it suffice with pleasure.

RoseEllen. A with as with confess consent comforted let a melon be an accountable by with a time to be for it.

Supposing they were finally never killed together and they both lived longer how times are they to keep with it.

Chorus of Wellingtonians. Here have a chance to present a lake and let it make a fasten with a catapult and see. Seeds are flown flying and harshly a lake is a jet of water.

There are fifteen women. Fifteen weakening weakening Mabel. Mabel marble distract heather.

Julian is bold whether there is or is not not accountable.

Helen is meadowed with out or with hospitality.

Arthur is felt tightly in redress.

John is nearly succeeding and would look.

Camille cool if a man has a name a man named Camille a man named Camille yet.

RoseEllen is astonished.

Ellen comes to be amount to it.

Gessler made allow.

Fasten a double with welcome and Friday they will come welcome.

SCENE VI

If they had made their wills they had and they had left it to each other which they did they might have been killed together and if they had the children of which he was not the father would not have inherited anything from their mother nor from their father their mother having inherited from their father and the law presuming that if they are killed together the man lives longer.
Chorus of Baltimoreans.

Nothing is found out ably.

They believe that seeing is believing.

They believe that if they wait they are waiting.

They believe that may be they do.

They believe that outwardly with care they will come Thursday and not wait until Saturday.

Make a dent.

SCENE VII

It is doubtful whether they are one and one.

It is doubtful whether they are one and one.

It is doubtful whether they are one and one. It is doubtful whether they are one and one.

It is doubtful whether they are one and one.

Railroad time railroad time.

A railroad in a tunnel.

A railroad within and in a tunnel. A railroad within and in a tunnel. A railroad within in within in a railroad with in in within. A railroad within a within a tunnel without a tunnel a railroad without a tunnel.

SCENE VIII

Called credit.

SCENE IX

Creditable.

SCENE X

He prefers her in Baltimore. She prefers her in Baltimore.

SCENE XI

Very likely they are to move about.
Very likely they are to move about.
A scene in Baltimore with Baltimore a scene with Baltimore a scene in Baltimore a scene a scene of a scene with and of seen Baltimore.
Fast and wound fast and wound they must do their share.
Say much in stretches.
Scene Baltimore.
Baltimore May marry.

SCENE XII

Not lost it.
RoseEllen with well in a point in appoint a councilor or a counselor or a tutor or a better feeling authority in propositions in relation to saving and by all with merriment plenty of course advantages with Friday a man and Ferdinand colors hopes and hopeful and at last and remained if they were willing to be welcome inadmissible without oriole a complaint.

SCENE XIII

An advantage.

Harry who is ill.

Ella who is after every little while very comfortable.

Nelly who owns remaining very far reaching.

Frank who has a return every day in the fastening of a ribbon in an attachment for the reunion of palaces and appointments within call.

After that many manage to have the time to be always ready.

Scene XIV

If in between they care to be Europeans if in between they care to be Europeans in Atlanta there will be after all Geneva in Africa. And about what about what are they referring to.

RoseEllen is always happy to hear and Europeans know that they are after all not having a beginning a middle an ending on a black butterfly without fluttering a black and a butterfly without floating a butterfly black with a grey white border which is not fluttering but flying, a butterfly can fly very high over the water and over the trees and not so well with a very little breeze any solution can be indeed indeed carry all, they may have a train going in and out.

Act Last

Because without with carry a train in and out of a tunnel well tunnel well.

Act Five

Farther.

Father than an act.

Farther in farther.

Than another act.

Makes a medicine seemingly audacious and perused.

Peruvia and precluded.

Rather precautionary in supper and surprise supple in competition in rectilinear in counterpane and at a most than wither a cloud unsupportably dismay with sweeter for the nine in eradication they make mine whine in appliances for the most cause as pronounceably irreplaceable for the financeer.

Helen did they call aloud and say what makes it partake of left to right in vertical with and without their plan if they have not heard of it.

Very nearly Julian.

Come Jonas come and plan half come and to be troubled with a cannot land in interrogation with might it be found irreplaceable in their on their account.

Avery never does believe in twins.

SCENE II

If they were accidentally killed together it would be allowed that it could be believed that if it were possible he would have been living longer and now it would not make any difference and she would could be killed first.

RoseEllen is never hurried.

Neither is Julian.

Chorus of Baltimoreans is never not prevailed for the moment in commission which did if it happens make plenty of in detail with particular in appointment that they were fancied as by nearly really display gracious if so Mary.

Mary.   Mary is so gracious.

Desdina.   Will they have to have a talk with them.

Raymond.   Let out without a brother who is tall when they are very much better than if they could be called about in Rome. Rome is a distance. So is Switzerland and Italy and so is Scotland and England.

RoseEllen Ellen Ferdinand and Maybelle. How are happier happinesses in happen to be fair.

They are fair in leaving it without doubt not as they used to. Chorus of willows and also of little pears.

How are Howard and his cousin with a cousin as a man. With his cousin and have it just couple it out of return in regard to advancing lain for a restful in interdependence they reclothed.

A little Julian.

A larger Louis.

Allowed Amy.

All but very well.

Very well I thank you.

How are Howards left to pale. She is very excitable.

If it does not make any difference will he will she marry them will they will they provide cloth for part of the time.

There is no to do.

Chorus of Baltimoreans not any more in a twitter that time has passed.

One thousand or two framed friendly or few with ready recall of appearing with a winter and window in repairs.

And so out loud.

Their many.

If it is veritable that if they die by an accident they will be killed sooner as much with out Howard and loaves of wishes. Loaves of wishes make water melon. In a hurry. A chorus of Baltimoreans may do may be they may do.

A MOVIE

Stein was among the first modern writers to author a film-script, or at least a text subtitled to suggest that it could become a film-script—or at least a conceptual film-script.—R. K.

> Eyes are a surprise
> Printzess a dream
> Buzz is spelled with z
> Fuss is spelled with s
> So is business.

The UNITED STATES is comical.

Now I want to tell you bout the Monroe doctrine. We think very nicely we think very well of the Monroe doctrine.

American painter painting in French country near railroad track. Mobilisation locomotive passes with notification for villages.

Where are American tourists to buy my pictures sacre nom d'un pipe says the american painter.

From *Operas and Plays* (1932).

American painter sits in cafe and contemplates empty pocket book as taxi cabs file through Paris carrying French soldiers to battle of the Marne. I guess I'll be a taxi driver her in gay Paree says the american painter.

Painter sits in studio trying to learn names of streets with help of Bretonne peasant femme de menage. He becomes taxi driver. Ordinary street scene in war time Paris.

Being lazy about getting up in the mornings he spends some of his dark nights in teaching Bretonne femme de menage peasant girl how to drive the taxi so she can replace him when he wants to sleep.

America comes into the war american painter wants to be american soldier. Personnel officer interviews him. What have you been doing, taxiing. You know Paris, Secret Service for you go on taxiing.

He goes on taxiing and he teaches Bretonne f. m. english so she can take his place if need be.

One night he reads his paper under the light. Policeman tells him to move up, don't want to wants to read.

Man comes up wants to go to the station.

Painter has to take him. Gets back, reading again.

Another man comes wants to go to the station. Painter takes him.

Comes back to read again. Two american officers come up. Want to go to the station.

Painter says Tired of the station take you to Berlin if you like. No station.

Officers say give you a lot if you take us outside town on way to the south, first big town.

He says alright got to stop at home first to get his coat.

Stops at home calls out to Bretonne f. m. Get busy telegraph to all your relations, you have them all over, ask have you any american officers staying forever. Be back to-morrow.

Back to-morrow. Called up by chief secret service. Goes to see him. Money has been disappearing out of quartermaster's department in chunks. You've got a free hand. Find out something.

Goes home. Finds f. m. Bretonne surrounded with telegrams and letters from relatives. Americans everywhere but everywhere. She groans. Funny Americans everywhere but everywhere they all said. Many funny Americans everywhere. Two Americans not so funny here my fifth cousin says, she is helping in the hospital in Avignon. Such a sweet american soldier. So young so tall so tender. Not very badly hurt but will stay a long long time. He has been visited by american officers who live in a villa. Two such nice ladies live there too and they spend and they spend, they buy all the good sweet food in Avignon. "Is that something William Sir," says the Bretonne f. m.

Its snowing but no matter we will get there in the taxi. Take us two days and two nights you inside and me out. Hurry. They start, the funny little taxi goes over the mountains with and without assistance, all tired out he is inside, she driving when they turn down the hill into Avignon. Just then two Americans on motor cycles come on and Bretonne f. m. losing her head grand smash. American painter wakes up burned, he sees the two and says by God and makes believe he is dead. The two are very helpful. A team comes along and takes american painter and all to hospital. Two Americans ride off on motor cycles direction of Nimes and Pont du Gard.

Arrival at hospital, interview with the wounded American who described two american officers who had been like brothers to him, didn't think any officers could be so chummy with a soldier. Took me out treated me, cigarettes everything fine.

Where have they gone on to, to Nimes.

Yes Pont du Gard.

American painter in bed in charge of french nursing nun but manages to escape and leave for Pont du Gard in mended taxi. There under the shadow of that imperishable monument of the might and industry of ancient Rome exciting dual. French gendarme amerian painter, taxi, f. m. Bretonne, two american crooks with motor cycles on which they try to escape over the top of the

Pont du Gard, great stunt, they are finally captured. They have been the receivers of the stolen money.

After many other adventures so famous has become the american painter, Bretonne femme de menage and taxi that in the march under the arch at the final triumph of the allies the taxi at the special request of General Pershing brings up the rear of the procession after the tanks, the Bretonne driving and the american painter inside waving the american flag Old Glory and the tricolor[.]

CURTAIN.

FILM

The importance of "Film" is that it was apparently written originally in French. Few other major American writers have published texts written in languages other than English, though many authors born in Europe have written in other tongues.—R. K.

Deux sœurs qui ne sont pas sœurs

Au coin d'une rue d'un boulevard extérieur de Paris une blanchisseuse d'un certain âge avec son paquet de linge qu'elle était en train de livrer, s'arrête pour prendre dans ses mains et regarder la photo de deux caniches blancs et elle la regarde avec ardeur. Une automobile de deux places stationnait le long du trottoir. Tout à coup, deux dames en descendent et se précipitent sur la blanchisseuse en demandant à voir la photo. Elle la fait voir et les deux dames sont pleines d'admiraton jusqu'au moment où une jeune femme qui est coiffée comme si elle venait d'avoir un prix au concours de beauté et après s'être égarée dans la rue, passe et à ce mo-

---

From *Operas and Plays* (1932).

ment voit l'auto vide, se dépêche d'entrer et se met à pleurer. A ce moment, les deux dames entrent dans l'auto et jettent la jeune femme dehors. Elle tombe contre la blanchisseuse qui commence à la questionner, et l'auto, conduite par les deux dames part, et tout à coup la blanchisseuse voit qu'elle n'a plus sa photo. Elle voit un jeune homme et elle lui raconte tout de suite l'histoire.

Quelques heures plus tard, devant un bureau de placement, rue du Dragon, il y a une autre blanchisseuse plus jeune avec son paquet de linge. La voiture des deux dames approche, s'arrête, et les deux dames descendent et font voir à la blanchisseuse la photo des deux caniches blancs. Elle regarde avec plaisir et excitation, mais c'est tout. Juste à ce moment la jeune femme du prix de beauté approche pousse un cri de joie et se précipite vers la voiture. Les deux dames entrent dans leur auto et, en entrant, laissent tomber un petit paquet, mais toujours elles sont en possession de la photo et elles partent précipitamment.

Le surlendemain la première blanchisseuse est encore dans sa rue avec son paquet de linge et elle voit la jeune femme du prix de beauté approcher avec un petit paquet à la main. Et en même temps elle voit le jeune homme. Ils sont tous les trois alors ensemble et tout à coup elle passe, l'auto, avec les deux dames et il y a avec elles un vrai caniche blanc et dans la bouche du caniche est un petit paquet. Les trois sur le trottoir le regarde passer et n'y comprennent rien.

HOW WRITING IS WRITTEN

What I want to talk about to you tonight is just the general subject of how writing is written. It is a large subject, but one can dis-
cuss it in a very short space of time. The beginning of it is what
everybody has to know: everybody is contemporary with his period. A very bad painter once said to a very great painter, "Do what
you like, you cannot get rid of the fact that we are contemporaries."
That is what goes on in writing. The whole crowd of you are contemporary to each other, and the whole business of writing is the
question of living in that contemporariness. Each generation has to
live in that. The thing that is important is that nobody knows what
the contemporariness is. In other words, they don't know where
they are going, but they are on their their way.

Each generation has to do with what you would call the daily
life: and a writer, painter, or any sort of creative artist, is not at all
ahead of his time. He is contemporary. He can't live in the past,
because it is gone. He can't live in the future because no one knows
what it is. He can live only in the present of his daily life. He is expressing the thing that is being expressed by everybody else in their

From *The Choate Literary Magazine* (February 1935).

daily lives. The thing you have to remember is that everybody lives a contemporary daily life. The writer lives it, too, and expresses it imperceptibly. The fact remains that in the act of living, everybody has to live contemporarily. But in the things concerning art and literature they don't have to live contemporarily, because it doesn't make any difference; and they live about forty years behind their time. And that is the real explanation of why the artist or painter is not recognized by his contemporaries. He is expressing the time-sense of his contemporaries, but nobody is really interested. After the new generation has come, after the grandchildren, so to speak, then the opposition dies out: because after all there is then a new contemporary expression to oppose.

That is really the fact about contemporariness. As I see the whole crowd of you, if there are any of you who are going to express yourselves contemporarily, you will do something which most people won't want to look at. Most of you will be so busy living the contemporary life that it will be like the tired business-man: in the things of the mind you will want the things you know. And too, if you don't live contemporarily, you are a nuisance. That is why we live contemporarily. If a man goes along the street with horse and carriage in New York in the snow, that man is a nuisance; and he know[s] it, so now he doesn't do it. He would not be living, or acting, contemporarily: he would only be in the way, a drag.

The world can accept me now because there is coming out of *your* generation somebody they don't like, and therefore they accept me because I am sufficiently past in having been contemporary so they don't have to dislike me. So thirty years from now I shall be accepted. And the same thing will happen again: that is the reason why every generation has the same thing happen. It will always be the same story, because there is always the same situation presented. The contemporary thing in art and literature is the thing which doesn't make enough difference to the people of that generation so that they can accept it or reject it.

Most of you know that in a funny kind of way you are nearer your grandparents than your parents. Since this contemporariness is always there, nobody realizes that you cannot follow it up. That is the reason people discover—those interested in the activities of other people—that they cannot understand their contemporaries. If you kids started in to write, I wouldn't be a good judge of you, because I am of the third generation. What you are going to do I don't know any more than anyone else. But I created a movement of which you are the grandchildren. The contemporary thing is the thing you can't get away from. That is the fundamental thing in all writing.

Another thing you have to remember is that each period of time not only has its contemporary quality, but it has a time-sense. Things move more quickly, slowly, or differently, from one generation to another. Take the Nineteenth Century. The Nineteenth Century was roughly the Englishman's Century. And their method, as they themselves, in their worst moments, speak of it, is that of "muddling through". They begin at one end and hope to come out at the other: their grammar, parts of speech, methods of talk, go with this fashion. The United States began a different phase when, after the Civil War, they discovered and created out of their inner need a different way of life. They created the Twentieth Century. The United States, instead of having the feeling of beginning at one end and ending at another, had the conception of assembling the whole thing out of its parts, the whole thing which made the Twentieth Century productive. The Twentieth Century conceived an automobile as a whole, so to speak, and then created it, built it up out of its parts. It was an entirely different point of view from the Nineteenth Century's. The Nineteenth Century would have seen the parts, and worked towards the automobile through them.

Now in a funny sort of way this expresses, in different terms, the difference between the literature of the Nineteenth Century and the literature of the Twentieth. Think of your reading. If you look at it from the days of Chaucer, you will see that what you might call the "internal history" of a country always affects its use of writing. It makes a difference in the expression, in the vocabulary, even in the handling of grammar. In Vanderbilt's amusing story in your *Literary Magazine*, when he speaks of the fact that he is tired of using quotation marks and isn't going to use them any more, with him that is a joke; but when I began writing, the whole question of punctuation was a vital question. You see, I had this new conception: I had this conception of the whole paragraph, and in *The Making of Americans* I had this idea of a whole thing. But if you think of contemporary English writers, it doesn't work like that at all. They conceive of it as pieces put together to make a whole, and I conceived it as a whole made up of its parts. I didn't know what I was doing any more than you know, but in response to the need of my period I was doing this thing. That is why I came in contact with people who were unconsciously doing the same thing. They had the Twentieth Century conception of a whole. So the element of punctuation was very vital. The comma was just a nuisance. If you got the thing as a whole, the comma kept irritating you all along the line. If you think of a thing as a whole, and the comma keeps sticking out, it gets on your nerves; because, after all, it destroys the reality of the whole. So I got rid more and more of commas. Not because I had any prejudice against commas; but the comma was a stumbling block. When you were conceiving a sentence, the comma stopped you. That is the illustration of the question of grammar and parts of speech, as part of the daily life as we live it.

The other thing which I accomplished was the getting rid of nouns. In the Twentieth Century you feel like movement. The Nineteenth Century didn't feel that way. The element of movement was not the predominating thing that they felt. You know that in your lives movement is the thing that occupies you most—you feel movement all the time. And the United States had the first instance of what I call Twentieth Century writing. You see it first in Walt Whitman. He was the beginning of the movement. He didn't see it very clearly, but there was a sense of movement that the European was much influenced by, because the Twentieth Century has become the American Century. That is what I mean when I say that each generation has its own literature.

There is a third element. You see, everybody in his generation has his sense of time which belongs to his crowd. But then, you always have the memory of what you were brought up with. In most people that makes a double time, which makes confusion. When one is beginning to write he is always under the shadow of the thing that is just past. And that is the reason why the creative person always has the appearance of ugliness. There is this persistent drag of the habits that belong to you. And in struggling away from this thing there is always an ugliness. That is the other reason why the contemporary writer is always refused. It is the effort of escaping from the thing which is a drag upon you that is so strong that the result is an apparent ugliness: and the world always says of the new writer, "It is so ugly!" And they are right, because it *is* ugly. If you disagree with your parents, there is an ugliness in the relation. There is a double resistance that makes the essence of this thing ugly.

You always have in your writing the resistance outside of you and inside of you, a shadow upon you, and the thing which you must express. In the beginning of your writing, this struggle is so tremendous that the result is ugly; and that is the reason why the followers are always accepted before the person who made the revolution. The person who has made the fight probably makes it seem ugly, although the struggle has the much greater beauty. But the followers die out; and the man who made the struggle and the quality of beauty remains in the intensity of the fight. Eventually it comes out all right, and so you have this very queer situation which always happens with the followers: the original person has to have in him a certain element of ugliness. You know that is what happens over and over again: the statement made that it is ugly— the statement made against me for the last twenty years. And they are quite right, because it *is* ugly. But the essence of that ugliness is the thing which will always make it beautiful. I myself think it is much more interesting when it seems ugly, because in it you see the element of the fight. The literature of one hundred years ago is perfectly easy to see, because the sediment of ugliness has settled down and you get the solemnity of its beauty. But to a person of my temperament, it is much more amusing when it has the vitality of the struggle.

In my own case, the Twentieth Century, which America created after the Civil War, and which had certain elements, had a definite influence on me. And in *The Making of Americans*, which is a book I would like to talk about, I gradually and slowly found out that there were two things I had to think about; the fact that knowledge is acquired, so to speak, by memory; but that when you know anything, memory doesn't come in. At any moment that you are conscious of knowing anything, memory plays no part. When any of you feels anybody else, memory doesn't come into it. You have the sense of the immediate. Remember that my immediate forebears were people like Meredith, Thomas Hardy, and so forth, and you will see what a struggle it was to do this thing. This was one of my first efforts to give the appearance of one time-knowledge, and not to make it a narrative story. This is what I mean by immediacy of description: you will find it in *The Making of Americans*, on page 284: "It happens very often that a man has it in him, that a man does something, that he does it very often that he does many things, when he is a young man when he is an old man, when he is an older man." Do you see what I mean? And here is a description of a thing that is very interesting: "One of such of these kind of them had a little boy and this one, the little son wanted to make a collection of butterflies and beetles and it was all exciting to him and it was all arranged then and then the father said to the son you are certain this is not a cruel thing that you are wanting to be doing, killing things to make collections of them, and the son was very disturbed then and they talked about it together the two of them and more and more they talked about it then and then at last the boy was convinced it was a cruel thing and he said he would not do it and the father said the little boy was a noble boy to give up pleasure when it was a cruel one. The boy went to bed then and then the father when he got up in the early morning saw a wonderfully beautiful moth in the room and he caught him and he killed him and he pinned him and he woke up his son then and showed it to him and he said to him 'see what a good father I am to have caught and killed this one,' the boy was all mixed up inside him and then he said he would go on with his collection and that was all there was then of discussing and this is a little description of something that happened once and it is very interesting."

I was trying to get this present immediacy without trying to drag in anything else. I had to use present participles, new constructions of grammar. The grammar-constructions are correct, but they are changed, in order to get this immediacy. In short, from that time I have been trying in every possible way to get the sense of immediacy, and practically all the work I have done has been in that direction.

In *The Making of Americans* I had an idea that I could get a sense of immediacy if I made a description of every kind of human being that existed, the rules for resemblances and all the other things, until really I had made a description of every human being—I found this out when I was at Harvard working under William James.

Did you ever see that article that came out in *The Atlantic Monthly* a year or two ago, about my experiments with automatic writing? It was very amusing. The experiment that I did was to take a lot of people in moments of fatigue and rest and activity of various kinds, and see if they could do anything with automatic writing. I found that they could not do anything with automatic writing, but I found out a great deal about how people act. I found there a certain kind of human being who acted in a certain way, and another kind who acted in another kind of way, and their resemblances and their differences. And then I wanted to find out if you could make a history of the whole world, if you could know the whole life history of everyone in the world, their slight resemblances and lack of resemblances. I made enormous charts, and I tried to carry these charts out. You start in and you take everyone that you know, and then when you see anybody who has a certain expression or turn of the face that reminds you of some one, you find out where he agree or disagrees with the character, until you build up the whole scheme. I got to the place where I didn't know whether I knew people or not. I made so many charts that when I used to go down the streets of Paris I wondered whether they were people I knew or ones I didn't. That is what *The Making of Americans* was intended to be. I was to make a description of every kind of human being until I could know by these variations how everybody was to be known. Then I got very much interested in this thing, and I wrote about nine hundred pages, and I came to a logical conclusion that this thing could be done. Anybody who has patience enough could literally and entirely make of the whole world a history of human nature. When I found it could be done, I lost interest in it. As soon as I found definitely and clearly and completely that I could do it, I stopped writing the long book. It didn't interest me any longer. In doing the thing, I found out this question of resemblances, and I found making these analyses that the resemblances were not of memory. I had to remember what person looked like the other person. Then I found this contradiction: that the resemblances were a matter of memory. There were two prime elements involved, the element of memory and the other of immediacy.

The element of memory was a perfectly feasible thing, so then I gave it up. I then started a book which I called *A Long Gay Book* to see if I could work the thing up to a faster tempo. I wanted to see if I could make that a more complete vision. I wanted to see if I could hold it in the frame. Ordinarily the novels of the Nineteenth Century live by association; they are wont to call up other pictures than the one they present to you. I didn't want, when I said "water", to have you think of running water. Therefore I began by limiting my vocabulary, because I wanted to get rid of anything except the picture within the frame. While I was writing I didn't want, when I used one word, to make it carry with it too many associations. I wanted as far as possible to make it exact, as exact as mathematics; that is to say, for example, if one and one make two, I wanted to get words to have as much exactness as that. When I put them down they were to have this quality. The whole history of my work, from *The Making of Americans*, has been a history of that. I made a great many discoveries, but the thing that I was always trying to do was this thing.

One thing which came to me is that the Twentieth Century gives of itself a feeling of movement, and has in its way no feeling for events. To the Twentieth Century events are not important. You must know that. Events are not exciting. Events have lost their interest for people. You read them more like a soothing syrup, and if you listen over the radio you don't get very excited. The thing has got to this place, that events are so wonderful that they are not exciting. Now you have to remember that the business of an artist is to be exciting. If the thing has its proper vitality, the result must be exciting. I was struck with it during the War: the average dough-boy standing on a street corner doing nothing—(they say, at the end of their doing nothing, "I guess I'll go home")—was much more exciting to people than when the soldiers went over the top. The populace were passionately interested in their standing on the street corners, more so than in the St. Mihiel drive. And it is a perfectly natural thing. Events had got so continuous that the fact that events were taking place no longer stimulated anybody. To see three men, strangers, standing, expressed their personality to the European man so much more than anything else they could do. That thing impressed me very much. But the novel which tells about what happens is of no interest to anybody. It is quite characteristic that in *The Making of Americans*, Proust, *Ulysses*, nothing much happens. People are interested in existence. Newspapers excite people very little. Sometimes a personality breaks through the newspapers—Lindbergh, Dillinger—when the personality has vitality. It wasn't what

Dillinger *did* that excited anybody. The feeling is perfectly simple. You can see it in my *Four Saints.* Saints shouldn't do anything. The fact that a saint is there is enough for anybody. The *Four Saints* was written about as static as I could make it. The saints conversed a little, and it all did something. It did something more than the theatre which has tried to make events has done. For our purposes, for our contemporary purposes, events have no importance. I merely say that for the last thirty years events are of no importance. They make a great many people unhappy, they may cause convulsions in history, but from the standpoint of excitement, the kind of excitement the Nineteenth Century got out of events doesn't exist.

And so what I am trying to make you understand is that every contemporary writer has to find out what is the inner time-sense of his contemporariness. The writer or painter, or what not, feels this thing more vibrantly, and he has a passionate need of putting it down; and that is what creativeness does. He spends his life in putting down this thing which he doesn't know is a contemporary thing. If he doesn't put down the contemporary thing, he isn't a great writer, for he has to live in the past. That is what I mean by "everything is contemporary". The minor poets of the period, or the precious poets of the period, are all people who are under the shadow of the past. A man who is making a revolution has to be contemporary. A minor person can live in the imagination. That tells the story pretty completely.

The question of repetition is very important. It is important because there is no such thing as repetition. Everybody tells every story in about the same way. You know perfectly well that when you and your roommates tell something, you are telling the same story in about the same way. But the point about it is this. Everybody is telling the story in the same way. But if you listen carefully, you will see that not all the story is the same. There is always a slight variation. Somebody comes in and you tell the story over again. Every time you tell the story it is told slightly differently. All my early work was a careful listening to all the people telling their story, and

I conceived the idea which is, funnily enough, the same as the idea of the cinema. The cinema goes on the same principle: each picture is just infinitesimally different from the one before. If you listen carefully, you say something, the other person says something; but each time changes just a little, until finally you come to the point where you convince him or you don't convince him. I used to listen very carefully to people talking. I had a passion for knowing just what I call their "insides". And in *The Making of Americans* I did this thing; but of course to my mind there is no repetition. For instance, in these early *Portraits*, and in a whole lot of them in this book (*Portraits and Prayers*) you will see that every time a statement is made about someone being somewhere, that statement is different. If I had repeated, nobody would listen. Nobody could be in the room with a person who said the same thing over and over and over. He would drive everybody mad. There has to be a very slight change. Really listen to the way you talk and every time you change it a little bit. That change, to me, was a very important thing to find out. You will see that when I kept on saying something was something or somebody was somebody, I changed it just a little bit until I got a whole portrait. I conceived the idea of building this thing up. It was all based upon this thing of everybody's slightly building this thing up. What I was after was this immediacy. A single photograph doesn't give it. I was trying for this thing, and so to my mind there is no repetition. The only thing that is repetition is when somebody tells you what he has learned. No matter how you say it, you say it differently. It was this that led me in all that early work.

You see, finally, after I got this thing as completely as I could, then, of course, it being my nature, I wanted to tear it down. I attacked the problem from another way. I listened to people. I condensed it in about three words. There again, if you read those later *Portraits*, you will see that I used three or four words instead of making a cinema of it. I wanted to condense it as much as possible and change it around, until you could get the movement of a human being. If I wanted to make a picture of you as you sit there, I would wait until I got a picture of you as individuals and then I'd change them until I got a picture of you as a whole.

I did these *Portraits*, and then I got the idea of doing plays. I had the *Portraits* so much in my head that I would almost know how you differ one from the other. I got this idea of the play, and put it down in a few words. I wanted to put them down in that way, and I began writing plays and I wrote a great many of them. The Nineteenth Century wrote a great many plays, and none of them are now read, because the Nineteenth Century wanted to put their novels on the stage. The better the play the more static. The minute you try to make a play a novel, it doesn't work. That is the reason I got interested in doing these plays.

When you get to that point there is no essential difference between prose and poetry. This is essentially the problem with which your generation will have to wrestle. The thing has got to the point where poetry and prose have to concern themselves with the static thing. That is up to you.

SENTENCES AND PARAGRAPHS

"Sentences and Paragraphs" is less an exposition on writing than a meditation in which one thought reminds her of another, rather than leading to another.—R. K.

A Sentence is not emotional a paragraph is.

Dates of what they bought.

They will be ready to have him. We think so.

He looks like a young man grown old. That is a sentence that they could use.

I was overcome with remorse. It was my fault that my wife did not have a cow. This sentence they cannot use.

A repetition of prettiness makes it repeated. With them looking.

A repetition of sweetness makes it not repeating but attractive and making soup and dreaming coincidences. The sentence will be

From *How to Write* (1931).

saved. He raises his head and lifts it. A sentence is not whether it is beautiful. Beautiful is not thought without asking as if they are well able to be forgiving.

George Maratier in America.

The sexual life of Genia Berman.

A book of George Hugnet.

The choice of Eric Haulville.

The wealth of Henri d'Ursel.

The relief of Harry Horwood.

The mention of Walter Winterberg. The renown of Bernard Faÿ. The pleasure of prophecy concerning René Crevel. Titles are made of sentences without interruption. Sucking is dangerous. The danger of sucking.

With them.

In itself.

Within itself. A part of a sentence may be a sentence without their meaning. Think of however they went away.

It looks like a garden but he had hurt himself by accident.

Every sentence has a beginning. Will he begin.

Every sentence which has a beginning makes it be left more to them.

I return to sentences as a refreshment.

Howard opposes them less.

That is nice.

George is wonderfully well.

How does he like ability.

A sentence should be arbitrary it should not please be better.

It should not be disturbed.

A sentence has colors when they mean I liked it as selling salt should be very little used in dishes.

That is one of the best I have done.

Pleasantly or presently.

How or have. A sentence is.

Made or make a meaning.

Now feebly commence a sentence.

How has he hurried. That is a paragraph because it means yes. How has he hurried.

Now for a sentence. Welcome to hurry. That is either a sentence or a part of a sentence if it is a part of a sentence the sentence is he is welcome to hurry. Welcome is in itself a part of a sentence. She prefers them. I have told her where the place which is meant is.

Welcome when they come. Are they welcome when they come. A sentence instead of increases. It should be if they are. Welcome when they come. That so easily makes a paragraph. Try again.

They made made them when they were by them. This is a sentence. It has no use in itself because made is said two times.

Way-laid made it known as quince cake. This is a perfect sentence because it refers to regretting. They regret what they have given. So far there is no need for a paragraph. I cannot see him. This is a paragraph.

Think of a use for a paragraph. A sentence is exhausted by have they been there with him.

A useful and useful if you add house you have a paragraph. He looks like his brother. That is a whole sentence.

Dogs get tired and want to sleep. This is not a sentence to be abused.

He has had his portrait painted by a Frenchman a Dutchman an Englishman and an American.

Pleases by its sense. This is a fashion in sentences.

A dog which you have never had before has sighed. This is a fixture in sentences it is like a porcelain in plaster. All this together has no reverses. What is the difference between reserve and reverse. They can be beguiled.

Beguiled and belied. It was famous that a woman who was a wife to him.

A veritable hope. Hurry with a sentence.

This are our announcements.

A sentence. She owes him to her.

A sentence. He ought to own mines.

He heard her come in. Laughed is a word.

If a word reminds you that is a preparation which they do in time so that it is with all.

Candied is a word we were mistaken she can have a lake.

There is no use in weapons of precision for them formerly.

Think of imagination as has to do for you. Door handles which he likes.

Now there is no use in stopping when they went in.

She mentioned edging edging is used in having sewing surrounding something. It is very difficult to think twice.

This is very well done because it does not stop.

Eggs are of fish and fowl. This is perfectly reasonable. Tell them how to finish.

Now this is a new paragraph. The ending tell them how to finish makes it an importance.

First-rate has relation to tires. How are they.

That is a way to please a paragraph. Think if you can. I find it difficult to know yes or no. I find no difficulty in yes I said no. I said I would and I did. I did not used to.

This is an ordinary paragraph made different by content.

As they asked for it. Why is as they asked for it a sentence.

Think of how do you do as very necessary.

He gave it to them to-day. Now think carefully of monstrosity. He gave it to them to give away. Which one threw it away.

It is to be certain that love is lord of all.

This sentence has hope as origin.

A tapestry made easy by being seen.

Think of all these sentences and not to be annoyed.

After all what is the difference between it and you. Everybody has said they are happy.

If two sentences make a paragraph a little piece is alright because they are better apart. They are as a pleasure as out loud. Now think.

A paragraph such as silly.

That is alright.

So there we are just as all the same.

No not out loud never accrue as allowed.

What does he mean by eating.

There you are. There are marks where he went away.

What does he do by himself. There you are. Left left left right left he had a good job and he left.

Buy a pair and with them do this for them which they like as well.

It is very necessary to be held by Fanny.

Now all this is still sentences. Paragraphs are still why you were selfish.

Shell fish are what they eat. This is neither a paragraph nor a sentence.

When it is there it is out there. This is a sentiment not a sentence.

Now that is something not to think but to link. A little there. I lost a piece of my cuff button and I found it. This is not a sentence because they remain behind.

Now that is it. I have it. They do not leave it because they do send it. Now the minute you do more you make a subject of a severance. A sentence has been heard. Now listen. Have it made for me. That is a request. A sentence is proper if they have more than they could. They could. Without leaving it. A sentence makes not it told but it hold. A hold is where they put things. Now what is a sentence. A sentence hopes that you are very well and happy. It is very selfish. They like to be taken away. A sentence can be taken care of. The minute you disperse a crowd you have a sentence. They were witnesses to it even if you did not stop. There there is no paragraph. If it had a different father it would have.

I heard how they liked everybody and I said so too.

That is not a sentence and you see just why it is not why it should be.

Once when they were nearly ready they had ordered it to close.

This is a perfect example and it is not because it is a finish it is not ended nor is it continued it is not fastened and they will not neglect. There you are they will not neglect and yet once again they have mustaches. Think well do they grow any taller after they have a beard. They do although all experience is to the contrary.

Once when they were nearly ready they had ordered it to close.

This is one of the series of saving the sentence.

Remarks are made.

The courtiers make witty remarks.

They payed where they went.

Habits of which they are the owners are those they have without it being to them of any aid.

It is February.

They add it up.

He does not sound like me.

Nor do I sound like him.

Think that a sentence has been made.

I am very miserable about sentences. I can cry about sentences but not about hair cloth.

Now this is one way of relenting.

Think of a sentence. A whole sentence. Who is kind. We have known one who is kind. That is a very good sentence.

A separate cushion is not as comfortable.

This is a sentence that comes in the midst not in the midst of other things but in the midst of the same thing.

They have that as flourishes.

That is a sentence that comes by obedience to intermittance.

That is the cruelest thing I ever heard is the favorite phrase of Gilbert.

Saving the sentence volume one.

Or three

The difference between a short story and a paragraph. There is none.

They come and go. It is the cruelest thing I ever heard is the favorite phrase of Gilbert. And he is right. He has heard many cruel things and it is the cruelest thing that he has heard.

It is very hard to save the sentence.

Part of it is explained.

I like evidence of it.

He is to get away as usual.

Music is nondescript.

This is a sentence. They have taken exception to this statement because there will be exceptions when words are harbingers of means, by which they made names. He accompanied words by musical tunes.

How are houses crowded. A crowd contemplate moving. This is a commonplace sentence facing they will object.

It is a pleasure to play with a dog.

Bower is a secluded place where they had names. Find their names. All this meets the objection.

A little bit of way and she comes to say that he is the best taken care of anyway.

This is a light sentence with positive joy and so they have it. Do understand and to understand. This is so light it is an emotion and so a paragraph. Yes so a paragraph.

A man. One man. Of interest to one man. They say they will find it interesting.

How are ours received. That is a question which they make. Now think of a sentence. All these are parts. One man makes four children. He is not taught without care.

This sentence comes to the same place as all they said.

Now what is the difference between a sentence and I mean.

The difference is a sentence is that they will wish women.

Do you all see.

Now here is a sentence.

Are they coming back. That is not a sentence.

A sentence is from this time I will make up my mind.

Then they have hurried.

A sentence can be three things they can use. A sentence can be three things made with hurry.

Come and see me.

Come Thursday and you will see them.

Wait for what you are waiting for.

By the time that it is here they have had it and it is what they selected.

I like what they give me. Now all these sentences have been made with their assistance.

Now make a sentence all alone.

They remember a walk. They remember a part of it. Which they took with them.

Now who eases a pleasure.

I ought to be a very happy woman.

Premeditated meditation concerns analysis. Now this is a sentence but it might not be.

Premeditated. That is meditated before meditation.

Meditation. Means reserved the right to meditate.

Concerns. This cannot be a word in a sentence. Because it is not of use in itself.

Analysis is a womanly word. It means that they discover there are laws.

It means that she cannot work as long as this.

It is hard not to while away the time.

It is hard not to remember what it is.

With them they accord in the circumstances.

Sentences make one sigh.

There were three kinds of sentences are there. Do sentences follow the three. There are three kinds of sentences. Are there three kinds of sentences that follow the three.

If his ear is back is it drying. One says there are three kinds of sentences and every other one is just alike. Butter spreads thinly.

They made it be away as they went or were sent. This is a mixture of a memory and a reproduction. This is never noisy.

Nothing is noisy.

How are a sentence is the same.

If it is very well done they make it with butter. I prefer it not with butter.

What is a sentence with tears. Is she using red in her tapestry red in her tapestry. All these sentences are so full of with glass, glass is held it can make coffee so too. Now then what is it.

A sentence is Humbert with him.

There are so few kings. He was so funny.

He was so funny. That is a sentence.

She resembled him. Now that you see is because of it it is not so, she was exactly like her. Exactly alike her. If you forget a paragraph.

Hop in hope for.

Neglecting.

I will write to Christian Berard.

It is alright.

Once or twice it does not make any difference.

Does not make any difference.

Let us meditate.

Does not make any difference.

They fasten that they are not by noticing.

He would not hurt even if it does bother his teeth by it. Now think carefully whether they say it.

I would use a sentence if I could.

Why does it not please me to be sitting here.

Who likes to hear her hear of them. See how bad that is.

A sentence is saved not any sentence no not any sentence at all not yet.

It is not very easy to save a sentence. The sentence that is the one they are saving if they are lucky which has been predicted to them.

Never ask any one what a sentence is or what it has been.

It is of no interest if you know what it has to do with it.

Come back to complacency.

What is a sentence.

If he has wished. Wild and while.

A sentence says that the end of it is that they send in order to better themselves in order to sentence. A sentence is that they will have will they be well as well. What is a sentence. A sentence is tardily with them at a glance as an advance. Listen to this. It does make any difference if his voice is welling they will be well if they receive their welcome with as without as well with it.

It is all a relief.

Everything is worth while with a pudding an angel made of pudding.

Do you see why I am happy.

Happy is to find what it does. What is it it does.

What is the difference between a question and answer. There is no question and no answer. There is an announcement. There is at the outset.

Have never had the outset.

We feel that if we say we we will go.

This a simple meaning. A sentence that is simple in a cross with a meaning.

A sentence says you know what I mean. Dear do I well I guess I do.

Keep away from that door and go back there, that has not a meaning that has an association does he do so he does but not by guess work or difference there is no difference.

I think there which I wish here.

For no movement.

It does make any difference if a sentence is not in two.

We change from Saturday to to-day.

She thinks that she can wish that she can have it be there.

What is a sentence. A sentence is not a fair. A fair is followed by partake. This does make a sentence.

Think how everybody follows me.

A sentence makes them all not an avoidance of difficulty. A sentence is this. They never think before hand if they do they lay carpets. Lay carpets is never a command. You can see that a sentence has no mystery. A mystery would be a reception. They receive nothing. In this way if it finishes. This is so obviously what they will do. Obviously what they will do is no mistake because we did not know it. We did not know it is not a mistake either. Leave it alone is not theirs as a mistake. Artificially is what they call when they call out. Who knows how many have been careful. Sentences are made wonderfully one at a time. Who makes them. Nobody can make them because nobody can what ever they do see.

All this makes sentences so clear I know how I like them.

What is a sentence mostly what is a sentence. With them a sentence is with us about us all about us we will be willing with what a sentence is. A sentence is that they cannot be carefully there is a doubt about it.

The great question is can you think a sentence. What is a sentence. He thought a sentence. Who calls him to come which he did.

The Earles parlor was a parlor in a house in Lynn. Does it make any difference if a sentence is balanced it does and it does not.

The balancing of a sentence is mound and round. They will thank you anywhere. What is a sentence. A sentence is a duplicate. An exact duplicate is depreciated. Why is a duplicated sentence not depreciated. Because it is a witness. No witnesses are without value. Even which it may be they do not know that their right hand is their right hand nor their left hand which is their left hand.

A sentence then can easily make a mistake. A sentence must be used. Who has had a sentence read for him. He will be pleased with what he has and has heard. This is an exceedingly pretty sentence which has been changed.

I did not expect to be interested but I am. Now the whole question of questions and not answer is very interesting. The whole thing about all day is not at all when they were owned. What is a question. To thank for a question is no mistake.

We change from Saturday to to-day.

NEXT.
LIFE AND LETTERS
OF MARCEL DUCHAMP

A family likeness pleases when there is a cessation of resemblances. This is to say that points of remarkable resemblance are those which make Henry leading. Henry leading actually smothers Emil. Emil is pointed. He does not overdo examples. He even hesitates.

But am I sensible. Am I not rather efficient in sympathy or common feeling.

I was looking to see if I could make Marcel out of it but I can't.

Not a doctor to me not a debtor to me not a d to me but a c to me a credit to me. To interlace a story with glass and with rope with color and roam.

How many people roam.

Dark people roam.

Can dark people come from the north. Are they dark then. Do they begin to be dark when they have come from there.

Any question leads away from me. Grave a boy grave.

What I do recollect is this. I collect black and white. From the standpoint of white all color is color. From the standpoint of

From *Geography and Plays* (1922).

black. Black is white. White is black. Black is black. White is black. White and black is black and white. What I recollect when I am there is that words are not birds. How easily I feel thin. Birds do not. So I replace birds with tin-foil. Silver is thin.

Life and letters of Marcel Duchamp.

Quickly return the unabridged restraint and mention letters.

My dear Fourth.

Confess to me in a quick saying. The vote is taken.

The lucky strike works well and difficultly. It rounds, it sounds round. I cannot conceal attrition. Let me think. I repeat the fullness of bread. In a way not bread. Delight me. I delight a lamb in birth.

FORENSICS

They will have nothing to do with still. They will had that they have head of the skill with which they divided them until they knew what they were doing without it.

A dog who has been washed has been washed clean with our aid in our absence.

After a long decision they will wait for what she does.

She chose to be helped by their coming here.

No distress in elegance.

Quarrels may wear out wives but they help babies.

We will hope they will not wear out wives.

It is an appointment that he will keep in singing for them and they keep an appointment.

They say it would have been better.

To invite.

Would it have been better.

To say.

Would it have been better

To show

Them this.

From *How to Write* (1931).

Forensics are a plan by which they will never pardon. They will call butter yellow. Which it is. He is. They will call birds attractive. Which they are. They are. They will also oblige girls to be women that is a round is a kind of hovering for instance.

Forensics may be because of having given.

They made all walk.

They say is it better to follow than to presume. Shown as shutters.

Now what is forensics. Forensics is eloquence and reduction.

It is they who were in a hurry.

She made Caesar leave it to Caesars.

What is forensics.

Forensics is a taught paragraph.

Paragraphs.

Will they cause more as the middle classes.

Does it make any difference to her that he has taken it. Of course it does although as she was considerate of me she did not manage it. This is forensics.

Everything makes spaces.

I agreed to everything.

This was not my business.

And yet I am not puzzled.

Because I was obedient.

Now think of forensics.

What are forensics establishing.

Forensics. I say I will obey her.

Forensics. She will reveal him.

Forensics. And they will come at them.

With him.

Now think of forensics as an argument.

Does he mind forensics if it is edited.

I can see that she can see to change one for three.

Now is this forensics for me.

When she can see she can cease to pursue how do you do. What is forensics forensics is an argument to be fought.

Ask for him. Do not ask for him.

Ask this for him.

It is very patient to ask this for him. Patient.

Forensics. How are and will she finish one before the other. If she does it will be satisfactory. There is no argument in forensics.

Just about why they asked her she bought it.

What is forensics. Did you meet Bruce yes but I did not mention it. If there had been a cause.

Shall we. A necessity.

Having been nervous was anticipated.

They might be and have spilt syrup.

What are forensics. Forensics are elaborated argument. Mister Bruce.

Elaborate argument.

There is a difference between a date and dreary.

Snow at an angle can fall.

But will she.

They may go.

At a certain gate.

For them to call.

Will she need a title.

Must they copy a matter.

Or would they call a cloth annul.

Categoric or a thought.

Heavenly just as bought.

Forensics are double.

They dispute a title and they dispute their trouble.

A title is made for defense. It did not defend him nor did I. I always do.

PART TWO.

Partly a defense.

Have you come in.

Yes I have but I am not in which is a pity.

PART THREE.

Just why does she mean me.

What are forensics.

Do not be persuaded that you have heard something that has caused you not to come. Theodore can give in to at least one.

That is not forensics because there are not two. He made forty thousand in two.

Yes which they did.

Forensics are the words which they like. They must be careful.

Once who was through.

Should think with you.

Which once she was through.

With it.

Enlightenment.

Forensics is an argument.

Does it make any difference if they are alike. That is an argument.

Forensics leads to reputation.

How about forensics.

It is farther which is for mixed happy in better.

Hear me.

She should be worthy of being careful.

And must it be felt.

They admire in the sense of lose that they thought.

With her.

She may be called amiable in fancy.

All this interests him with forensics.

What is the difference between him and his friend.

It is all alike forensics disposes of that.

Should he.

By their advice should he.

If he followed their advice.

That is not forensics forensics has nothing to do with advice and why. Now forensics has only to do with the difference between inconvenience and disgrace. There is no chance to better gather. It is able and beneficial. She made an argument do and after all she did frame. No pleasure in an accusation. Did I say she would go.

All this is conclusion.

What is forensics.

They need pleasure singly.

PART II

A parlor is a place.

Who knows why they feel that they had rather not gather there.

PART III

Will he ask them why she chose this. If they do he will be disappointed in her being so withdrawn and reminded and when will two meet one. The necessity. Further. Should hurry be advantageous more in coming than in going in adding and following. Should he be they worship welling. Their emotion welled up but admittedly they were admiring.

Forensics are plainly a determination.

Does and do all include obstinacy.

Particularly for pleasure in clarity.

She makes hours.

Well what do you believe. Do you believe in ease in understanding. Do you believe in favors in accomplishment. Do you believe that they regard with forbearance their increase of rectification nor do they they bewilder and but whether in fancy they charge them and consistently they are better without followers. They should be charity without call. No noise makes tranquility a burden with help and a trouble to them to end well. Very well I thank you is why they were generous. Think forensically. How I doubt.

It is more than a pleasure to dream more than a pleasure. To dream.

Were he to manage to whom would there be an obligation to oblige.

Part IV

If they think well of selling and they do who do they refuse for you of whom. Which they do.

An argument is sustained.

Has he meant to call out loud for his mother and not in disuse married or rather meant to marry. Should it be that with which they are startled. All arguments are helped with no insistence and she says. I will not positively deny, why. Better than they have the privilege of decrying them.

What is an argument. What are forensics. What are master pieces. What are their hopes. An argument is this. I have it. They reserve it. They do not answer at once. Forensics is this. Better come when it rains, better come when it rains, and rains, better come and puzzle that they have been within and it rains who have all by the time and not also to go.

They had no argument without doubt.

What are master pieces. Master pieces are when he has been cold and has been softly so and now has turned over.

Forensics are a remedy in time. So have thousands. A master piece of strategy. An argument of their deliberation. The forensics of abuse which has not been written. No thought of their search.

Part V

She said I should be ready she was. I reply she was ready I was ready and we both went. Forensically this leads to establishment of a difference I beg to differ. Rather more than I beg to differ.

Our tower.

That is a fault

Forensics may bestow what they ought.

Shall judgments be perfect.

She came and bought one. Oh thank you. This makes a subject for forensics. She came and bought one. Oh thank you. And then they rest. She came. And bought one. Oh thank you. And then they rest. Forensics is in the state. They do feel that they are included in a state. In a state. A state is a piece of a part. Which they make added. Forensics is so true.

A state apart.

Will they content will they contend. Milk. Will they think that they meant made an instance of shut her for them a time.

It is very easy to make forensics. Anxious.

At last I am writing a popular novel. Popular with whom. They may be popular with them. Or more ferociously.

Forensics consists not in hoping to have this destroyed. As much as why not.

Partly why not. Forensics is an adaptation of trilogy. She is useful therefor she is not martyred. And they are correct or why do they so.

Forensics consists in disposing of violence by placating irony.

For that there is this use. Follow for mean. To mean to cover following by they mean to be at one and then they mean to follow with following their meaning.

She reads passionately for him in means. And they invite partly for him in means and so they ask appointments for him in means to carry on their pleasure in usage. How are ours entangled. Nobody can be declared for them formerly. Forensics reside in the power to receive many more often in use.

If I asked if it were so would the answer make them know that answering with intuition is what forensics are in vanishing. And have they vanished or been vanishing. Which they do not do. Because some are still doing something in answering.

Hurry hurry him do. This is not forensics because it is not added. Forensics establishes which is that they will rather than linger and so they establish. Follow me first they went there after they had been with him. This is forensics made into a certainty.

It is very extraordinary in forensics that they can be right which they are as they mean they add to compare. And so they win in fusion that so they oblige pleasure in advancement. Think of forensics, think placidly of forensics.

Who can come to this in pleasure and believe that they will have their certainty. When they leave they must be[s]tow this on and with them which they relish. In which way they resolve to abolish devastation for them as planned. It is made more nearly eaten which is very close to his watching. And so they know that they are patient in progress. This makes forensics independent. It is very easy to see that he has been bowed by constraint because he waits. This is forensics illuminated.

What is a forensic bird. A bird considered forensically is very close to admiration. In consequence to have it said leave and carry, a bird leaves and a bird carries. Birds leave and carry. And gradually as if in indifference. Birds leave and birds carry. As if in indifference. Forensics chooses that they conclude. In carrying and in choosing and in leaving birds leave birds carry birds choose, birds in leaving birds in choosing, birds in carrying conclude the carrying the choosing and the leaving. As reasonably. And so forensics begins again.

Make it be mine partly can not enter into forensics.

If she is sitting quietly and it is known will they correct this in explaining. Forensics as we are told are always bold.

No no indeed not they and forensics can be held at bay.

This is a forensic sentence. She meant not to think of what would be the use to which that which was done would be put. She refused to think of the use to which that which was done would be put. And in the struggle because preparatorily there need not be a struggle in the meantime and with significance a struggle is separated irremediably with outburst. And yet it is all occasionally. For them it is and might. For instance forensics does not use nor deny nor imply it refuses to curve. In that way there is abundance.

She said she liked it best and did she like it best or did she change her mind upon seeing the other. This is a question and answer and forensics will gather that they were familiar with the answer. Yes they would think very well of them both. And she would be very happy in having accounted for it. This is forensics mildly. And yet it can be recognised.

She knew that they could care to leave forty more there. Forensics is in use when calling further they arouse misuse of their action as having appealed to it for them to requite them. It is better to have it lost than if it had remained two. So she says in her pleasure of their detention. And then. It will be changed to their advantage. This is the way that they do not need pleasure in forensics. Pleasure is their capacity to choose well known rings. And they covet a brooch and love a brook and neglect broods and all of it will measure theirs as much. Retain them. Follow another. And but whether. They could continue. To countenance them.

Should it be reasoned that they will plan their trophy in winter. She made such light as there was fatter.

A climax is better than farther. And so forensics choose. And never. To differ. Forensics asserts that calm in time is their remedy. Just as is an obligation to reinforce presence of their protection.

How can they use policy of persuasion. Listen to hints. Forensics begins with union and organisation. After that. Advance in volume.

They shall stretch. Their conclusions. From here. To there. They will. Prepare. Efficaciously. Just as much. As they have been. In the habit. Of anticipating. Melodiously. In reference. To their analysis. In a garden. Admire forensics.

If in the meaning of their connection. They disturb. Without it. As much. As they generously instil. Into them. In their allowance. Of whether. They will partly fail.

Forensics is a distribution unequally.

Explain why it matters. That they must bewilder. With whatever. They could crowd. As treasure. And so they fastened. Window curtains. Forensics makes regaining wholly a feather in meditation.

Just when they please.

Forensics is established.

Just why they met. They will bemoan, they will excuse they will reverse they will comply with them as a cause. And wealth, they will use energy in very much with which they will have caused their ought, ought they to comply, made it as predetermined, vouchsafed, or with the cause of their relief, that they once knew. It is a gradual cause. They will be perfectly in love with doves and woods. And very much what they had hoped. In singing.

Forensics can be so delicately heard.

What did she do with fire. She almost put fire to forensics. As useful. As usual. As vagrant. As appointed. As veiled. And as welcome. In their plenty. This may be there. And they will dwell upon it.

This may not be there and they will not venture not to dwell in this way more upon it. They may be very able to cover it without a change of leading it from this to that in violence. In which. They may encounter. All that they. May trust.

For them there is no escape. Forensics may pale. It often does. And such as it. Is more than very often their return. Do not be cautious in readiness.

Just why. They like. What they do.

Forensics is richly in a hurry.

They fasten the best ways on their detachment.

A detachment of troops. Who can. Be careful. Of a. Detachment. Of troops. And if they are. What is it. That they leave there. As they leave alike. It. Alike. As a bother. To them. This can show. That they. Must. Accept. A denial. They have authority. For all. That they want. As their. Treasure. And. Do they. Hope. To show. Something. For it. Without. An appointment. Just when they went. Usefully. In their. Destruction. In. Enjoyment.

Such forensics can lately take shape.

Just plan their use. Then carry it out in principle. Find it a favorable moment. To advance. Their interests. Moreover. Just at once. Which is. By their account. That they will have it as a blemish. In theirs. In unison. An advantage to forsake. Which they will. As they may glean. More facts. For which. By their ordinary values. They will be practically. As far apart. Forensics may be athirst for gold. It may with them battle and die. It can as much bequeath and condole. For them. To merit. That they. Should console. Them.

BIBLIOGRAPHY, 1904–1929

by Gertrude Stein

What makes this self-assessment special is, first, the fact that no other major modern writer ever published such a list. They didn't need to do so if they had regular publishers whose publicists would do the work. Since most of Stein's manuscripts were not published for many years, this text becomes a guide to when she thought she wrote texts that didn't appear in print for many years. (Often, according to Stein scholars, she made mistakes in dating, needless to say perhaps.)

THREE LIVES 1904, 1905
 Grafton Press New York. 1909.
1000 copies printed 279 pages
 John Lane London bound
300 copies Grafton printing
1920
 Boni and Boni New York
1927

First 200 pages appeared
Transatlantic, Paris, April 1924.
January 1925. 60 pages
translated into french to appear
Edition de la Montagne January
1929.

MAKING OF AMERICANS
 1906–1908 *Contact Edmond* Paris
1905. 500 copies 925 pages

A LONG GAY BOOK
 1909–1912 Beginning printed
in the *Dial* 1926

From *transition* (February 1929).

MANY MANY WOMEN 1910

G. M. P. 1911–1912

JENNY HELEN HANNAH
PAUL AND PETER 1912

TWO 1910–1912

TENDER BUTTONS 1913
  Claire Marie New York 1915.
  1000 copies 78 pages.
    Reprinted *Transition* no. 14,
  1928
    35 Portraits 1908–1912

A MAN

FIVE OR SIX MEN

TWO WOMEN *Contact Collection*
  Paris 1925

ITALIANS in *Geography and Plays*
  Four Seas Co. Boston 1922

ORTA OR ONE DANCING

MATISSE *Camera Work* New York
  August 1912

PICASSO *Camera Work* New York
  August 1912

FOUR PROTEGEES

MEN

NADELMAN *Larus* Boston 1925

A PAINTER

ELISE SURVILLE

FOUR DISHONEST ONES

A KIND OF WOMEN

A FAMILY in *Geography and Plays*

ADA   "   "   "

JULIA MARLOW

FROST in *Useful Knowledge, Payson
  and Clarke* New York 1928

PURMAN

RUSSELL

PACH

CHALFIN

HARRIET. FEAR

HESSEL

ROCHE in *Geography and Plays*

CONSTANCE FLETCHER in
  Geography and Plays.

HARRIET MAKING PLANS

PLAYING

STORYETTE OF H. M.

RUE DE RENNES

BON MARCHE WEATHER

MI-CAREME

FLIRTING AT THE BON-MARCHE

GALERIE LAFAYETTE *Rogue* New York March, 1915.

MISS FURR AND MISS SKEENE in *Geography and Plays* *Vanity Fair* 1925

1913

PORTRAIT OF MABEL DODGE Privately printed 300 copies Florence 1913 in *Camera Work* New York 1913.

PORTRAIT OF GIBB in *Oxford Magazine* 1920 in *Geography and Plays.*

PORTRAIT OF CONSTANCE FLETCHER in *Geography and Plays*

SCENES IN RELATION in *Geography and Plays.*

PUBLISHERS in *Geography and Plays*

PORTRAIT OF F. B. in *Geography and Plays.*

PORTRAIT OF PRINCE B. D. in *Geography and Plays.*

ENGLAND in *Geography and Plays.*

WHAT HAPPENED A PLAY in *Geography and Plays*

ONE (VAN VECHTEN) ALMOST A PLAY in *Geography and Plays*

ARTICLE,   "   "   "

WHITE WINES A PLAY in *Geography and Plays*

BRAQUE in *Geography and Plays*

MARSDEN HARTLEY AND SO FORTH in *Geography and Plays*

OLD AND OLD

SUSIE ASADO in *Geography and Plays*

MRS. THURSBEY *The Soil* New York 1917

A CURTAIN RAISER in *Geography and Plays*

MIGUEL

SIMONS A BOUQUET

IN GENERAL

THANK YOU

A SWEET TAIL in *Geography and Plays*

CARNAGE

YET DISH

AMERICANS in *Geography and Plays*

IN

IN THE GRASS. ON SPAIN in *Geography and Plays*

GUILLAUME

CARRY

FRANCE in *Geography and Plays*

GO IN GREEN

SIMON

BE TIME VINE

IRMA

A LIDE CLOTHES

MRS. EDWARDES

PRECIOCILLA in *Composition as Explanation* Hogarth Press London 1926

SACRED EMILY in *Geography and Plays*

1914

MEAL ONE

EMP LACE

SERIES

TILLIE

CURTAIN LET US

DATES

FOUR

FINISHED ONE

OVAL

ONE OR TWO

CRETE

IS ONE

WEAR in *Broom* Rome January 1923

GENTLE JULIA

PRINTED LACE

AT

NEW HAPPINESS

MRS WHITEHEAD in *Geography and Plays.*

LOCKERIDGE

MRS. EMERSON in *Close Up* Territet 1927

TUBENE

BIRD JET

ONE SENTENCE

1915

NOT SIGHTLY A PLAY in *Geography and Plays*

PINK MELON JOY in *Geography and Plays*

JOHNIE GREY in *Geography and Plays*

STUDY NATURE

POSSESSIVE CASE

NO

MONSIEUR VOLLARD ET CEZANNE *New York Sun* October 10th 1915

WHEN WE WENT AWAY

FARRAGUT in *Useful Knowledge*

HOW COULD THEY MARRY HER

IF YOU HAD THREE HUSBANDS *Broom* Rome Jan. April June 1922 in *Geography and Plays*

THIS ONE IS SERIOUS

HE DIDN'T LIGHT THE LIGHT

DAVID DAISY AND APPOLONIA

INDEPENDENT EMBROIDERY

I HAVE NO TITLE TO BE SU[C]CESSFUL

HE SAID IT A MONOL[O]GUE in *Geography and Plays*

1916

MALLORCAN STORIES in
  Geography and Plays

LOOK AT US

MEXICO A PLAY in *Geography and
  Plays*

DECORATIONS

A POEM ABOUT WALBERG in
  Geography and Plays

ALL SUNDAY

1917

LIFTING BELLY

MISS CRUTWELL

A KING OR SOMETHING. A
  PLAY in *Geography and Plays*

MARRY NETTIE

COUNTING HER DRESSES in
  Geography and Plays

HAVE THEY ATTACKED
  MARY. HE GIGGLED *Vanity
  Fair* June 1917 100 privately
  printed New York 1917

AN EXERCISE IN ANALYSIS.
  A PLAY

I CAN FEEL THE BEAUTY

WILL WE SEE THEM AGAIN

WHY CAN KIPLING SPEAK

1918

ONE HAS NOT LOST ONE'S
  MARGUERITE *Blue Jay*
  Baltimore April 1926

WHY WIN WINGS

IN THEIR PLAY

CAN YOU BELIEVE BETTER

WHAT IS THE NAME OF A
  RING

IN THE MIDDLE OF A DAY

DO YOU LIKE YOUR SUIT

THE FORD

CALL IT A TABLE

THIRD DAY NOT THIRSTY

CAN CALL US

CAN YOU SEE THE NAME

EXCEPTIONAL CONDUCT

1919

1920

IRELAND

WOULD

A MOVIE

POLISH

THE REVERY OF THE
ZIONIST

A LEAGUE *Life* Sept[.] 1920 in
Geography and Plays.

MORE LEAGUE *Oxford Magazine*
May 7th 1920

EVENTS

A HYMN

THE PSYCHOLOGY OF
NATIONS OR WHAT ARE
YOU LOOKING AT in
Geography and Plays

DAUGHTER

NEXT. LIFE AND LETTERS.
MARCEL DUCHAMP in
Geography and Plays

NAMES OF FLOWERS

RICH AND POOR IN
ENGLISH

PHOTOGRAPHS

SCENERY

COAL AND WOOD

LAND OF NATIONS (Subtitle
AND ASK ASIA) in *Geography
and Plays*

DEVELOP SPANISH

LAND RISING

A PLAY IN CIRCLES

VACATION IN BRITTANY
Little Review Spring 1922

WOODROW WILSON in *Useful
Knowledge*

1921

B. B. OR THE BIRTHPLACE
OF BONNES *Little Review*
Autumn 1922

Moral tales of 1920–1921

NEST OF DISHES

EMILY CHADBOURNE in
Useful Knowledge

NOT A HOLE

CURTAINS DREAM

DINNER

COURTING

KITES

READINGS

SEPARATED

ATTACKS

JOKES FOR JESSIE

DOLPHIN

LITTLE PILLOWS

SINGING TO A MUSICIAN

FINISH CONSTANCE

SONATINA FOLLOWED BY
  ANOTHER

CURRENTS

MARY

CAPTURE SPLINTERS

A LITTLE CREAM

THINK AGAIN

READ A NEW CURRANT

TODAY WE HAVE A
  VACATION

SONNETS THAT PLEASE

REREAD ANOTHER. A PLAY

1922

OBJECTS LIE ON A TABLE. A
  PLAY

SAINTS AND SINGING. A
  PLAY.

FINER THAN MELANCTHA

I FEEL A REALLY ANXIOUS
  MOMENT COMING

MILDRED'S THOUGHTS
American Caravan 1926

DIDN'T NELLY AND LILY
  LOVE YOU

AMERICAN BIOGRAPHY in
  Useful Knowledge

AN INSTANT ANSWER OR
  ONE HUNDRED
  PROMINENT MEN in
  Useful Knowledge

JO DAVIDSON *Vanity Fair* 1922

A SINGULAR ADDITION.
SEQUEL TO ONE
HUNDRED PROMINENT
MEN

A SAINT OF SEVEN in
*Composition as Explanation Hogarth
Essays.*

LEND A HAND. FOUR
RELIGIONS in *Useful
Knowledge.*

WHY ARE THERE WHITES
TO CONSOLE

A VALENTINE. TO
SHERWOOD ANDERSON
in *Useful Knowledge Little Review*
Spring 1923

PRUDENCE CAUTION AND
FORESIGHT. A STORY OF
AVIGNON

IF HE THINKS. A
NOVELETTE OF
DESERTION *transition* Dec.
1927

LILY LIFE

ERIK SATIE

TALKS TO SAINTS IN SAINT
REMY

1923

PROCESSION

FOR TEN

PRAISES

HAROLD LOEB

FOURTEEN ANONYMOUS
PORTRAITS

CEZANNE

AN INDIAN BOY *The Reviewer*
Richmond Virginia Jan. 1926

PRECEPTS

A LIST INSPIRED BY AVERY
HOPWOOD

CAPITAL CAPITALS *This Quarter*
Paris No. 1 Vol. 1 1925

JONAS JULIAN CAESAR AND
SAMUEL

ELUCIDATION *transition* Paris
March 1927

A VILLAGE *Galerie Simon* 1928.
100 copies illustrated by Elie
Licaux.

PRACTICE IN ORATIONS

SUBJECT CASES. THE BACK
GROUND OF A
DETECTIVE STORY

AM I TO GO OR I'LL SAY SO.
A PLAY IN PLACES

HE AND THEY. HEMINGWAY
Ex-Libris Paris 1923

A BOOK CONCLUDING
WITH AS A WIFE HAS A
COW *Galerie Simon* Paris 1927
100 copies illustrated by Juan
Gris *transition* June 1927

VAN OR TWENTY YEARS
AFTER. SECOND
PORTRAIT OF CARL VAN
VECHTEN *The Reviewer*
Richmond Virginia April 1924
in *Useful Knowledge*

ARE THERE ARITHMETICS
Eights Week Oxford May 1927

NEW

IF I TOLD HIM. A
COMPLETED PORTRAIT
OF PICASSO *Vanity Fair* 1923

GEOGRAPHY

AS EIGHTY. A DISPUTATION

ARE THERE SIX OR
ANOTHER QUESTION in
Useful Knowledge

STUDIES IN
CONVERSATION *transition*
September 1927

CODY AND BRENNER

EQUALLY SO. A
DESCRIPTION OF ALL
INCIDENTS

1924

WHEREIN THE SOUTH
DIFFERS FROM THE
NORTH in *Useful Knowledge*

A BIRTHDAY BOOK

IN WHICH HOUSE DID HE
LIVE

WHEREIN IOWA DIFFERS
FROM KANSAS in *Useful
Knowledge*

ELECTED AGAIN

THE DIFFERENCE
BETWEEN THE
INHABITANTS OF
FRANCE AND THE
UNITED STATES in *Useful
Knowledge*

MADE A MILE AWAY *transition*
November 1927

MILDRED ALDRICH
  SATURDAY

AND SO TO CHANGE SO. A
  FANTASY ON THREE
  CAREERS

BIRTH AND MARRIAGE

DAHOMY or AS SOFT A
  NOISE

PICTURES OF JUAN GRIS
  Little Review Autumn 1924

THE BRAZILIAN ADMIRAL'S
  SON

EMMET ADDIS THE
  DOUGHBOY. A PASTORAL
  in *Useful Knowledge*

FIFTEENTH OF NOVEMBER.
  T. S. ELIOT *The New Criterion*
  Jan. 1926 *Georgian Stories* 1926

COLOURED AS COLOURS. A
  GIFT

DESCRIPTIONS OF
  LITERATURE The *As Stable
  Press* 1926. 100 copies New
  York *transition* Summer 1928

WHICH ONE WILL

TO CALL IT A DAY

MAN RAY

NEAR EAST OR CHICAGO. A
  DESCRIPTION in *Useful
  Knowledge*

AFTER AT ONCE

LIKE THAT A COMEDY

A HISTORY OF HAVING A
  GREAT MANY TIMES
  NOT CONTINUED TO BE
  FRIENDS

1925

EARLY AND LATE

EDITH SITWELL in *Composition
  as Explanation* Hogarth Press
  London

WAR OR MORE in *Useful
  Knowledge*

BUSINESS IN BALTIMORE in
  Useful Knowledge

USEFUL KNOWLEDGE
  AMONG NEGROES in
  Useful Knowledge

THIRD

A NOVEL

PHENOMENA OF NATURE

1926

JEAN COCTEAU in *Composition as Explanation Hogarth Essays* London

COMPOSITION AS EXPLANATION **Address delivered before** *Oxford and Cambridge Literary Societies The Dial* Oct. 1926 *Hogarth Essay Series* London 1926 *Hogarth Essays Doubleday and Doran* 1927.

EDITH SITWELL AND HER BROTHERS THE SITWELLS

ALLEN TANNER in *Useful Knowledge*

AN ACQUAINTANCE WITH DESCRIPTION in Press *Seizen Press* London 225 numbered and signed copies

PAVLICK TCHELITCHEF

LIPCHITZ *Art Magazine* London 1926

1927

PATRIARCHAL POETRY

REGULAR REGULARLY IN NARRATIVE

DUCHESS OF BOHAN

A DIARY

OPERA FOUR SAINTS IN THREE ACTS

FELICITY IN MOON-LIGHT

TWO SPANIARDS

BY THE WAY

HURLBUT

RELIEVE

ONE SPANIARD *transition* June 1927

ADMIT

AN ADVANTAGE

LOVE A DELIGHT

WITH A WIFE

THREE SITTING HERE *Close up* Territe 1926

LIFE AND DEATH OF JUAN GRIS *transition* June 1927

LUCY CHURCH AMIABLY

A BOUQUET

1928

FINALLY GEORGE A VOCABULARY

DAN BAFFEL A NEPHEW *transition* March 1928

TO VIRGIL AND EUGENE

A LYRICAL OPERA

ARTHUR A GRAMMAR

JANE HEAP

THE D'AIGUYS

NOT PAISIEUX A PLAY

THEIR WILLS. A BOUQUET. AN OPERA

GEORGE HUGNET

CHRISTIAN BERARD

VIRGIL THOMSON

THE SENTENCE

1929

BERNARD FAŸ

SOURCES

Introducing originally appeared in *Useful Knowledge*. Published by Payson and Clarke, New York, 1928.

Advertisements originally appeared in *Geography and Plays*. Published by The Four Seas Company, Boston, 1922.

Business in Baltimore originally appeared in *Useful Knowledge*. Published by Payson and Clarke, New York, 1928.

A Family of Perhaps Three originally appeared in *Geography and Plays*. Published by The Four Seas Company, Boston, 1922.

An Instant Answer or A Hundred Prominent Men originally appeared in *Useful Knowledge*. Published by Payson and Clarke, New York, 1928.

Old and Old originally appeared in *Operas and Plays*. Published by Plain Edition, Paris, 1932.

A Collection originally appeared in *Geography and Plays*. Published by The Four Seas Company, Boston, 1922.

A Patriotic Leading originally appeared in *Useful Knowledge*. Published by Payson and Clarke, New York, 1928.

IIIIIIIIII. originally appeared in *Geography and Plays.* Published by The Four Seas Company, Boston, 1922.

The Superstitions of Fred Anneday, Annday, Anday: A Novel of Real Life originally appeared in *The Nassau Lit* (December 1935).

If You Had Three Husbands originally appeared in *Geography and Plays.* Published by The Four Seas Company, Boston, 1922.

Rooms originally appeared in *Tender Buttons.* Published by Claire-Marie, New York, 1914.

We Came. A History originally appeared in *Readies for Bob Brown's Machine.* Published by Roving Eye Press, Cagnes-sur-Mer, 1931.

Many Many Women originally appeared in *G. M. P.*, 1932.

Wherein Iowa Differs from Kansas and Indiana originally appeared in *Useful Knowledge.* Published by Payson and Clarke, New York, 1928.

France originally appeared in *Geography and Plays.* Published by The Four Seas Company, Boston, 1922.

Wherein the South Differs from the North originally appeared in *Useful Knowledge.* Published by Payson and Clarke, New York, 1928.

Americans originally appeared in *Geography and Plays.* Published by The Four Seas Company, Boston, 1922.

American Biography And Why Waste It originally appeared in *Useful Knowledge.* Published by Payson and Clarke, New York, 1928.

Lend a Hand or Four Religions originally appeared in *Useful Knowledge.* Published by Payson and Clarke, New York, 1928.

Three Sisters Who Are Not Sisters: A Melodrama originally appeared in *The Gertrude Stein First Reader and Three Plays.* Published by M. Fridberg, Dublin, 1946.

Are There Six or Another Question originally appeared in *Useful Knowledge.* Published by Payson and Clarke, New York, 1928.

SOURCES

Objects Lie on a Table: A Play originally appeared in *Operas and Plays*. Published by Plain Edition, Paris, 1932.

Civilization: A Play originally appeared in *Operas and Plays*. Published by Plain Edition, Paris, 1932.

At Present: A Play originally appeared in *Operas and Plays*. Published by Plain Edition, Paris, 1932.

The First Reader originally appeared in *The Gertrude Stein First Reader and Three Plays*. Published by M. Fridberg, Dublin, 1946.

Are There Arithmetics originally appeared in *Oxford 1927* (May 28, 1927).

A Bouquet. Their Wills. originally appeared in *Operas and Plays*. Published by Plain Edition, Paris, 1932.

A Movie originally appeared in *Operas and Plays*. Published by Plain Edition, Paris, 1932.

Film, *Deux soeurs qui ne sont pas soeurs* originally appeared in *Operas and Plays*. Published by Plain Edition, Paris, 1932.

How Writing Is Written originally appeared in *The Choate Literary Magazine* (February 1935).

Sentences and Paragraphs originally appeared in *How to Write*. Published by Plain Edition, Paris, 1931.

Next. Life and Letters of Marcel Duchamp originally appeared in *Geography and Plays*. Published by The Four Seas Company, Boston, 1922.

Forensics originally appeared in *How to Write*. Published by Plain Edition, Paris, 1931.

Bibliography, 1904–1929 originally appeared in *transition*, February 1929.

ABOUT THE EDITOR

Since beginning to publish in national magazines in 1961, **Richard Kostelanetz** has contributed poems, stories, articles, reviews, and experimental prose to hundreds of magazines both in the United States and abroad. He has written roughly fifty books of criticism, cultural history, and creative work, in addition to editing more than three dozen anthologies of art and exposition. Among the recent books authored by him are *Wordworks: Poems Selected and New; Minimal Fictions; One Million Words of Booknotes, 1958–1993; A Dictionary of the Avant-Gardes; Radio Writings; Fillmore East: Recollections of Rock Theater; Politics in the African-American Novel; John Cage (Ex)plain(ed)*; and *John Cage: Writer.* New books edited by him include *A Portable Baker's Biographical Dictionary of Musicians; Writing on Philip Glass; AnOther E. E. Cummings; A Frank Zappa Companion*; and *A B. B. King Companion.*

Individual entries on Mr. Kostelanetz appear in *Contemporary Poets, Contemporary Novelists, Postmodern Fiction, Baker's Biographical Dictionary of Musicians, Webster's Dictionary of American Authors*, and *Encyclopedia Britannica*, among other distinguished directories. Entries featuring his post-Steinian fiction appear in *A Reader's Guide to Twentieth-Century Writers* and the *Merriam-Webster Encyclopedia of Literature*, among other compendia. Long active in alternative literary publishing, he cofounded Assembling Press in 1970 and founded Future Press in 1977 and Archae Editions in 1978. Living in New York, where he was born, he still needs $1.50 (U.S.) to take a subway.